DATA MANAGEMENT AND INTERNET COMPUTING FOR IMAGE/PATTERN ANALYSIS

The Kluwer International Series on
ASIAN STUDIES IN COMPUTER AND INFORMATION SCIENCE

Series Editor

Kai-Yuan Cai

Beijing University of Aeronautics and Astronautics, Beijing, CHINA

Also in the Series:

COMMON WAVEFORM ANALYSIS: ***A New and Practical Generalization of Fourier Analysis***, *by Yuchuan Wei and Qishan Zhang;* ISBN: 0-7923-7905-5

DOMAIN MODELING-BASED SOFTWARE ENGINEERING: ***A Formal Approach***, *by Ruqian Lu and Zhi Jin;* ISBN: 0-7923-7889-X

AUTOMATED BIOMETRICS: ***Technologies and Systems***, *by David D. Zhang*; ISBN: 0-7923-7856-3

FUZZY LOGIC AND SOFT COMPUTING, *by Guoqing Chen, Mingsheng Ying, Kai-Yuan Cai*; ISBN: 0-7923-8650-7

INTELLIGENT BUILDING SYSTEMS, *by Albert Ting-pat So, Wai Lok Chan*; ISBN: 0-7923-8491-1

PERFORMANCE EVALUATION, PREDICTION AND VISUALIZATION OF PARALLEL SYSTEMS *by Xingfu Wu*; ISBN: 0-7923-8462-8

ROBUST MODEL-BASED FAULT DIAGNOSIS FOR DYNAMIC SYSTEMS *by Jie Chen and Ron J. Patton;* ISBN: 0-7923-8411-3

FUZZY LOGIC IN DATA MODELING: ***Semantics, Constraints, and Database Design*** *by Guoqing Chen;* ISBN: 0-7923-8253-6

SOFTWARE DEFECT AND OPERATIONAL PROFILE MODELING *by Kai-Yuan Cai;* ISBN: 0-7923-8259-5

DATA MANAGEMENT AND INTERNET COMPUTING FOR IMAGE/PATTERN ANALYSIS

by

David Zhang
Hong Kong Polytechnic University

Xiaobo Li
University of Alberta

Zhiyong Liu
National Natural Science Foundation of China

SPRINGER SCIENCE+BUSINESS MEDIA, LLC

ISBN 978-0-7923-7456-5 ISBN 978-1-4615-1527-2 (eBook)
DOI 10.1007/978-1-4615-1527-2

Library of Congress Cataloging-in-Publication Data

A C.I.P. Catalogue record for this book is available
from the Library of Congress.

Printed on acid-free paper.

CONTENTS

PREFACE *xi*

ACKNOWLEDGEMENTS *xiv*

1 OVERVIEW **1**

1.1 PRIP and IAP 1

1.2 IAP Dada Management in PRIP Computations 2

1.3 Internet Computing for PRIP 4

1.4 PRIP Applications 5

1.5 Book Perspective 6

REFERENCES 10

Part I SOFTWARE MANAGEMENT: MODELS & ALGORITHMS

2 ISSUES OF DATA MANAGEMENT **15**

2.1 IAP Input Data Format 15

2.2 Local Data Movement 19

2.3 Regional Data Movement 23

2.4 Global Data Movement 23

2.5 Regular and Irregular Data Movement 26

2.6 IAP Data Movement on Parallel Machines 27

2.7 Conclusion 29

REFERENCES 30

3 TYPICAL PRIP ALGORITHMS AND IAP DATA MANAGEMENT 33

3.1 Introduction 33
3.2 Linear Spatial Filtering 34
3.3 Morphological Filtering 38
3.4 Hough Transform 41
3.5 Labeling 55
3.6 Conclusion 59
REFERENCES 60

4 NEURAL EVOLUTION MODEL FOR GRAY LEVEL IMAGE RESTORATION 63

4.1 Introduction 63
4.2 MES Image Restoration Model 64
4.3 Improvements of ES Operators 65
4.4 Neural Evolution Algorithm (NEA) 67
4.5 Simulations and Comparisons 69
4.6 Conclusion 74
REFERENCES 75

5 PARTIAL FRACTAL MODEL FOR HYBIRD IMAGE CODING 77

5.1 Introduction 77
5.2 Basic Fractal Mapping 79
5.3 Partial Fractal Mapping 81
5.4 A General Framework for Hybrid Fractal-based Image Coding Systems 85
5.5 A Hybrid Image Coding System 86
5.6 Simulations and Conclusions 91
REFERENCES 94

6 BEST NEIGHBORHOOD MADLE FOR BLOCK-BASED IMAGE CODING 97

6.1 Introduction 97

6.2 Model Definition 98
6.3 Algorithm Implementation 100
6.4 ES-BNM Algorithm 103
6.5 Simulations and Comparisons 105
6.6 Conclusion and Discussion 111
REFERENCES 111

7 IMPULSE NOISE REMOVAL ALGORITHMS FOR IAP 115
7.1 Introduction 115
7.2 Noise Model and Impulse Detector 116
7.3 Polynomial Approximation (PA) Filter 119
7.4 Adaptive Order PA (AOPA) Filter 121
7.5 Simulations and Comparisons 125
7.6 Conclusion 131
REFERENCES 131

Part II HARDWARE MANAGEMENT: ARCHITECTURES & RESOURCE SHARING

8 INTERNET RESOURCE SHARING 133
8.1 Introduction 133
8.2 Software Resources 134
8.3 Hardware Resources 136
8.4 Image and Multimedia Databases on the Internet 144
8.5 Conclusion 146
REFERENCES 147

9 PARALLEL PROCESSING FOR IMAGE RESTORATION 151
9.1 Introduction 151
9.2 JBNM Algorithm 152
9.3 Parallel Computation 158
9.4 Experimental Results and Analysis 161

9.5 Conclusion 164
REFERENCES 164

10 IMAGE STORAGE MANAGEMENT ON PARALLEL COMPUTERS 167
10.1 Introduction 167
10.2 Linear Parallel Memory Systems 169
10.3 XOR Storage Schemes 175
10.4 Conclusion and Discussion 188
REFERENCES 191

11 DATA MANAGEMENT FOR SEQUENTIAL COMPUTER SYSTEMS 195
11.1 Introduction 195
11.2 Reuse Ratio Analysis 198
11.3 Performance Improvement from Cache Optimization 204
11.4 XOR Cache Mapping 208
11.5 Conclusion 216
REFERENCES 218

12 PERMUTATION ROUTING FOR INTER-CONNECTION NETWORK 221
12.1 Introduction 221
12.2 Two-stage Routing for BPC Permutations 222
12.3 Routing LC Permutations on MIMD Hypercubes 235
12.4 Setting up *N* Independent Paths for LC-Permutations 248
12.5 Conclusion 258
REFERENCES 260

Part III TYPICAL EXAMPLES: APPLICATIONS & IMPLEMENTATIONS

13 COMPRESSION CODING FOR IAP DATA 265
13.1 Introduction 265

13.2 Quadtree Compression and an Improved Reconstruction Phase 269

13.3 Wavelet Compression and Vector Quantization 281

13.4 The Performance of ModLVQ Algorithm 289

13.5 Conclusion 292

REFERENCES 293

14 REDUCTION OF BLOCKING EFFECTS AND REMOVAL OF IMPULSE NOISE 297

14.1 Introduction 297

14.2 Blocking Effect Reduction Algorithm 298

14.3 Experimental Results 300

14.4 Progressive Switching Median Filter for the Removal of Impulse Noise 303

14.5 Impulse Noise Detection and Removal Using Fuzzy Techniques 309

14.6 Conclusion 313

REFERENCES 314

15 IMAGE RESTORATION FROM INTERNET TRANSMISSION CORRUPTION 317

15.1 Introduction 317

15.2 Restoration Algorithm 320

15.3 Experimental Results 321

15.4 Performance Analysis 324

15.5 Conclusion 327

REFERENCES 327

16 ENCRYPTION CODING FOR IAP DATA 331

16.1 Introduction 331

16.2 Secret-key Encryption Algorithms 334

16.3 Public-key Encryption Algorithms 337

16.4 Image and Video Encryption Coding 338

16.5 Partial Encryption of Quadtree Compressed Images 344

16.6 Partial Encryption of Wavelet Compressed Images 351
16.7 Partial Encryption of Videos 354
16.8 Conclusion 356
REFERENCES 357

INDEX 361

PREFACE

Image processing and pattern recognition (PRIP) have found more and more applications in many areas, ranging from engineering, industry, medicine, education and the military. Most image and pattern (IAP) operations are computation and memory intensive. Recently, the rapid growth of Internet technology has changed the IAP field in several ways. Multimedia systems on Internet demand for high quality images in large quantities, which urges the research in more efficient data compression, storage and communication, as well as faster computation and operation. The public network environment and security consideration pushes forward data encryption research. On the other hand, Internet is also changing the field of IAP computing by providing a variety of shared resources, including hardware, software and image databases. Dealing with those new challenges and new opportunities in Internet IAP computing is the objective of this book.

The wide range of practical applications has been raising interesting theoretical questions for PRIP researchers. And powerful computers made possible for sophisticated IAP algorithms and stimulated further theoretical research. Therefore, IAP methods are being invented everyday, and new books are covering more advanced PRIP technology. A number of books gave detailed algorithms and programs for mostly low-level image processing. However, main attention is still mostly on the IAP target, as if it is purely local, with no discussion on the new demands and new facilities brought by Internet. There are very few books focusing on the data management issues and Internet computing aspect of PRIP research.

Internet made global resource sharing feasible for almost everyone. IAP computation can now take advantage of the net and access hardware, software and image databases in the world, including different parallel computer architectures and a large number of dedicated PRIP computers. In this book, we are intended to present a comprehensive overview of the state of the art in the above areas, and intends to give detailed *case studies* emphasizing: how IAP data are distributed and exchanged on sequential and parallel machines; how the data communication patterns in low- and higher-level IAP computing differ from general numerical computation, what problems they cause, and what opportunities they provide; how the images and matrices should be stored, accessed and distributed on different types of machines connected to Internet; and how Internet resource sharing and data transmission change traditional IAP computing.

The book is organized as follows. Chapter 1 of the book gives a brief overview for IAP tasks and related computational issues. We discuss why the data management issues are important, and what kinds of software and hardware methods are being considered in this book.

Part I of the book, Chapters 2 through 7, is on a number of software approaches to IAP computing. We first outline several issues of data management and give some definitions and notations. Then we describe several representative data communication patterns and related algorithms and software approaches, including low, intermediate and high level PRIP computations, evolutionary method for grayscale image restoration, partial fractal mapping, best neighborhood matching for the image coding, and impulse noise removal. The image coding algorithms discussed here are dealing with a number of important issues in Internet IAP data formatting. The noise removal and image restoration are also critical issues in IAP data communication and recovery.

In Part II, Chapter 8 through 12, is on architecture and implementation. A number of sample approaches are discussed: parallel processing for image restoration, storage schemes on parallel and sequential computer systems, and routing algorithms on data permutations. A wide range of architectures has been covered here, which reflect the variation of the resources being shared on Internet. Memory management issues are discussed in particular. Different machine types have different data storage and access situations. Data permutation is another necessary step in accessing the IAP data.

From Chapters 13 through 17, Part III presents a few applications of Internet PRIP computing, including a low bit rate image compression, corrupted image restoration, partial image encryption, and progressive color image transmission scheme. Coding, transmission and recovery are all important in real applications, especially for IAP data. Most of the approaches discussed here can also be used for general numerical and symbolic Internet computing.

This book is not a primer in data management and internet computing, in that a certain amount of prior knowledge, such as pattern recognition and image processing, is assumed. It is our hope that this book will contribute to our understanding of this new and exciting discipline: Data Management and Internet Computing for Image/Pattern Analysis.

David D. Zhang
Xiaobo Li
Zhiyong Liu

Hong Kong Polytechnic University
Kowloon, HongKong

ACKNOWLEDGEMENTS

During years of cooperation many colleagues have contributed to the development of the ideas presented in this book. It is difficult to mention them all. We wish to express our gratitude to Prof. Zhi-Qiang Liu, Prof. Xiangzhen Qiao, Dr. Zhou Wang, Dr. Zhe Wang, Wen Li, Ka-Ming Leung, Dave MacLeod, Bob Gregorish, Qitao Gan, Monroe Thomas, Dr. Xiaoqing Qu, Jason Knipe, Howard Cheng, and Joseph Modayil. We also want to thank Prof. Dave Clyburn, Guangming Lu, Bin Li, Li Yu and Lisheng Xu for their invaluable assistance in the preparation of this book. The financial support from UGC/CRC and CERG Grants from Hong Kong government and the Canadian Natural Sciences and Engineering Research Council under Grant OGP9198 is greatly appreciated.

SERIES EDITOR'S ACKNOWLEDGMENTS

I am pleased to acknowledge the assistance to the editorial work by Beijing University of Aeronautics and Astronautics and the National Natural Science Foundation of China

Kai-Yuan Cai
Series Editor
Department of Automatic Control
Beijing University of Aeronautics and Astronautics
Beijing 100083
China

Chapter 1

OVERVIEW

In this chapter, we give a brief overview of the field of *Pattern Recognition and Image Processing* (PRIP), concentrating on the data management aspect. Section 1.1 introduces the data entities that PRIP deals with: *images and patterns* (IAP). Section 1.2 is devoted to basic IAP data management issues. The Internet PRIP computation issues are discussed in Section 1.3 , and some representative applications are outlined in Section 1.4. Section 1.5 presents the organization of the book.

1.1 PRIP and IAP

An *image* is a picture of a scene taken by a camera. The image data often take the form of a two-dimensional (2-D) integer array. An *image processing* system takes in an image and produces another image that is an improved version of the original input. An *image analysis* system, also called a *computer vision* system, which usually contains an image processing element in its early stage, takes an input image and generates an understanding of it, as shown in Figure 1.1 [24, 25, 29, 30, 31, 32, 35, 39, 41], This understanding can be in the form of a description (a sentence), such as "The picture has a car on the left and a house on the right," or in the form of some data structure, such as a tree. Indeed, PRIP provides a way to make a computer see or to give a robot an eye.

Understanding the objects in a picture requires recognition. A well-studied area, *Pattern Recognition*, consists of many powerful techniques [25, 38, 39, 52]. A pattern recognition system considers each input item as a *pattern*, and the output is usually a label, assigned to the input pattern, pointing to a known category or class. For example, if the input image is a picture of a written character, the output could be "That character is a letter H." More generally speaking, a pattern to be recognized could be in a form other than image. It can be a one-dimensional temporal signal, such as a sound wave or a video of some hand gesture conveying

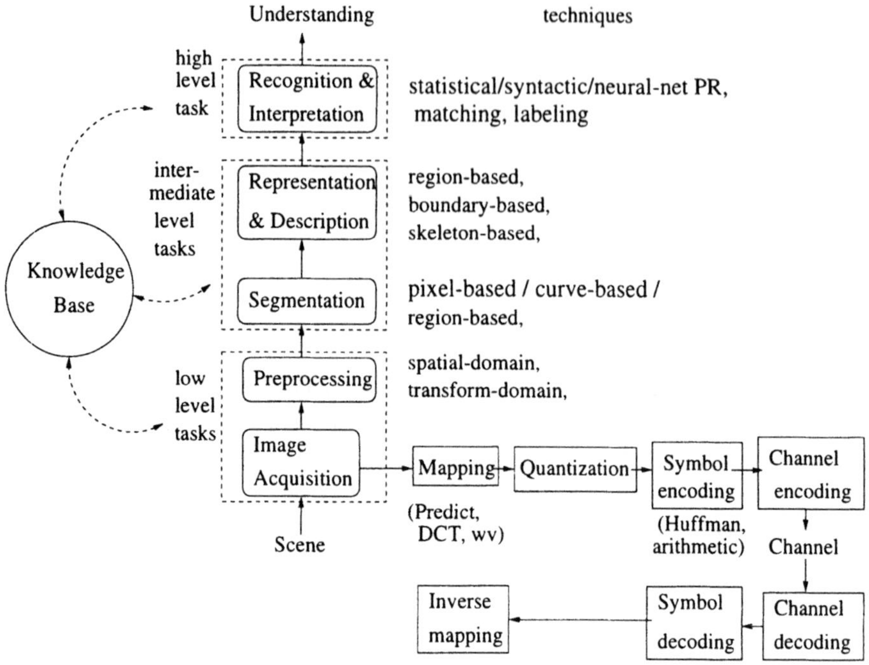

Figure 1.1. A typical computer vision system

a certain message. To represent a pattern in a digital computer, a vector or a matrix of some kind is usually used.

Image processing and pattern recognition (PRIP) are both active research areas and both have found wide applications in industry, engineering, medicine, agriculture, education, and the military. These two disciplines are closely related and share a great many methods and algorithms, usually requiring heavy computation and intensive memory access.

1.2 IAP Data Management in PRIP Computations

The major topics in image processing include *image enhancement*, *image restoration* and *image segmentation* [26, 31, 33, 34]. Enhancement operations deal with the pixels in an image. The objective is to reduce noise and improve the image for either visual inspection or further machine processing. Over-exposed or under-exposed pictures can be improved by *histogram transformation*, e.g., *histogram equalization*, which shifts the gray levels of the image pixels to reveal useful details in a scene. A *thinning* operation [48] extracts the skeleton of a line-like object in the image, such as the strokes of a character, to simplify the consequent recognition task. Image restoration is the process of taking an image with a known degradation and restoring it to its original appearance. Both enhancement and restoration take an image as input and produce another image as output. The input and output are approximately of the same size and type. The intermediate data structures involve vectors and matrices of other sizes and types, such as a histogram array. In enhancement and restoration computations, a large amount of data communication is local within the neighborhood of a pixel, but some global communications also take place, such as in histogram operations and image transforms.

During processing, one often needs to use simple image manipulation operations, such as re-sampling, shifting, rotation, shrinking, and expansion. These operations usually require little or no intermediate data structures and only a few steps of global communication.

Image compression coding is another type of low-level processing [27]. To serve the heavy demand for storing and transmitting a continuously increasing number of images of ever-increasing size, compressing an image into a smaller size but keeping its quality becomes crucial. Spatial-domain compression methods generate a data structure to directly represent the input image but with its redundancy eliminated or reduced [37, 45, 46, 47, 49]. Transform-domain methods convert the input image into a set of coefficients and then record the coefficients in a data structure. The Discrete Cosine Transform (DCT) and the wavelet transforms have been used [21, 22, 23, 28, 36, 40, 42, 43]. Generally speaking, transform-domain methods are more powerful and require more global data communications.

Higher level vision tasks deal with regions or curves instead of pixels. *Segmentation* is often considered as the first intermediate-level operation. It divides an image into disjoint regions, and each region can be recognized or classified later. Directly categorizing the pixels into regions often uses exploratory data analysis tools such as *clustering* [53, 54]. When a single feature is used in clustering, the process is also called *thresholding*. In these operations, a number of intermediate data structures, such as matrices, vectors or linked lists forming trees, are involved. The generation of these matrices requires heavy local and global operations. Region-based image segmentation techniques such as *region growing* group neighboring pixels into regions and let the region expand in size by taking in more adjacent pixels. There are heavy local data communications, and most of them are independent of each other. Curve-based segmentation connects edge points in the image to form the boundaries of the objects. Because it deals with much fewer pixels, the computation can be faster. But the data communication pattern is more irregular and more global.

The *Hough transform* and the *Active Contour* models are examples of curve-based segmentation methods.

In pattern recognition [38, 44], two types of matrices are usually involved: the pattern matrix and the proximity matrix. A pattern matrix is a two-dimensional array. Each row can represent a pattern and each column a feature. For example, if an image of a human face is a pattern, and the "eigen-face" approach is used, the first 50 coefficients of the eigen transform of the face could be the feature values. A proximity matrix is a square matrix with the (i, j)-th entry being the similarity or distance between pattern i and pattern j. Hierarchical clustering operates mostly on this proximity matrix. As many proximity measures are symmetric, this matrix is also symmetric and only half of it needs to be stored and processed. This triangular shape of the matrix creates certain challenges in the operation and data movement, but also provides efficiency and convenience.

1.3 Internet Computing for PRIP

The traffic on the Internet is increasing rapidly. One estimate is that it doubles every 100 days [19]. The widespread use of the Internet provides PRIP researchers with tremendous opportunities and convenience for the following reasons:

- A great number of PRIP <u>software</u> tools and packages are available on the Internet. Besides commercial software products, there are also many research and experimental programs available on-line [2, 3, 6, 7, 9, 11, 14, 15]

- Many pipeline and multiprocessor <u>computer systems</u> are serving government organizations, education/research institutions and industrial labs [18, 20]. Many of them also provide remote access through the Internet to researchers for academic and educational purposes. A large number of heavy PRIP computations can be shifted to remote supercomputers through the Internet. This has made it possible for research groups to explore much more complex and powerful PRIP methodologies. The Internet has also made it possible to access information on special-purpose PRIP hardware devices. Finding a suitable frame grabber or an embedded vision processor could require only one or two steps on a Web search engine [8, 10, 13, 17].

- The resources the Internet presents to PRIP workers also include numerous <u>image databases</u> [1, 4, 5, 12, 16]. PRIP research and testing cannot be done without a rich collection of input images or videos. Easy access to many different types of data collections world-wide is available to everyone with an Internet connection.

A detailed discussion of Internet resource sharing for PRIP computation is given in Chapter 8.

1.4 PRIP Applications

PRIP technologies have found applications in many areas [50]. One of the oldest and most extensively studied application area is optical character recognition. Recognizing printed and hand-written characters is critical to automatic document processing. Related techniques, such as page segmentation and various thinning algorithms have also been developed.

PRIP has been used heavily in medical imagery and medical diagnosis. Automatic examination of chest x-rays and mammograms can help detect warning signs of cancer. The early diagnosis of various diseases can benefit directly from powerful PRIP algorithms. Automated biometrics have utilized many PRIP methods, such as image segmentation, feature selection and pattern classification [51].

Aerial and satellite picture interpretation is another active area for PRIP application. Cloud pattern analysis in weather forecasting, earth resource study, land-use recording, geophysical exploration, and crop prediction have employed different types of PRIP techniques. PRIP algorithms are also used in seismic image analysis for oil resource analysis and earth-quack forecast.

In industrial automation, PRIP is actually the eyes and ears of the robots. It allows a robot to determine the position, size, shape and orientation of real objects. Humans receive over 90% of information about their surroundings through vision. And the ability of recognizing patterns is one of the key features of intelligent behavior. Naturally, vision and PRIP ability is extremely important to a mobile robot in obtaining information from environment and making decisions. Lately, PRIP technology has been used in evaluating meat quality and control the processing of agriculture products. In the transportation area, PRIP has found applications in traffic scene analysis and automatic vehicle control.

This book presents several sample PRIP applications in a wide range, from the low-level image processing (e.g., enhancement or coding), mid-level operations (e.g., image segmentation), to higher-level operations (e.g., object labeling and pattern recognition). General filtering is discussed, and so are some special types of filters (polynomial approximation filter, adaptive order PA filter, and progressive switching median filter). Abstract data distribution and communication models are discussed, together with algorithms, implementations and some experimental results. We intent to paint a rather colorful "image" of the field of PRIP and give readers a clear impression of their data management "patterns."

1.5 Book Perspective

The book is organized as follows. Chapter 1 of the book gives a brief overview for PRIP tasks and related computational issues. We discuss why the data management issues are important, and what kinds of software and hardware methods are being considered in this book.

Part I of the book, Chapters 2 through 7, is on a number of software approaches to PRIP computing. We first outline several issues of data management and give some definitions and notations. Then we describe several representative data communication patterns and related algorithms and software approaches, including low, intermediate and high level PRIP computations, evolutionary method for grayscale image restoration, partial fractal mapping, best neighborhood matching for the image coding, and impulse noise removal. The image coding algorithms discussed here are dealing with a number of important issues in the Internet IAP data formatting. The noise removal and image restoration are also critical issues in IAP data communication and recovery.

Chapter 2 is on specific issues of IAP data management. IAP data are mostly in the form of vectors and matrices. In many cases, PRIP operations involve heavy computations and demand for large memory spaces. The following questions are discussed: (1) what are the frequently used data movement and distribution patterns, (2) how they differ from general numerical computations, (3) what difficulties they can cause us, and (4) what advantages and opportunities they may provide.

Chapter 3 give four typical PRIP algorithms, including two low-level image processing operations: linear filtering and binary morphological filtering, one mid-level image segmentation operation: the Hough transform, and one higher-level operation: object labeling. These algorithms cover a number of common data distribution and movement patterns.

Chapter 4 introduces a novel image restoration method by using modified evolution strategy (MES). We first review the background of image restoration and some useful concepts associated with it. A MSE image restoration model is then made. Three main improvements consist of coordinate descending mutation, "survival of the fittest" selection rule and hybrid evolution strategies are presented. Theoretical analysis and experimental results demonstrate the efficiency of the proposed method.

The fractal image compression technique models a natural image using a contractive mapping called fractal mapping in the image space. In Chapter 5, we first introduce the concept of fractal mapping and some useful concepts associated with it. The fractal image coding algorithm is compatible with other image coding methods. A new mapping in the image space called partial fractal mapping is proposed in this chapter. Then we develop a general framework of fractal-based hybrid image coding encoding/decoding systems and a new hybrid image coding scheme where non-fractal coded regions are used to help the encoding of fractal coded regions. Experiments show that the proposed system performs better than the quadtree-based fractal image coding algorithm and the JPEG image compression standard at high compression ratios larger than 30.

Imperfect transmission of block-coded images often results in lost blocks. In Chapter 6, we introduce a novel error concealment method called Best Neighborhood Matching (BNM) which is presented by using a special kind of information redundancy – block-wise similarity within the image. The proposed algorithm can utilize the information of not only neighboring pixels, but also remote regions in the image. The model definition is presented in this chapter. Very good restoration results are obtained by experiments.

In Chapter 7, a novel filtering algorithm is presented to restore images corrupted by impulsive noise. As a pre-processing procedure of the noise cancellation filter, an improved impulse detector is used to generate a binary flag image which gives each pixel a flag indicating whether it is an impulse. We describes the impulse noise model assumed by our experiments and presents an iterative impulse detection algorithm which provides us with more accurate detecting results than those of previously proposed methods.

Part II of the book, Chapters 8 through 12, is on computation resources, especially on the architecture and implementation issues. A number of sample approaches are presented: parallel processing for image restoration, storage schemes on parallel and sequential computer systems, and routing algorithms on data permutations. A number of parallel and distributed architectures are discussed, reflecting the variation of the resources being shared on the Internet. Memory management issues are discussed in particular. Different machine types have different data storage and access situations. Data permutation is another necessary step in accessing the IAP data.

In Chapter 8, we present a brief overview of the computation resources on the Internet and discuss a number of related issues. Various examples for image database are also given in this chapter. The Internet has made the hardware and software computational resources available for the PRIP communities world-wide. The tremendous number of image databases can be on the fingertips of any PRIP programmer. To make a full use of the rich resources becomes critically important in IAP data management and PRIP technology research and development. A careful investigation and in-depth design can take a full advantage of this rich resource on the Internet.

In Chapter 9, based on the BNM model in Chapter 6, we propose an improved fast implementation method, named Jump and look all round the JBNM algorithm. It has illustrated that the computing time in JBNM can be reduced to 1/6 of that by BNM while the similar restored image quality is remained. Some experimental results are given in this chapter. To speed-up our algorithm again, a parallel JBNM is proposed and performance analysis related to our parallel algorithms developed.

In Chapter 10, we will discuss some techniques for the design of parallel memory systems. Some background information for parallel memory systems will be first introduced. Linear skewing schemes are then described as an example. XOR schemes will be finally introduced.

As the advances in hardware technology, the gap between fast CPU and the slow memory system is increased severely also in sequential computer systems. Hierarchical memory systems are used in sequential computers to bridge the gap. Cache is a widely used mechanism n the memory hierarchy. But it has been found that cache performance is not satisfying for many important application algorithms since its hit ratio is very low for many frequently data access patterns due to conflict use of the cache lines. This problem shares some similarity with the problem of memory module access conflict in parallel memory systems discussed in Chapter 10. In addition, some special issue (data reuse rate) need to be considerate in cache systems. We will discuss the cache line conflict problem and some techniques to solve it in Chapter 11.

Interconnection networks provide communication facility for parallel processing systems. In order to reduce communication overhead (both hardware overhead and time overhead), interconnection networks and corresponding routing techniques have been one of the key issues in the research of parallel and distributed processing systems. Chapter 12 introduces some permutation routing algorithms for hypercubes. The algorithms have a common feature that they can avoid conflicts in the message transmission process. Also they are simple for their implementation.

Part III of the book, Chapters 13 through 17, presents a few applications of Internet PRIP computing, including a low-bit rate image compression, corrupted image restoration, partial image/video encryption, and progressive color image transmission scheme. Coding, transmission and recovery are all important in real applications, especially for IAP data management and PRIP computations. Most of the approaches discussed here can also be used for general numerical and symbolic Internet computing.

Chapter 13 deals with an important issue in IAP data management for Internet PRIP computations: compression coding. Because of the large data volume and the need for fast transmission (sometimes almost real-time), compression coding is critical. We give an overview on the motivation ("why") and the general approaches ("how") to IAP data compression. As an example for the spatial-domain methods, we present two improvements to the reconstruction phase of a quadtree compression algorithm. We also discuss a vector quantization scheme that works for a transform-domain compression algorithm.

In Chapter 14, we propose a new approach for removing blocking artifacts in reconstructed block-encoded images. The key of the approach is using piecewise similarity within different parts of the image as a prior to give reasonable modifications to the block boundary pixels. This makes our approach different from traditional ones which are often developed by applying some kinds of smoothing constraints on local regions. Experimental results show that our approach well achieves enhanced decoding for JPEG-decoded images both objectively and subjectively. We also introduce the progressive switching median filter for the removal of impulse noise and the impulse noise removal using fuzzy techniques.

In Chapter 15, we present a new algorithm which can remove impulse noise from corrupted images while preserving details. The algorithm is fundamentally different from the traditional methods in that it can utilize the information of not only a local window centered about the corrupted pixel but also some remote regions in the image. Experimental results indicate that our algorithm outperforms many existing techniques.

Storing and transmitting IAP data in the Internet environment is different from the traditional communication due to the open nature of the Internet. Data encryption coding is desirable, and sometimes necessary, to ensure security for certain applications. Various encryption coding methods have be proposed to protect multimedia data on the Internet. Chapter 16 briefly describes basic concepts of encryption and a number of well-known encryption algorithms, then concentrates on a *partial encryption* scheme for images and videos.

References

[1] *http://ant.edb.miyakyo-u.ac.jp/Taxo_E/F80903.html.*

[2] *http://bersoft.com/bimagem/index.htm.*

[3] *http://documents.cfar.umd.edu/imageproc/.*

[4] *http://umbra.nascom.nasa.gov/images/latest.html.*

[5] *http://wieck.com/public/.*

[6] *http://www-dsp.rice.edu/splib.*

[7] *http://www.aai.com.*

[8] *http://www.alacron.com/index.htm.*

[9] *http://www.clemex.com.*

[10] *http://www.coreco.com/corecodefault.html.*

[11] *http://www.cs.cmu.edu/afs/cs/project/cil/ftp/html/v-source.html.*

[12] *http://www.cs.ualberta.ca/ kenw/photos.html.*

[13] *http://www.datacube.com/.*

[14] *http://www.euresys.com/SoftwareTools/eVision.htm.*

[15] *http://www.inf.ufes.br/ thomas/home/tooldiag.html.*

[16] *http://www.lib.colum.edu/commwais.html.*

[17] *http://www.matrox.com/imgweb/genesism.htm.*

[18] *http://www.netlib.org/benchmark/top500.html.*

[19] *http://www.tbook.com/n/Harry_Newton/Newton_s_Telecom _Dictionary_The_1578200539.htm.*

[20] *http://www.top500.org/ORSC/2000/overview00.html.*

[21] M. Antonini, M. Barlaud, P. Mathieu, and I. Daubechies. Image coding using wavelet transform. *IEEE Trans. Image Proc.*, 1(2):205–220, 1992.

[22] Y. Arai, T. Agui, and M. Nakajima. A fast DCT-SQ scheme for images. *Trans. of the IEICE*, 71(11):1095, 1988.

[23] A. Averbuch, D. Lazar, and M. Israeli. Image compression using wavelet transform and multiresolution decomposition. *IEEE Trans. Image Proc.*, 5(1):4–15, 1996.

[24] G. Awcock. *Applied Image Processing.* Macmillan Press, 1994.

[25] S.T. Bow. *Pattern Recognition and Image Processing.* Marcel Dekker, 1992.

[26] K. Castleman. *Digital Image Processing.* Prentice Hall, 1996.

[27] R.J. Clarke. *Digital Compression of Still Images and Video.* Academic Press, 1995.

[28] L.H. Croft and J.A. Robinson. Subband image coding using watershed and watercourse lines of the wavelet transform. *IEEE Trans. Image Proc.*, 3(6):759–771, 1994.

[29] F. Dailey. *Image Technology: State of the Art.* Computer Technology Research, 1992.

[30] B. Furht. *Video and Image processing in Multimedia Systems.* Kluwer Academic Publishers, 1995.

[31] R.C. Gonzalez and R.E. Woods. *Digital Image Processing.* Addison-Wesley, 1992.

[32] R.M. Haralick and L.G. Shapiro. *Computer and Robot Vision.* Addison-Wesley, 1992.

[33] J. Illingworth and J. Kittler. The adaptive Hough transform. *IEEE Trans. on Patt. Anal. and Machine Intell.*, PAMI-9(5):690–698, 1987.

[34] J. Illingworth and J. Kittler. A survey of the Hough transform. *Computer Vision, Graphics, and Image Processing*, 44:87–116, 1988.

[35] B. Jahne. *Digital Image Processing: Concepts, Algorithms, and Scientific Applications.* Spring-Verlag, 1995.

[36] J. Knipe and X. Li. An improved lattice vector quantization scheme for wavelet compression. *IEEE Trans. Signal Proc.*, 46(1):239–243, 1998.

[37] J. Knipe and X. Li. On the reconstruction of quadtree data. *IEEE Trans. Image Proc.*, 7(12):1653–1660, 1998.

[38] M. Nadler and E. Smith. *Pattern Recognition Engineering.* John Wiley & Sons, 1993.

[39] N. Pavel. *Fundamentals of Pattern Recognition.* Marcel Dekker, 1993.

[40] W.B. Pennebaker and J.L. Mitchell. *JPEG Still Image Data Compression Standard.* Van Nostrand Reinhold, 1993.

[41] J. Russ. *The Image Processing handbook, 3rd ed.* CRC Press, 1999.

[42] A. Said and W.A. Pearlman. A new fast and efficient image codec based on set partitioning in hierarchical trees. *IEEE Trans. Circuits and Systems for Video Tech.*, 6:243–250, 1996.

[43] D.G. Sampson, E.A.B. da Silva, and M. Ghanbari. Wavelet transform image coding using lattice vector quantization. *Electronics Letters*, 30(18):1477–1478, 1994.

[44] J. Schurmann. *Pattern Classification: a unified view of statistical and neural approaches.* John Wiley & Sons, 1996.

[45] E. Shusterman and M. Feder. Image compression via improved quadtree decomposition. *IEEE Transactions on Image Processing.*, 3(2):207–215, 1994.

[46] P. Strobach. Tree-structured scene adaptive coder. *IEEE Trans. Commun.*, 38(4):477–486, 1990.

[47] P. Strobach. Quadtree-structured recursive plane decomposition coding of images. *IEEE Trans. Sig. Proc.*, 39(6):1380–1397, 1991.

[48] C.Y. Suen and P. Yang. *Thinning methodlogies for pattern recognition.* World Scientific, 1994.

[49] G.J. Sullivan and R.L. Baker. Efficient quadtree coding of images and video. *IEEE Transactions on Image Processing*, 3(3):327–331, 1994.

[50] R.J. Thierauf. *Image processing systems in business: a guide for MIS professionals and end users.* Quorum Books, 1992.

[51] D. Zhang. *Automated Biometrics: Technologies and Systems.* Kluwer Academic Publishers, 2000.

[52] D. Zhang, L. Deng, and M. Elmasry. A pipelined ANN architecture for speech recognition. In *VLSI Artificial Neural Networks Engineering*, pages 297–315. Kluwer Academic Publishers, 1994.

[53] D. Zhang, K. Kamel, and M. Elmasry. Fuzzy clustering neural network (FCNN): Competitive learning algorithm and parallel architecture. *The International Journal of Intelligent and Fuzzy Systems*, 2:289–298, 1994.

[54] D. Zhang, M. Kamel, and M. Elmasry. A parallel ANN arichitecture for fuzzy clustering. In *VLSI Artificial Neural Networks Engineering*, pages 277–296. Kluwer Academic Publishers, 1994.

Chapter 2

ISSUES OF DATA MANAGEMENT

IAP data are mostly in the form of vectors and matrices. In many cases, PRIP operations involve heavy computations and demand for large memory spaces. This chapter looks into the following issues:

- what are the frequently used data movement and distribution patterns,
- how they differ from general numerical computations,
- what difficulties they can cause us, and
- what advantages and opportunities they may provide.

2.1 IAP Input Data Format

The input to a PRIP system is usually an image in the form of a two-dimensional integer array. Each number represents the grayscale or color of a pixel in the picture of a real scene. The early stage image processing, also called "low-level image processing", is mostly iconic and based on individual pixels or small groups of pixels. The intermediate-level processing involves large groups of pixels in the form of curves or regions. High-level processing uses more abstract numerical and symbolic data. The intermediate and higher level processing employ various data structures, such as real and complex vectors, matrices and linked lists [2, 3, 6, 8, 9, 10, 13, 17].

PRIP systems take in images of different formats. A large number of image coding formats have been used. The most common ones include JPEG, TIFF, GIF, and PGM. Table 2.1 gives a few examples. A detailed list of these formats with brief descriptions can be found at [1]. Typical image sizes range from several hundred rows and columns to several thousand rows and columns. For example, many existing gray-level images use an 8-bit mode to represent up to 256 gray-levels for each pixel.

Different images may contain different numbers of gray-levels. Figure 2.1 shows four examples. The first one is an ultrasound image used in meat quality grading. It is originally in a TIFF format with 234 × 260 pixels. The second picture, 151 by 225, is a part of an outdoor scene, taken by a regular optical camera and then digitized on a scanner. The third one is an indoor scene of size 384 by 256, taken by a digital camera. The last image is a "standard" photograph of a portrait, downloaded from the Internet. This image has been used by researchers [11] for various tests in image processing and coding.

Table 2.1. Some common image formats

Name	Brief description
BMP, BMP24, DIB	bitmap format
DCM	read-only medical image format
DPI, EPS, EPSF, EPSI, EPT	Adobe PostScript format
GIF, GIF87	8-bit color format
JBIG	binary image format
JPEG, JPEG24	grayscale/color format, lossy

Color images are often represented in a 24-bit mode. The 24 bits for each pixel is an index to a 4 × 8 × 4 color map. Figure 2.2 is a picture taken by a control camera looking at a set of "baby" plants. A vision system examines each plant and determines if it is healthy. Color information is crucial in this application. There are 400 × 400 pixels in the original image.

Traditionally, an image of 512 by 512 is said to have a "television-quality" in terms of resolution [9]. Along with the rapid increase of computer power, images with higher resolution and greater gray-level/color separation become more and more commonplace. For example, Kodak DC260 Zoom Camera in 1998 produces images of 768 × 512. The more recent Cannon EOS-D30 digital camera takes pictures of two different sizes: 2160 × 1440 and 1440 × 960. The raw format of the former requires 3.4 MB of storage, and the compressed form takes 1.3 MB or 0.7 MB depending on the parameters. The later can be compressed to 0.7 MB or 0.4 MB.

In some PRIP computations, such as the Fast Fourier Transform (FFT), the matrix size is often converted to powers of two. When the raw input image is of other sizes, rows or columns of zeros are padded. The same padding is used in image compression when wavelet transforms are used to facilitate the generation of a multi-resolution pyramid. The matrix sizes being powers of two is an interesting feature of image processing, which makes it different from general numerical computation.

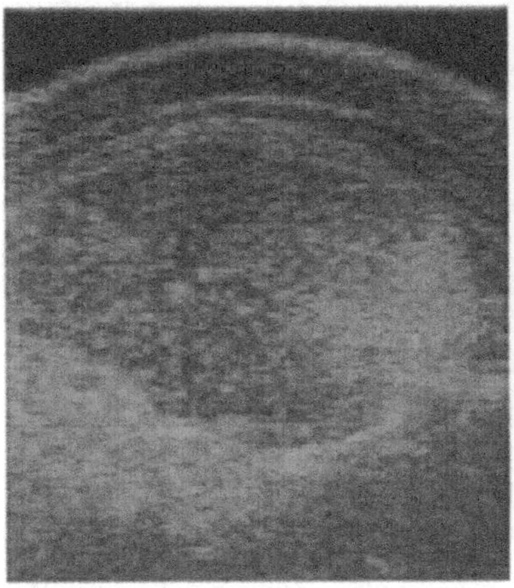

(a) Ultrasound image of pig muscle

(b) Outdoor scene

(c) Indoor scene

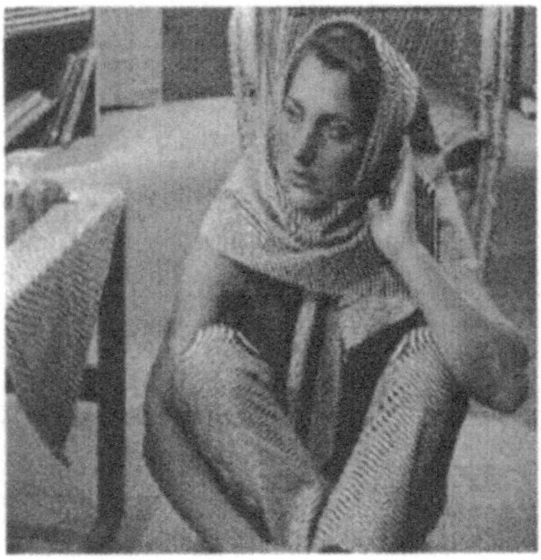

(d) Teapot

Figure 2.1. Gray-level image examples

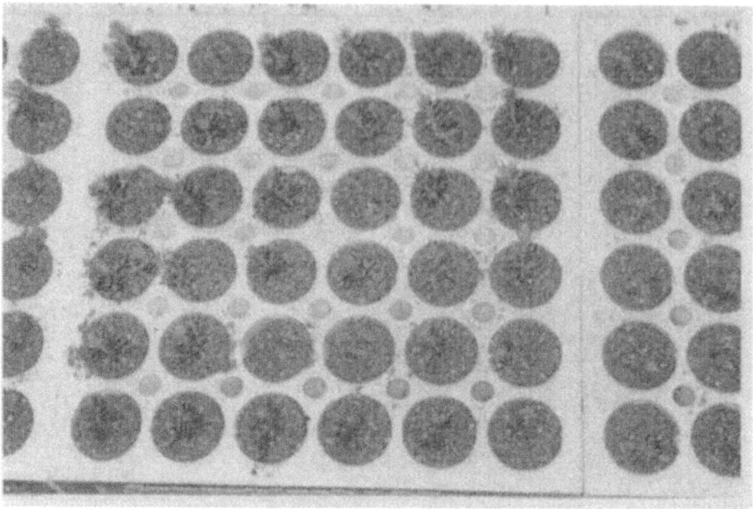

Figure 2.2. A grayscale version of a color image ("baby" trees)

The internal data structure for some PRIP operations can be three-dimensional or higher dimensional matrices. Because of the large size of the images and matrices, some programmers choose to reuse arrays of the initial image for later processing. Advanced high-level programming languages like JAVA make parts of such practice automatic and simpler, but a large number of C programs currently in use can still take advantage of a good understanding of the relation between the initial data structure and the data requirement in later processing. In higher-level PRIP operations, vectors and matrices are commonly used to store "patterns" and their relations, as well as their labels, such as the pattern matrix, the similarity matrix, and labeling vectors. The size and format of these matrices vary from application to application. Table 2.2 gives a few examples.

Table 2.2. Arrays used in PRIP

IAP data	Type and size
Histogram	1-D integer array, size 32 to 256.
Fourier transform result	The same as the image, real or complex.
Spatial filter	2-D integer array of R by C, usually $R, C < 10$.
Pattern matrix	2-D real array, $>$ 100 rows, tens of columns.
Proximity matrix	2-D real array, $>$ 100 rows and columns.
Labeling vector	1-D integer array, a few hundreds elements.
Co-occurrence matrix	2-D or 3-D square array, 32 to 256 rows/cols.

$D(0,1)$	$D(0,2)$	$\cdots\cdots\cdots$	$D(0,N-1)$
	$D(1,2)$	$\cdots\cdots\cdots$	$D(1,N-1)$
		$\cdots\cdots$	$\cdots\cdots$
		$\cdots$	$\cdots\cdots$
		$\cdots$	$D(N-2,N-1)$

Figure 2.3. An upper triangle of a distance matrix D

Because of the symmetry of most commonly used proximity measures, the proximity matrix is usually symmetric and it is sufficient to store only the upper (or lower) triangle. For a set of N patterns, $\{P(i,*) \mid 0 \leq i < N\}$, the Minkowski metric between $P(s,*)$ and $P(t,*)$, $0 \leq s,t < N$, is defined as

$$D_k(s,t) = \left(\sum_j |P(s,j) - P(t,j)|^k\right)^{1/k} \quad \text{where } k \geq 1 \qquad (2\text{-}1)$$

and the distance matrix is an $N \times N$ matrix D. When $k = 1$, it is called the "city-block distance". When $k = 2$, it is the Euclidean distance. The upper triangle of D, $\{D(s,t) \mid 0 \leq s < t < N\}$, is shown in Figure 2.3. Storing this triangular matrix in a 1-D array will require some index calculations. For example, if a 1-D array T is used, elements $T[0]$ through $T[M]$, $M = N(N-1)/2$, will be filled, and $D(i,j)$ is stored in $T[p]$ with

$$p = i(N - \tfrac{i+1}{2}) + (j - i - 1) \qquad (2\text{-}2)$$

The PRIP programmer must weigh the trade-off between the storage saving and the computation speedup before deciding on using a 1-D array or the full 2-D $N \times N$ array.

Storing the above matrices requires a special attention of a programmer, on both parallel and sequential computers. Naive definition and initialization of the matrices may lead to a significant reduction in computation efficiency.

2.2 Local Data Movement

The most commonly used local operation in PRIP is the spatial neighborhood operation. Usually, a neighborhood around pixel $X(i,j)$ is $N(i,j)$, which is defined as a rectangular sub-image around the pixel location (i,j). That is,

$$N_{r,c,h,v}(i,j) = \{X(s,t) \mid i - r \leq s \leq i + h,\ j - c \leq t \leq j + v\} \qquad (2\text{-}3)$$

$X(i,j)$	$X(i,j+1)$

(a)

$X(i,j)$	$X(i,j+1)$
$X(i+1,j)$	$X(i+1,j+1)$

(b)

Figure 2.4. Two simple neighborhoods

$X(5,8)$,	$X(5,9)$,	$X(5,10)$,	$X(5,11)$,	$X(5,12)$,
$X(6,8)$,	$X(6,9)$,	$X(6,10)$,	$X(6,11)$,	$X(6,12)$,
$X(7,8)$,	$X(7,9)$,	$X(7,10)$,	$X(7,11)$,	$X(7,12)$

Figure 2.5. A 3 by 5 neighborhood centered at (6,10)

This neighborhood is determined by four parameters: r, c, h, and v. For example, $r = c = h = 0$ and $v = 1$ gives a 1×2 neighborhood, shown in Figure 2.4(a). Another simple neighborhood with $r = c = 0$, $h = v = 1$ is give in Figure 2.4(b).

When $r = h$ and $c = v$ the neighbor is centered at the pixel (i, j) and forms a rectangle of $(2r + 1) \times (2c + 1)$. For example, $N_{1,2,1,2}(6, 10)$, or simply denoted as $N_{3\times5}(6, 10)$, contains the 15 pixels as shown in Figure 2.5.

Most commonly used neighborhoods are symmetric and square in shape, i.e., $r = c = h = v$. A basic neighborhood operation is *template matching*, also called spatial filtering, masking, correlation, or convolution. Precisely speaking, there is a sign difference between correlation and convolution, but the data access patterns are basically the same. The result of a neighborhood operation is defined as

$$Y(i,j) = F(N(i,j)). \tag{2-4}$$

That is, the value of every pixel in the output image Y at location (i, j) is completely determined by a function F of the neighborhood $N(i, j)$. In other words, to generate the result value at location (i, j), only the pixels in $N(i, j)$ need to be examined. The function F can be a linear combination (weighted sum) or a non-linear operation, such as maximum, minimum, or a statistic (e.g., median). Regardless the nature of the operation, the data movement and distribution directions are very similar. With a symmetric neighborhood ($r = h$ and $c = v$), $X(i, j)$ is only used in the computation of $Y(s, t)$ when $(s, t) \in N(i, j)$ except the cases along the image margins. If those values are stored in memory of

$X(5,8)$,	$X(5,9)$,	$X(5,10)$,	$X(5,11)$,	$X(5,12)$,
$X(6,8)$,	$X(6,9)$,	$X(6,10)$,	$X(6,11)$,	$X(6,12)$,
$X(7,8)$,	$X(7,9)$,	$X(7,10)$,	$X(7,11)$,	$X(7,12)$

Figure 2.6. Two overlapping 3×3 neighborhoods: $N(6,9)$ and $N(6,11)$

a single processor computer, all the values involved in generating one output need to be fetched rapidly, preferably in one cycle. That is, these values should be in cache at the same time. Related issues are discussed in later chapters. If a parallel computer with multiple memory modules is used, storing pixels of one neighborhood in different memory modules may provide a faster access. Which memory stores which pixel, and which processor will use this pixel, will be presented in the later chapters in detail.

The neighborhoods of adjacent pixels overlap. For example, $N(i,j)$ and $N(i,j+1)$ of size $(r+h+1) \times (c+v+1)$ share $r+h+1$ elements, as demonstrated in Figure 2.6. This neighborhood overlapping (element sharing) is also a special characteristic of image processing, different from typical operations in general numerical computations, such as matrix multiplication or Gaussian elimination. If the shared elements are stored in the same block in the memory with the new neighborhood, the computation of the new neighbor does not need to access memory as often. However, the cache conflict problems have to be carefully examined. In a multi-memory system, the shared pixel values can be stored in local registers for the next computation step. Median filtering gives a typical example of the utilization of shared neighborhood elements. The result of that filter is the statistical median of all neighborhood values. In the computation of the median value at position $(i, j+1)$, the pixels in the region shared with $N(i,j)$ need not to be sorted again.

Another feature of the data movement in local PRIP operations is the margin treatment. Consider an input image of size $R \times C$. The computation of any $Y(i,j)$ with $i < r$, $i > (R-1-r)$, $j < c$, or $j > (C-1-c)$ will require an extension of the reference neighborhood $N(i,j)$. Figure 2.7 depicts a one-dimensional case. To carry out the neighborhood operations in the same way as other places, a *wrap-around* or a *reflection* can be used. In a wrap-around treatment, each row of pixels can be considered as a ring. The right-most pixel serves as the immediate left neighbor of the left-most pixel, etc., as shown in Figure 2.7(a). This is a common practice, especially in the Fourier transform. The reason for this is not only computational convenience but also the assumption of the

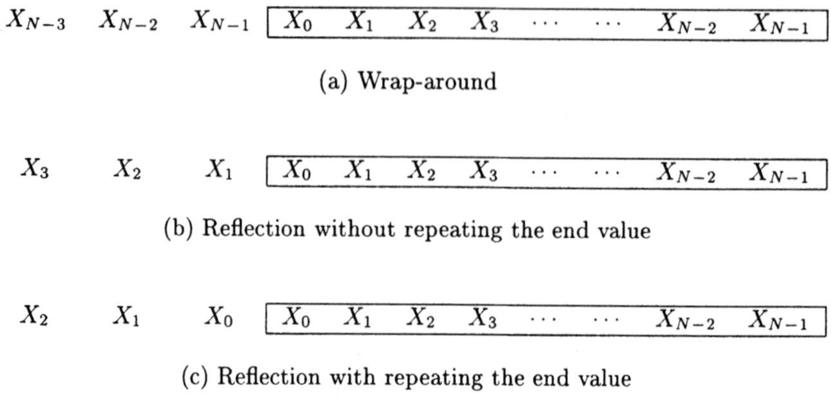

Figure 2.7. The left margin of a 1-D image and two types of extension

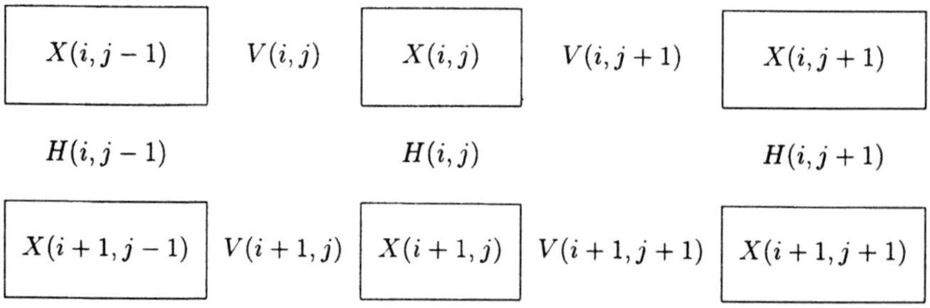

Figure 2.8. Crack edge definition and data communication pattern

periodicity of the input signal, which is the basis for the Fourier analysis. In a reflection treatment, the pixels immediately next to the margin are reused, as given in Figure 2.7(b) and (c). On a parallel machine, data shifting and exchange between connected processors and memory modules can be tricky. The wrap-around treatment of the marginal pixels can be a natural choice for a mesh or cube connected computer, but very difficult for some other types of networks.

An alternative way of looking at images at the pixel level is the "crack-edge" view. In this view, an "edge" is not *on* a pixel, but *in between* pixels, as shown in Figure 2.8. For example, the horizontal crack-edge $H(i, j-1)$ is the difference between $X(i, j-1)$ and $X(i+1, j-1)$, and the vertical crack-edge $V(i, j)$ is the difference between $X(i, j-1)$ and $X(i, j)$. Crack-edge detection and relaxation algorithms on various computer models have been proposed [12, 14].

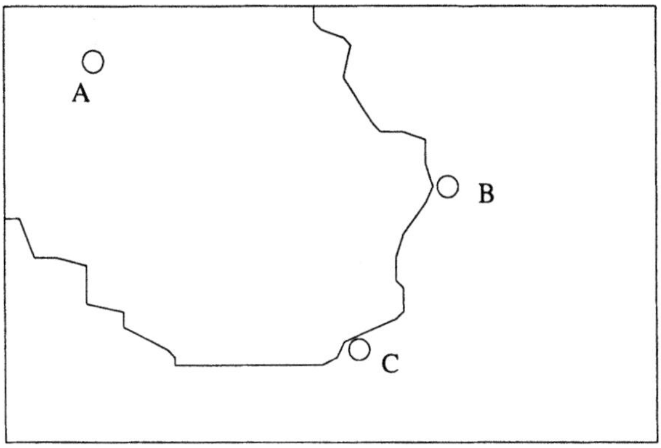

Figure 2.9. The value of the seed pixel A affects the merging decision of pixels B and C.

2.3 Regional Data Movement

Data communication at a long distance (many pixels) can occur in two ways. One is through propagation. In a repeated spatial filtering, such as a low-pass filtering followed by an edge detection, then a morphological erosion, can propagate information from one pixel to other pixel positions several steps away. Larger filters and structuring elements make this propagation faster. A more direct "long distance" data communication can happen in an intermediate level operation, such as region growing. If the criterion for taking a new pixel into a existing region is to compare its value (gray-level, color or texture) to the original seed of the region, the seed value must be known many pixel positions away, as shown in Figure 2.9. In the decision making for points B and C, the value of A, the original seed, is needed. If the merging criterion is to compare the new pixel with the centroid of the existing region, theoretically, all pixels in the region contribute to the decision. The updating of the centroid may involve pixels far away from each other if the region can grow in many different directions. Keeping a record of the centroid and using it for many different directions can be a challenging problem.

2.4 Global Data Movement

Global communications are necessary for some low-level image processing and almost all intermediate-level vision tasks. One example is the histogram computation. In image $\{X(i,j),\ 0 \leq i,j \leq N-1\}$, each pixel takes value from 0 to $K-1$. A histogram is a discrete probability function (multiplied by the total number of pixels) stored in an integer array

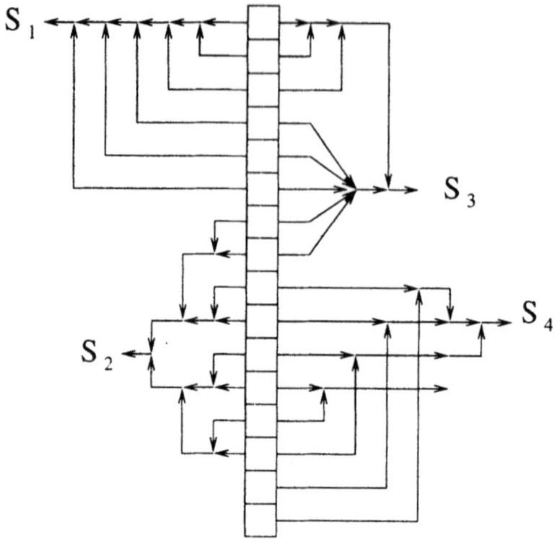

Figure 2.10. Global summation orderings

$H(m)$, $0 \leq m < K$ with $H(m)$ being the number of pixels having gray level m. Every value of H depends on the whole image, not any particular neighborhood. This global summation can be done in different orders as show in Figure 2.10. For example, S_1 takes in one value at a time, S_2 forms a binary tree, S_3 are built from group sums, and the group sums can be sums of smaller groups. The different summation orders can make a significant difference in accuracy and computation efficiency, especially when multiple processors and multiple memory modules are involved.

Another example of global computation is the Discrete Fourier Transform (DFT), as defined in [9],

$$F(u) = \frac{1}{N}\sum_{x=0}^{N-1} f(x)e^{-j2\pi ux/N} \tag{2-5}$$

where $f(x)$ is the original 1-D signal, $\{f(x) \mid 0 \leq x \leq N-1\}$, and the result is a vector of N complex numbers, $\{F(u) \mid 0 \leq u \leq N-1\}$, and $j = \sqrt{-1}$. The fast Fourier Transform (FFT) is defined as

$$F(u) = \frac{1}{M}\left[F_{even}(u) + F_{odd}(u)W_{2M}^{u}\right], \tag{2-6}$$

$$F_{even}(u) = \frac{1}{M}\sum_{x=0}^{M-1} f(2x)W_{M}^{ux}, \tag{2-7}$$

$$F_{odd}(u) = \frac{1}{M}\sum_{x=0}^{M-1} f(2x+1)W_{M}^{ux}, \tag{2-8}$$

$$W_N = e^{-j2\pi/N}, \; M = N/2. \tag{2-9}$$

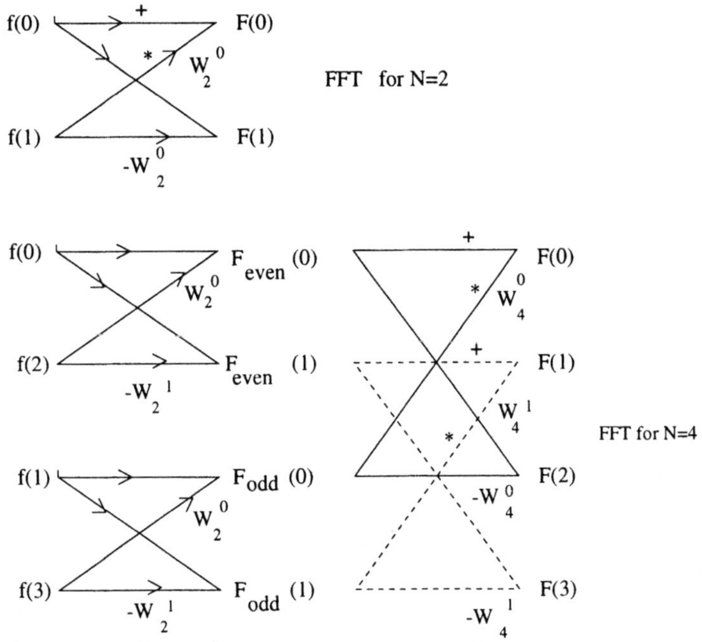

Figure 2.11. FFT butterfly data communication pattern for $N = 2$ and $N = 4$

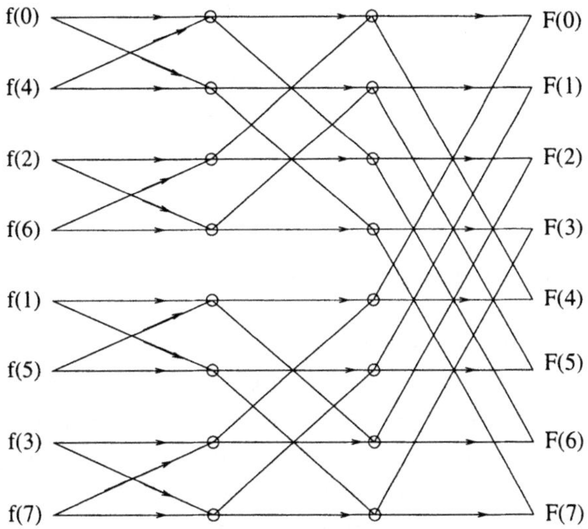

Figure 2.12. FFT butterfly data communication pattern for $N = 8$

FFT requires a "butterfly" data communication. This "butterfly" pattern in the cases of $N = 2$ and $N = 4$ are shown in Figure 2.11. The case of $N = 8$ is shown in Figure 2.12. The two-dimensional FFT is done

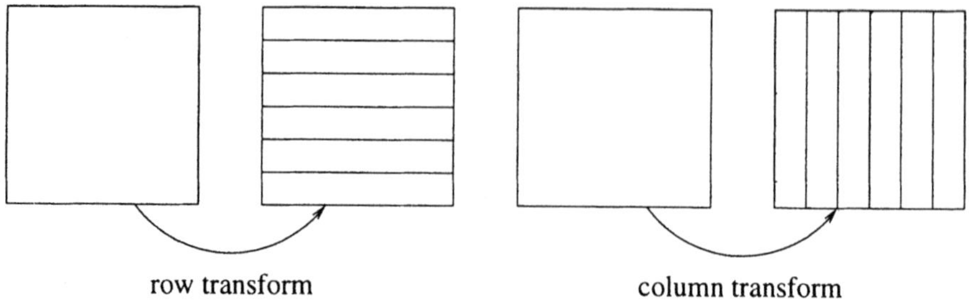

Figure 2.13. The steps in a 2-D FFT

by applying a 1-D FFT on each row separately, replacing the pixels with the FFT results, then applying a 1-D FFT on the columns. Figure 2.13 depicts this process.

Both the histogram and the FFT computations are commonly used. Because of the fundamental importance of the FFT, a great number of FFT algorithms have been proposed for almost every existing sequential and parallel machine. The basic computation steps in the FFT have also been used for other transforms, such as the discrete Walsh transform and the discrete Hadamard transform.

All these global computations can take advantage of parallel computers and their interconnection networks. Some network models, such as the hypercube, have better inherent global communication abilities. A standard mesh network employs a step-wise propagation, and "enhanced mesh networks" have certain types of global links, such as a shared bus for an entire row or column.

2.5 Regular and Irregular Data Movement

The data communication and computation in the filtering, histogram and the FFT computations are regular in the sense that the operation steps are fixed and they are dependent only on the *size* but not the *values* of the input image. Single Instruction stream Multiple Data stream (SIMD) parallel computers are especially suitable for this type of operations. Since the operation steps are completely predictable, the performance of those tasks is known beforehand.

Some PRIP tasks involve irregular communication patterns, thus their execution order and speed are not completely predictable. A typical example is the region growing operation in which every region may grow in its own speed and along specific directions, as indicated in Figure 2.14. If some parts of the image are completely homogeneous, as on the upper-

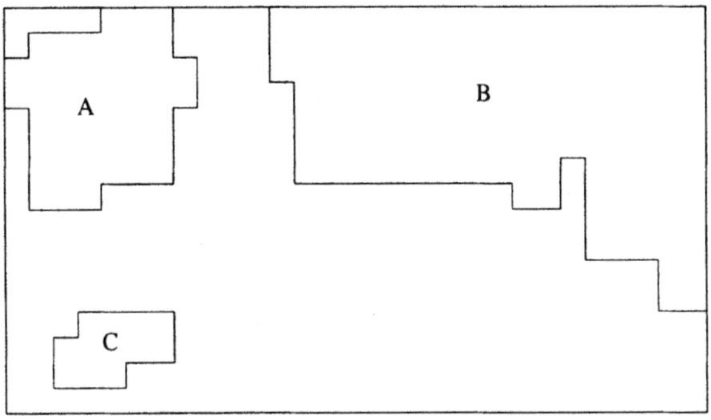

Figure 2.14. In region growing, the regions in a homogeneous part (upper-right) of the image can grow into a large region and take longer time than in other parts (e.g., the lower-left portion of the image

right corner of the image in Figure 2.14, a seed B can easily expand through a large area and take a long time. The image parts with many strong edges can stop merging much earlier and have to wait, as in the lower-left part of that example image. If a parallel machine is used and the image pixels are distributed spatially to the processors, some processors could idle for a long time. The dynamic load balancing can be highly desirable in this case.

2.6 IAP Data Movement on Parallel Machines

In a relatively small sequential computer, a large image and intermediate matrices may not be able to reside in the central memory all at the same time. At least they may not be put in cache at once. This affects the PRIP operations with global data movements more seriously than those operations involving mostly local communications. When real-time PRIP computations are required, the memory access may become a bottleneck. Later chapters of this book discuss this problem to a certain extent.

On a parallel computer, the PRIP operations with mostly regular data movements can be handled very well by many types of interconnection network [4, 5, 18, 19, 20]. With a SIMD machine, each processing element (PE) has a small local memory for data but no program memory, and a number of direct links to other PEs. Data exchanges, especially global data communications, can be an interesting design topic that is completely different for every type of interconnection network. On a hypercube machine, the only allowable data communications take place between two PEs with a direct link. In other words, all the data transfer

	$j = 00$	01	10	11
$i = 000$	$r = 0$ 00000	1 00001	2 00010	3 00011
001	4 00100	5 00101	6 00110	7 00111
010	8 01000	9 01001	10 01010	11 01011
011	12 01100	13 01101	14 01110	15 01111
$i = 100$	$r = 16$ 10000	17 10001	18 10010	19 10011
101	20 10100	21 10101	22 10110	23 10111
110	24 11000	25 11001	26 11010	27 11011
111	28 11100	29 11101	30 11110	31 11111

Figure 2.15. The PEs of a 32 processor cube are listed with their indices r in both binary and decimal forms, and with their conceptual row and column indices i and j

Procedure Broadcast (A, x, y) {
  for $(l = x; l >= y; l-)$ {
    $A(r^{(l)}) \leftarrow A(r), (r_l = 0)$
  }
}

Figure 2.16. A parallel procedure for broadcasting contents in register A

must take the following shape

$$B(p^{(k)}) \longleftarrow A(p)$$

where $A(p)$ is a local register on PE(p) and $B(p^{(k)})$ is a local register on PE(q) with q being almost identical to p except bit k.

A hypercube computer with 2^{n+m} PEs can be used to store an image of size $2^n \times 2^m$. For example, when $n = 3$ and $m = 2$, the PEs can be visualized as a 8×4 array, as depicted in Figure 2.15. Broadcasting contents of register A along one of the dimensions can be done with the procedure listed in Figure 2.16. When $x = n + m - 1$ and $y = m$, that procedure will replicate the contents in register A of the PEs in row 0 to those of all other rows on the machine in Figure 2.15. Figure 2.17 demonstrates a row-to-row broadcasting on that machine. The procedure in Figure 2.18, with parameters $x = n+m-1$ and $y = m$, rotates upwards

	initial	$l=4$	$l=3$	$l=2$
$i=000$	0	0	0	0
001	1	1	1	0
010	2	2	0	0
011	3	3	1	0
100	4	0	0	0
101	5	1	1	0
110	6	2	0	0
111	7	3	1	0

Figure 2.17. The content of register A of each PE at each step during broadcasting

```
Procedure RotateUp (A, x, y) {
  for (l = x; l >= y; l--) {
    A(r^(l)) ← A(r), (r_k = 0 for all k < l)
  }
}
```

Figure 2.18. A parallel procedure for rotating the contents in register A

	initial	$l=4$	$l=3$	$l=2$
$i=000$	0	4	2	1
001	1	1	1	2
010	2	2	4	3
011	3	3	3	4
100	4	0	6	5
101	5	5	5	6
110	6	6	0	7
111	7	7	7	0

Figure 2.19. The content of register A of each PE at each step during rotation

the contents of the columns in the above machine. Figure 2.19 presents the details. Other data communication patterns and procedures can be seen in many parallel algorithm papers and books, such as [7, 15, 16].

2.7 Conclusion

This chapter has discussed a number of common IAP data formats and frequently used data movement/distribution patterns. Some of the movements are similar to general numerical computations, such as accessing rows and columns of a pattern matrix. Some movements and distribution patterns are special to PRIP, such as the margin treatments. Many data movements in low-level PRIP computations are local, such as in the filtering operations. The global IAP data communications, such as those in the FFT algorithm, can take advantage of a parallel computer and its powerful interconnection network. The irregular data movements, such as those in a region growing and in a tree-search type of matching algorithm, require a special attention in order to maintain system efficiency.

References

[1] *http://www.simplesystems.org/ImageMagick/www/formats.html.*

[2] G. Awcock. *Applied Image Processing.* Macmillan Press, 1994.

[3] S.T. Bow. *Pattern Recognition and Image Processing.* Marcel Dekker, 1992.

[4] P. Chaudhuri. *Parallel Algorithms: Design and Analysis.* Prentice-Hall, 1992.

[5] M. Cosnard. *Parallel Algorithms and Architectures.* Van Nostrand Reinhold, 1995.

[6] F. Dailey. *Image Technology: State of the Art.* Computer Technology Research, 1992.

[7] Z. Fang, X. Li, and L. Ni. On the communication complexity of generalized 2-d convolution on array processors. *IEEE Trans. on Computers*, 38(2):184–194, 1989.

[8] B. Furht. *Video and Image processing in Multimedia Systems.* Kluwer Academic Publishers, 1995.

[9] R.C. Gonzalez and R.E. Woods. *Digital Image Processing.* Addison-Wesley, 1992.

[10] B. Jahne. *Digital Image Processing: Concepts, Algorithms, and Scientific Applications.* Spring-Verlag, 1995.

[11] J. Knipe and X. Li. An improved lattice vector quantization scheme for wavelet compression. *IEEE Trans. Signal Proc.*, 46(1):239–243, 1998.

[12] E. Leung and X. Li. Parallel processing approaches to edge relaxation. *Pattern Recognition*, 21(6):547–558, 1988.

[13] N. Pavel. *Fundamentals of Pattern Recognition.* Marcel Dekker, 1993.

[14] J.M. Prager. Extracting and labeling boundary segments in natural scenes. *IEEE Trans. Pattern Anal. Mach. Intell.*, PAMI-2(1):16–27, 1980.

[15] X. Qu and X. Li. Parallel template matching algorithms. In *1988 International Conference on Parallel Processing*, pages 223–226, 1988.

[16] S. Ranka and S. Sahni. *Hypercube Algorithms.* Springer-Verlag, 1990.

[17] J. Russ. *The Image Processing handbook, 3rd ed.* CRC Press, 1999.

[18] J. Smith. *The Design and Analysis of Parallel Algorithms.* Oxford University Press, 1993.

[19] D. Vernon. *Parallel Computer Vison.* Ellis Horwood, 1992.

[20] D. Zhang. Survey for special purpose computer of pattern recognition and image processing (PRIP). *Journal of Automation*, (1):84–92, 1989.

Chapter 3

TYPICAL PRIP ALGORITHMS AND IAP DATA MANAGEMENT

In this chapter, we give four typical PRIP algorithms, including two low-level image processing operations: linear spatial filtering and binary morphological filtering, one mid-level image segmentation operation: the Hough transform, and one higher-level operation: object labeling. These algorithms cover a number of common data distribution and movement patterns.

3.1 Introduction

Filtering is the most commonly used and most well-studied PRIP operation. Almost every single PRIP application requires some kind of filtering, at least at the beginning stage. Some popular filtering operations have been built into image acquisition software packages.

The Hough transform is an image segmentation method. It involves an intermediate matrix called the accumulator array. This method is powerful in detecting parametric or nearly parametric curves, even when the curves are only partially visible in the input image. The implementation of the algorithm is straightforward and the parameter control is relatively easy. There are several variations of the original Hough transform that improve the computation efficiency.

Object labeling is an understanding of the image objects (usually the resulting regions from the image segmentation process). Different algorithms have been proposed for various computer models.

In this chapter, the basic steps of those operations are described first, followed by example applications. The data storage and communication patterns in each case have unique characteristics and require different treatments. Usually, Single Instruction stream and Single Data stream (SIMD) computers are more useful for lower level PRIP operations because of the local and regular data communication patterns, and Multiple Instruction stream and Multiple Data stream (MIMD) comput-

$W(-r,-c)$	......	$W(-r,0)$	......	$W(-r,v)$
......	......	......	......	......
$W(0,-c)$	......	$\boxed{W(0,0)}$	......	$W(0,v)$
......	......	......	......	......
$W(h,-c)$	......	$W(h,0)$	......	$W(h,v)$

Figure 3.1. A template of size $(r+h+1) \times (c+v+1)$ centered at $(0,0)$

ers are more suitable for handling the irregular and global data movement in the higher-level PRIP operations. Here, we give a brief discussion of two parallel algorithms: a SIMD filtering algorithm and a MIMD labeling algorithm.

3.2 Linear Spatial Filtering

The linear filtering in the spatial domain, also called the *template matching* operation, is defined as

$$Y(i,j) = \sum_{s=-r}^{h} \sum_{t=-c}^{v} X(i+s, j+t) \cdot W(s,t),$$
$$r \leq i < R-h, \; c \leq j < C-v \qquad (3\text{-}1)$$

where X is an input image of $R \times C$, Y is the output image of $(R-r-h) \times (C-c-v)$, "$\cdot$" denotes multiplication, and W is the template of size $(r+h+1) \times (c+v+1)$, which is also called "window" or "filter", as shown in Figure 3.1.

In most cases, the template is symmetric, that is, $r = h$ and $c = v$, as defined in most textbooks. However, asymmetric filters (e.g., 1×2 and 2×2 templates) do exist, as mentioned in Chapter 2. Different filters define different operations. A typical symmetric 3×3 low-pass filter is an averaging with W defined as in Figure 3.2(a). A simple symmetric high-pass filter is given in Figure 3.2(b). A "high-boost" ([5] p196) enhancement filtering is to add a certain percentage of the result of high-pass filtering to the original image. Figure 3.3 demonstrates the effect of filtering. Part (a) is an input image of a traffic intersection. Part (b) shows a high-boost filtering result. Part (c) shows the low-pass filtering effect.

The sequential implementation of a linear filtering has four levels of nested loops: i, j, s, and t, where i and j are the row/column indices for the image Y, and s, t are for the filter (template) W, as shown in Figure 3.4.

1/9	1/9	1/9
1/9	1/9	1/9
1/9	1/9	1/9

(a)

−1/9	−1/9	−1/9
−1/9	8/9	−1/9
−1/9	−1/9	−1/9

(b)

Figure 3.2. A 3×3 averaging (low-pass) filter and a 3×3 high-pass filter, both in spatial domain

(a) original image

(b) an enhanced version (high-pass filtering result added to the original)

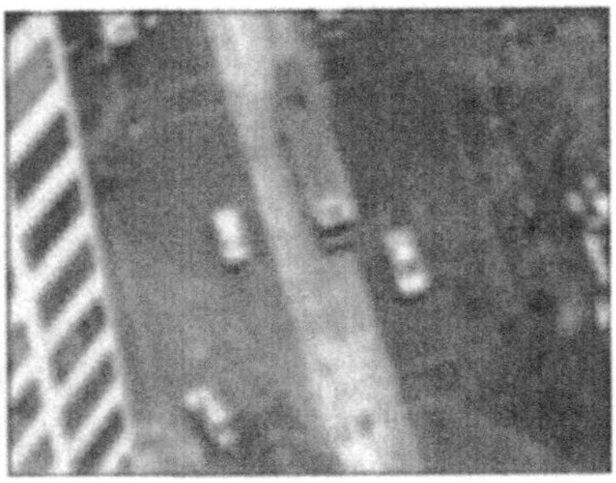

(c) a blurred version (low-pass filtering result)

Figure 3.3. Examples of linear filtering results on a traffic intersection image

```
for (i = r; i < R - h; i++) {
    for (j = c; j < C - v; j++) {
        Y(i,j) = 0;
        for (s = (-r); s <= h; s++) {
            for (t = (-c); t <= v; t++) {
                Y(i,j) += X[i+s][j+t] * W[s][t];
            }
        }
    }
}
```

Figure 3.4. Template matching pseudo code (sequential)

−1	−2	−1
0	0	0
−1	−2	−1

−1	0	1
−2	0	2
−1	0	1

(a) Sobel edge detector ([5] p199)

1	1	1
1	1	1
1	1	1
0	0	0
−1	−1	−1
−1	−1	−1
−1	−1	−1

1	1	1	0	−1	−1	−1
1	1	1	0	−1	−1	−1
1	1	1	0	−1	−1	−1

(b) two masks to detect boundaries but not thin lines

Figure 3.5. Edge detector examples

Linear filters have been used to detect various features of the image. A tremendously large number of edge detection filters have been proposed. Figure 3.5(a) shows the popular Sobel edge detectors. Using the Sobel detectors on an image similar to that in Figure 3.3(a), the road markers (pedestrian crossing lines), as well as the vehicle outlines, can be picked up. A closer examination of the images reveals that the street markers are two or three pixels wide. In a vehicle detection system, to distinguish thin lines from the boundary between homogeneous regions, the 7×3 and 3×7 filters in Figure 3.5(b) are proposed [12], and produced the edge detection result in Figure 3.6(c).

(a) original image

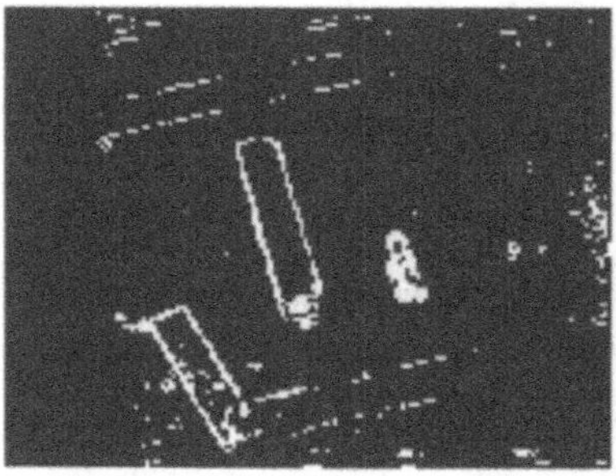

(b) the result of using Sobel operator

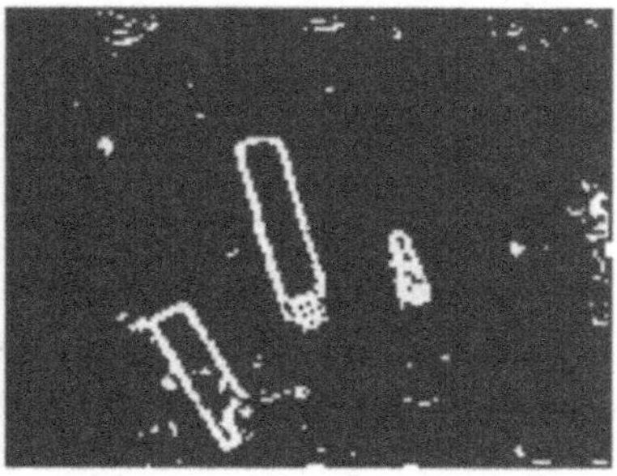

(c) the result of using the 7×3 and 3×7 masks

Figure 3.6. Edge detection results using operators given in the previous figure

+	*			
	*			
	*	*		
*				

(a)

+		*		
		*		
		*	*	
	*			

(b)

Figure 3.7. Input binary image X and a translation X_w

3.3 Morphological Filtering

There are various types of non-linear filtering. Binary morphological filtering operations are defined below. Let $X = \{X(i,j)\}$ be a set of input pixels with value 1. Figure 3.7(a) depicts a 5×5 binary image:

$$X = \{(0,1), (1,1), (2,1), (2,2), (3,0)\}. \tag{3-2}$$

All other input pixels have the value 0. The upper-left corner, (0,0), is designated as the "origin". The translation of the above X by a point $w = (0,1)$ is

$$(X)_w = \{x + w \mid x \in X\} = \{(0,2), (1,2), (2,2), (2,3), (3,1)\}, \tag{3-3}$$

Figure 3.7(b) shows $(X)_w$. The origins are marked as "+" and the set elements are marked as "*".

A collection of points, $W = \{w\} = \{W(s,t)\}$, called the *structuring element*, is used in a similar way that a template is used in the linear filtering operations. The binary dilation of X by W is defined as the union of the translations of X by the elements of W, i.e.,

$$X \oplus W = \bigcup_{w \in W} (X)_w \tag{3-4}$$

Consider $W = \{(0,0), (0,1)\}$ with (0,0) being its origin. In other words, this filter W is of size 1 by 2. In the formulation of Equation (3-1) of Section 3.2, it has $r = h = c = 0$ and $v = 1$. For the same X above, $X \oplus W$ is shown in Figure 3.8.

A binary erosion of X by W is the set of locations for the origin of W such that W is completely contained in X. That is,

$$X \ominus W = \{x \mid (W)_x \subseteq X\} = \bigcap_{w \in W} (X)_{-w}. \tag{3-5}$$

In the above example, $X \ominus W$ would be just a single point at (2,1).

+	*	*		
	*	*		
	*	*	*	
*	*			

Figure 3.8. An example of binary dilation $X \oplus W$

Figures 3.9(a) through (e) give an example for the application of binary erosion and dilation in a traffic scene analysis system. The input to the vision system is a pair of images, U and V. Image V is taken by a video camera installed above the intersection. Image U is a reference picture that is taken by the same camera when the intersection is empty (with no vehicles). A simple image subtraction, $|U-V|$, is used to detect the changes hoping to spot the vehicles present in V. A morphological filtering operation is employed to eliminate noise and to connect the pixels belong to the same vehicle. Figures 3.9(a) and (b) show images U and V, respectively. In Part (c), the white pixels in $|U - V|$ are the ones in $|U-V|$ with a value above a pre-determined threshold. A binary erosion operation is applied to this thresholded difference image, and its result is presented in Figure 3.9(d). Small groups of isolated pixels have been eliminated. A binary dilation filtering is applied to the erosion result producing an image shown in Figure 3.9(e). Here, the pixels form connected regions that correspond to actual vehicles. In real applications, the binary morphological operations can be modified to fit specific needs. For example, the erosion operation above is actually a modified version, which is defined below (K is the input image):

$$K_1(i,j) = 1 \text{ only if } K(i,j) = 1 \text{ and at least two neighbors are also } 1.$$

A full description of the linear and non-linear filtering operations used in this traffic scene analysis system can be found in [12].

A direct implementation of a binary dilation operation has four levels of nested loops: i, j, s, and t, where i and j are the row/column indices for the image Y , and s, t are for W. A pseudo-code algorithm is given in Figure 3.10.

It is obvious that the data communication pattern in a morphological filtering is the same as in a linear filtering. Because of the independence between the operations in non-overlapping neighborhoods, the spatial-domain filtering is among the first PRIP operations to be made parallel. Numerous parallel algorithms have been proposed for almost

(a) reference image U (empty intersection)

(b) image V of the intersection with vehicles

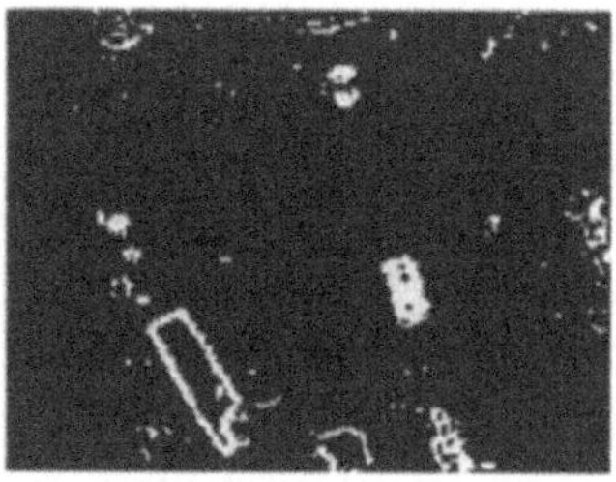

(c) thresholded $|U - V|$

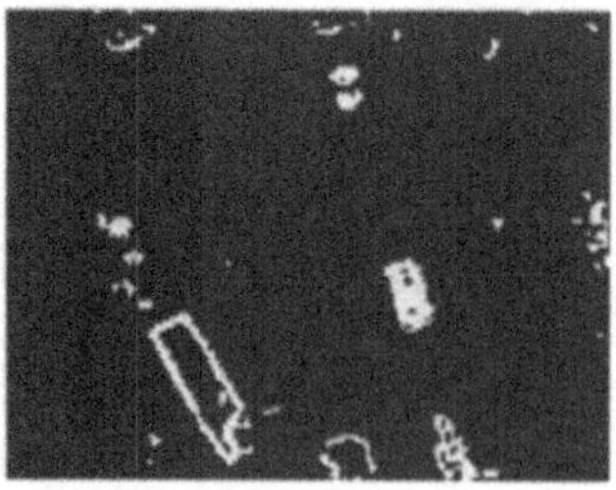

(d) after modified erosion

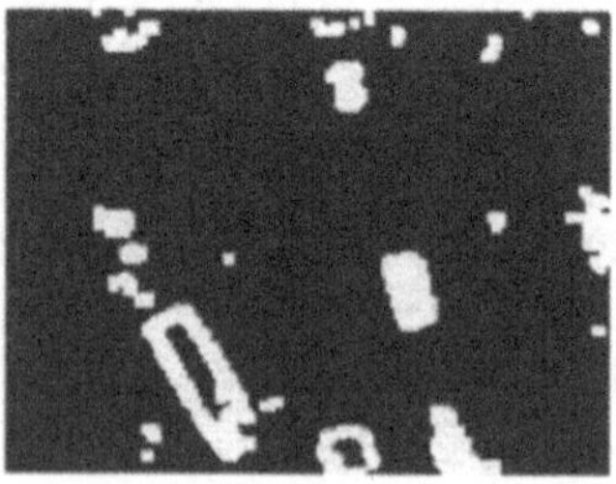

(e) after dilation

Figure 3.9. Morphological filtering on frame difference

```
for (i = r; i < R - h; i++) {
    for (j = c; j < C - v; j++) {
        Y[i][j] = 0;
        if (X[i][j]==1) {
            for (s = (-r); s <= h; s++) {
                for (t = (-c); t <= v; t++) {
                    if (W[s][t]==1) Y[i + s][j + t] = 1;
                }
            }
        }
    }
}
```

Figure 3.10. Java-like pseudo-code for binary dilation

every possible type of multiprocessor computer. Based on the Gray code communication pattern, hypercube template matching algorithms have been proposed for various SIMD and MIMD machines in 1980s. Ranka and Sahni [16] presents the algorithms for the cases where N^2 processors are available and $O(M)$ or $O(1)$ memory are attached to each processor, where $N \times N$ is the image size and $M \times M$ is the template size. As an example, Figure 3.11 provides another filtering algorithm for a SIMD hypercube machine with N^2 PEs and M^2 local memory cells per PE. Since filtering is only carried out in the spatial-domain when M is small, say, $M = 3$ or $M = 5$, $M \times M$ is a realistic local memory size and it allows a full utilization of the inherent data parallelism of the operation. The procedure QU88 involves five local registers: register A of PE(i, j) stores the input pixel value $(X(i, j))$, register C contains the final result pixel, and registers B, D, E are used to accumulate the partial results. The routines called from QU88 are given in Figure 3.12. Detailed explanations and examples can be seen in [15].

3.4 Hough Transform

The second example algorithm discussed in this chapter is the Hough transform that is frequently used for detecting curves or shapes in an image. Usually, an edge detection procedure produces an edge map where every pixel position has a value representing the edge-ness of its neighborhood. This edge map goes through a thresholding process and only the "strong" edges remain. Each strong edge is associated with a set of points in a parameter space, and "votes" for those parameter points.

```
Procedure QU88(A,B,C,D,E)
{
  B(p)=0; C(p)=0; D(p)=0; E(p)=0;
  MAR(p)=0; // set memory address register
  for (t = 0; t < M; t++) {
    for (s = o; s < M; s++) {
      CMAR=a+t*M+s; // set CM address
      M[MAR(p)] = CM[CMAR];
      MAR(p)++;
    }
  }
  alongColumn;
  ROTATE(D,m,n-1,0); C(p)=C(p)+D(p);
  ROTATE(E,m,n-1,0); B(p)=B(p)+E(p);
  ROTATE(B,n+m,2n-1,0); C(p)=C(p)+B(p);
}
```

Figure 3.11. Template matching algorithm QU88 on hypercube SIMD machines with N^2 PEs and M^2 local memory cells per PE

For example, any straight line passing through a fixed point (x, y) in the image space must have the format

$$x \cos A + y \sin A = r \tag{3-6}$$

as shown in Figure 3.13. That is, in the parameter space (r, A), there is a curve associated with the image space point (x, y). Many points on a straight line have the same values for r and A, therefore contribute to a same location of the parameter space. In other words, the points in the image space "vote" for the points in the parameter space. The intersection of curves in the parameter space represents straight lines in the image space. Consequently, detecting straight lines in the image space has become a problem of detecting points in the parameter space with a high number of "votes". The discrete representation of the parameter space is a 2-D array. The size and range of that 2-D array have to be chosen carefully. In other words, the definition and selection of the array for the parameter space is crucial in the Hough transform. Figure 3.14 depicts the correspondence between the input image lines and the curves in the parameter space, and demonstrates the idea of "voting". Figure 3.14(a) is the thresholded edge map. Parts (b), (c) and (d) are the accumulator array H at three different resolution: 125×45, 500×180, and 250×90. When the accumulator cells are too coarse, as in Part (b), the location of the peaks are not precise. When the cells are too fine, as

```
Procedure alongColumn
{
    t = 0; withinColumn(A, C, B, t);
    for (l = 0; l < m; l++) {
        A(p^(l) ⟵ A(p);
        t = (t + 2^l) mod M (p_l = 0);
        t = (t − 2^l) mod M (p_l = 1);
        withinColumn(A, C, B, t)  (p_l = 0);
        withinColumn(A, D, E, t)  (p_l = 1);
        F = false;
        U = l;
        GrayColumn(U, F);
    }
}

Procedure withinColumn (A, C, B, t)
{
    s = 0;
    MAR(p) = t * M;
    C(p) = C(p) + A(p) * M[MAR(p)];
    for (k = n; k < n + m; l++) {
        A(p^(k) ⟵ A(p);
        s = s + 2^(k−n) mod M (p_k = 0);
        s = s − 2^(k−n) mod M (p_k = 1);
        MAR(p) = t * M + s;
        C(p) = C(p) + A(p) * M[MAR(p)] (p_k = 0);
        B(p) = B(p) + A(p) * M[MAR(p)] (p_k = 1);
        F = false;
        U = k − n;
        GrayRow(U, F);
    }
    A(p^(n+m−1) ⟵ A(p);
}
```

Figure 3.12. Procedures called from QU88

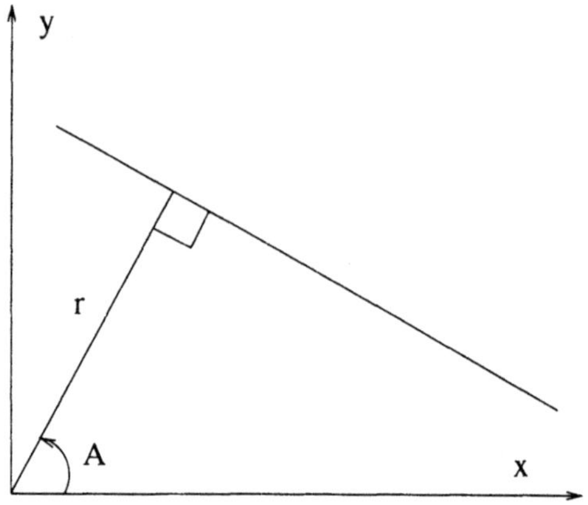

Figure 3.13. (A, r) representation of a straight line

in Part (c), only a very small number of cells can actually receive enough votes to become detectable peaks. The resolution in Part (d) gives the best result in this particular case.

Figure 3.15 (a) and (b) show two real images. Parts (c) and (d) are the thresholded edge difference images (subtracting the empty intersection image, before the morphological operations). The inputs to the Hough transform are given in parts (e) and (f). The results of the Hough transform are marked as gray lines in parts (e) and (f). Note the vehicle on the lower-left part of each image. In the case of (e), the Hough result correctly mark the vehicle outline and the noisy "arm" sticking out can no longer ruin the centroid and shape computation. That "arm" is actually a pedestrian walking by. In the case of part (f), a vehicle is partially covered by a tree, thus the edge map shows a box with one end being very heavy. Without the Hough transform, the centroid of the box would have been too close to the heavy end instead of at the true center of the vehicle.

The Hough transform has been used to detect other curves. To detect circles, a 3-D parameter space is used. A point (x, y) is on a circle with parameter (a, b, c) with:

$$(x - a)^2 + (y - b)^2 = c. \tag{3-7}$$

The parameters a and b are the center of a circle, and c is the radius. Figure 3.16(a) shows the side-view of a truck. The circular shape of the wheels can be easily detected using the above form of the Hough transform. In this case, the matrix for the parameter space can be su-

(a) Four lines

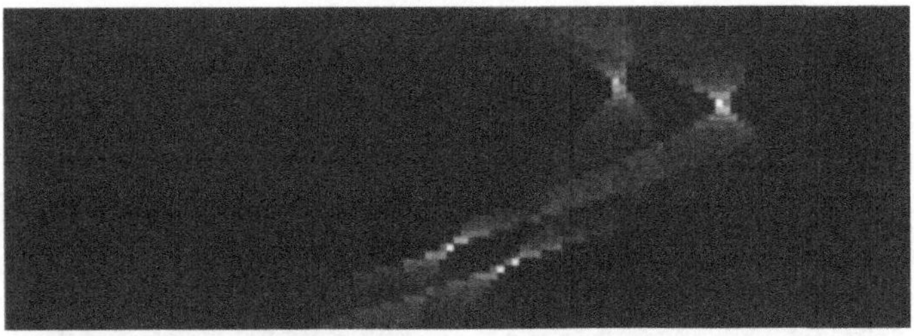

(b) A coarse array H (125×45)

(c) A fine array H (500×180)

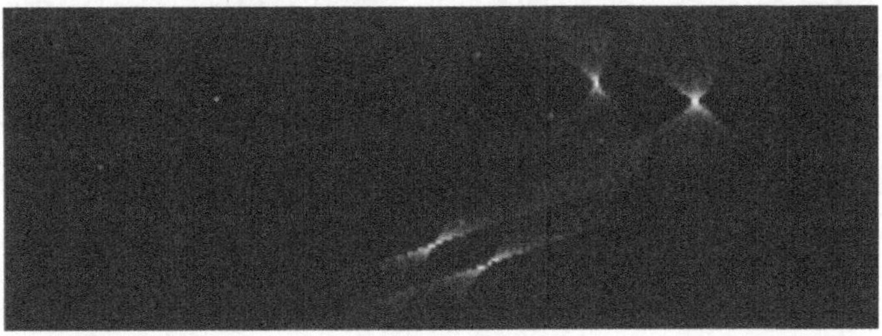

(d) Array H (250×90)

Figure 3.14. Hough accumulator array H in different resolutions

(a) A pedestrian is walking near the vehicle at lower-left

(b) The vehicle at lower-left is partially covered by a tree

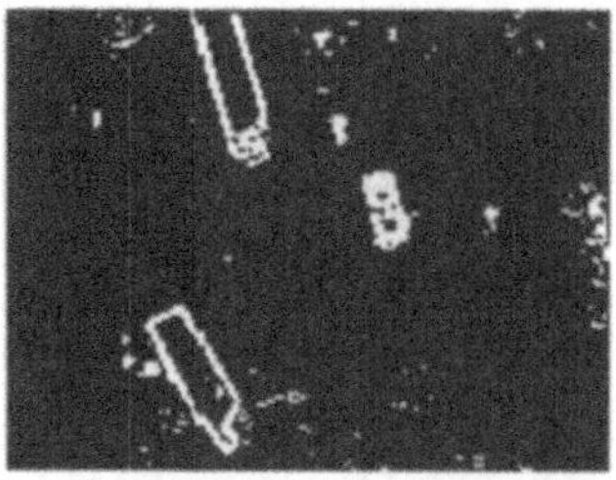

(c) Thresholded edge difference (subtracting the empty intersection)

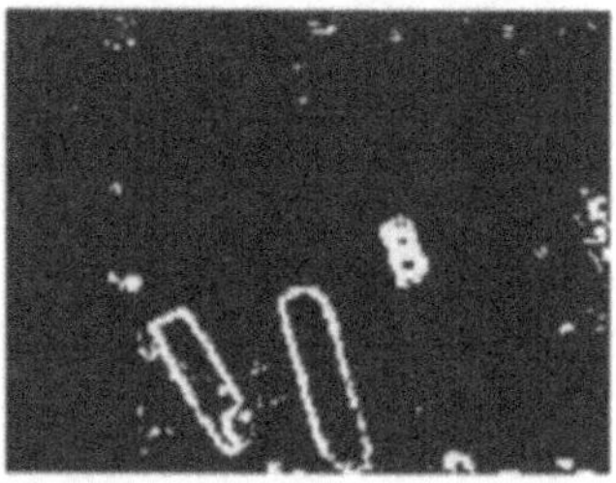

(d) Thresholded edge difference (subtracting the empty intersection)

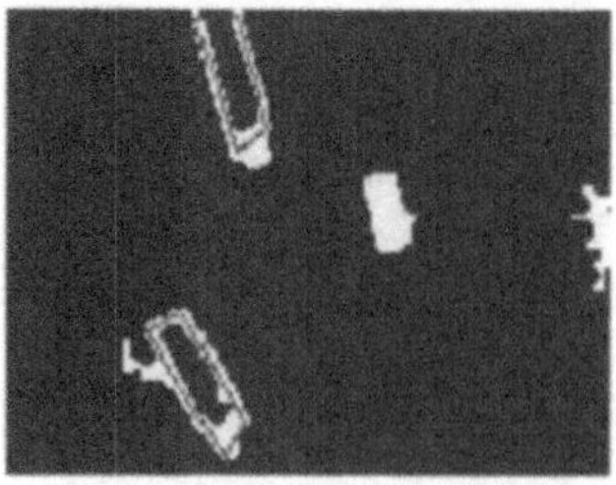

(e) The input and output of Hough transform

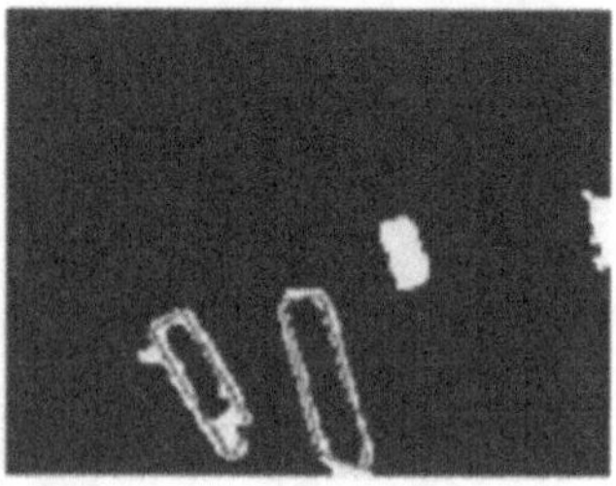

(f) The input and output of Hough transform

Figure 3.15. Hough transform correctly detects the outline of a vehicle despite of the shape distortion

(a) Side view of a truck

(b) The edge map where the circles are clearly visible and easily detected by Hough transform

Figure 3.16. Wheel detection using circle Hough transform

perimposed on the input image, with a and b aligned with x and y, the coordinates of the input image.

The Hough transform has also been used to detect arbitrary non-parametric shapes [1]. A rigid object of any shape can be detected regardless the position, rotation and scale changes. A variation of that scheme could be used for detecting somewhat "elastic" shapes. That is, the shape of the objects can encapsulate some degree of deformability. Let's introduce the idea of a "well-behaved shape" (*WBS*), which is any simple shape for which there exists a reference location L such that a ray drawn from L at any angle will pass through exactly one point on the perimeter of the shape. Every convex shape is well-behaved. Some concave shapes can also be a *WBS* as illustrated in Figure 3.17. In Fig-

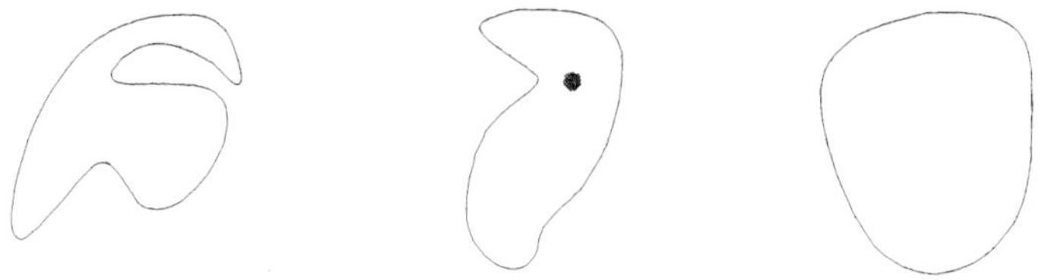

(a) (b) (c)

Figure 3.17. Some closed shapes. (a) Neither well-behaved nor convex; (b) well-behaved but not convex; (c) well-behaved and convex

ure 3.17*(b)*, a small region exists (represented by the shaded circle) in which a suitable L may be found. The *WBS* concept can be easily extended to accommodate open shapes (i.e. curve segments). Thus, if a closed shape happens not to be well-behaved, it can be decomposed into a finite number of well- behaved open shapes, each with its own reference location.

To achieve the attribute of elasticity, it is necessary merely to add an extra radius component to the vector, so that each entry in the data structure now contains an angle θ, a minimum radius r_1 and a maximum radius r_2. In Figure 3.18, the shaded area represents the region of deformability for the shape. A point at a distance d from the reference location is considered to be part of the shape provided $r_1 \leq d \leq r_2$ for the given angle, i.e. it falls somewhere within the shaded region. Since it is possible to set $r_1 = r_2$ for any (or all) of the vectors in the data structure, the elastic model is clearly a superset of all well-behaved rigid shapes that can be represented in Ballard's scheme [1].

This elastic model is used with the Hough transform to detect eyeglasses in an "ID- type" input image containing a single upright human face. The presence of eyeglasses could disturb many face recognition al-

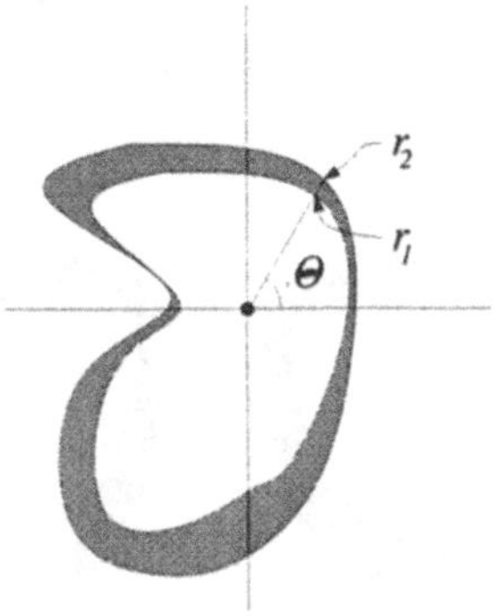

Figure 3.18. The elastic model of a simple shape

gorithms, especially the steps for locating the eyes. Directly detecting the eyeglasses helps correctly locate the eye position and facilitate the normalization of the face in terms of size and orientation, which can be crucial in the later face recognition or verification process.

Developing a template for eyeglasses is accomplished by selecting a set of 13 representative images. Some observed measurements of those test images are tabulated in Table 3.1.

Table 3.1. Statistics contributing to eyeglasses template design (distances in pixels)

CHARACTERISTIC	MINIMUM	MAXIMUM	AVERAGE
Horizontal extent	35	44	39.3
Vertical extent	29	38	34.2
Center-to-center distance	46	53	48.5
Tilt angle	$-3.4°$	$4.1°$	$0.6°$

The horizontal and vertical extent measures are the average bounding box dimensions for each of the left and right lens in the image. The center-to-center distance is the distance between the bounding box centers for each of the two lenses. The tilt angle is the angle made by the center-line of the glasses with respect to the horizon. All left lenses are normalized to eliminate any tilt angles and all centers aligned. The term "left" here refers to the lens that is physically located on the left side of the image, and not to the lens over the subject's left eye. The resulting single image of a left lens (appears to be a very thick frame) is flipped to create a mirror-image copy to produce the right lens. Two lenses are positioned so that their centers are the desired 48.5 pixels apart. The assembled composite shape template is depicted in Figure 3.19.

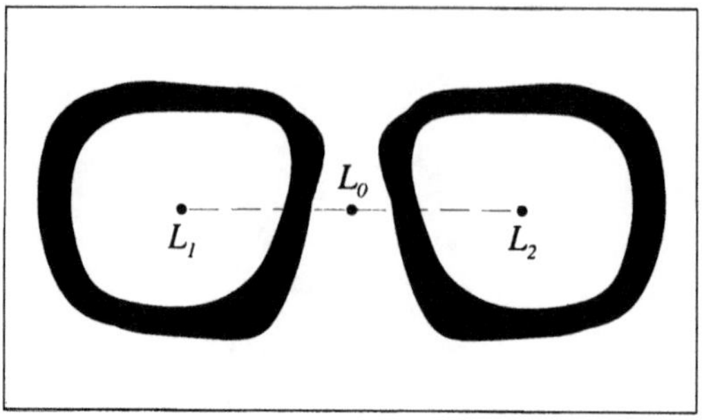

Figure 3.19. Applying the elastic shape model to the eyeglasses template

Since the template consists of two closed, well-behaved shapes, it is convenient to store the vectors for each lens as a list sorted according to increasing angle, that makes it possible to perform a binary search on the template entries at run-time, thereby making the Hough transform phase of the program more efficient.

Several line detection masks, shown in Figure 3.20, are used to extract lines, including the eyeglasses frame lines. Note that these line

-1	-1	-1	-1	-1
0	0	0	0	0
2	2	2	2	2
0	0	0	0	0
-1	-1	-1	-1	-1

(a) 0°|180°

-1	0	2	0	-1
-1	0	2	0	-1
-1	0	2	0	-1
-1	0	2	0	-1
-1	0	2	0	-1

(b) 90°|270°

0	-1	-1	0	2
-1	-1	0	2	0
-1	0	2	0	-1
0	2	0	-1	-1
2	0	-1	-1	0

(c) 45°|225°

2	0	-1	-1	0
0	2	0	-1	-1
-1	0	2	0	-1
-1	-1	0	2	0
0	-1	-1	0	2

(d) 135°|315°

Figure 3.20. Masks used for detecting (a) horizontal, (b) vertical, (c) & (d) diagonal lines

detectors serve the purpose opposite to those described in the vehicle detection case in Section 3.2. Figure 3.21 shows the result of a template matching with those line masks and the result after applying a "response attenuation factor". The attenuation factor is derived from two individ-

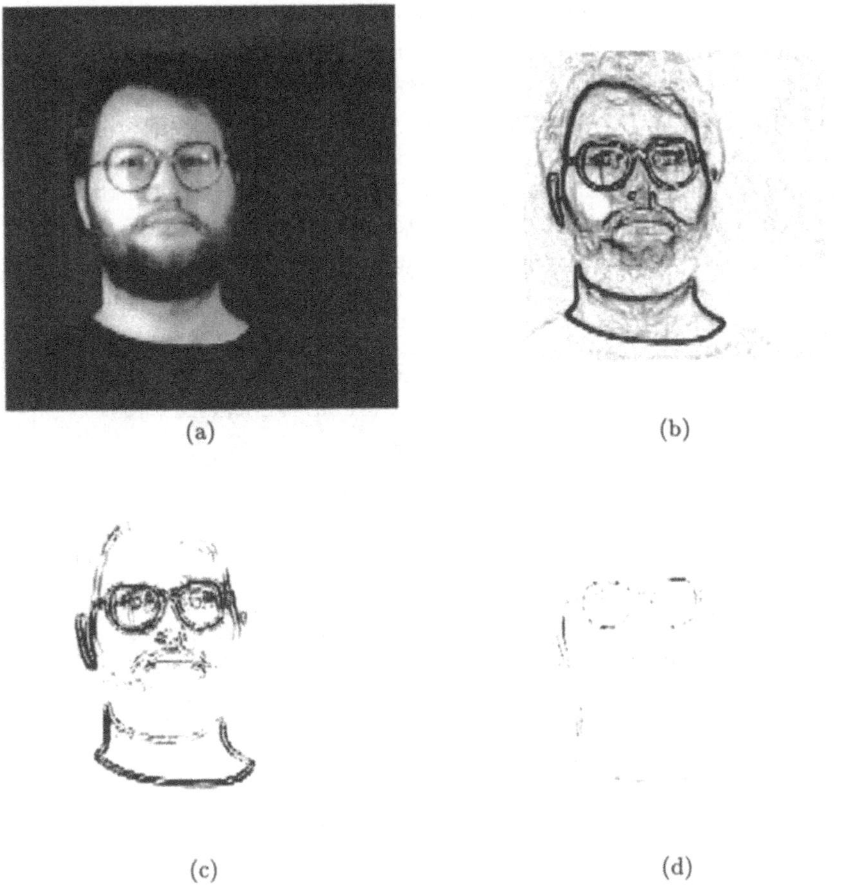

Figure 3.21. Effect of response attenuation on line detection. (a) Original image; (b) response of Sobel edge detector; (c) raw response of line detector; (d) attenuated line response

ual components: a comparison of average intensities on either side of the line on which the current pixel is assumed to lie; and a measure of the degree of smoothness or evenness of all of the pixels comprising the potential line.

The strength and orientation arrays obtained from the line detector form the input to the Hough transform. In this step, the basic Hough transform accumulates in parameter space the strength of each pixel in the line image that exceeds a certain threshold. Every such pixel p is potentially part of the rim of one of the lenses in the eyeglasses to be detected. But p is at some unknown distance from the actual center of the lens, so the transform must accumulate line strength values at all of the cells where a potential center could reside. The program searches through the template for the angle that is closest to the orientation value for p and extract the two radius values r_1 and r_2 for this angle. The accumulator then increments all of the cells that lie in a straight line at distances between r_1 and r_2 from p. Because p is a line pixel, it could very well be oriented in the opposite direction, so the procedure is repeated for the angle that is 180° greater than the orientation normal for p. Figure 3.22 provides a graphic view of the behavior of the Hough

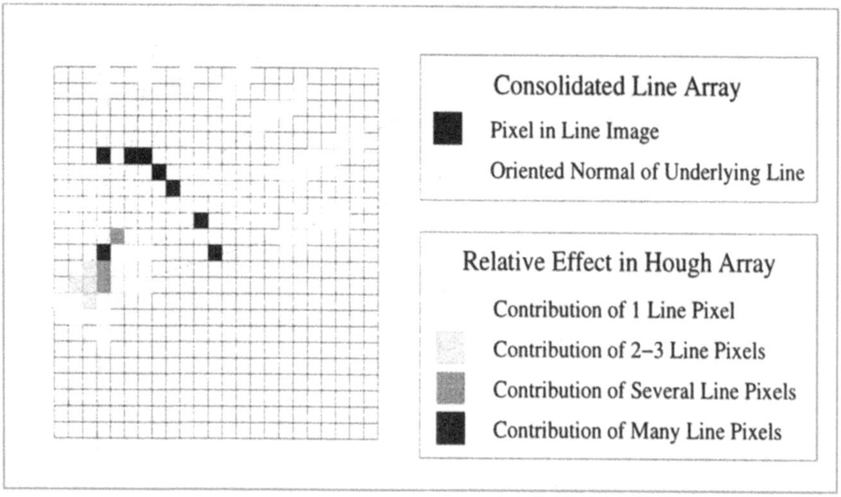

Figure 3.22. A view into the Hough Transform accumulator array

transform on a small portion of an image. For pictorial purposes, the accumulator array is assumed to be positioned directly above an imaginary line image that contains both the strength and the orientation data for each line pixel. The solid black squares represent pixels in the line image, while the shaded squares represent Hough accumulator cell values. For simplicity, it is assumed momentarily that the eyeglasses template represents a simple shape consisting of only a single lens. The immediate interpretation of the image is that the accumulator cell with the darkest shaded square corresponds to the location with the highest likelihood of being a center for this single lens. That is, if we were in the process of detecting the right lens, then the darkly shaded square might correspond to a potential location for center L_2 of Figure 3.19.

In the actual case, however, the accumulator cells must be offset so that we are incrementing the potential centers for the entire template. Considering Figure 3.19 once again, we see that L_1 is at 180° and some distance d from L_0 and that L_2 is at 0° and the same distance d from L_0. Since this information is inherent in the template data structure, the correction to the accumulator array is quite straight forward.

Besides the accumulated strength, a secondary "integrity count" array is maintained to keep track of the number of pixels that contribute to each accumulator cell. After the basic strength accumulation has finished, the accumulator cells are updated as follows:

$$A_{ij} \leftarrow A_{ij} + wC_{ij}, \tag{3-8}$$

where A_{ij} is the accumulator cell, C_{ij} is the integrity count for the corresponding cell, and w is an experimentally determined weighting factor applied to each count value.

The test set consists of 39 test pictures in which the subjects are wearing glasses. A Hough transform procedure using the elastic template constructed above is applied and 10 most likely positions for the glasses center are reported. The groups of the accumulator cells are analyzed. The following list of user-defined parameters are used:

- The line detection percentile threshold is $LP = 95$;
- The Hough transform accumulator threshold is $HT = 25$; and
- The integrity count weight factor is $WF = 80$.

The test results are tabulated in Table 3.2. With respect to the position error in the entire sample, the method correctly finds 32 of the 39 centers to within 5 pixels of the observed center. In the remaining seven pictures, six centers are found to be within 8 pixels, and one center occurs at our acceptability limit of 10 pixels.

Figure 3.23 depicts the results from a number of typical images from our sample. The orthogonal cross in each image is the center point as chosen by the program; it represents the center of the accumulator group with the largest number of contributing accumulator cells. Beneath each image is a 3-tuple $\langle e, s, c \rangle$, where e is the error of the program-selected center compared to the visually observed center, s is the accumulated strength for the group, and c is the accumulated integrity count for the group. Of particular interest is the high degree of variability in the images—the program is able to locate the glasses quite accurately irrespective of gender, race, facial expression, head position, size of the head relative to image size, presence or absence of facial hair, or overall image quality.

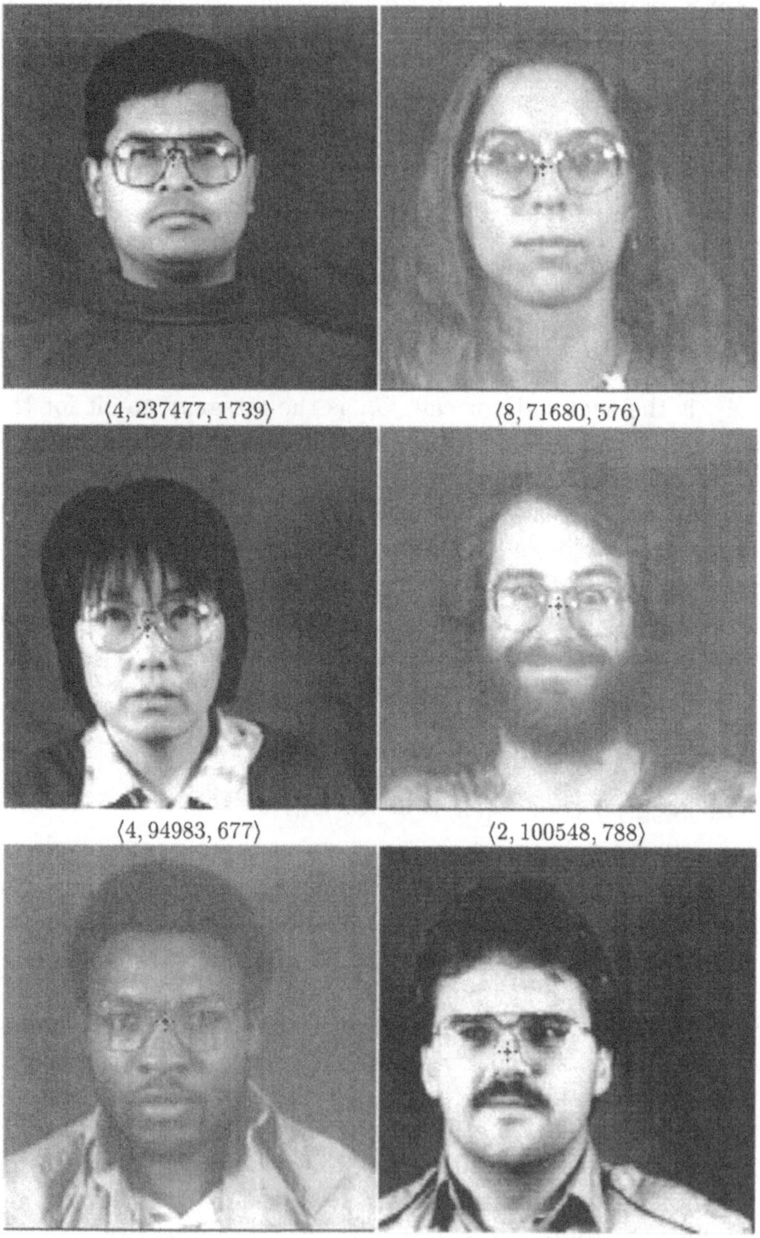

⟨4, 237477, 1739⟩ ⟨8, 71680, 576⟩

⟨4, 94983, 677⟩ ⟨2, 100548, 788⟩

⟨4, 27585, 227⟩ ⟨10, 45437, 277⟩

Figure 3.23. Results obtained on typical images

The standard Hough transform is computation intensive because it involves a complete evaluation of the parameter space. Speeding up the computation can be beneficial or even crucial in certain applications. A number of variations of the Hough transform aiming at reducing the computation load have been proposed, such as the adaptive Hough transform [8, 9], the randomize Hough transform [18], the pyramid Hough transform [10], and the probabilistic Hough transform [11]. The Hough transform algorithms on parallel computers [3, 4, 14] have also been proposed.

Table 3.2. Results of experiments based on cell grouping

CHARACTERISTIC	MINIMUM	MAXIMUM	AVERAGE
13 Representative Images			
Group size	37	69	59.0
Accumulated strength	35,429.7	266,404.3	140,747.3
Accumulated integrity count	222	1814	987.9
Position error	1	5	3.1
26 Additional Images			
Group size	31	67	51.3
Accumulated strength	27,585.5	179,943.3	78,373.5
Accumulated integrity count	210	1340	565.4
Position error	1	10	4.1
Entire Sample			
Group size	31	69	53.9
Accumulated strength	27,585.5	266,404.3	99,164.7
Accumulated integrity count	210	1814	706.2
Position error	1	10	3.8

3.5 Labeling

After image segmentation, the image regions may correspond to real objects in the scene. Recognizing the objects often means to label the image regions. This scene labeling problem can be addressed as the *Consistent labeling problem* (CLP). CLP has attracted a great attention in the computer vision and artificial intelligence areas. Finding a (possibly unique) assignment of l labels to m objects could have $O(l^m)$ possibilities. A normal image may have tens or even hundreds of regions. A reasonably complex line drawing can easily have 50 to 100 line segments. In general, however, heuristics or domain-dependent knowledge can be applied to make the problem tractable. CLP could be defined as follows [7]:

- A set of units $U = \{u_1, \cdots, u_m\}$.
- A set of labels $\Lambda = \{\lambda_1, \cdots, \lambda_l\}$.

- A set $T \subseteq U^n$ of all n-tuples of units which mutually constrain one another.
- A set $R \subseteq (U \times \Lambda)^n$ of all $2n$-tuples $(u_1, \lambda_1, \cdots, u_n, \lambda_n)$ where $(\lambda_1, \cdots, \lambda_n)$ is a legal labeling of units $(u_1, \cdots, u_n)$.

A labeling of the objects in U is a function $f : U \longrightarrow \Lambda$ such that for all $u_{i_1}, \cdots, u_{i_n} \in T$, $((u_i, f(u_{i_1})), \cdots, (u_{i_n}, f(u_{i_n}))) \in R$.

Consider an example of CLP with six units (could be six image regions or six line segments) and two possible labels (could be "vehicle" and "background") below:

$$
\begin{aligned}
U &= \{0,1,2,3,4,5\}, \\
\Lambda &= \{\lambda_0 = a, \lambda_1 = b\}, \\
R &= \{(0,a,1,a,2,a),(0,a,1,b,2,b),(0,a,1,b,2,a),(0,a,1,a,2,b), \\
&\quad (0,b,1,a,3,b),(0,a,1,a,3,b),(0,a,1,b,3,b),(0,b,1,b,3,b), \\
&\quad (1,a,2,b,4,a),(1,a,2,b,4,b),(1,b,2,a,4,a),(1,b,2,a,4,b), \\
&\quad (1,a,3,a,4,a),(1,a,3,b,4,b),(1,b,3,a,4,b),(1,b,3,b,4,b), \\
&\quad (4,a,5,a),(4,b,5,a),\}
\end{aligned}
$$

Six binary numbers, W_0 through W_5, are established with bit k relating to the k-th label. In other words, $W_i(k) = 1$ indicates that λ_k is a permissible label for u_i. For the above example, the W_i's all take the form of "11" to begin with.

The set R is represented as the following array:

index	tuple-size	unit tuple	possible labeling of the tuple
0	3	(0, 1, 2)	$(a,a,a) \to (a,b,b) \to (a,b,a) \to (a,a,b)$
1	3	(0, 1, 3)	$(b,a,b) \to (a,a,b) \to (a,b,b) \to (b,b,b)$
2	3	(1, 2, 4)	$(a,b,a) \to (a,b,b) \to (b,a,a) \to (b,a,b)$
3	3	(1, 3, 4)	$(a,a,a) \to (a,b,b) \to (b,a,b) \to (b,b,b)$
4	2	(4, 5)	$(a,a) \to (b,a)$

The arrow ("→") denotes a linked list. Those arrays and linked lists facilitate further manipulations leading to a solution to the CLP. This data structure is just as useful as other IAP data formats (e.g., the rectangular integer array for images and pattern matrices, the triangle matrix for proximity matrices), especially for higher-level vision computations.

Tree search and filtering [13] are the two basic approaches to CLP. If there exits any solution, tree search is guaranteed to find it. Many different filtering algorithms have been applied to reduce the possible labels each unit could take, i.e., to simplify the constraint relation set R, before and during the tree search. In the above example, the constraints

```
Procedure seqDep1(L, u)
labeling L;
object u;
{
    for (each label for object u) {
        assign label to object u in labeling L;
        if (label violates any constraints)
            next label;
        else if (u is the last object)
            print labeling L;
        else
            seqDep1(L, u + 1);
    }
    return;
}
```

Figure 3.24. A sequential depth-first search algorithm

defined for the tuple (0, 1, 2) preclude u_0 from ever having λ_1 (b). Thus the constraints (b, a, b) and (b, b, b) for the tuple (0, 1, 3) can be removed. This filtering process is applied several times until no more constraints can be removed from the R structure:

index	tuple-size	unit tuple	possible labeling of the tuple
0	3	(0, 1, 2)	$(a, a, a) \rightarrow (a, b, b) \rightarrow (a, b, a) \rightarrow (a, a, b)$
1	3	(0, 1, 3)	$(a, a, b) \rightarrow (a, b, b)$
2	3	(1, 2, 4)	$(a, b, b) \rightarrow (b, a, b)$
3	3	(1, 3, 4)	$(a, b, b) \rightarrow (b, b, b)$
4	2	(4, 5)	(b, a)

The binary words W_i's are now modified accordingly and become {01, 11, 11, 10, 10, 01}.

The performance of CLP depends strongly on the order in which the units are placed in the tree search. It is crucial to place the units with most constraints close to the root. Reducing the amount of branching at the early part of the tree can minimize the effort of backtracking. For the above example, the search order of 0, 3, 4, 5, 1, 2 has a depth-first search path length of 16, while the order 0, 1, 2, 3, 4, 5 has a path length of 34. The pseudo code of a sequential depth-first tree search algorithm is given in Figure 3.24.

On a multiprocessor computer, the sequential depth-first search procedure can be carried out to a specified depth and then parallel tasks on

```
parDep1( boolean prime, labeling partLbl, object u )
{
  if( u is deeper into tree than the specified depth ) {
    add partLbl to list L;
    return;
  }
  for( each label for object u ) {
    assign label to object u in partLbl;
    if( label violates any constraints )
      next label;
    else if( u is the last object ) {
      print labeling;
      return;
    }
    else parDep1 ( FALSE, partLbl, u+1, depth );
  }
  if( prime ) // having a list of partial labelings L {
    parallel( i = 1 : # of partial labelings in L )
    parDep1( TRUE, L(i), u+depth );
  }
  return;
}
```

Figure 3.25. A parallel depth-first search algorithm

the remaining branches can be launched. Each of the parallel tasks can then recursively search its piece of the tree to a specified depth and launch more parallel tasks. At the terminal nodes, any remaining labelings can be printed out as solutions. That is, the algorithm is divided into stages, and each stage consists of a sequential search to a prescribed depth, enumerating all partial solutions. Once this is done, the remaining partial solutions will be handled in parallel by performing another staged search. The pseudo code of this algorithm is given in Figure 3.25. Figure 3.26 illustrates the stages, the sequential and parallel portions of this algorithm.

The parallel depth-first search algorithm can be implemented on a MIMD computer or on a network of workstations. Some of such experiments are reported in [6] and [17]. A variety of line-drawing labeling problems are tested. The numbers of objects (line segments) are 9, 20, 33, and 54. The lines meet each other forming a vertex mutually con-

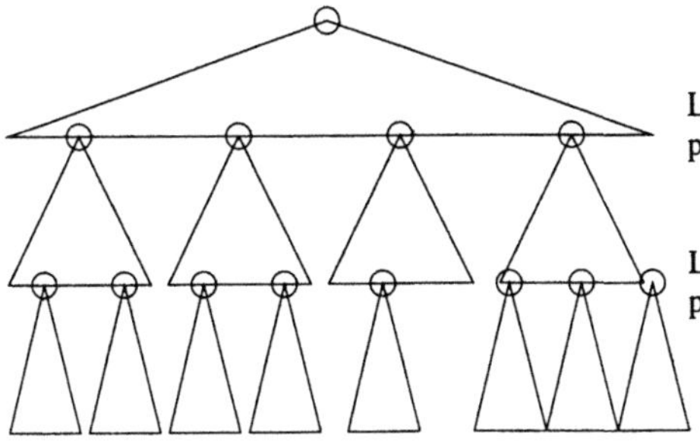

Figure 3.26. The stages of a parallel tree search algorithm

strain one another. In one set of experiments, a network of 16 Sun 3/80 workstations, connected via Ethernet, was used. Heterogeneous network could also be used. Intranet and Internet computers usually have a tremendous number of idle cycles and thus provide a low cost option to parallel computing. Another set of experiments were run on an MIMD 64 processor Myrias SPS-2 [2]. A brief report of the speedups is given in Table 3.3.

Table 3.3. Speedup results

		speedup
SPS-2	8 PE's	8
	16 PE's	11
	32 PE's	26
	64 PE's	33
workstations	4 PE's	3.6
	8 PE's	7.5
	16 PE's	11.3

3.6 Conclusion

This chapter has presented a number of typical PRIP algorithms. They are among the most commonly used procedures. The data structures and data communication patterns involved in those algorithms are representatives of the ones used in the majority of PRIP applications. The lower-level PRIP procedures can take advantage of the inherent data locality and make a full use of SIMD parallel computer architectures. Higher-level PRIP operations employ several different data structures and they are more suitable for MIMD computers.

References

[1] D.H. Ballard. Generalizing the Hough transform to detect arbitrary shapes. *Pattern Recognition*, 13(2):111–122, 1981.

[2] M. Beltrametti, K. Bobey, R. Manson, M. Walker, and D. Wilson. Pams/sps-2 system overview. In *Supercomputing Symposium*, pages 63–71, 1989.

[3] A. Choudhary and R. Ponnusamy. Implementation and evaluation of Hough transform algorithms on s shared memory multiprocessor. *Journal of Parallel and Distributed Computing*, 12(2):178–188, 1991.

[4] M. Farretti. The generalized Hough transform on mesh-connected computers. *Journal of Parallel and Distributed Computing*, 19(1):51–57, 1993.

[5] R.C. Gonzalez and R.E. Woods. *Digital Image Processing.* Addison-Wesley, 1992.

[6] R. Gregorish, X. Li, and J. Schaeffer. Parallel object labeling in mimd and distributed environments. In *Pattern Recognition: Architectures, Algorithms and Applications*, pages 55–74.

[7] R.M. Haralick and L.G. Shapiro. *Computer and Robot Vision.* Addison-Wesley, 1992.

[8] J. Illingworth and J. Kittler. The adaptive Hough transform. *IEEE Trans. on Patt. Anal. and Machine Intell.*, PAMI-9(5):690–698, 1987.

[9] J. Illingworth and J. Kittler. A survey of the Hough transform. *Computer Vision, Graphics, and Image Processing*, 44:87–116, 1988.

[10] J. Jolion and A. Rosenfeld. An o(logn) pyramid Hough transform. *Pattern Recognition Letters*, 9(4):343–350, 1989.

[11] N. Kiryati, Y. Eldar, and A. Bruckstein. A probabilistic Hough transform. *Pattern Recognition*, 24(4):303–316, 1991.

[12] X. Li, Z. Liu, and K. Leung. Detection of vehicles from traffic scenes using fuzzy intergrals. *Pattern Recognition*, to appear.

[13] B. Nudel. Consistent-labeling problems and their algorithms: expected-comp lexities and theory-based heuristics. *Artificial Intelligence*, pages 135–178, 1983.

[14] S. Olariu, J. Schwing, and J. Zhang. Computing the Hough transform on reconfigurable meshes. *Image and Vision Compting*, 11(10):623–630, 1993.

[15] X. Qu and X. Li. Parallel template matching algorithms. In *1988 International Conference on Parallel Processing*, pages 223–226, 1988.

[16] S. Ranka and S. Sahni. *Hypercube Algorithms.* Springer-Verlag, 1990.

[17] M. Thomas and X. Li. Experiments in parallel scene labeling. In *Proceedings of Vision Interface '91*, pages 64–73, Calgary, Canada, 1991.

[18] L. Xu, E. Oja, and P. Kultanen. A new curve detection method: Randomized Hough Transform (RHT). *Pattern Recognition Letters*, 11(5):331–338, 1990.

Chapter 4

NEURAL EVOLUTION MODEL FOR GRAY LEVEL IMAGE RESTORATION

This chapter introduces a novel image restoration method by using modified evolution strategy (MES). We first review the background of image restoration and some useful concepts associated with it. A MSE image restoration model is made in Section 4.2. Three main improvements that consist of coordinate descending mutation, "survival of the fittest" selection rule and hybrid evolution strategies are presented in Section 4.3. Neural evolution algorithm is introduced in Section 4.4. Theoretical analysis and experimental results in Section 4.5 demonstrate the efficiency of the proposed method. In Section 4.6, we draw a conclusion.

4.1 Introduction

Image restoration refers to finding an estimate of an image from the degraded recording. Generally, image restoration is regarded as an ill-conditioned problem. Bayesian estimation and the regularization methods are two classical formulations where a priori information (constraints) is incorporated in order to deal with such difficulty. Both methods lead to very large and constrained optimization problems. Traditionally, the data are transformed into the frequency domain to achieve realistic solutions. However, the feasibility of frequency domain processing is limited by several factors such as space-invariance, stationary, and so on. In fact, most of the existing image restoration methods are based on some global optimization criteria. The typical optimization models based on Hopfield or Hopfield-like networks were introduced by Zhou et al [1].

Evolution strategies (ES) mimic the basic principle of the evolutionary process and are powerful in many difficult real-world optimization problems [2]. This chapter presents an image restoration method based on modified evolution strategy (MES), which has the advantages of fault tolerance and no requirement of wide sense stationary assumption. The MES image restoration method proposed in this chapter has the ability to escape from the local optimums and yield good approximate solution. Since searching optimal solution in the complex and large space still is a bottleneck of the practical evolution strategies [3], the computational complexity of gray level image restoration will restrict the ES implementation. In this chapter, we use MES method to improve traditional evolution strategies (TES) by proposing coordinate descending mutation operator, "survival of the fittest" selection rule and hybrid evolution strategies. The main purpose of these improvements is to guarantee the performance of MES in image restoration, reduce the complexity of searching space and improve the convergence speed at the same time.

4.2 MES Image Restoration Model

For a linear shift-invariant degraded system, the image degradation is normally modeled as [4]

$$g = H * f + n \tag{4-1}$$

where H is the "blur matrix", $*$ represents the convolution operator, n is the signal independent additive white noise, f and g are the original and degraded images, respectively. There are many kinds of optimization criteria for image restoration. Usually the optimization procedure is presented by a constrained square error function, i.e.,

$$E = \left\| g - H * \hat{f} \right\|^2 + \rho \left\| D * \hat{f} \right\|^2 \tag{4-2}$$

where $\hat{f}$ is the estimate of the original image, ρ is a constant and D is a Laplacian operator. The estimate of the original image is obtained by minimizing Equation (4-2). We can employ ES as the optimization technique in image restoration. Equation (4-2) denotes the fitness function, Φ. A population at generation t, $P(t)=\{\vec{a}_1(t),\ldots,\ \vec{a}_n(t)\}$, consists of individuals, $\vec{a}_i(t)$, where n is the population size. In this chapter, one individual (parent or offspring), $\vec{a}_i(t)$, denotes an estimate of the original image, and each dimension of $\vec{a}_i(t)$ represents the gray level value of one pixel, from 0 to 255. An initial population, $P(0)$, is generated by the degraded image through adding Gaussian distributed random numbers. After Gaussian mutation, the new children are obtained. Among these children, we can select the individuals with higher qualification as the new parents to get next generation. This circulation will be going on and then the individuals be changing better, so that the estimate of the image represented by the individual is gradually near to the best one of the original image.

4.3 Improvements of ES Operators

In TES, all the dimensions are optimized simultaneously, hence it is not easy to find the optimum in the search space of large sized gray level images. Some modification should be made to guarantee the employment of ES according to the characters of image restoration. Three modified ES operators are described as follows:

Coordinate Descending Mutation

The coordinate descending mutation operator, m_{cd}, is used here to reduce the computational complexity. Coordinate descending mutation comes from the mathematical conception of coordinate descending optimization. Owing to the strong interrelation of the neighbor pixels, in this chapter, one pixel and its 8-neighbor pixels are regarded as a "partial individual" and its fitness, Φ_p, is called "partial fitness". Coordinate descending mutation operator, m_{cd}, means to select one pixel of the image while other pixels keep constant, and add Gaussian mutation to the selected pixel. After coordinate descending mutation, only Φ_p is calculated as the criterion of evolutionary operation. The pixel is sequentially selected one after another. After all the pixels are operated, the fitness of the whole individual, Φ, is evaluated. If the decrease of Φ becomes less than some certain criterion, the evolution process stops.

The search complexity is greatly reduced by using m_{cd}. This improvement makes it possible for applying ES to restore large sized gray level images. In addition, the computational complexity of Φ_p is much smaller than that of Φ. This is because the fitness function must be calculated after every mutation, but the adoption of Φ_p can speed up the evolution process sharply after numerous iterations.

The search space for the TES can be defined as

$$P_1 = 256^{w\times h}. \tag{4-3}$$

While that of our MES with coordinate descending is

$$P_2 = 256 \times w \times h. \tag{4-4}$$

Then, the ratio of these two complexities is

$$Ratio = \frac{2^{8\times(w\times h-1)}}{w\times h} \tag{4-5}$$

where w and h represent the width and height of the image, respectively. It is clear that the complexity ratio will almost increase exponentially when the image size is further enlarged.

"Survival of the Fittest" Selection Rule

This rule requires that a child becomes a new parent once its Φ_p is higher or equal to that of the parent; otherwise, the parent keeps unchanged. Though the evolution procedure is always towards the increase direction of the fitness that avoids the redundant search, our method is not directly to some certain local optimum with the acceptance of the first better mutation.

$(\mu+\lambda)-$ES and $(\mu,\lambda)-$ES are two main streams of ES, where μ and λ $(1\leq\mu\leq\lambda)$ are the number of parents and children, respectively. In $(\mu+\lambda)-$ES, μ parents are used to create λ offspring and all solutions compete for survival, with the best being selected as the parents of the next generation. In $(\mu,\lambda)-$ES, only λ offspring compete for survival, and the parents are completely replaced each generation. While selecting the new parents, μ old parents and λ children should be kept at the same time. Since the computer memory is limited, the larger μ and λ, the more difficult for the computer to simulate. However, the proposed "survival of the fittest" selection performs like $(\mu+\lambda)$-ES with a variant λ, where the competition is done between parent and child one by one. Only two individuals need to be saved other than $\mu+\lambda$ $(1\leq\mu\leq\lambda)$. In order to save the computer memory, we also let $\mu=1$ and the maximum of λ be equal to 50.

Hybrid Evolution Strategies

Rapid convergence and reliable global convergence behavior are two contradictory requirements. With losing the parents experience, $(\mu,\lambda)-$ES is easily to escape from the local optimal solutions, while its convergence speed may be slow. Selecting μ better individuals from the union of parents and offspring, $(\mu+\lambda)-$ES guarantees a monotonically improving performance, but it is easy to fall into the local optimum space. We use the integration of $(\mu+\lambda)-$ES and $(\mu,\lambda)-$ES to speed up the convergence, and increase the probability of finding the optimum solution at the same time.

Firstly, $(\mu+\lambda)-$ES is performed to proximate the optimum quickly as described above. When the fitness function sinks into the local optimum, based on the local optimum, $(\mu,\lambda)-$ES is used to re-initialize the population in the next generation in order to escape from the local optimum area. This is similar to the "disaster" of nature. After re-initialization, $(\mu + \lambda)$ −ES is still used to search another optimum solution. As we know, exhaustive enumeration method is impractical. After several "disasters", the best individual is selected as the satisfactory solution. Using the operators introduced above, the description of our MES image restoration method is given below:

$t = 0$;
initialize $P(0) = \{ \vec{a}_1(0) \}$;
evaluate $P(0) = \{ \Phi(\vec{a}_1(0)) \}$;
while ($\iota (P(t)) \neq$ true) {
　　while ($i \leq w \times h$) {
　　　$\lambda = 0$;
　　　while ($\lambda < 50$) {
　　　　coordinate descending mutate
　　　　$P'(t) = \{ \vec{a}_1'(t) \} = m_{cd}(\vec{a}_1(t))$;
　　　　evaluate "partial fitness" $P'(t) = \{ \vec{a}_1'(t) \}$: $\{ \Phi_p(\vec{a}_1'(t)) \}$;
　　　　"survival of the fittest" select;
　　　　if ($\Phi_p(\vec{a}_1'(t)) \leq \Phi_p(\vec{a}_1(t))$) $\{ P(t+1) = P'(t) \}$
　　　　else $\{ P(t+1) = P(t) \}$
　　　　$\lambda = \lambda + 1$;
　　　　}
　　　$i = i + 1$;
　　　}
　evaluate $P'(t) = \{ \Phi(\vec{a}_1'(t)) \}$;
　$t = t + 1$;
　if ($\iota(+,) =$ true) {re-initialize $\vec{a}_1(t)$ }
　}

where $\iota(+,)$ and $\iota(P(t))$ denote the re-initialization and stop criterion, respectively.

4.4 Neural Evolution Algorithm (NEA)

For a linear shift-invariant degraded system, the image degradation is normally modeled as Equation (4-1). There are many kinds of optimization criteria for image restoration. Usually the optimization procedure is defined by a constrained square error function in Equation (4-2). In this section, a neural evolution algorithm is defined in the following.

Integration of HNN and ES

There are two main operators in ES, Gaussian mutation and recombination, where the former acts as the deterministic function in simulated evolutionary processes [5]. In this chapter, we define that each individual can be generated by the following two steps: (1) Adding 30% Gaussian mutation to one individual, which will be regarded as the initial sample of the HNN method; and (2) Employing HNN in our algorithm in order to converge into local optimums of the fitness function. In this way, an effective restoration result can be obtained. According to the local optimization character of neural networks, it is obvious that this result represents a local optimum of Equation (4-2).

Selection Rule

During the image restoration procedure, its fitness, Φ, is evaluated as the criterion of the survival of this individual. The "survival of the fittest" selection rule requires that once the fitness of an individual is higher or equal to that of the parent, this child becomes a new parent; otherwise, the parent is kept unchanged. Though the evolution procedure makes the solution always move towards the increase direction of the fitness that avoids the redundant search, our algorithm does not directly approximate the local optimum with the acceptance of the first better mutation.

$(\mu+\lambda)$-ES ($\mu \geq \lambda \geq 1$) is one of the major forms of traditional ES. It means that μ best individuals are selected out of the set of μ parents and λ children. That is to say, μ old parents and λ children should be saved at the same time for the selection of new parents. Usually, the memory space in computer is limited, hence it is a difficult task to simulate both μ and λ individuals, especially when they are large ones. However, in our "survival of the fittest" selection, the competition can be done between parent and child one by one. It is not necessary to save $\mu+\lambda$ individuals at the same time, but only two. This performs like $(\mu+\lambda)$-ES with a variant λ. We also let $\mu=1$ in order to save the computer memory, and set the maximum value of λ to 50.

Image Restoration Algorithm

This algorithm using the strategy of neural evolution, mentioned above, can be described as follows:

$t = 0$;

initialize $P(0) = \{ \vec{a}_1(0) \}$;

evaluate $P(0) = \{ \Phi(\vec{a}_1(0)) \}$;
while not terminate
{
$\lambda = 0$;
while ($\lambda < 50$)
{
$P'(t) = 30\%$ Gaussian mutate $P(t)$;
$P''(t) =$ HNN restore $P'(t)$;
evaluate $P''(t) = \{ \Phi(\vec{a}_1''(t)) \}$;
"survival of the fittest" select:
if $(\Phi(\vec{a}_1''(t)) \leq \Phi(\vec{a}_1(t)))$ $\{ P(t+1) = P''(t) \}$
else $\{ P(t+1) = P(t) \}$;
$\lambda = \lambda + 1$;
}
$t = t + 1$;
}

4.5 Simulations and Comparisons

Experimental Results: MES

Based on Equations. (4-3)-(4-4), Table 4.1 shows the search complexity of TES and MES method for the restoration of 256 gray level images with the size of 16×16 and 32×32. Their computational complexity ratio is described in Equation (4-5). As an example, for an image of size 32×32, the complexity of TES is almost 2^{8K} times larger than that of our MES method. We can also consider larger image with the size 128×128, where this ratio approximately rises to 2^{128K}. It is clear that MES method can greatly reduce the complexity of the search space.

The following experiments continually demonstrate the necessity of the proposed improvements. The computational time between TES and MES method is compared under very similar peak signal-to-noise ratio (PSNR) improvement. For the image of size 16×16, the restoration time of our MES method is 3.6s, but the TES restoration method is 20.5s; As to the image of size 32×32, by using MES method, the restoration time is 23.1s, while TES is 2142.5s (See Table 4.1). To larger image, such as more than 64×64, the convergence time of traditional ES restoration method is intolerable, however our method can still work well. Those improvements proposed in Section 4.3 guarantee the application of ES to image restoration.

Table 4.1. Comparison of TES and MES method with different image sizes

Image Restoration Method	Image Size			
	16×16		32×32	
	Time (s)	Complexity	Time (s)	Complexity
MES	3.6	2^{16}	23.1	2^{18}
TES	20.5	2^{2K}	2142.5	2^{8K}

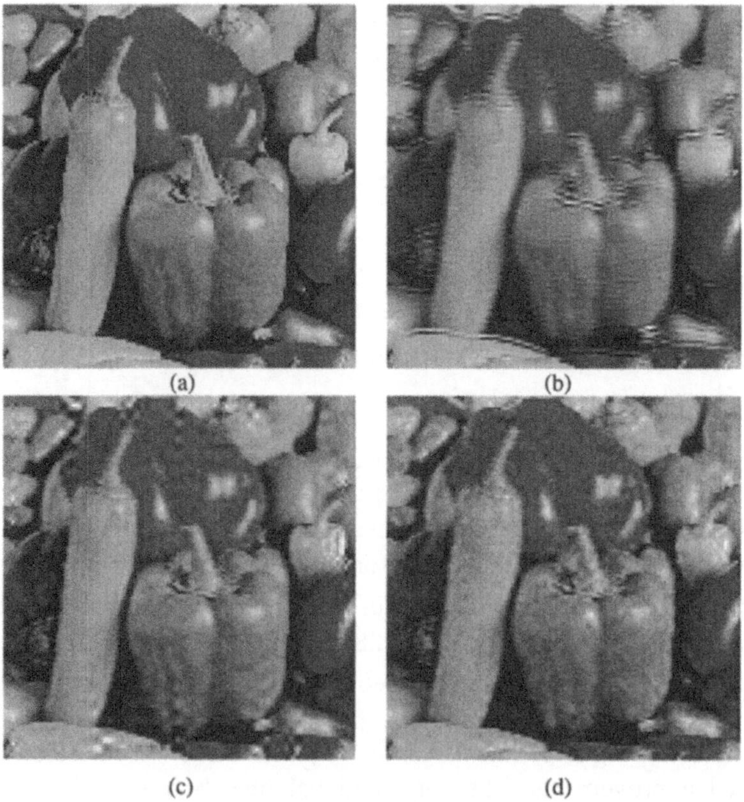

Figure 4.1. Comparison of MES and Hopfield network restoration method. (a) Original "Peppers" image, (b) Degraded image, (c) The restored image using Hopfield network method, and (d) The image restored using our MES method

Hopfield network is now widely employed in image restoration method. Because of its advantages of fault tolerance and no requirement of wide sense stationary (WSS) assumption, Hopfield network image can obtain higher quality restored images than traditional methods, such as Wiener filter and SVD pseudoinverse. So, we make some comparisons to the popular Hopfield network method. The original "peppers" image shown in Figure 4.1(a) is of size 128×128 with 256 gray levels. Figure 4.1(b) shows the degraded image with quantization noise. The experiments were implemented under the same conditions. The first and last 4 rows and columns were taken as the boundary [1] and the constant ρ in Equation (4-1) is set to 0.005. Figure 4.1(c) shows the restored image using Hopfield network method. The restoration using our MES method is given in Figure 4.1(d). The PSNR improvement of Figure 4.1(c) is 6.5 dB and that of Figure 4.1(d) is 7.5 dB. As to object evaluation, Figure 4.1(c) has ringing effects due to the intensively waved degradation. Owing to the random search mechanism of ES, our MES method can get visually and subjectively good image no matter whatever degraded model is.

Experimental Results: NEA

The proposed algorithm has been applied to many image restoration applications. In order to analyze their performance, we compare the image restoration quality of NEA with that of HNN, and also give the restoration results of both NEA and ES under the same computational time.

As an example in this paper, two typical images, "Lena" and "Plane", are shown in Figure 4.2. They are 256 gray level images with dimension 128×128. We also re-sample the original images to other three different sizes, viz., 16×16, 32×32 and 64×64. All of them are used as our test set to evaluate the performance of NEA, HNN and ES. The objective criterion between the restored image and the degraded image is the peak signal-to-noise ratio (PSNR).

The comparative restoration results based on Figure 4.2(a) and its three kinds of re-sampled images are shown in Table 4.2. We see, under the same computational time, NEA can obtain much better restoration results than ES. Note that given enough computation time, ES can also get high quality estimates, but it becomes too much time consuming (and not much useful) from the point of practical image restoration. For example, it will take a few hours to approach 6.95 dB in 128×128 image restoration. In addition, Table 1 illustrates that the PSNR difference between NEA and ES increases with the increase of the image size. This means that for restoration of a large size image, NEA can get satisfactory results quickly while ES needs much more time. The experimental results demonstrate that the local searching ability of NEA is more efficient than that of ES by using HNN.

(a) (b)

Figure 4.2. Two typical gray level images with the size of 128×128. (a) "Lena" image, (b) "Plane" image

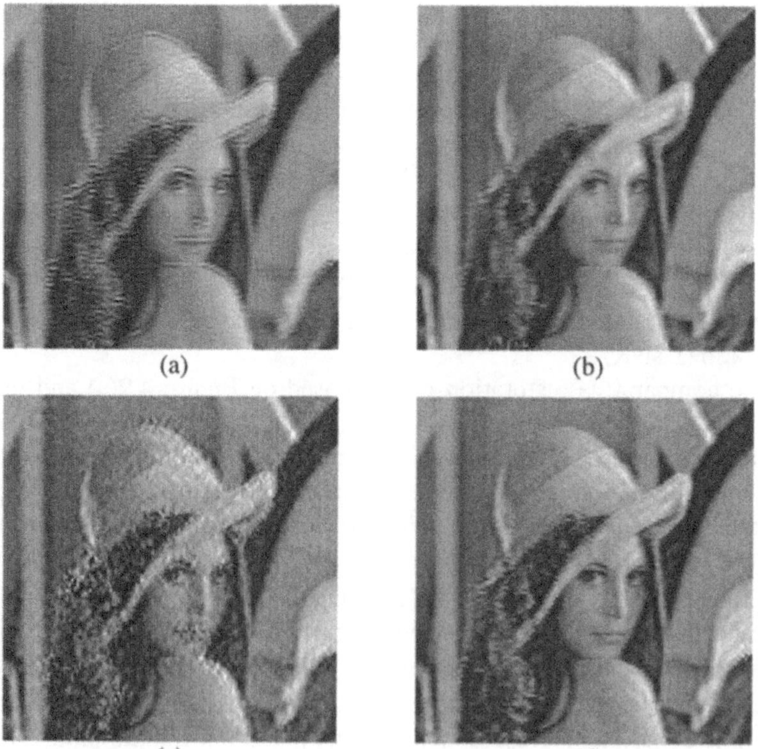

(a) (b) (c) (d)

Figure 4.3. Restoration performance for image "Lena". (a) Degraded image of "Lena" and the restored images based on (b) HNN method, (c) ES method only (time: 109s), and (d) NEA (time: 109s)

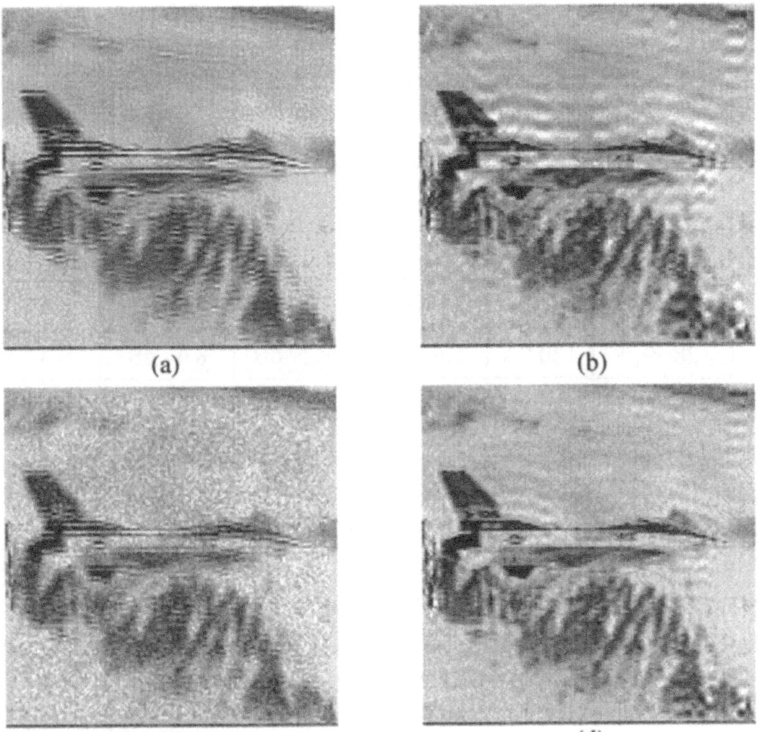

(a) (b) (c) (d)

Figure 4.4. Restoration performance for image "Plane". (a) Degraded image of "Plane" and the restored images based on (b) HNN method, (c) ES method only (time: 120s), and (d) NEA (time: 120s)

Table 4.2. Comparative restoration results in PSNR among NEA, ES and HNN for Figure 4.2(a) and its re-sampled images

Image	*NEA vs. ES*			*NEA vs. HNN*	
Size	*Time*	NEA	ES	NEA	HNN
16 ×16	1.0 s	2.08 dB	0.78 dB	2.08 dB	1.47 dB
32 ×32	17.0 s	3.83 dB	1.95 dB	3.83 dB	2.81 dB
64 ×64	85.0 s	5.33 dB	1.31 dB	5.33 dB	4.51 dB
128 ×128	109.0 s	6.95 dB	1.03 dB	6.95 dB	5.80 dB

Table 4.3. Comparative restoration results in PSNR among NEA, ES and HNN for Figure 4.2(b) and its re-sampled images

Image	*NEA vs. ES*			*NEA vs. HNN*	
Size	*Time*	NEA	ES	NEA	HNN
16×16	0.4 s	4.80 dB	0.64 dB	4.80 dB	2.75 dB
32×32	16.0 s	6.41 dB	1.87 dB	6.41 dB	4.62 dB
64×64	90.0 s	7.66 dB	1.72 dB	7.66 dB	5.55 dB
128×128	120.0 s	8.44 dB	1.29 dB	8.44 dB	6.31 dB

Considering the construction of NEA, it is no doubt that the computational time of NEA will be longer than HNN, but with the population search mechanism, NEA has more chance to explore the better results. Table 4.2 also illustrates the comparisons of NEA and HNN. The PSNR of NEA is higher than HNN. For example, the PSNR of NEA can be 1.15dB higher than that of HNN when a 128×128 image is restored. In addition, Table 4.3 gives the restoration results based on Figure 4.2(b) and its re-sampled images, which can also well demonstrate the superiority of NEA.

We show the restoration images in both Figures. 4.3-4.4 to make use of human subjective judgement. As a performance analysis between NEA and HNN, the result of NEA in Figures 4.3-4.4(d) is comparable to HNN in Figures 4.3-4.4(b). Under the same computational time, the results of both ES and NEA are shown in Figures 4.3-4.4(c) and Figures 4.3-4.4(d), respectively. Their PSNR and computational times are shown in Tables 4.2-4.3. The simulation results show that the proposed NEA method not only performs better in objective criterion, but also gives visually good results.

4.6 Conclusion

Based on ES, this chapter has proposed a novel method for restoring gray level images. By means of approximately decreasing the computational complexity exponentially, the proposed coordinate descending mutation operator makes it possible for applying ES to large sized gray level image restoration. "Survival of the fittest" selection rule and hybrid strategies are also efficient to speed up the convergence and guarantee the satisfactory solution. In addition, combining ES and HNN, a novel NEA have been described and applied to the much less than of ES, especially, for large dimensional images. NEA also can obtain better quality than HNN method.

The simulation results illustrate the effectiveness of our both MES and NEA methods.

References

[1] Y.T. Zhou, R. Chellappa, A. Vaid and B.K. Jenkins, "Image Restoration Using a Neural Network", *IEEE trans. on ASSP*, 36(7):1141-1151, 1988.

[2] D.B. Fogel, *Evolutionary Computation: Toward a New Philosophy of Machine Intelligence*, IEEE Press, Piscataway, 1995.

[3] T. Back, U. Hammel and H.P. Schwefel, "Evolutionary Computation: Comments on the history and Current State", *IEEE Trans. On Evolutionary Computation*, 1(1):3-16, 1997.

[4] W.K. Pratt, *Digital Image Processing*, John Wiley & Sons, 2nd ed., New York, 1973.

[5] D.B. Fogel and J.W. Atmar, "Comparing genetic operators with Gaussian mutations in simulated evolutionary process using linear systems", *Biological Cybernetics*, 63:111-114, 1990.

[6] R. Chellappa (ed.), *Digital Image Processing*, IEEE Computer Society Press, 1992.

[7] R.C. Gonzalez, *Digital Image Processing*, Addison-Wesley,1992.

[8] J.C. Russ, *The Image Processing Handbook*, Roca Raton: CRC Press,1995.

[9] D. Zhang, *Neural Network System Design Methodology*, Tsinghua University Press, 1996.

[10] G.A. Carpenter and S. Grossber, *Neural Networks for Vision and Image Processing*, The MIT Press, Cambridge, 1992.

Chapter 5

PARTIAL FRACTAL MODEL FOR HYBRID IMAGE CODING

The fractal image compression technique models a natural image using a contractive mapping called fractal mapping in the image space. In this chapter, we first introduce the concept of fractal mapping and some useful definitions. In Section 5.2, we demonstrate that the fractal image coding algorithm is compatible with other image coding methods. A new mapping in the image space, called partial fractal mapping is proposed in Section 5.3. A general framework of fractal-based hybrid image coding encoding/decoding systems is presented in Section 5.4. Section 5.5 proposes a new hybrid image coding scheme, which non-fractal coded regions are used to help the encoding of fractal coded regions. Experiments in Section 5.6 show that the proposed system performs better than the quadtree-based fractal image coding algorithm and the JPEG image compression standard at high compression ratios larger than 30.

5.1 Introduction

The concept of fractal was introduced by Mandelbrot [1] as an alternative to the traditional Euclidean geometry mainly for dealing with shapes generated by nature. In recent years, the interest of applying this theory has been steadily growing. A recent trend in computer graphics and image processing has been to use Iterated Function System (IFS) to generate and describe both man-made fractal-like structures and natural images. Barnsley et al. were the first to present the concept of fractal image compression using IFS [2]. A fully automatic image compression algorithm for real world gray scale images called Fractal Block Coding (FBC) was proposed by Jacquin [3, 4]. Jacquin's algorithm has been studied, refined and improved in recent years, many important research results on this topic are collected in Fisher's book [5]. As Jacquin indicated in [4], the main point of FBC is that it can capture and exploit a special kind of image redundancy — piecewise self-similarity in images, which is not used by traditional image coding techniques. Since natural images are not exactly self-similar, the image will be formed of properly transformed "parts" of itself [5]. The fractal code of the image is actually the collection of these transformations, which are called fractal transformations. Usually, fractal transformations can be represented by fewer bits than the original image, so a fractal code is a compression of the original image, sometimes with very high compression ratios.

Nevertheless, fractal representations are not always very efficient for image compression. For example, the fractal compression method usually needs much more bits to encode very "flat" regions than other simpler methods. Taking advantage of the powerful compression ability of fractal coding while at the same time avoiding its inefficiency for some kinds of regions seems contradictory. A way to solve this problem is to develop a hybrid system where only some parts of the image are encoded using fractal techniques and the remaining parts are modeled using other methods, so that the merits of different approaches can be combined and the overall coding efficiency is improved. There have been some examples for such kind of hybrid systems. In Jacquin's primary work [3, 4], he used only dc components to encode *shade blocks* (smooth with no significant gradient). Ø ien et al. reported that it might be advantages to encode the complex regions (sharp edges and textures) of an image with FBC and smooth regions with a block-DCT encoder [4]. Laurencot and Jacquin compared FBC with LBG [6] based VQ scheme. Their results appeared that for sharp-edge blocks, FBC performs better than VQ, but the results are very similar for texture blocks, with perhaps a slight advantage for VQ coding of texture block [4, 7].

It should be noted that all of the above mentioned hybrid systems assume that the fractal image coding algorithm is compatible with other methods. However, no explanation on the compatibility had been given. Since in fractal block coding, the encoding of every block is highly related with other blocks in the image, if only a proportion of the blocks are coded using fractal method, could the remaining non-fractal-coded blocks destroy the whole fractal code?

In this chapter, by introducing the concept of partial fractal mapping, we provide some mathematical explanations on how and why a hybrid fractal image coding system can work. A general framework of the hybrid system is then proposed. According to such a framework, many different hybrid image coding schemes can be derived. Actually, all the above mentioned hybrid systems are only some special cases of it. The framework also gives us something that is new to those previously proposed algorithms: 1) Non-fractal-coded regions can be used to help the encoding of the fractal-coded regions to improve the overall coding efficiency; 2) Non-fractal-coded regions can be encoded using not only block-based but also non-block-based algorithms; 3) The domain pool used by the fractal-coded blocks can be reduced. Finally, we provide an example of the new hybrid system and give some experimental results.

Symbols

R^M :	The M-dimensional Cartesian product of the real numbers
ϕ, ψ, θ:	Images (or elements in R^M)
$d_{\max}$:	The $d_{\max}$ metric of two elements in R^M
d_2:	The d_2 metric of two elements in R^M
Ω:	The set of sample point indexes in a signal
W:	Basic fractal mapping
W^P :	Partial fractal mapping
■ :	End of proof

5.2 Basic Fractal Mapping

A digital signal ϕ with M sample points can be viewed as an element in R^M, where R^M denotes the M-dimensional Cartesian product of the real numbers. Let $\Omega=\{1, 2, \ldots, M\}$ represents the set of sample point indexes in the signal. We can denote $\phi \in R^M$ and $\phi = (\phi(1), \phi(2), \ldots, \phi(M))^T$. In this chapter, the signal ϕ refers to an image and R^M refers to the image space that is the collection of all possible images. When we use sub-indexes on ϕ such as ϕ_1 and ϕ_n, we mean they are different images. For convenience, one-dimensional model is used in this chapter. Nevertheless, the discussions and theorems presented below are also applicable or can be easily adapted to two-dimensional or higher-dimensional cases.

In R^M, we define the following two kinds of metrics:

$$\forall \phi_1, \phi_2 \in R^M \qquad d_{\max}(\phi_1, \phi_2) = \max_{j \in \Omega} |\phi_1(j) - \phi_2(j)| \tag{5-1}$$

$$\forall \phi_1, \phi_2 \in R^M \qquad d_2(\phi_1, \phi_2) = \Big(\frac{1}{M} \sum_{j=1}^{M} |\phi_1(j) - \phi_2(j)|^2\Big)^{1/2} \tag{5-2}$$

Then we have two complete metric spaces of $(R^M, d_{\max})$ and (R^M, d_2). It is easy to prove

$$\forall \phi_1, \phi_2 \in R^M \qquad d_2(\phi_1, \phi_2) \leq d_{\max}(\phi_1, \phi_2) \tag{5-3}$$

The image is partitioned into N non-overlapping sub-pieces $R_i \subset \Omega$ (i=1,2,..., N). In the fractal image coding literature, R_i is also called a range block. Let r_i be the number of pixels in R_i ($M = \sum_{i=1}^{N} r_i$), then we have

$$\Omega = \bigcup_{i=1}^{N} R_i \quad \text{and} \quad R_i \cap R_j = \varnothing \quad (i \neq j) \tag{5-4}$$

Each R_i corresponds to a transformation W_i, which transforms another sub-piece in the image $D_i \subset \Omega$ to the position of R_i, where D_i is also called a domain block and we use d_i to represent the number of pixels in D_i. W_i is a combination of the extracting transformation E_i, the geometrical transformation G_i, the luminance transformation L_i and the putting transformation P_i. They are illustrated as follows:

E_i: $R^M \rightarrow \mathcal{R}^{d_i}$ is to extract the domain block D_i from the image.

G_i: $\mathcal{R}^{d_i} \rightarrow \mathcal{R}^{r_i}$ includes the action of spatial contraction and rotation, that maps block of size D_i to block of size R_i and rotate it in some way. Usually d_i is a multiple of r_i, so that every pixel j in R_i corresponds to K pixels $j_1, j_2, \ldots, j_K$ in D_i. The pixel value of j is determined by the weighted average of corresponding pixel values in D_i, that is

$$z_R(j) = \sum_{k=1}^{K} a_{j_k} \bullet z_D(j_k), \tag{5-5}$$

where z_R and z_D are the gray values in R_i and D_i, respectively. (a_{j_1}, a_{j_2}, ..., a_{j_K}) is the weight vector that satisfies $\sum_{k=1}^{K} a_{j_k} = 1$.

L_i: $\mathcal{R}^{r_i} \rightarrow \mathcal{R}^{r_i}$ is a luminance transformation which modifies each pixel one by one using a uniform one-dimensional gray value mapping l_i: $R \rightarrow R$, $z \rightarrow l_i(z)$. If

$$\exists\, 0 \leq s < 1, \forall i \in [1, N], \ \forall z_1, z_2 \in R, \quad |l_i(z_1) - l_i(z_2)| < s \bullet |z_1 - z_2| \tag{5-6}$$

then l_i is a one-dimensional contractive mapping. P_i: $\mathcal{R}^{r_i} \rightarrow R^M$ is to put the processed image block back into the image at the position of R_i and set the remaining part of the image to be all zero.

By applying the transformations in order of E_i, G_i, L_i and P_i, we can achieve the combined transformation of

$$W_i: R^M \rightarrow R^M, \qquad W_i(\phi) = P_i L_i G_i E_i(\phi). \tag{5-7}$$

The collection of all W_i is called an Iterated Function System: IFS={W_1, W_2, ..., W_N}. The function of IFS can also be viewed as an overall fractal mapping W on the image, which is the sum of all W_i :

$$W: R^M \rightarrow R^M, \qquad W(\phi) = \sum_{i=1}^{N} W_i(\phi). \tag{5-8}$$

If all l_i's are contractive, it can be proved that W is a contractive mapping in (R^M, $d_{\max}$), that is

$$\forall \phi_1, \phi_2 \in R^M \quad d_{max}(W(\phi_1), W(\phi_2)) \leq s \bullet d_{max}(\phi_1, \phi_2), \tag{5-9}$$

where $0 \leq s < 1$ is called the contractive factor of W. According to the Contraction Mapping Theorem in complete metric space, W has the following properties:

Property 1 There exists a unique attractor image $\phi \in R^M$, such that

$$W(\phi) = \phi \tag{5-10}$$

Property 2 Iteratively apply W to any initial image $\phi^{(0)}$ in R^M, the attractor image can be eventually obtained:

$$\forall \phi^{(0)} \in R^M \qquad \lim_{n \to \infty} W^{\circ n}(\phi^{(0)}) = \phi \tag{5-11}$$

where $\phi^{(n)} = W^{\circ n}(\phi^{(0)}) = \underbrace{W(W(\cdots(W(\phi^{(0)}))))}_{n \ times}$.

Property 3 The collage theorem: $\forall \psi \in R^M$, if for $\varepsilon > 0$, we have $d_{max}(W(\psi), \psi) \leq \varepsilon$, then

$$d_{max}(\phi, \psi) \leq \frac{\varepsilon}{1-s} \tag{5-12}$$

These three properties are the bases of fractal image coding algorithms. If we have an image ψ to be encoded, then the encoding is to find a fractal mapping W, which makes the error between $W(\psi)$ and ψ as small as possible. When decoding, W is applied iteratively to an arbitrary initial image $\phi^{(0)}$, then we obtain an image sequence $\phi^{(0)}$, $\phi^{(1)}$, ... , $\phi^{(n)}$, ... and the attractor image ϕ is eventually achieved, which is our reconstructed image. According to the collage theorem, the difference between ϕ and ψ can be controlled by the error between $W(\psi)$ and ψ. In practice, even if some of the l_i's are non-contractive, the iteration procedure can still converge to an attractor image. Although such kind of convergence is very difficult to be mathematically proved, the usage of non-contractive l_i has been widely adopted by many fractal image coding systems. More discussions are given by Fisher in [9].

5.3 Partial Fractal Mapping

If only part of the image is coded using fractal method, then Equation (5-4) should be modified. First, we partition the whole image Ω into two parts Ω_1 and Ω_2

$$\Omega = \Omega_1 \cup \Omega_2 \qquad \text{and} \qquad \Omega_1 \cap \Omega_2 = \varnothing \tag{5-13}$$

where only Ω_1 part is modeled using fractal method and Ω_2 part is encoded using any other method. Ω_1 can be further partitioned:

$$\Omega_1 = \bigcup_{i=1}^{N_1} R_i \qquad \text{and} \qquad R_i \cap R_j = \varnothing \quad (i \neq j) \tag{5-14}$$

Under such a partitioning, we have $\sum_{i=1}^{N_1} r_i < M$. Obviously, $M - \sum_{i=1}^{N_1} r_i$ is the number of pixels in Ω_2.

For the non-fractal coded part Ω_2, we use a constant function mapping C: $R^M \to R^M$, so that $\forall \phi \in R^M$, we always have $C(\phi)=\theta$, where θ is a constant vector in R^M and satisfies $\forall j \in \Omega_1$, $\theta(j)=0$.

For the fractal coded part Ω_1, the process is similar to that in Section 5.2 for basic fractal encoding. For each R_i, we find the appropriate W_i and D_i. As to a certain R_i, its corresponding D_i may in Ω_1 or in Ω_2, or part of it in Ω_1, and the remaining part in Ω_2.

We call the collection of W_i (i=1, … , N_1) a partial Iterated Function System: $\text{IFS}^P=\{W_1, W_2, \ldots, W_{N_1}\}$. The combination of IFS^P and the constant mapping C compose a partial fractal mapping:

$$W^P: R^M \to R^M$$

$$W^P(\phi) = C(\phi) + \sum_{i=1}^{N_1} W_i(\phi) = \theta + \sum_{i=1}^{N_1} W_i(\phi). \tag{5-15}$$

Now we discuss the properties of W^P.

Theorem 1 W^P is a contractive mapping in $(R^M, d_{\max})$.

Proof: $\forall \phi_1, \phi_2 \in R^M$

$\forall j \in \Omega$

if $j \in R_i \subset \Omega_1$, then

$$\left|(W^P\phi_1)(j) - (W^P\phi_2)(j)\right| = \left|v_i\left(\sum_{k=1}^{K} a_{j_k}\phi_1(j_k)\right) - v_i\left(\sum_{k=1}^{K} a_{j_k}\phi_2(j_k)\right)\right|$$

$$\overset{(6)}{<} s\cdot\left|\sum_{k=1}^{K} a_{j_k}\phi_1(j_k) - \sum_{k=1}^{K} a_{j_k}\phi_2(j_k)\right| = s\cdot\left|\sum_{k=1}^{K} a_{j_k}\left[\phi_1(j_k) - \phi_2(j_k)\right]\right|$$

$$\leq s\cdot\sum_{k=1}^{K} a_{j_k}\left|\phi_1(j_k) - \phi_2(j_k)\right| \leq s\cdot\sum_{k=1}^{K} a_{j_k}\cdot \max_{j=1,\cdots,M}\left|\phi_1(j) - \phi_2(j)\right|$$

$$= s\cdot \max_{j=1,\cdots,M}\left|\phi_1(j) - \phi_2(j)\right| = s\cdot d_{\max}(\phi_1, \phi_2) \tag{5-16}$$

if $j \in \Omega_2$, then

$$\left|(W^P\phi_1)(j)-(W^P\phi_2)(j)\right| = |\ \theta(j)\ \text{-}\ \theta(j)\ | = 0 \le s\cdot d_{\max}(\phi_1,\phi_2) \quad (5\text{-}17)$$

$$\therefore \quad \max_{j=1,\cdots,M}\left|(W^P\phi_1)(j)-(W^P\phi_2)(j)\right| \le s\cdot d_{\max}(\phi_1,\phi_2) \quad (5\text{-}18)$$

i.e., $$d_{\max}(W^P(\phi_1),W^P(\phi_2)) \le s\cdot d_{\max}(\phi_1,\phi_2) \ \blacksquare \quad (5\text{-}19)$$

According to Theorem 1 and the Contractive Mapping Theorem in complete metric space, we can prove that in (R^M, d_{max}) space, W^P satisfies the three properties of W described in Section 5.2.

In real applications, we are more concerned with the d_2 metric. However, in (R^M, d_2), it is difficult to prove the contractivity of either W or W^P, but we have the following theorems.

Theorem 2 There are a basic fractal mapping W and a partial fractal mapping W^P in (R^M, d_2) space, where the IFS^P of W^P is a subset of the IFS of W (i.e., the encoding of Ω_1 part of W^P is exactly the same as the corresponding part of W). If W is a contractive mapping, then W^P is also a contractive mapping.

Proof: $\forall \phi_1, \phi_2 \in R^M$
Because W is contractive in (R^M, d_2), $d_2(W(\phi_1),W(\phi_2)) \le s\cdot d_2(\phi_1,\phi_2)$
Thus we have

$$d_2(W^P(\phi_1),W^P(\phi_2)) = \Big(\frac{1}{M}\sum_{j=1}^{M}\left|(W^P\phi_1)(j)-(W^P\phi_2)(j)\right|^2\Big)^{1/2}$$

$$= \Big(\frac{1}{M}\sum_{j\in\Omega_1}\left|(W\phi_1)(j)-(W\phi_2)(j)\right|^2 + \frac{1}{M}\sum_{j\in\Omega_2}\left|\theta(j)-\theta(j)\right|^2\Big)^{1/2}$$

$$\le \Big(\frac{1}{M}\sum_{j=1}^{M}\left|(W\phi_1)(j)-(W\phi_2)(j)\right|^2\Big)^{1/2}$$

$$= d_2(W(\phi_1),W(\phi_2)) \le s\cdot d_2(\phi_1,\phi_2) \ \blacksquare \quad (5\text{-}20)$$

Theorem 2 demonstrates that W^P is more likely to be contractive than W in (R^M, d_2) space.

Theorem 3 In (R^M, d_2) space, W^P has a unique attractor image ϕ, such that $W^P(\phi) = \phi$

Proof:
Existence:
From the properties of W^P in (R^M, d_{max}) space, we know that there exists a $\phi \in R^M$ that makes $d_{max}(W^P(\phi),\phi) = 0$, then we have

$$d_2(W^P(\phi),\phi) \overset{(3)}{\le} d_{\max}(W^P(\phi),\phi) = 0 \quad (5\text{-}21)$$

$\therefore$ In (R^M, d_2) space, $W^P(\phi) = \phi$.

That is to say, W^P has the same attractor image ϕ in both $(R^M, d_{\max})$ and (R^M, d_2).
Uniqueness:
If there exist two different attractors ϕ_1, ϕ_2 of W^P in (R^M, d_2) space:

$$\phi_1 \neq \phi_2, \quad W^P(\phi_1) = \phi_1 \text{ and } W^P(\phi_2) = \phi_2 \tag{5-22}$$

then $$[d_2(W^P(\phi_1), \phi_1)]^2 = \frac{1}{M}\sum_{j=1}^{M}\left|(W^P\phi_1)(j) - \phi_1(j)\right|^2 = 0 \tag{5-23}$$

Obviously, $\forall j \in \Omega, \quad |(W^P\phi_1)(j) - \phi_1(j)| = 0$

so, $$\max_{j=1,\cdots,M} |(W^P\phi_1)(j) - \phi_1(j)| = 0, \text{ i.e., } d_{\max}(W^P(\phi_1), \phi_1) = 0 \tag{5-24}$$

$\therefore$ ϕ_1 is an attractor of W^P in $(R^M, d_{\max})$ space.

For the same reason, ϕ_2 is also an attractor in $(R^M, d_{\max})$ space.
But we have assumed $\phi_1 \neq \phi_2$. This is contradictory to the theorem that the attractor of W^P in $(R^M, d_{\max})$ space is unique. ■

Theorem 4 if ϕ is the attractor of W^P in (R^M, d_2) space, then

$$\forall \phi^{(0)} \in R^M \qquad \lim_{n\to\infty}(W^P)^{\circ n}(\phi^{(0)}) = \phi \tag{5-25}$$

Proof: According to Property 2 of W^P in $(R^M, d_{\max})$ space,

$$\forall \varepsilon > 0, \ \exists N, \ \forall n > N, \qquad d_{\max}((W^P)^{\circ n}(\phi^{(0)}), \phi) < \varepsilon \tag{5-26}$$

so, $$d_2((W^P)^{\circ n}(\phi^{(0)}), \phi) \overset{(3)}{\leq} d_{\max}((W^P)^{\circ n}(\phi^{(0)}), \phi) < \varepsilon \tag{5-27}$$

$\therefore$ $$\lim_{n\to\infty}(W^P)^{\circ n}(\phi^{(0)}) = \phi \quad ■ \tag{5-28}$$

Theorem 3 and Theorem 4 prove that W^P still satisfies Property 1 and Property 2 in (R^M, d_2) space. The difference from those in $(R^M, d_{\max})$ space is that we can not prove the collage theorem (Property 3). However, the error between the original image and the reconstructed image still can be controlled: $\forall \psi \in R^M$, if $\exists \varepsilon > 0$, such that $d_{\max}(W^P(\psi), \psi) \leq \varepsilon$, then we have

$$d_2(\phi, \psi) \overset{(3)}{\leq} d_{\max}(\phi, \psi) \leq \frac{\varepsilon}{1-s}. \tag{5-29}$$

5.4 A General Framework for Hybrid Fractal-based Image Coding Systems

According to the construction and properties of W^P, we get a general hybrid fractal image coding framework which is shown in Figure 5.1. First, an image partitioning algorithm segment the whole image into two parts Ω_1 and Ω_2. Ω_2 is encoded using some other techniques. Its decoding result is the item of θ in Equation (5-15). The Ω_1 part is encoded using fractal method. The output codes include the fractal code of Ω_1 (*a*), the code of Ω_2 part (*b*) and the segmentation information code (*c*). When decoding, the segmentation information is first decoded, then we decode Ω_2 and get θ. Finally, the fractal code is iteratively applied to reconstruct part Ω_1 and we achieve our reconstructed image.

The framework of Figure 5.1 provides us with much flexibility for real implementation. The flexibility exists in almost every section of the encoding side:

1) The image partitioning algorithm.

2) The encoding of the image partitioning information. Obviously, this information must be encoded using lossless methods.

3) The encoding of the non-fractal-coded region Ω_2. Not just block-based methods can be used as those in previous hybrid image coding systems. Actually, almost any image coding techniques can be chosen.

4) The fractal image coding of Ω_1, which includes the selection of parameters, domain pool and the searching procedure, etc.

5) Sometimes the decoding result of Ω_2 can be used to predict some fractal parameters for the encoding of Ω_1, so that the coding efficiency of Ω_1 can be improved. We show this in Figure 5.1 using the dashed lines.

Apparently, many different hybrid image coding schemes can be derived from the general framework shown in Figure 5.1. Examples include those published in [3, 6, 7]. In the next section, we give another example which shows more merits of our hybrid method.

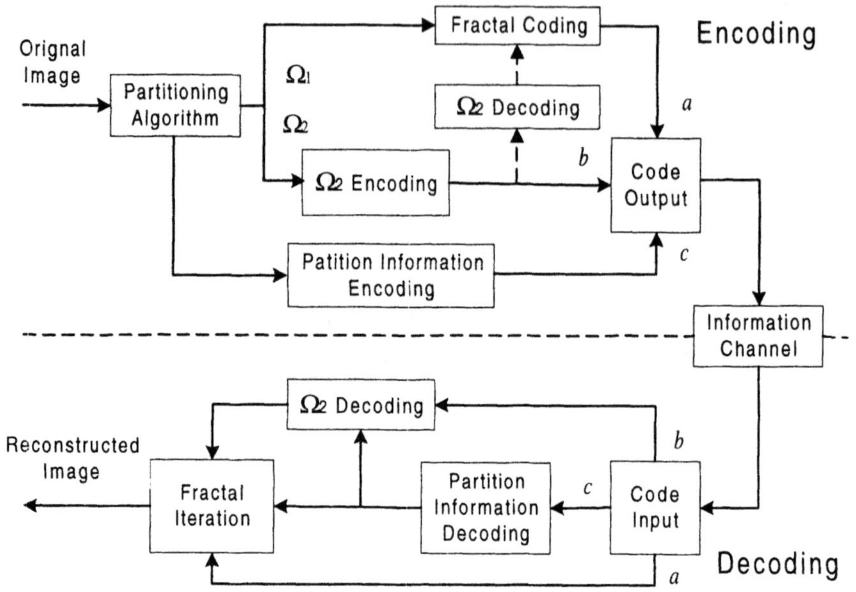

Figure5.1. A general framework of the hybrid image encoding/decoding systems

5.5 A Hybrid Image Coding System

The image to be encoded is partitioned into non-overlapping equal-sized blocks. Each block is categorized into one of the following four classes:

1) A large smooth region which is composed of at least 2 of connected adjacent blocks and can be approximated sufficiently well by a uniformly gray region.

2) A large smooth region which is composed of at least 2 of connected adjacent blocks and·can be sufficiently approximated by a plane (i.e., linear approximation).

3) An isolatedly coded block simply approximated by a uniformly gray block.

4) An isolatedly coded block modeled by fractal-based method.

Two bits are needed for each block to catalogue it into one of the four classes. We use a lossless adaptive arithmetic coding algorithm presented in [12] to further compress this information.

Image Partitioning

First, a *Sobel* operator (refer to [11]) is applied to the original image and we obtain an edge image. An example of the edge image of "Lena" is shown in Figure 5.2. Second, the edge image is partitioned into non-overlapping equal-sized 8×8 blocks. An 8×8 block may have many edge pixels or only a few or no edge pixels. A threshold T_S of the number of edge pixels is used to determine whether the block is smooth or complex. Next, we use a region growing algorithm to merge adjacent smooth blocks (A block's top, right, bottom and left blocks are called its adjacent blocks). The region growing is an iterative procedure. We first select a smooth block from the image. If any of its 4 adjacent blocks is also smooth, then the middle block and the adjacent blocks are merged into a smooth region and the merged adjacent block becomes a new selected smooth block. The same merging process is applied to each of the new selected smooth blocks. The iteration continues so that the merged region grows as much as possible with at least two or sometimes hundreds of complete 8×8 blocks. For the ease of encoding, we restrict each merged region to be within a local 64×64 block region. An example of image partitioning and merging result for the standard image "Lena" is shown in Figure 5.3.

Figure 5.2. Edge image of "Lena"

Except for the large smooth regions, the remaining parts of the image are all isolated blocks which will be encoded using block-based algorithms. These blocks are likely to be complex, but some of them may be smooth because a smooth block with no adjacent smooth block can not be merged into a large smooth region.

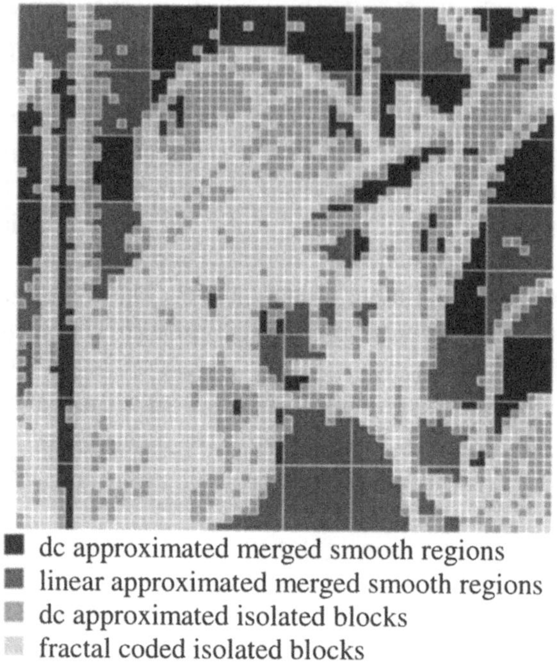

Figure 5.3. An example of image partitioning and merging result for "Lena" 512×512

Approximation of Merged Smooth Regions

For each merged smooth region, we first simply try to approximate it by a uniformly gray region with gray level equal to its mean value m. If the resulting MSE is less than a threshold T_{E1}, the dc component of the region is quantized and stored. Otherwise, we use a plane to approximate it. Plane approximation means to use a linear equation $\hat{z} = ax + by + c$ to model the region. The optimal parameters can be easily obtained under the condition of minimum squared error between the approximation plane and the original region. We can also easily prove that

$$c = m - a\bar{x} - b\bar{y} \tag{5-30}$$

where m is the mean value (dc component) of the region, $\bar{x}$ and $\bar{y}$ are the averages of x and y within the region, respectively. Then the plane equation can be rewritten as

$$\hat{z} = ax + by + c = a(x - \bar{x}) + b(y - \bar{y}) + m \tag{5-31}$$

We encode a, b and m to represent the plane.

Prediction of dc Components of Isolated Blocks

The dc component of an isolated block is correlative with its neighborhood regions. We use the average of the dc components of its 8 surrounding blocks as a prediction of the dc component of the surrounded block. If all isolated blocks have all of their surrounding blocks in merged smooth regions, the prediction is simple. However, an isolated block may have less than 8 surrounding blocks in merged smooth regions, thus its dc component can not be directly predicted. We use a progressive procedure to solve this problem. In the initial image, the merged smooth regions are covered using the approximation method described in Section 5.2 and the isolated blocks are left uncovered. The procedure consists of several steps. The output of each step is used as the input of the next step. In Step 1, for each isolated block, if all of its 8 surrounding blocks have been covered, we compute the average of the dc components of these 8 blocks as a prediction of its dc component. The difference between the real dc component and the predicted dc component is stored. Then the block is covered with a uniformly gray value equal to its real dc component. Step 2, 3, 4, ... are the same as Step 1 except that the uncovered blocks are allowed to be covered if they have 7, 6, 5, ... instead of 8 surrounding blocks covered. This procedure continues until all isolated blocks have been covered.

Normally, the difference between the real dc component and the predicted dc component is a value near zero. This kind of distribution allows us to code dc components more efficiently. If the absolute value of the difference between the real and predicted dc components is less than 16, we use 5 bits to code the difference. Otherwise, we use 8 bits to directly encode the real dc component. One extra bit is used to make a classification. If p represents the proportion of the 5 bits coded dc components in all dc components, then the average number of bits needed to code a dc component is $5p+8(1-p)+1=9-3p$. Since the dc components are useful for the encoding of isolated blocks including fractal-coded blocks, this prediction procedure can be viewed as a way where non-fractal-coded regions are used to help the encoding of fractal-coded regions.

Encoding of Isolated Blocks

For each isolated block, we also first simply try to approximate it by a uniformly gray block with gray level equal to its dc component. If the resulting MSE is less than a threshold T_{E2}, we do not need any extra bit to code it because its dc component has been predicted and quantized using the method described in Section 5.3. Otherwise, we encode it using a modified fractal block coding (FBC) method called Fractal Block Coding in Residue Domain (FBCRD). A detailed description of FBCRD is presented in [10]. FBCRD is, in some ways, similar to a fractal image coding algorithm proposed by Øien and Lepsøy [8]. Both of them can get faster decoding than basic FBC and store the scaling factor and the dc component instead of the scaling factor and the offset for luminance transformations. This is beneficial with respect to encoding. FBCRD also has something different from Øien and Lepsøy's algorithm. When decoding, the dc component of the domain block is dynamically computed and is variable in each iteration, while in Øien and Lepsøy's algorithm, it is a fixed value. This difference frees FBCRD from several constraints on Øien and Lepsøy's algorithm:

1) There is no constraint on the image partitioning method.

2) It is not necessary for the domain block to be made up of an integer number of complete range blocks.

3) More important for our usage, FBCRD can be applied in a hybrid system where only part of the image is fractal-coded. In this kind of systems, since a domain block may cover some non-fractal coded regions, the dc component of the block can only be computed dynamically.

In our hybrid system, all fractal-coded blocks are complex blocks, thus more likely to be approximated by complex domain blocks. This allows us to exclude smooth domain blocks from the domain pool. If a domain block dose not contain any pixel of any fractal-coded block, we regard it as a smooth domain block and exclude it from the domain pool. The reduction of domain pool leads to two improvements with respect to encoding. First, smaller domain pool means less encoding time. Second, smaller domain pool allows us to use fewer bits to encode the position shift for the geometrical transformations.

Decoding and Postprocessing

At the decoder, the block classification information is the first to be decoded. Then large smooth regions are merged and covered using dc or linear approximation method. A progressive procedure corresponding to that in the encoder is applied to decode the dc components of isolated blocks and cover them with uniformly gray blocks. The result of this progressive procedure is our initial image for fractal decoder iterations. Then FBCRD based decoding procedure is iteratively applied and more detailed information in fractal coded blocks is gradually emerged through iterations. The iteration is terminated when we achieve a satisfactory image. In each fractal decoder iteration, non-fractal-coded regions are kept unchanged.

To reduce the discontinuities at the block and region boundaries, we use a simple smooth algorithm similar to that introduced by Fisher in [9] to minimize these artifacts. That is, if the pixel values on either side of a boundary are u and v, then they are replaced by $\frac{3}{4}u+\frac{1}{4}v$ and $\frac{1}{4}u+\frac{3}{4}v$, respectively. This algorithm is applied only to boundary pixels of large smooth regions and isolated blocks. The internal pixels of either large regions or isolated blocks are kept unaltered.

5.6 Simulations and Conclusions

We use some 8 bits/pixel gray scale images to test our hybrid system. Peak Signal-to-Noise Ratio (PSNR) is used to make an objective evaluation. In our hybrid system, each 8×8 block needs 2 bits to be classified into one of four classes. Usually, this classification information can be compressed by 25~40% by using adaptive arithmetic coding algorithm [12]. We use 8 bits to code the dc component for a dc approximated large smooth region and 8 bits to code each of the 3 parameters for a linear approximated merged smooth region. For isolated blocks, the proportion p is typically around 0.65, so $9-3p\approx 7$ is the average number of bits for a dc component. For a fractal-coded block, we use 6 bits to code scaling factor and 3 bits to code symmetry. Since the domain pool is condensed, the bits needed for the position of domain block is reduced from 10 bits to 9 bits. Averagely, a total of about 25 bits are needed for each fractal-coded block including the bits for its dc component.

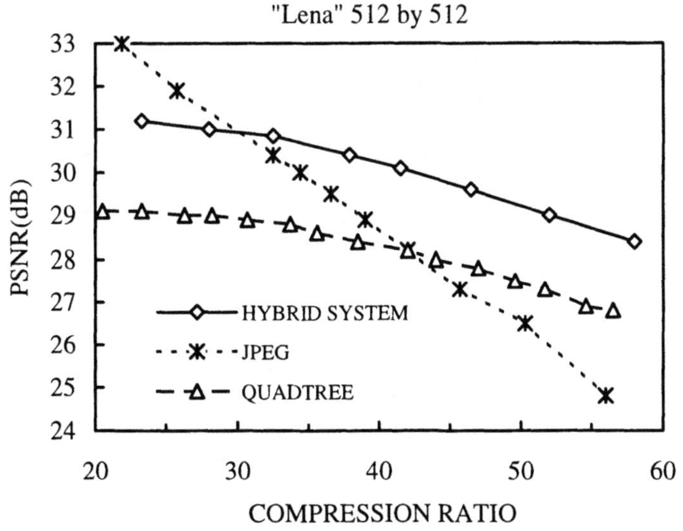

Figure 5.4. A comparison of compression results for image "Lena" 512×512

The selection of the three threshold parameters T_S, T_{E1} and T_{E2} can be used to control the tradeoff between high compression ratio and good image quality. If T_S is higher, more blocks will be regarded as smooth, thus we will obtain higher compression ratio but lose more image details. Similarly, if T_{E1} and T_{E2} are higher, more blocks or regions will be simply represented using a uniformly gray region and the compression will be higher, but approximation becomes less efficient. Figure 5.4 shows PSNR versus compression ratios and compares our hybrid system with Fisher's quadtree fractal block coding method [9] and the JPEG still image coding standard [13]. It appears that our hybrid system performs better than the fully fractal-coded quadtree method in a wide range of compression ratios. JPEG is better at low compression ratios, but the hybrid system outperforms JPEG at high compression ratios larger than 30. Figure 5.5 and Figure 5.6 show the decoded images of "Lena" and "Peppers" by our hybrid system, the quadtree method and the JPEG standard at similar compression ratios. In the hybrid system, the threshold parameters are set to T_S=0, T_{E1}=32 and T_{E2}=64, respectively. In Figure 5.7, some enlarged areas of the decoded images by the hybrid system and the quadtree method are provided, where the areas are extracted from Figure 5.5. Our hybrid system appears major improvements with respect to the subjective quality of the reconstructed images.

Figure5.5. Original and decoded "Lena" images. Upper-left: Original image; Upper-right: Quadtree decoded image, Compression ratio = 35.6, PSNR = 28.6dB; Lower-left: JPEG decoded image, Compression ratio = 36.6, PSNR = 29.5dB; Lower-right: Decoded image by the hybrid system, Compression ratio = 37.9, PSNR = 30.4dB

Another benefit from our hybrid system is the save of encoding and decoding computation time. The reason is manifold. First, the number of fractal coded blocks is reduced compared with fully fractal block coding algorithm, while the encoding of other regions is much faster. Second, the domain pool for fractal block coding is reduced. Since most of the encoding time of fractal image compression systems is used in searching for suitable domain blocks in the domain pool, smaller domain pool means less encoding time. Third, smaller domain pool allows us to use fewer bits to code the position shift for the geometrical transformations. Experimentally, only 20%~60% the encoding time of the fully fractal block coding algorithm is needed. Finally, the number of decoder iterations is less than the fully fractal coding algorithm due to the good convergence property of FBCRD.

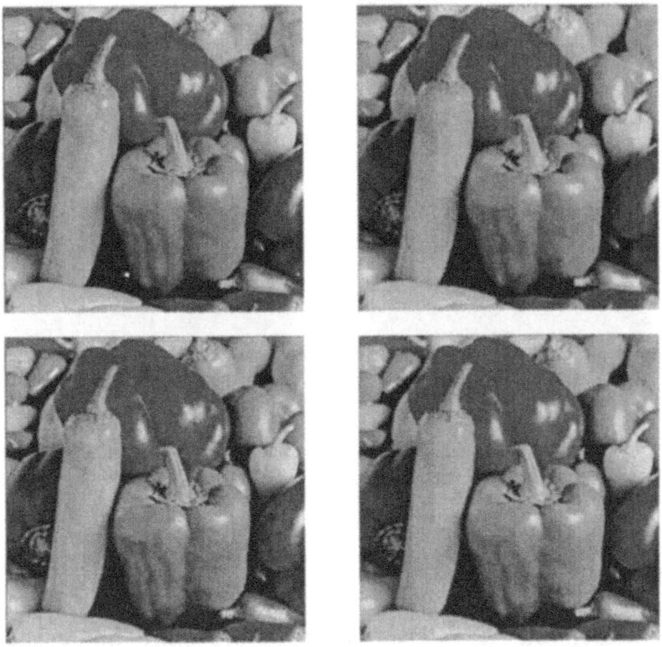

Figure 5.6. Original and decoded "Peppers" images. Upper-left: Original image; Upper-right: Quadtree decoded image, Compression ratio = 34.3, PSNR = 28.7dB; Lower-left: JPEG decoded image, Compression ratio = 34.0, PSNR = 29.7dB; Lower-right: Decoded image by the hybrid system, Compression ratio=35.0, PSNR=30.5dB

In this chapter, we propose the concept of partial fractal mapping and introduce a general framework for a class of fractal-based hybrid image coding systems. In addition, a real hybrid system is presented where non-fractal-coded regions are used to help the encoding of fractal-coded regions. Experiments show that our hybrid system outperforms the JPEG image compression standard at high compression ratios. We believe that under our general framework, the compression result can be further improved by combining fractal technique with other more sophisticated methods.

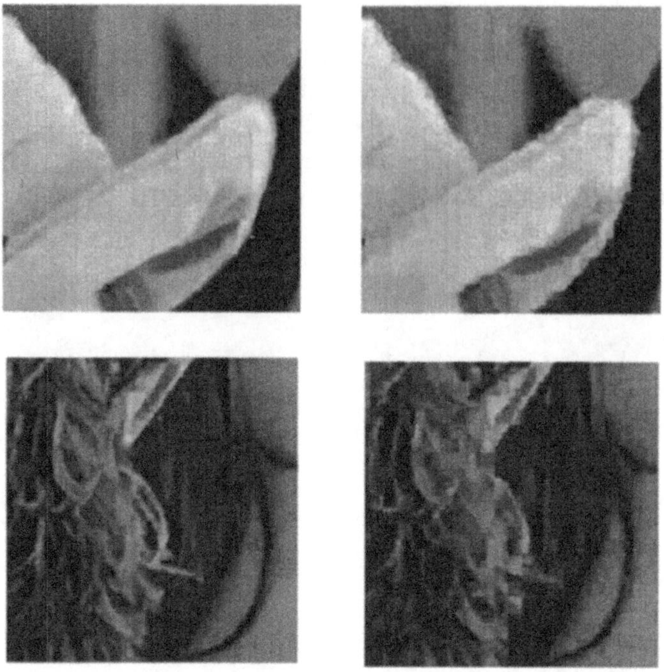

Figure 5.7. Enlarged areas of "Lena" image. Left: decoded image areas by the hybrid system; Right: quadtree decoded image areas

References

[1] B.B. Mandelbrot, *The Fractal Geometry of Nature*, San Francisco: W.H. Freeman, 1983.

[2] M.F. Barnsley, *Fractals Everywhere*, New York: Academic Press, 1988.

[3] A.E. Jacquin, "Image coding based on a fractal theory of iterated contraceptive image transformations", *IEEE Trans. Image Process.*, 1(1): 18-30, Jan. 1992.

[4] A.E. Jacquin, "Fractal image coding: a review", *Proceedings of the IEEE*, 81(10):1451-1465, Oct. 1993.

[5] Y. Fisher, ed., *Fractal Image Compression: Theory and Application*, New York: Springer-Verlag, 1994.

[6] Y. Linde, A. Buzo, and R.M. Gray, "An algorithm for vector quantizer

design", *IEEE Trans. Commun.*, COM-28:84-95, Jan. 1980.

[7] T. Laurencot and A.E. Jacquin, "Hybrid image block coders incorporating fractal coding and vector quantization, with a robust classification scheme", *AT&T Tech. Memo.*, Feb. 1992.

[8] G.E. Øien, and S. Lepsøy, "Fractal image coding with fast decoder convergence", *Signal Processing*, 40:105-117, 1994.

[9] Y. Fisher, "Fractal image compression with quadtrees", in *Fractal Image Compression: Theory and Applications to Digital Images*, Y. Fisher, ed., New York: Springer-Verlag, 1994.

[10] Z. Wang and Y.L. Yu, "Fractal block coding in residue domain," *China Journal of Electronics,* 14(3):236-240, 1997.

[11] X.K. Zhou, ed., *Practical Microcomputer Image Processing*, Beijing: Beijing Univ. of Aeronautics and Astronautics Press, 1994.

[12] I.H. Witten, R.M. Neal, and J.G. Cleary, "Arithmetic coding for data compression", *Communications of the ACM*, 30(6):520-540, Jun. 1987.

[13] G.K. Wallace, The JPEG Still Picture Compression Standard, *Communications of the ACM*, 34(4):30-44, April 1991.

Chapter 6

BEST NEIGHBORHOOD MODEL FOR BLOCK-BASED IMAGE CODING

Imperfect transmission of block-coded images often results in lost blocks. In this chapter, we introduce a novel error concealment method called Best Neighborhood Matching (BNM), which is presented by using a special kind of information redundancy — block-wise similarity within the image. The proposed algorithm can utilize the information of not only neighboring pixels, but also remote regions in the image. The model definition and algorithm implementation are presented in Section 6.2 and Section 6.3, respectively. ES-BNM Algorithm is also defined in Section 6.4. Theoretical analysis and experimental results in Section 6.5 demonstrate the efficiency of the proposed method. In Section 6.6, we draw a conclusion.

6.1 Introduction

Recently, many image coding algorithms have been developed to reduce the bit rate for digital image and video representation and transmission. Among them, block-based techniques have proved to be the most practical and are adopted by most existing image and video compression standards such as JPEG [1], MPEG [2] and H.261 [3]. Since real-world communication channels are not error free, the coded data transmitted on them may be corrupted. Block-based image coding systems are vulnerable to transmission impairment. Loss of a single bit often results in loss of a whole block and may cause consecutive block losses.

Error concealment is aimed at masking the effect of these missing blocks to create subjectively acceptable images. So far many error concealment methods have been proposed [4-10]. Some of them have the capability of detecting damaged blocks before recovering them [7] while the others must be supported by an appropriate transform format and/or an error detection algorithm that helps to identify damaged blocks [6, 8, 9]. Some of them are developed for DCT-based image coding methods [7, 10] while some others can be applied to any block-based approaches [5, 8, 9]. Some of them only deal with still images [8, 9] while the others can be used on image sequences or on both still images and image sequences [4, 7]. In this correspondence, we introduce a new error concealment algorithm which 1) assumes we know which information is received correctly and which is not; 2) can be applied to any block-based image coding system, i.e., independent of block encoding approach; 3) only recovers lost blocks for gray scale still images.

Although there exists much difference in previously published methods, they can be categorized into one framework. First, all of them used the information of only neighboring pixels as the source to generate pixel values of the missing blocks. Second, they rely on some pre-defined constrains on the spectra or structures of the lost blocks. The reconstructed blocks should be smoothly connected with adjacent regions either in spatial or in transform domain. Consequently, a well recovered lost block is often a smooth block, a sharp edge block or a stripe block with very consistent directions. The concealment algorithm is a low-pass filter or directionally low-pass filter in nature.

The technique proposed in this correspondence is fundamentally different from the previous framework. It is developed by making use of a special kind of priori information — block-wise similarity within the image. By taking advantage of such kind of information redundancy, the fractal block coding (FBC) technique, a very promising technique for high compression ratios, was developed [11, 12]. The FBC algorithm introduced a practical way to find block-wise self-similarities within natural images. In this correspondence, we will use a similar way to find block-wise similarities. However, our algorithm can not be called *fractal* because the word "fractal" in "fractal image compression" means self-similarity at every different scale while we are trying to utilize block-wise similarities at the same scale.

6.2 Model Definition

Let x_{ij} and $x_{ij}^{(new)}$ represent the pixel values at position (i, j) in the damaged image and the restored image, respectively. Since we know which blocks in the image are received correctly and which are not, it is easy to give each pixel a binary flag f_{ij} indicating whether it is lost, i.e., $f_{ij} = 1$ means (i, j) is missing and $f_{ij} = 0$ means it is good. The goal of our error concealment algorithm is to give each missing pixel with $f_{ij} = 1$ a new value which can comply with our visual sense. In this section, we first introduce a class of block-wise luminance transformations. The BNM algorithm is then developed by making use of such kind of transformations.

Consider an $N \times N$ block in the image with its up-left corner at position (i, j). The block can be represented as $\{ x_{i+m,j+n} \mid 0 \le m \le N-1, 0 \le n \le N-1\}$. A block-wise luminance transformation on the block is defined as:

$$x_{i+m,j+n} \rightarrow v(x_{i+m,j+n}) \qquad \text{for all } 0 \le m \le N-1, 0 \le n \le N-1, \qquad (6\text{-}1)$$

where v is a one-dimensional real valued function. Some possible selections of v are listed below:

$\forall z \in \boldsymbol{R}$ ($\boldsymbol{R}$ denotes the set of real number),

$$v(z) = z \qquad \text{(direct matching);} \qquad (6\text{-}2)$$

$$v(z) = a_0 + a_1 z + \cdots + a_p z^p \qquad (p\text{-order matching, } p \ge 1). \qquad (6\text{-}3)$$

An $N \times N$ image block with its up-left corner at (k, l) in the damaged image may contain both good pixels and missing pixels, so the block can be divided into two parts — the lost part and the good part. In our BNM algorithm, the good part is also called the neighborhood of the lost part or the matching part of the whole block because we will apply a matching test on it. The number of pixels in the matching part can be calculated as:

$$n_M = \sum_{m=0}^{N-1} \sum_{n=0}^{N-1} (1 - f_{k+m,l+n}). \qquad (6\text{-}4)$$

Such an $N \times N$ block with both lost part and matching part is called a range block. To recover the lost part of it, a searching procedure is applied within a large range in the image. The purpose of the searching procedure is to find a good $N \times N$ block (no pixel is missing) in the image which can best approximate the matching part of the range block through an appropriate block-wise luminance transformation. We call the good block a domain block. The Mean Square Error (MSE) between the transformed domain block and the range block in the matching part is used as the criterion to evaluate the matching result:

$$\text{MSE}_M = \frac{1}{n_M} \sum_{m=0}^{N-1} \sum_{n=0}^{N-1} (1 - f_{k+m,l+n}) \cdot (v(x_{i+m,j+n}) - x_{k+m,l+n})^2 \qquad (6\text{-}5)$$

Each of the candidate domain block in the image will result in its corresponding MSE_M. The one with the best matching result, i.e. with the minimal MSE_M, is our ultimate choice. When two domain blocks are of the same MSE_M, the one closer to the lost block is the winner. Finally, the lost part of the range block is replaced by the corresponding part of the transformed domain block, while the good part of the range block is kept unchanged:

$$x^{(new)}_{k+m,l+n} = \begin{cases} x_{k+m,l+n} & if \ f_{k+m,l+n} = 0 \\ v(x_{i+m,j+n}) & if \ f_{k+m,l+n} = 1 \end{cases} \quad \text{for all } 0 \le m \le N-1, 0 \le n \le N-1. \tag{6-6}$$

Briefly speaking, the BNM algorithm for a lost block can be summarized as the following five steps:

1) Extract a lost block from the image together with its neighborhood as a range block.
2) Search for a good candidate domain block with the same size of the range block in a searching range within the image.
3) Try to match the neighborhood of the lost block with the domain block through a block-wise luminance transformation.
4) Compete for the best match (i.e., find the minimal MSE_M) among all the candidate domain blocks.
5) Recover the lost block using the pixel values transformed from the corresponding part of the winning domain block.

6.3 Algorithm Implementation

For the real application of the BNM algorithm, there remain some choices which include:

1) the size N of range and domain blocks as well as the composition of the range blocks;
2) the searching range, i.e., given a range block, which part of the image is searched for candidate domain blocks;
3) the choice of the luminance matching function v.

In our simulations, the test images are 8 bits/pixel gray level images. Two cases of damaged images are generated by randomly discarding some 8×8 blocks from the original images. In the first case, the lost blocks are restricted to be isolated, i.e., all of their 8 surrounding blocks are good blocks; In the other case, no restriction is applied, so that some adjacent missing blocks may be connected into big lost regions.

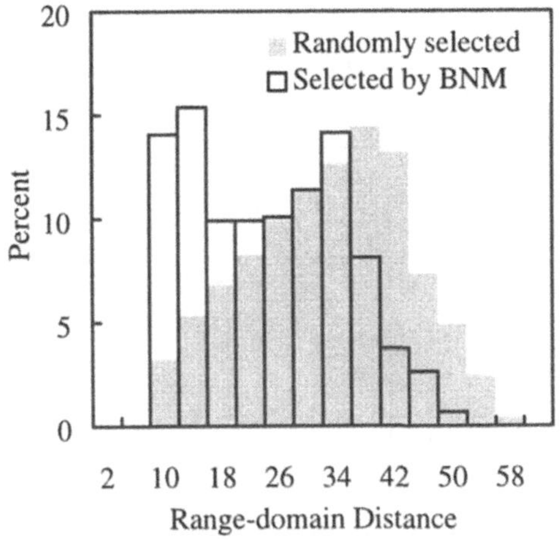

Figure 6.1. Statistics on randomly selected and BNM selected range-domain distance. The data are obtained from the test where "Barb" is corrupted with isolated block losses and with a block loss rate of 10%

In our implementations, the sizes of all range and domain blocks are set to be 10×10, i.e., $N = 10$. We put the 8×8 lost block at the center of a range block, thus the matching part of the range block is a one pixel wide boundary around the lost block. This is why we call the matching part the neighborhood of the lost block. When competing for the best match for a certain range block, both a near domain block and a remote domain block may become the winner. Figure 6.1 shows a statistic result in percentage on range-domain distance for two cases. In the first case, the domain blocks are randomly selected from the searching range, while in the other case, the domain blocks are found by the BNM algorithm. It appears that near domain blocks are more likely to be chosen by the BNM algorithm, but remote domain blocks (sometimes with a distance of over 40) may also be highly correlative with the range block. The searching range in the image should be neither too small (lose some well matched remote domain block) nor too large (lead to high computation burden or absurd matching). In our implementations, the searching range is an 80×80 square region with the range block locating at its center. Figure 6.2 illustrates the structure of lost block, range block, domain block and the searching range block.

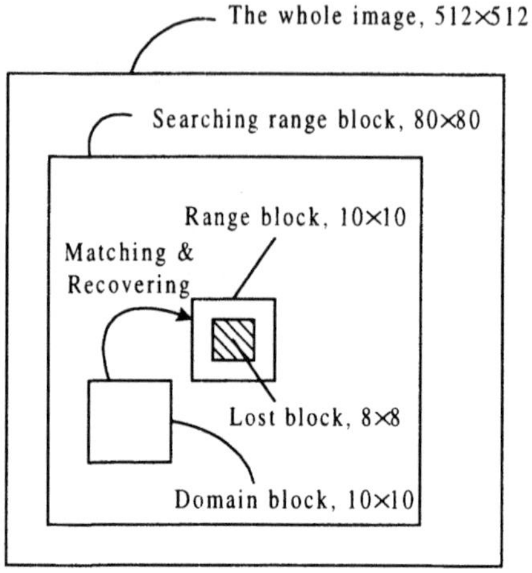

Figure 6.2. The structure of lost block, range block, domain block and searching range block with their default sizes

The matching function v is the core of the luminance transformation. The direct matching function $v(z) = z$ does not change pixel values and the p-order ($p \geq 1$) matching function try to match the values of the pixels in the range blocks through polynomial approximations. The parameters a_0, a_1, $\cdots$, a_p are selected to minimize MSE_M. They can be obtained by solving the equations:

$$\begin{cases} \partial \mathrm{MSE}_M / \partial a_0 = 0 \\ \partial \mathrm{MSE}_M / \partial a_1 = 0 \\ \vdots \\ \partial \mathrm{MSE}_M / \partial a_p = 0 \end{cases} \tag{6-7}$$

For the 1-order case, the solution is :

$$\begin{cases} a_1 = \dfrac{n_M \cdot \sum\limits_{m=0}^{N-1}\sum\limits_{n=0}^{N-1}(1-f_{k+m,l+n}) \cdot x_{k+m,l+n} \cdot v(x_{i+m,j+n}) - \sum\limits_{m=0}^{N-1}\sum\limits_{n=0}^{N-1}(1-f_{k+m,l+n}) \cdot x_{k+m,l+n} \cdot \sum\limits_{m=0}^{N-1}\sum\limits_{n=0}^{N-1}(1-f_{k+m,l+n}) \cdot v(x_{i+m,j+n})}{n_M \cdot \sum\limits_{m=0}^{N-1}\sum\limits_{n=0}^{N-1}(1-f_{k+m,l+n}) \cdot (v(x_{i+m,j+n}))^2 - \left(\sum\limits_{m=0}^{N-1}\sum\limits_{n=0}^{N-1}(1-f_{k+m,l+n}) \cdot v(x_{i+m,j+n})\right)^2} \\ a_0 = \dfrac{1}{n_M}\left[\sum\limits_{m=0}^{N-1}\sum\limits_{n=0}^{N-1}(1-f_{k+m,l+n}) \cdot x_{k+m,l+n} - a_1 \cdot \sum\limits_{m=0}^{N-1}\sum\limits_{n=0}^{N-1}(1-f_{k+m,l+n}) \cdot v(x_{i+m,j+n})\right] \end{cases} \tag{6-8}$$

The direct matching may be more practical in some applications because no parameters need to be calculated. However, its restoration result is not so good as those of 1-order or high order matching functions. It should be mentioned that, high order matching function, although can give smaller MSE_M, can not always get eventual restoration result better than that of low order matching function. The reason is that it may falsely lead to absurd recovery. In other words, two blocks that are not so similar may become very similar through a high order matching function. Actually, the 1-order matching function is always the best in our experiments. We use it in the following simulations.

6.4 ES-BNM Algorithm

In our original implementation of the BNM algorithm, the search for an appropriate domain block in the image is conducted by an exhaustive search procedure. That is to say, all the possible domain blocks in the search range are tried one by one. Such a search procedure results in long computation time. Since the search procedure of BNM can be considered as a combination optimization problem, ES may be a good choice to improve the efficiency of BNM searching.

EAs mimic the process of natural evolution. They are based on the collective learning process within a population of individuals, each of which represents a search point in the solution space. The individuals evolve toward better regions of the search space by means of randomized selection, mutation, and recombination process [13]. Though there are some distinction between "evolutionary" and "genetic" algorithm in EAs, it seems more appropriate to think of a common set of design elements for building powerful evolutionary algorithm [14]. Here we employs ESs as the optimization technique.

Mutation is one of the main operators of ESs, which is often performed independently on each vector element by adding a normally (Gaussian) distributed random value with expectation zero and some standard deviation. Recombination may also be applied for the self-adaptive ability of the algorithm [15]. However Gaussian mutation takes the primary role in generating new structures and exploring possible solution regions, so we use it as the only operator to generate new individuals.

Based on the considerations mentioned above, we propose an evolution strategy best-neighborhood-matching (ES-BNM) algorithm. Owing to the powerful searching ability of ES, ES-BNM should be more effective than the full searching method in BNM. The description of an evolutionary optimization approach involves the following operations.

Representation of the Individual

All pixels in the searching range are defined as a search space. Each individual is represented by a 2-dimensional vector $\vec{x}=\{x_1, x_2\}$, where x_1 and x_2 represent x-axis value and y-axis co-ordinate value of the up-left pixel in the range block and domain block, respectively.

Fitness Function

The MSE_M shown in Equation (6-5) is selected as the fitness function, which represents the different between the domain and the range block. The smaller the MSE_M, the more similar between domain block and range block.

Evolutionary Operators

We choose Gaussian mutation operator as the unique operator to explore new solution regions.

Selection Rule

If the child is better than the parent, it becomes the new parent of the next generation, or a counter is increased. The maximum of the counter is set to a certain number. If one child becomes a new parent, the counter is set to zero. If the maximum counter is reached, it means that the parent is not very powerful and this parent will be rejected. After that a new one is re-generated and the counter is set to zero.

For each loss block, the searching, matching and competing operations are carried out as follows (see Figure 6.2):

1) *Initialize the Parent and the Fitness Functions*

   The initial value of the individual is the x-axis value and y-axis value of the left-up corner of the range block. Set the fitness of the initial parent to a large value ($> MSE_M$ for all the rest domain blocks);

2) *Generate Child*

   Add Gaussian numbers to the two dimensions of the parent in order to get a new child, which corresponds to one domain block;

3) *Calculate the Fitness*

   Match the given region of the range block and domain block, and regard the MSE_M between these two blocks as the fitness of this domain block;

4) *"Survival of the Fittest" Selection Rule*

If the MSE_M of the child is smaller than that of the parent, recover the loss pixels of the range block with those of the domain block; otherwise, reject this child, and go to Step 2;

5) *Judge the Terminate Criterion*
If the terminate criterion is satisfied, turn to the next range block; otherwise, go to Step 2.

These five steps are used sequentially to recover each loss block.

6.5 Simulations and Comparisons

BNM Results

The peak signal-to-noise ratio (PSNR) is used to give a quantitative evaluation on the quality of the reconstructed image. As mentioned before, two cases of corrupted images are considered in this correspondence. In the case of isolated block losses, we recover the lost blocks one by one using the BNM algorithm. A problem with regard to the usage of the BNM algorithm is that when the lost block is close to the image boundaries, the 80×80 searching range block may exceed the image boundaries. In such a case, we move the searching range block into the image until its boundary reaches the image boundary. For contiguous block losses, the restoration scheme is more complex because we can not assume a completely good boundary (neighborhood) for a missing block. To solve this problem, we

1) exclude the missing pixels in the one pixel wide boundary of a missing block from the matching part of the range block, thus the matching test is applied on the remaining good boundary pixels only.
2) recover the damaged image through a progressive procedure which is composed of several steps. The missing blocks recovered in the current step are considered as good blocks in the subsequent steps. By using such a progressive procedure, the more a lost block holds good boundary pixels, the earlier it is recovered.

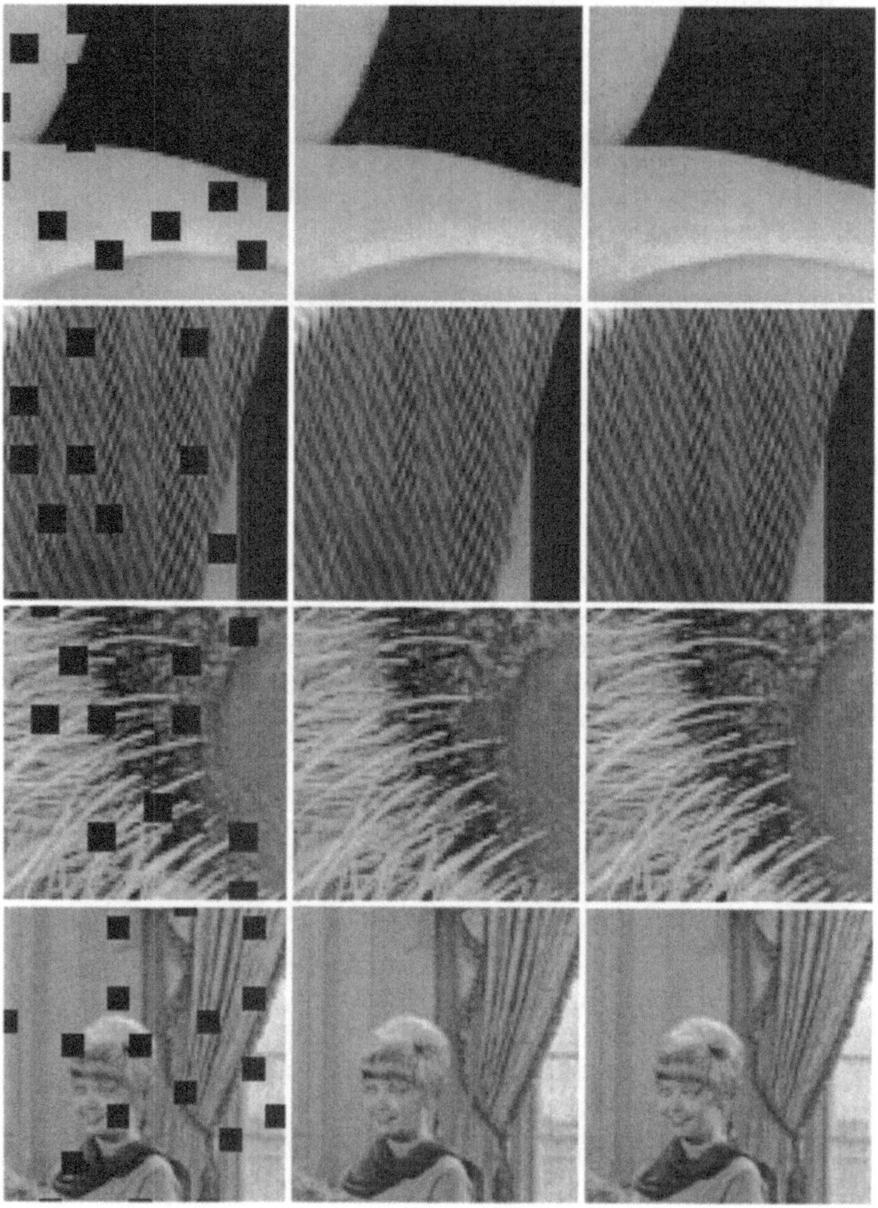

Figure 6.3. Examples for various kinds of image details. The first row: sharp edge area; The second row: texture area; The third row: very complex area; The forth row: small object and stripe area. Left column: damaged; Middle column: restored; Right column: original areas extracted from standard images "Peppers", "Barb", "Mandrill" and "Couple" (from top to bottom), respectively

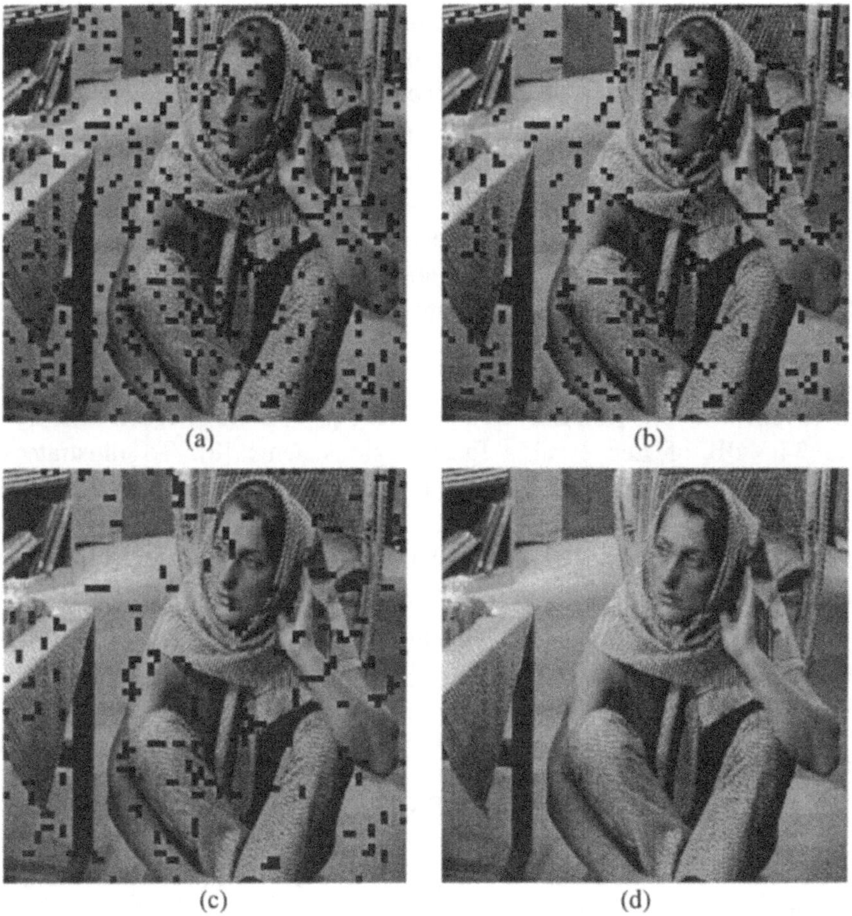

Figure 6.4. (a) Damaged image "Barb" with contiguous block losses and with block loss rate of 15%, PSNR = 14.74dB, (b) after Step 1, PSNR = 16.00 dB, (c) after Step 2, PSNR = 17.47 dB, and (d) reconstructed image after Step 4, PSNR = 32.84 dB

Table 6.1. PSNR performance for different kinds of methods with the block loss rates ranging from 2.5% to 15.0%

Error Concealment Algorithm	Block Loss Rate					
	2.5 %	5.0 %	7.5 %	10.0 %	12.5 %	15.0 %
Without concealment	22.79 dB	19.44 dB	17.67 dB	16.43 dB	15.31 dB	14.64 dB
Dc concealment	36.56 dB	32.94 dB	31.39 dB	29.95 dB	29.19 dB	28.01 dB
Direct BNM	41.14 dB	38.97 dB	36.31 dB	35.46 dB	33.61 dB	32.32 dB
1-order BNM	41.77 dB	39.63 dB	37.64 dB	37.08 dB	34.97 dB	33.19 dB

The proposed restoration algorithm has been tested on some standard gray level images. The sizes of the lost blocks are fixed to be 8×8. A dc concealment algorithm is also developed to recover the lost blocks where we simply cover each lost block with uniform gray value equal to the average gray value of its 8 surrounding blocks. In Table 6.1, we present the restoration results for image "Barb" using dc concealment, direct BNM and 1-order BNM algorithms, respectively. The dc concealment algorithm can improve PSNR by a magnitude of about 13-14 dB while those for direct BNM and 1-order BNM algorithms are 18-20 dB and 19-21 dB, respectively. The PSNR performance of the 1-order BNM algorithm for image "Barb" with a block loss rate of 10% is 37.08 dB, which is a significant improvement over 31.2 dB of Sun's scheme [5], 32 dB of HCIE scheme [8] and 34.5 dB of Lee et al.'s fuzzy logic scheme [8]. To illustrate the subjective quality of our BNM algorithm, we show some enlarged examples for sharp edge areas, texture areas, very complex areas, stripe areas and small objects in Figure 6.3. The visual quality of the recovered blocks are very good even when the areas contain a lot of detail information. In Figure 6.4, we demonstrate the progressive procedure for contiguous block losses. Although some missing blocks are connected to large black regions, they are still recovered very well.

ES-BNM Results

The peak signal-to-noise ratio (PSNR) is used to give a quantitative evaluation on the quality of the reconstructed image. Only isolated 8×8 block losses are considered in this paper. The concealment results and the computation time of ES-BNM are compared to those of BNM. Standard 512×512, 256 gray level image "Barb" is selected as the test image.

Figure 6.5 shows the subject quality of our ES-BNM. Figure 6.5(a) is the original image "Barb", and Figure. 6.5(b) is the damaged image with a block loss rate of 10%. Figure 6.5(c) shows our experimental result of ES-BNM. The PSNR performance of the 1-order ES-BNM algorithm is 36.64dB (shown in Table 6.2), which is a significant improvement over 31.2 dB of Sun's scheme [5], 32dB of HCIE scheme [8] and 34.5 dB of Lee et al.'s fuzzy logic scheme [8].

Table 6.2. Comparisons of the concealment results with the loss ratio of 10%

Algorithm	*BNM*	*ES-BNM*	*Sun's*	*HCIE*	*Lee et al 's*
Concealment	37.08 dB	36.64 dB	31.2 dB	32 dB	34.5 dB

PSNR comparisons between BNM and ES-BNM for both the direct matching and the 1-order matching are shown in Figure. 6.6 and Figure 6.7, respectively. It is clear that the concealment results of these two algorithms are much closer. For example, the PSNR performance of the 1-order ES-BNM is close to 37.08dB of BNM [16]. However, owing to the powerful global searching character, the searching time of ES-BNM is only 0.36 times to that of BNM. Comparisons of computation time are shown in Table 6.3.

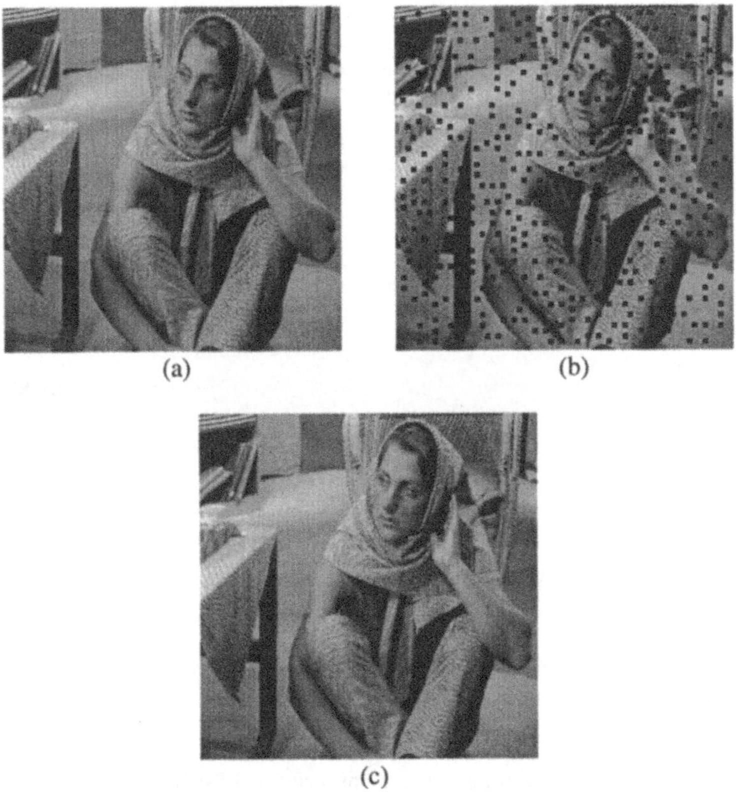

Figure 6.5. The concealment result of ES-BNM. (a) original image with the size of 512*512, (b) damaged image with a loss rate of 10% (16.43dB), and (c) the experimental result using ES-BNM (36.64dB)

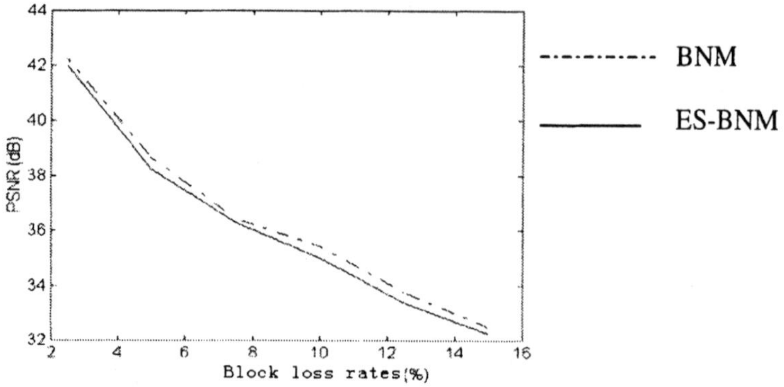

Figure 6.6. PSNR comparison between BNM and ES-BNM for the direct matching with block loss rates ranging from 2.5% to 15.0%

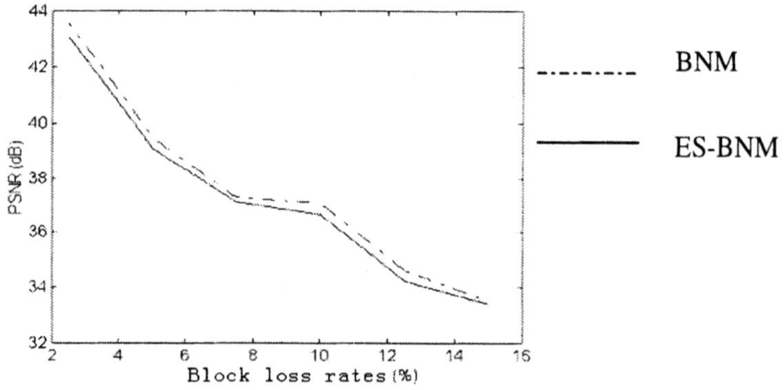

Figure 6.7. PSNR comparison between BNM and ES-BNM for the 1-order matching with the block loss rates ranging from 2.5% to 15.0%

Table 6.3. Comparisons of computational time between ES-BNM and BNM (*s: second*)

Error Concealment Algorithm	*Block Loss Rate*					
	2.5%	5.0%	7.5%	10.0%	12.5%	15.0%
Direct BNM	97.0 *s*	175.8 *s*	217.7 *s*	249.6 *s*	249.7 *s*	231.0 *s*
Direct ES-BNM	15.4 *s*	35.2 *s*	59.2 *s*	59.2 *s*	85.4 *s*	104.9 *s*
ES-BNM / BNM	0.16	0.20	0.22	0.24	0.34	0.45
1-order BNM	173.3 *s*	309.5 *s*	385.9 *s*	432.8 *s*	439.5 *s*	446.1 *s*
1-order ES-BNM	43.3 *s*	92.8 *s*	123.5 *s*	153.7 *s*	181.8 *s*	202.9 *s*
ES-BNM / BNM	0.25	0.30	0.32	0.36	0.41	0.45

6.6 Conclusion and Discussion

In this correspondence, a novel information loss restoration technique, BNM, is presented. The simulation results indicate that this algorithm provides significant improvement over existing algorithms in terms of both subjective and objective evaluations. It can make use of the information of not only neighboring regions, but also remote regions within the image. We think the ability to use long-range correlation is the main reason why it can outperform other algorithms. Another advantage is that the BNM algorithm does not apply any constraint on the spectra of local regions. We do not need to classify a missing block into one of several categories due to its neighborhood direction or complexity. Whatever the block looks like, it can be recovered using the same method. In other words, the BNM algorithm is inherently an adaptive algorithm.

The BNM algorithm is not restricted to the particular 8×8 block size. The reason to choose such a size in our simulations is that it is the size frequently used by a lot of proposed image and video coding techniques. Actually, the methodology described in this correspondence can be used for different shapes, sizes and transforms. Further improvements include developing fast searching algorithms and generalizing the BNM technique for color images, image sequences or other kinds of signals.

By merging ES into the BNM approach, a novel information loss restoration method for block-based image coding, ES-BNM is proposed. Both BNM and ES-BNM algorithms perform better than other existing approaches. They provide similar restored image quality while the ES-BNM algorithm costs much less time. From our experiments, the restored image quality is so good that we cannot distinguish the original image and restored one by our eyes if the block loss ratio is less than 10%. ES-BNM can also be viewed as a new successful application that demonstrates the powerful optimization ability of ES.

References

[1] G. Walleye, "The JPEG still image picture compression standard", *Commun. ACM*, 34(4):30-44, Apr. 1991.

[2] D. Le Gall, "JPEG: A video compression standard for multimedia applications", *Commun. ACM*, 34(4):46-58, Apr. 1991.

[3] M. Liou, "Overview of the p×64 kbit/s video coding standard", *Commun. ACM*, 34(4):59-63, Apr. 1991.

[4] Y. Wang and Q. Zhu, "Signal loss recovery in DCT-based image and video codecs", in *SPIE Proc. Visual Commun. Image Processing*, 1605:667-678, Nov. 1991.

[5] H. Sun, K. Challapali, and J. Zdepski, "Error concealment in digital simulcast AD-HDTV decoder", *IEEE Trans. on Consumer Electronics*, 38(3):108-118, Aug. 1992.

[6] W. M. Lam, A. R. Reibman, and B. Liu, "Recovery of lost or erroneously received motion vectors", in *Proc. ICASSP*, 5:417-470, 1993.

[7] W. M. Lam and A. R. Reibman, "An error concealment algorithm for image subject to channel errors", *IEEE Trans. on Image Processing*, 4(5):533-542, May 1995.

[8] X. Lee, Y. Q. Zhang, and A. Leon-Garcia, "Information loss recovery for block-based image coding techniques — a fuzzy logic approach", *IEEE Trans. on Image Processing*, 4(3):259-273, Mar. 1995.

[9] H. Sun and W. Kwok, "Concealment of damaged block transform coded images using projections onto convex sets", *IEEE Trans. on Image Processing*, 4(4):470-477, Apr. 1995.

[10] S.S. Hemami and T.H.Y. Meng, "Transform coded image reconstruction exploiting interblock correlation", *IEEE Trans. on Image Processing*, 4(7):1023-1027, July 1995.

[11] A. Jacquin, "Image coding based on a fractal theory of iterated contractive image transformations", *IEEE Trans. on Image Processing*, 1(1):18-30, Jan. 1992.

[12] Fisher, ed., *Fractal Image Compression - Theory and Applications*, New York: Springer-Verlag, 1994.

[13] V. Nissen, "Solving the Quadratic Assignment Problem with Clues from Nature", *IEEE Trans on Neural Networks*, 5(1):66-72, 1994.

[14] D.B. Fogel, "An Introduction to Simulated Evolutionary Optimization", *IEEE Trans on Neural Networks*, 5(1):3-14, 1994.

[15] T. Bäck, U. Hammel, and H.P. Schwefel, "Evolutionary Computation: Comments on the History and Current State", *IEEE Trans. on Evolutionary Computation*, 1(1):3-17, 1997.

[16] Z. Wang, Y.L. Yu and D. Zhang, "Best Neighborhood Matching - An Information Loss Restoration Technique for Block Based Image Coding

Systems," *IEEE Transactions on Image Processing*, 7(7):1056-1061, 1998.

Chapter 7

IMPULSE NOISE REMOVAL ALGORITHMS FOR IAP

In this chapter, a novel filtering algorithm is presented to restore images corrupted by impulsive noise. As a pre-processing procedure of the noise cancellation filter, an improved impulse detector is used to generate a binary flag image which gives each pixel a flag indicating whether it is an impulse. This flag image has two uses: 1) A pixel is modified only when it is considered as an impulse; otherwise, it is left unchanged. 2) Only the values of the good pixels are employed as useful information by the noise cancellation filter. Section 7.2 describes the impulse noise model assumed by our experiments and presents an iterative impulse detection algorithm which provides us with more accurate detecting results than those of previously proposed methods. To remove noises from the corrupted image, in Section 7.3, we propose a new filter called polynomial approximation (PA) filter which is developed by modeling a local region with a polynomial that can best approximate the region under the condition of least square error. Section 7.4 introduces an adaptive approach that can automatically determine the orders of the polynomials. The proposed two kinds of PA filters, fixed-order and adaptive-order PA filters, are tested on images corrupted by both fixed-valued and random-valued impulsive noise. Some further simulation and comparison results are given in Section 7.5. Finally, a brief conclusion is drawn in Section 7.6.

7.1 Introduction

Images are often contaminated by impulse noise during transmission through communication channels. It is important to eliminate noise in the images before some subsequent processing, such as edge detection, image segmentation and object recognition. So far a large variety of filtering algorithms have been proposed to perform an effective noise cancellation while preserving the image structure [1-12]. Typical examples include the neighborhood mean filter and the median filter. Nevertheless, because these filters are implemented uniformly across the image, they tend to modify both noise pixels and undisturbed good pixels, resulting in blurring of the image. To avoid the damage of good pixels, the switching strategy is introduced by some recently published work [1-3, 9-12], where impulse detectors are employed to pre-select the pixels that should be modified. This kind of techniques has proved to be more effective than uniformly applied methods.

The approach we are proposing also uses an impulse detector to categorize all the pixels in the image into two classes – noise pixels and good pixels, i.e., noise-free pixels. These classification results are used in two ways during the filtering procedure. First, only pixels indexed as impulses will be modified. Second, the filter uses merely the information of noise-free pixels as the source to estimate the corrupted pixel values.

To replace an impulse pixel with a new value, various methods can be developed to make an estimation. However, almost all previously published algorithms, as far as we know, replace the corrupted value with one from a local window or some linear combination of local samples. In other words, only ranking or statistic information of neighboring pixel values is employed. These kinds of information, we think, is not enough to represent the real structure, such as direction and curvature, of the local region. Substantially different from previous algorithms, our new approach is developed by modeling the local region using some function approximation algorithms, so that it can tell the structure of the local window. The center corrupted pixel is then replaced with a value that can best comply with the structural information. In particular, polynomial approximation technique is used in the chapter, which is easy to operate and is effective in modeling local regions.

7.2 Noise Model and Impulse Detector

Impulse Noise Model

Images may be contaminated by various sorts of noises. The type of noise considered by our algorithm is only impulsive noise whose value is generally independent of the strength of the image signal. Let o_{ij} and x_{ij} denote the gray levels at location (i, j) of the original image and the noisy image, respectively. Then for an impulse noise model with noise probability p_n, we have

$$x_{ij} = \begin{cases} o_{ij} & \text{with probability } 1 - p_n \\ n_{ij} & \text{with probability } p_n \end{cases}, \qquad (7\text{-}1)$$

where n_{ij} is a noise value independent from o_{ij}. In this chapter, two cases of noise distributions are considered. In the first case, the values of the corrupted pixels equal to the maximum or minimum of the allowed dynamic range with equal probability. This kind of noise is commonly referred to as salt-pepper noise. In the other case, the corrupted pixel values are uniformly distributed between the maximum and minimum allowed dynamic range. For 8bpp (bits/pixel) gray level images, the noise luminance of the first case corresponds to a fixed value of 0 or 255 with equal probability, while that of the second case corresponds to a random value uniformly distributed between 0 and 255.

Impulse Detector

Our impulse detection algorithm is developed based on two assumptions: 1) A noise-free image should be locally smoothly varying, and is separated by edges; 2) A noise pixel takes a gray value substantially larger than or smaller than those of its neighbors.

Sun and Neuvo introduced a simple and effective method to detect noises in their switch I scheme [3]. We briefly describe it as follows: Let x_{ij} represents the pixel values at position (i, j) in the corrupted image. To judge whether x_{ij} is an impulse pixel, we find the median value of the samples in the $(2L_d+1)\times(2L_d+1)$ window centered about it, i.e.,

$$m_{ij} = \mathrm{Med}\{\, x_{i-L_d,\, j-L_d}\,,\ \ldots\,,\ x_{i,j}\,,\ \ldots\,,\ x_{i+L_d,\, j+L_d}\ \}\,. \tag{7-2}$$

The difference between m_{ij} and $x_{i,j}$ is used to detect impulses:

$$f_{ij} = \begin{cases} 1 & \text{if } \left|x_{ij} - m_{ij}\right| \ge T_d \\ 0 & \text{else} \end{cases}\,. \tag{7-3}$$

Here T_d is a pre-defined threshold value. The binary value f_{ij} indicates whether (i, j) is considered as an impulse, i.e., $f_{ij}=1$ means (i, j) is a corrupted pixel; otherwise, (i, j) is noise-free.

This detection method is adopted by our algorithm. In addition, we also developed a modified version to improve detection accuracy. The modified version is implemented through an iterative manner where the noisy pixels detected in the current iteration are modified and used to help the detection of other noisy pixels in the subsequent iterations. A main advantage of such an iterative procedure is that some impulse pixels located in the middle of large noise blotches can also be properly detected and filtered. Let $x_{ij}^{(0)}$ denote the pixel value at position (i, j) in the initial noisy image and $x_{ij}^{(n)}$ represent the pixel value at position (i, j) in the image after the n-th iteration.

In the n-th iteration (n = 1, 2, ...), for each pixel $x_{ij}^{(n-1)}$, we also first find the median value of the samples in a $(2L_d+1)\times(2L_d+1)$ window centered about it:

$$m_{ij}^{(n-1)} = \text{Med}\,\{\, x_{i-L_d,j-L_d}^{(n-1)}, \ldots, x_{ij}^{(n-1)}, \ldots, x_{i+L_d,j+L_d}^{(n-1)} \,\}. \tag{7-4}$$

The difference between $m_{ij}^{(n-1)}$ and $x_{ij}^{(n-1)}$ is the criterion to determine whether $x_{ij}^{(n-1)}$ should be changed:

$$x_{ij}^{(n)} = \begin{cases} m_{ij}^{(n-1)} & \text{if } \left| x_{ij}^{(n-1)} - m_{ij}^{(n-1)} \right| \geq T_d \\ x_{ij}^{(n-1)} & \text{else} \end{cases}. \tag{7-5}$$

Suppose the iteration stops after the N_d-th iteration. The flag value f_{ij} is then given as:

$$f_{ij} = \begin{cases} 1 & \text{if } x_{ij}^{(0)} \neq x_{ij}^{(N_d)} \\ 0 & \text{else} \end{cases}. \tag{7-6}$$

Before the real implementation of our impulse detector, several parameters, L_d, T_d and N_d, should be pre-determined. In our simulations, 3×3 sized window always gives better results than larger windows, so we choose L_d = 1. However, it is not so easy to select T_d and N_d because they are sensitive to the type of the noise. Figures 7.1-7.2 show typical examples of the detection correct rates as functions of T_d and N_d for fixed-valued and random-valued impulsive noise, respectively. Here, if E is denoted as the number of good pixels that are correctly detected as good pixels, F as the number of noise pixels that are correctly detected as noise pixels and G as the total number of pixels in the image, then the detection correct rate is calculated as $(E + F) / G$. In Figures 7.1-7.2, it appears that the best results can be obtained from 2 or 3 iterations when the images are corrupted by fixed-valued noise, while for the case of random-valued noise, no iteration is needed, i.e., $N_d = 1$ is the best. It can be also observed that the best T_d for fixed-valued noise is larger than that for random-valued noise. According to the above facts, we always use $T_d = 35$ and $N_d = 3$ for fixed-valued impulse noise and $T_d = 20$ and $N_d = 1$ (i.e., no iteration) for random-valued impulse noise in the remaining part of this chapter.

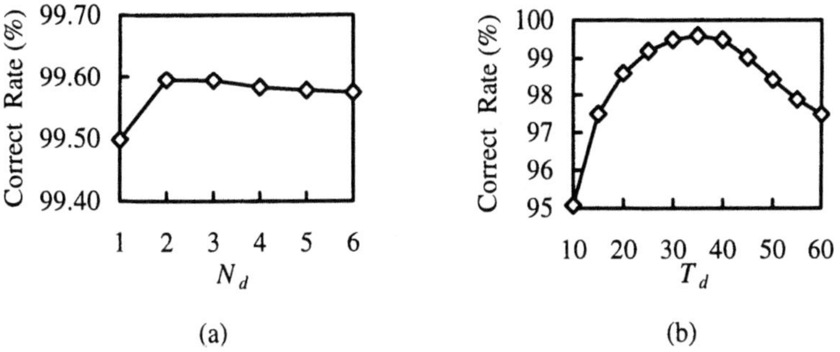

Figure 7.1. An example of the influence of detection parameters on the detection correct rate for fixed-valued impulse noise. The test image is "Lena" corrupted by 20% noise. (a) Correct rate as a function of N_d, where T_d is a fixed value of 35; (b) Correct rate as a function of T_d, where N_d is a fixed value of 3

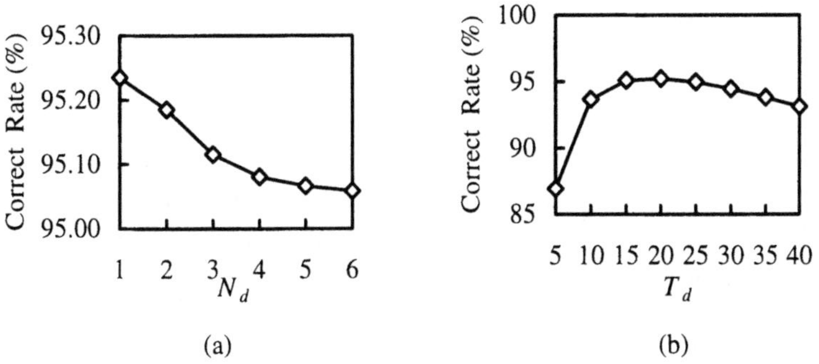

Figure 7.2. An example of the influence of detection parameters on the detection correct rate for random-valued impulse noise. The test image is "Lena" corrupted by 20% noise. (a) Correct rate as a function of N_d, where T_d is a fixed value of 20; (b) Correct rate as a function of T_d, where N_d is a fixed value of 1

7.3 Polynomial Approximation (PA) Filter

Consider a $(2L_f+1)\times(2L_f+1)$ square region centered about an impulse pixel (i_0, j_0) with $f_{i_0,j_0} = 1$. The pixels in it can be categorized into two classes — good pixels ($f_{ij} = 0$) and impulse pixels ($f_{ij} = 1$). Only good pixels are used by the PA filter which models the local region using a two-dimension polynomial. For simplicity, we shift the position of the center pixel (i_0, j_0) to (0, 0) and normalize the square region so that its top-left corner and bottom-right corner are located at (−1, −1) and (+1, +1), respectively:

$$y_{pq} = x_{ij}\,, \tag{7-7}$$

where y_{pq} is the pixel value under the new coordinate and we have

$$p = (i - i_0) / L_f \; ; \qquad q = (j - j_0) / L_f \; . \tag{7-8}$$

Then the approximation polynomial can be denoted as:

$$\hat{y}_{pq} = \sum_{m=0}^{K} \sum_{n=0}^{K-m} c_{mn} p^m q^n \, , \tag{7-9}$$

where $\{ c_{mn} \mid m = 0, \dots, K \; ; n = 0, \dots, m - K \}$ is a set of coefficients and K is the order of the polynomial. For example, a 2-order polynomial can be written as:

$$\hat{y}_{pq} = c_{00} + c_{10} p + c_{01} q + c_{20} p^2 + c_{02} q^2 + c_{11} pq \, . \tag{7-10}$$

The calculated value of $\hat{y}_{pq}$ can be used to estimate the value of x_{ij}:

$$\hat{x}_{ij} = \hat{y}_{pq} \, , \tag{7-11}$$

where

$$i = i_0 + p \cdot L_f \; ; \qquad j = j_0 + q \cdot L_f \; . \tag{7-12}$$

The set of coefficients $\{ c_{mn} \}$ should be well selected, so that the good pixels in the local region are best approximated under the condition of least square error. The square error is calculated as:

$$E = \sum_{i=-L_f}^{L_f} \sum_{j=-L_f}^{L_f} (1 - f_{ij})(x_{ij} - \hat{x}_{ij})^2 \, . \tag{7-13}$$

The minimum of E is achieved when the deviation of E with respect to every c_{mn} are all 0:

$$\partial E / \partial c_{mn} = 0 \quad (m = 0, \dots, K \; ; \;\; n = 0, \dots, K - m). \tag{7-14}$$

By solving these equations, the value of each c_{mn} can be obtained. Finally, the center pixel $x_{i_0 j_0}$ is replaced by the estimated value:

$$\hat{x}_{i_0 j_0} = \hat{y}_{00} = c_{00} \, . \tag{7-15}$$

As a special case, the 0-order PA filter has only one coefficient c_{00} and the solution of Equation (7-14) is simply

$$c_{00} = \frac{\sum_{i=-L_f}^{L_f} \sum_{j=-L_f}^{L_f} (1 - f_{ij}) x_{ij}}{\sum_{i=-L_f}^{L_f} \sum_{j=-L_f}^{L_f} (1 - f_{ij})}. \tag{7-16}$$

That is, c_{00} equals to the average value of the good pixels in the square region. Therefore, the 0-order PA filter can also be viewed as a noise-free neighborhood mean filter.

7.4 Adaptive Order PA (AOPA) Filter

A Study on Polynomial Order

Only two parameters, L_f and K, should be pre-defined before the application of the PA filter. Our simulations indicate that in most cases 5×5 sized square region is the best for the performance of the polynomial approximation algorithm, so we set $L_f = 2$. To determine the polynomial order K is not an easy task. The proper value of K depends on how many details are embraced in the local region and how much the region is corrupted. In this subsection, we investigate the performance of fixed-order PA (FOPA) filter where the value of K is invariable throughout the whole image. Then in the next subsection, an adaptive order PA (AOPA) filter is introduced where K is adjusted to comply with some local statistic features. In all the experiments, the test images are 512×512, 8bpp gray level images. Peak Signal-to-Noise Ratio (PSNR) is used to assess the filtering results:

$$\text{PSNR} = 10 \log_{10} \frac{255^2}{\frac{1}{r^2} \sum_{i=1}^{r} \sum_{j=1}^{r} (o_{ij} - t_{ij})^2} \tag{7-17}$$

where r is the size of the image ($r = 512$), o_{ij} and t_{ij} are the pixel values at position (i, j) within the original image and the test image, respectively.

In Tables 7.1-7.2, we list the filtering results of 0, 1, 2 and 3-order PA filters, where the original image "Lena" is corrupted with 10% ~ 30% fixed-valued and random-valued impulse noise, respectively. Basically, higher polynomial order, such as 2-order or 3-order, leads to higher PSNR. The reason is simple because higher order polynomials can reflect more complex characteristics, such as direction and curvature, of local regions. However, this is not always true especially when the noise rates are high. For instance, the PSNR performance of 2-order PA filter for 30% random-valued impulse noise is 30.87dB, which is substantially higher than 29.67dB of 3-order PA filter. We think the main reason is that low order polynomials are more robust than high order ones. To demonstrate it clearly, we give a simple one-dimension example (see Figure 7.3), where both a 2-order and a 3-order polynomial are used to estimate the point at 0.00 using the five sample points provided.

Table 7.1. Filtering results in PSNR for "Lena" corrupted with fixed-valued impulse noise

Filtering Algorithm	Percentage of Fixed-valued Impulse Noise				
	10%	15%	20%	25%	30%
0-order PA filter	36.60 dB	35.64 dB	34.65 dB	33.66 dB	32.31 dB
1-order PA filter	36.64 dB	35.65 dB	34.71 dB	33.69 dB	32.36 dB
2-order PA filter	39.48 dB	38.61 dB	37.44 dB	**36.26** dB	**34.22** dB
3-order PA filter	**39.63** dB	**38.79** dB	**37.56** dB	35.74 dB	33.03 dB
AOPA filter	39.60 dB –0.03 dB	38.79 dB 0.00 dB	37.57 dB +0.01 dB	36.27 dB +0.01 dB	34.21 dB –0.01 dB

Table 7.2. Filtering results in PSNR for "Lena" corrupted with random-valued impulse noise

Filtering Algorithm	Percentage of Random-valued Impulse Noise				
	10%	15%	20%	25%	30%
0-order PA filter	34.41 dB	33.34 dB	32.39 dB	31.41 dB	30.25 dB
1-order PA filter	34.44 dB	33.38 dB	32.38 dB	31.41 dB	30.23 dB
2-order PA filter	36.68 dB	35.30 dB	**33.99** dB	**32.59** dB	**30.87** dB
3-order PA filter	**36.80** dB	**35.32** dB	33.75 dB	32.12 dB	29.67 dB
AOPA filter	36.79 dB –0.01 dB	35.36 dB +0.04 dB	34.00 dB +0.01 dB	32.57 dB –0.02 dB	30.86 dB –0.01 dB

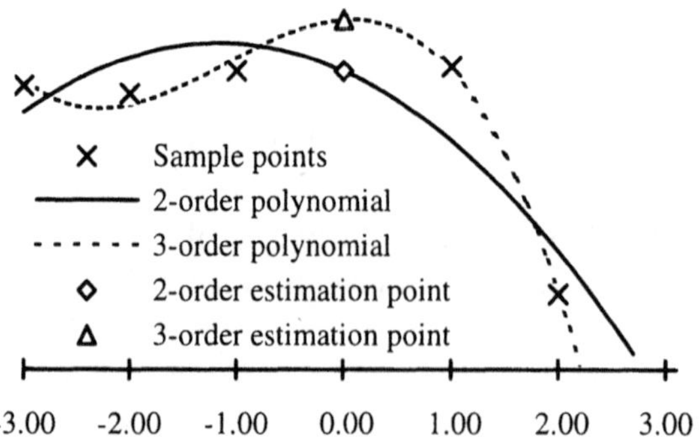

Figure 7.3. An example that demonstrates the approximation and estimation functions of 2-order and 3-order polynomials

Both of them are obtained under the condition of least square error. It can be observed that although the 3-order polynomial curve performs better in approximating the sample points, i.e., the curve is closer to the sample points, the estimated value for the point at 0.00 seems too high, not as good as that estimated by the 2-order polynomial. This phenomenon is sometimes called over-matching. Another drawback of high order PA is that it leads to high computation burden, which is not deserved especially when dealing with very smooth regions. For such kind of region, a 0-order or a 1-order polynomial is enough to give a good approximation within much less time.

Adaptive-Order PA (AOPA) Filter

For a certain region in the image, an appropriate choice of the polynomial order is determined mainly by two factors. The first is how many details the region contains and the second is how much the region is contaminated. Our AOPA filter is developed according to some quantitative evaluations on these two factors.

Before the description of the AOPA filter, however, we first define a detail estimation value $d_{i_0j_0}$ for each good pixel in the image. At (i_0, j_0) with $f_{i_0j_0} = 0$, we have

$$d_{i_0j_0} = x_{i_0j_0} - \frac{1}{M} \cdot \sum_{i=i_0-1}^{i_0+1} \sum_{j=j_0-1}^{j_0+1} (1 - f_{ij}) \cdot (1 - \delta_{i_0j_0}) \cdot x_{ij} \tag{7-18}$$

where

$$\delta_{i_0j_0} = \begin{cases} 1 & \text{if } i = i_0 \text{ and } j = j_0 \\ 0 & \text{otherwise} \end{cases}. \tag{7-19}$$

The calculation of $d_{i_0j_0}$ is equivalent to applying the following 3×3 mask to the image:

$$\begin{bmatrix} -\frac{1-f_{i_0-1,j_0-1}}{M} & -\frac{1-f_{i_0-1,j_0}}{M} & -\frac{1-f_{i_0-1,j_0+1}}{M} \\ -\frac{1-f_{i_0,j_0-1}}{M} & 1 & -\frac{1-f_{i_0,j_0+1}}{M} \\ -\frac{1-f_{i_0+1,j_0-1}}{M} & \frac{1-f_{i_0+1,j_0}}{M} & -\frac{1-f_{i_0+1,j_0+1}}{M} \end{bmatrix}, \tag{7-20}$$

where

$$M = 8 - \sum_{i=i_0-1}^{i_0+1} \sum_{j=j_0-1}^{j_0+1} f_{ij} \,. \tag{7-21}$$

Actually, such a mask can be viewed as a revised version of one of the Laplacian masks [1], which are useful in detecting lines, line ends and points over edges. The only difference is that it merely considers good neighboring pixels with $f_{ij} = 0$. In other words, the typical Laplacian mask is a special case of our revised version where all $f_{ij} = 0$. We call our new mask Noise-Free Laplacian filter which is capable of evaluate how many details a certain area of the image contains even under the condition that impulse noises exist in the image.

Now we describe how our AOPA filter determines the polynomial order. For an impulse pixel at position (i_0, j_0), we still use the information within a $(2L_f+1)\times(2L_f+1)$ window centered about it as the source to give an estimation on the pixel. First, we count how many good pixels are in the window:

$$R = \sum_{i=i_0-L_f}^{i_0+L_f} \sum_{j=j_0-L_f}^{j_0+L_f} (1 - f_{ij}) \,. \tag{7-22}$$

Second, a quantitative estimation on how much the local region is corrupted is given as:

$$u = \frac{R}{(2L_f + 1)^2} \,. \tag{7-23}$$

Next, a rough estimation on how many details the local region contains is calculated as follows:

$$v = \frac{1}{R} \cdot \sum_{i=i_0-L_f}^{i_0+L_f} \sum_{j=j_0-L_f}^{j_0+L_f} (1 - f_{ij}) \cdot \left| d_{ij} \right| \,. \tag{7-24}$$

Note that only good pixels in the window are considered. Our adaptive algorithm decides the order of the polynomial by combining the influences of both of these two factors u and v. The synthesized value is defined as:

$$s = u^a \cdot v^b \,, \tag{7-25}$$

where the use of a and b is to offer us with the flexibility to adjust the weights of u and v. Finally, the polynomial order is provided as:

$$\hat{y}_a = \begin{cases} \hat{y}_0 & \text{if } 0 \le s \le T_{s0} \\ \hat{y}_1 & \text{if } T_{s0} < s \le T_{s1} \\ \hat{y}_2 & \text{if } T_{s1} < s \le T_{s2} \\ \hat{y}_3 & \text{if } T_{s2} < s \end{cases}, \tag{7-26}$$

where $\hat{y}_a$, $\hat{y}_0$, $\hat{y}_1$, $\hat{y}_2$ and $\hat{y}_3$ denote the estimated value of the AOPA, 0-order PA, 1-order PA, 2-order PA and 3-order PA techniques, respectively. T_{s0}, T_{s1} and T_{s2} are threshold values that categorize $\hat{y}_a$ into one of four classes.

7.5 Simulations and Comparisons

Experiments of PA and AOPA Filters

To assess the performance of our algorithms, some computer simulations are carried out on several standard gray level images. In all the experiments concerning the AOPA filter, the parameters are selected as follows:

$$a = 3,\ b = 1,\ T_{s0} = 0.5,\ T_{s1} = 0.8 \ \text{ and } \ T_{s2} = 3.0 \tag{7-27}$$

Tables 7.1-7.2 give the PSNR performance of 0-order PA, 1-order PA, 2-order PA, 3-order PA and AOPA filters, where the original image "Lena" is corrupted with 10% ~ 30% fixed-valued and random-valued impulse noise, respectively. In each case, the best result among the 0, 1, 2 and 3-order PA filters is printed in bold. When the noise rate is low, the best result is usually obtained by the 3-order PA filter. However, with the increase of noise rate, 2-order PA filter gradually outperforms 3-order PA filter. The performance of AOPA filter traces the best result of the four FOPA filters. Its PSNR is sometimes slight higher or sometimes slightly lower than the best of the four. The last rows of the two tables present the differences of the PSNR performance between the AOPA filter and the best of the four FOPA filters. The absolute values of the differences are always very close to 0, ranging from 0.00 dB to 0.04 dB. Obviously, we will prefer the AOPA filter in real applications because for a given corrupted image, it is difficult for us to pre-determine which of the four FOPA filters is the best. In addition, in comparison with high-order FOPA filters, the AOPA filter may, in some way, save computing time because some of the regions are approximated by low-order polynomials. For example, for the case that the image "Lena" is corrupted by 30% fixed-valued impulse noise, 32.19% of the noise pixels are filtered by 0-order PA method, 23.05% by 1-order PA method, 38.71% by 2-

order PA method and only 6.04% are filtered by 3-order PA method. Since 0 and 1-order PA methods perform much faster than 2 and 3-order PA techniques, a lot of time can be saved by AOPA filter in comparison with pure 2 or 3-order PA filters. It is worth note that even though most of the noise pixels are not filtered by 2-order PA technique, the PSNR performance of the AOPA filter is very close to that of the 2-order PA filter which is significantly better than the other 3 FOPA filters.

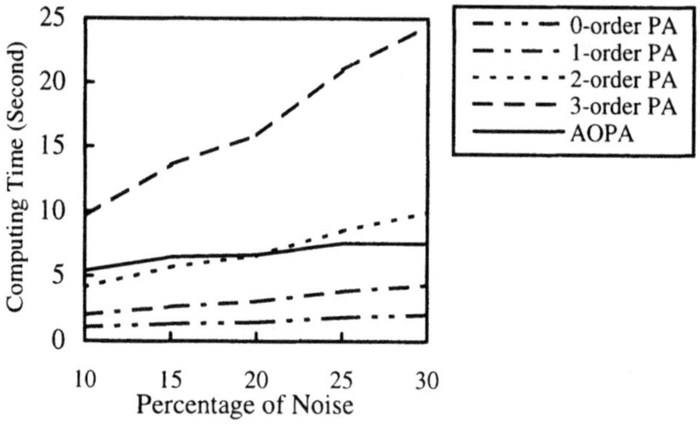

Figure 7.5. Comparison of computing time for various PA filters. The test image "Lena" is corrupted by fixed-valued impulse noise with a noise rate ranging from 10% to 30%. The simulations are conducted on a Pentium 166M PC computer

In Figure 7.5, we compare the performance speed of different PA filters, where the AOPA filter uses some extra time to classify each impulse pixel to be filtered by one of the four PA techniques. It appears that a 3-order PA filter always needs much more time than other PA filters. The computing time of AOPA filter is close to 2-order PA filter. When noise rate is low, the pure 2-order PA filter spends less time. We think such a litter bit of more time is deserved because the PSNR performance of AOPA filter is better than that of pure 2-order PA filter (See Table 7.2). When noise rate is high, 2-order PA filter needs more time than AOPA filter. In such a case, the AOPA and pure 2-order PA filters give almost the same PSNR results, while AOPA filter is better in saving time.

To demonstrate the visual quality of the filtering results, we show an enlarged area of "Lena" in Figure 7.6 where the image is corrupted by 20% fixed-valued impulse noise. It can be observed that the 1-order PA filter can give only rough approximation on the corrupted pixels while the AOPA filter tells much more details.

Table 7.3. Comparative restoration results in PSNR for 20% impulse noise for image "Lena". For fixed-valued impulse noise, impulses take on only the values 0 or 255 with equal probability. For random-valued impulse noise, impulse values are uniformly distributed between 0 and 255. See Reference

Filtering Algorithm	Fixed-valued Impulses	Random-valued Impulses
Median filter (3×3)	28.57 dB	29.76 dB
Median filter (5×5)	28.78 dB	28.59 dB
Median filter with adaptive length[2]	30.57 dB	31.18 dB
Rank conditioned rank selection filter[5]	31.36 dB	30.78 dB
Switch I median filter[3]	31.97 dB	31.34 dB
Switch II median filter[3]	29.96 dB	32.04 dB
Abreu et al. (*M*=1296) (inside training set)[10]	35.70 dB	33.37 dB
Fuzzy approach[11]	36.47 dB	33.78 dB
0-order PA filter	34.65 dB	32.39 dB
1-order PA filter	34.71 dB	32.38 dB
2-order PA filter	37.44 dB	33.99 dB
3-order PA filter	37.56 dB	33.75 dB
AOPA filter	37.57 dB	34.00 dB

In Table 7.3, we compare our PA filter with other state-of-the-art algorithms. Abreu et. al. reported many restoration results in PSNR for images corrupted by both 20% fixed-valued and random-valued impulse noises [10]. Some filtering results of a fuzzy approach developed by us are also provided [11]. We list some of those data and add the PSNR performance of our FOPA and AOPA filters into the table. It can be observed that for the case of fixed-valued impulse noise, the 2-order PA, 3-order PA and AOPA filters provide significant improvement over all the other approaches, while for the case of random-valued impulse noise, the 2-order PA, 3-order and AOPA filters are also the best and only the fuzzy approach [11] can compete with them. In Figures 7.7-7.8, we show some restored images obtained by different filtering methods which are the typical 3×3, 5×5 median filter, the switch I median filter [3] and our AOPA filter. In Figure 7.7, the test image "Bridge" is corrupted by 30% random-valued impulse noise, while in Figure 7.8, the test image "Peppers" is corrupted by 30% fixed-valued impulse noise. With a small window size of 3×3, the typical median filter misses many impulse pixels remaining in the image. When larger window size such as 5×5 is applied, almost all the impulses are removed, but many good pixels are also modified, resulting in blurring of the image. The Switch I median filter can well preserve good pixels while eliminating noise pixels, but still many impulses remained unaltered.

Dramatic restoration results are obtained by the AOPA filter. It can remove almost all of the noise pixels while preserve image details very well. It is also worth note that although the parameters are optimized for "Lena" image, good restoration results are still obtained for different types of images such as "Peppers" and "Bridge" under different occurrence rates of the impulse noise.

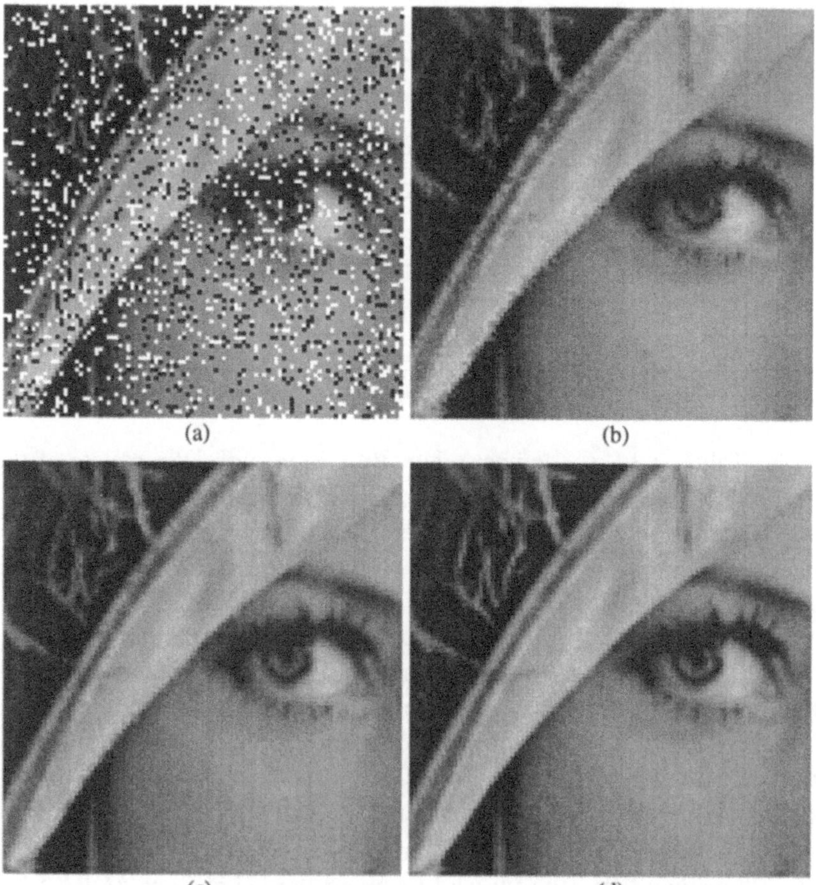

(a) (b) (c) (d)

Figure 7.6. (a) An enlarged area of "Lena" corrupted by 20% fixed-valued impulse noise, (b) Restoration result by 1-order PA filter, (c) Restoration result by AOPA filter, and (d) The original image area

Figure 7.7. Comparative restoration results for "Bridge" corrupted by 30% random-valued impulse noise. (a) The corrupted image, (b) Restored by 3×3 median filter, (c) Restored by 5×5 median filter (d) Restored by Switch I scheme, (e) Restored by AOPA filter, and (f) The original image of "Bridge"

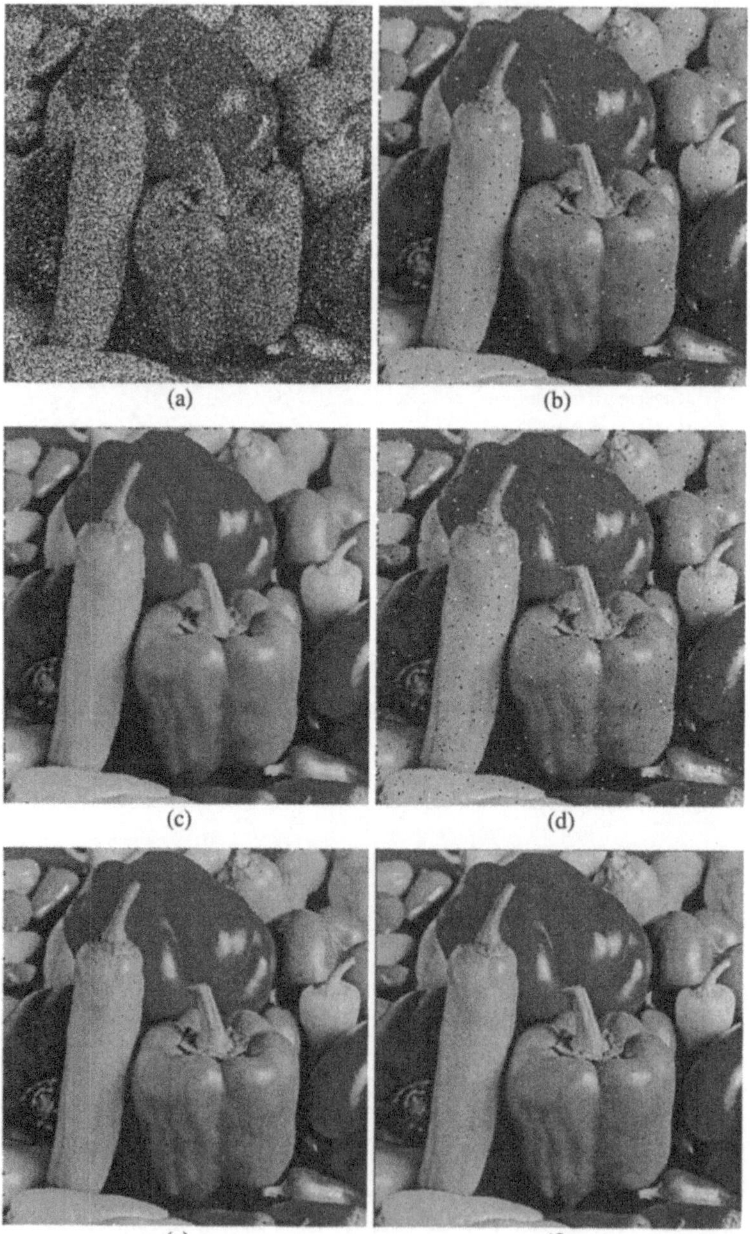

Figure 7.8. Comparative restoration results for "Peppers" corrupted by 30% fixed-valued impulse noise. (a) The corrupted image, (b) Restored by 3×3 median filter, (c) Restored by 5×5 median filter, (d) Restored by Switch I scheme, (e) Restored by AOPA filter, and (f) The original image of "Peppers"

7.6 Conclusion

In this chapter, a new impulse noise removal approach is introduced which is developed by using impulse detection and polynomial approximation techniques. The proposed impulse replacement method breaks through the traditional framework in that it is not designed by employing merely the ranking or statistic information and replacing the corrupted value with one from local window or some linear combination of local samples, but is implemented by modeling the local region using a polynomial, which is more powerful in representing the real structure of the region. An adaptive method is also presented which can automatically give an appropriate polynomial order for a local region. It has been proved to be very successful in obtaining good restoration results while saving computation time. Simulation results show that the proposed approach significantly outperforms many well-known techniques.

References

[1] S.T. Bow, *Pattern Recognition and Image Processing*, Marcel Dekker, Inc., New York, 1992.

[2] H. Lin, A.N. Willson, "Median filter with adaptive length," *IEEE Trans. Circuits and Systems*, 35(6):675-690, 1988.

[3] T. Sun and Y. Neuvo, "Detail-preserving median based filters in image processing," *Pattern Recognition Letters*, 15:341-347, 1994.

[4] R.C. Hardie and C.G. Boncelet, "LUM filters: A class of rank-order-based filters for smoothing and sharpening", *IEEE Trans. Signal Processing*, 41(3):1061-1076, 1993.

[5] R.C. Hardie and K.E. Barner, "Rank conditioned rank selection filters for signal restoration," *IEEE Trans. Image Processing*, 3(2):192-206, 1994.

[6] T. Sun M. Gabbouj and Y. Neuvo, "Center weighted median filters: Some properties and their applications in image processing," *Signal Processing*, 35:213-229, 1994.

[7] G. Ramponi, "The rational filter for image smoothing," *IEEE Signal Processing Letters*, 3(3):63-65, 1996.

[8] F. Russo and G. Ramponi, "A fuzzy filter for images corrupted by impulse noise," *IEEE Signal Processing Letters*, 3(6):168-170, 1996.

[9] L. García-Cabrera, M.J. García-Salinas, P.L. Luque-Escamilla, J. Martínez-Aroza, J.F. Gómez-Lopera and R. Román-Roldán, "Median-type filters with model-based preselection masks," *Image and Vision computing*, 14:741-752, 1996.

[10] E. Abreu, M. Lightstone, S.K. Mitra and K. Arakawa, "A new efficient approach for the removal of impulse noise from highly corrupted images," *IEEE Trans. Image Processing*, 5(6):1012-1025, 1996.

[11] D. Zhang and Z. Wang, "Impulse noise detection and removal using fuzzy techniques," *Electronics Letters*, 33:378-379, 1997.

[12] Z. Wang and D. Zhang, "Restoration of impulse noise corrupted images using long-range correlation," *IEEE Signal Processing Letters*, 5(1):5-8, 1997.

Chapter 8

INTERNET RESOURCE SHARING

In this chapter, we present a brief overview of the computation resources on the Internet and discuss a number of related issues. Section 8.2 is on software and Section 8.3 is on hardware. Various examples for image database are given in Section 8.4.

8.1 Introduction

In the late 1960s and early 1970s, organizations worldwide were using networks to connect computers together for both intra-organization and inter-organization communication. A large collection of networking hardware and software appeared. The Advanced Research Projects Agency (ARPA) of the Department of Defense in US started to connect a dozen main computer systems located at different universities and research institutions. This network was called the ARPAnet, the "grandparent" of Internet. The communication lines were operating at a then-stunning speed of 56KB instead of the 110 bits per second on a telephone line. The initial purpose is to let researchers share each other's computers. It rapidly became clear that the key benefit is simply enabling the researchers to communicate quickly and easily by e-mail on the net. The ARPA's communication protocols TCP/IP (the Transmission Control Protocol / the Internetworking Protocol) was developed and the current architecture of the Internet was created. Initially, the Internet was mainly for universities. Quickly, other organizations and companies are also connected. The bandwidth on the Internet has increased tremendously. The Internet has played a significant role in the economic prosperity during the last decade [50].

In 1990, the World Wide Web was developed that allows computer users to locate and view multimedia documents and especially allows researchers to be made instantly aware of the latest breakthroughs worldwide. The Internet and the Web make information conveniently accessible on almost any subject, and they have changed the nature of the way scientific research and commercial business are done. In 1993, less than 90,000 people used the Internet. In April 2001, there are over 300 million Internet users worldwide, according to the United States Internet Council's estimation [47]. The Internet and the World Wide Web can surely be listed among the most profound creations of humankind [50].

The Internet has made the global resource sharing feasible for everyone. PRIP computations can now take advantage of the rich resources all over the world, including software tools in almost every sub-area of PRIP, as well as various types of multiprocessor computers and special-purpose hardware. In the past decades, researchers have thoroughly studied sequential and parallel PRIP algorithms for many possible computer architectures. A great number of such algorithms and programs are readily available on the Internet. Many parallel and pipeline computers provide remote users with a tremendous computation power and can deliver high performance for PRIP applications. Many multimedia database systems with user-friendly search tools form colorful Web sites for downloading. In summary, PRIP researchers can easily find powerful software/hardware resources on the Internet, and enjoy a great deal of convenience in choosing test images as never before. On the other hand, the storage and transmission need and the open access of the Internet bring a number of challenging issues to our attention and demand for careful considerations.

8.2 Software Resources

What We Have

A number of companies provide on-line services in simple IAP data processing, such as high resolution scanning, image setting/finishing and large color poster printing. For example, *Cypher Digital Imaging* [28] offers access to their hardware facilities, including 36" wide Novajet, Novajet Pro42e 42" wide poster printers, and the latest Novajet 630 42" 600dpi printer. *Fairfield Imaging Limited* [45] provides software for visualization and image acquisition, annotation, measurement and analysis, mainly for bio-medical research and routine laboratory medicine workers. A similar company is *LizarTech* [37].

More general image processing and computer vision software packages are also widely available on the Internet. A number of sites provide lists or libraries of URLs for PRIP codes, such as the Rice University's SPLIB [14], the CMU's long list [25], and the ones maintained by UMD [4].

A large part of the on-line codes are for the following PRIP tasks:

- Low-level image processing on still images,
  such as camera calibration [8], edge detection, curve segmentation, hidden Markov model routines, texture classification, and mathematical morphology tools;
- Stereo processing,
  such as maximum-flow stereo algorithm and stereo corner matching;
- Optical flow computation,
- Range image processing,
- Intermediate-level processing,
  such as image segmentation, active contour; and
- Statistical pattern recognition, such as feature selection, extraction, normalization and classification rules [35].

Although most of the codes listed are for general purpose PRIP computations, some are written for specific applications, such as those for skin-cancer image segmentation [27] and those for document understanding [3].

Several places provide entire libraries of PRIP programs, such as *Intel open source computer vision library*, *Intel video capture card library* [9], and a number of large PRIP software packages prepared by universities (e.g., MIT, CMU, University of Maryland, Technical University of Denmark, and University of Calgary). Many of those codes are free for academic research. There are also a number of commercial software packages [2, 15, 21, 31].

The PRIP codes available on the Internet are written in many different computer languages (C, C++, Matlab, Java, Perl) under different operating systems (Unix, Linux, and Windows). Several sites also describe image processing scripting languages (e.g., PiXCL, geoPiXCL [46]). Some sites offer design help for PRIP researchers. For example, University of Westminster provides a site for filter design [5]. A user can enter the filter type (low-pass, high-pass, FIR, etc.) and a cut-off frequency, then the details of the designed filter (frequency responses) will be presented on the page.

PRIP researchers are still developing new algorithms and putting code on the Internet everyday. When one starts a PRIP project, the first step is usually to find and download some code instead of writing every line of the program from scratch. The Internet code sharing has already changed our research practice and partially freed us from rewriting many PRIP programs.

What We Need

Although there exist various search engines as well as carefully compiled lists and libraries for PRIP software resources on the Internet, none of them claim to be complete. A researcher or student still needs to conduct an intensive search and "surfing". Most of the free PRIP codes and even some commercial software are experimental in nature and do not guarantee correctness and efficiency. Users must do their own testing and evaluation. Different implementations of the same or similar PRIP algorithms provide healthy competition, but the repeated efforts waste both the developers' time and the end-users' time. More standardized and co-operative code sharing might be the next thing we want to see on the Internet. Especially a standard testing and comparison mechanism, including common testing image databases for various applications, would be a great help.

8.3 Hardware Resources

The Internet is a rich resource for hardware information. One can easily find introductions of specialized PRIP equipments from manufacturers' Web pages, such as [29, 23, 16, 38]. PRIP design tools are also available to provide a development environment, such as the PC based system at [41]. PRIP computations, especially the low-level image processing are computation and memory intensive, thus can take advantage of high-performance computing facilities. Hundreds of parallel and vector computers that exist all over the world are suitable for various levels of PRIP operations. Some of them can be accessed remotely and even provide a limited free time for scientific research. These supercomputers can be a powerful tool for a PRIP worker to experience complex algorithms that are impossible on their small computers.

Why Parallel

The inherent data locality and independence make parallel low-level PRIP operations possible and profitable. In the past decades, numerous parallel algorithms on many existing multiprocessor machines have been developed to cover almost every corner of the fields of numerical analysis and PRIP computations. A large number of dedicated computers and VLSI devices for PRIP have also been proposed and produced.

The following types of parallelism in PRIP have been identified [48, 51, 53]:

- *Pixel parallelism*: since digital images are sampled on a rectangular grid and stored as a two-dimensional array, each pixel can receive a series of operations independent from the rest of the image.

- *Neighborhood parallelism*: many low-level image processing operations involve only a small neighborhood of a pixel. That is, the result value of a pixel location is only a function of the pixels within a small neighborhood.

- *Bit-plane parallelism*: some image coding operations treat the gray level of each pixel as a sequence of bits. All the corresponding bits of the entire image form an image itself, called a bit-plane. An image with 256 gray levels per pixel could be viewed as eight separate binary bit-plane images. Sometimes, the operations can be performed on each bit-plane independently from other bit-planes. Color images and multi-channel images can also be treated in this manner.

- *Sequential-operation parallelism*: several low-level operators, such as filters, are applied to an image, one after another. Those operators can form a chain. All inputs and outputs of each stage of the chain are in the image form, and the output of previous stage is the input of the next stage. The operation of each stage is relatively independent.

- *Concurrent-operation parallelism*: several low-level operators (e.g., filters) can be applied to a single image and all the outputs are independent from each other. Based on the outputs, further combination and operations may take place.

- *Matrix-shape parallelism*: at some later stages of PRIP computations, certain operations may carry on with one part of a matrix, and other parts of the matrix can be used to store other information and perform other computations.

- *Decision-making parallelism*: a number of pattern classification and recognition operations can be viewed as a decision making process in the form of a search or comparison. For example, object labeling can be implemented as a tree search, and the nearest-neighbor classification involves calculations/comparisons of many distances. Most of those computation steps can be easily carried out in parallel.

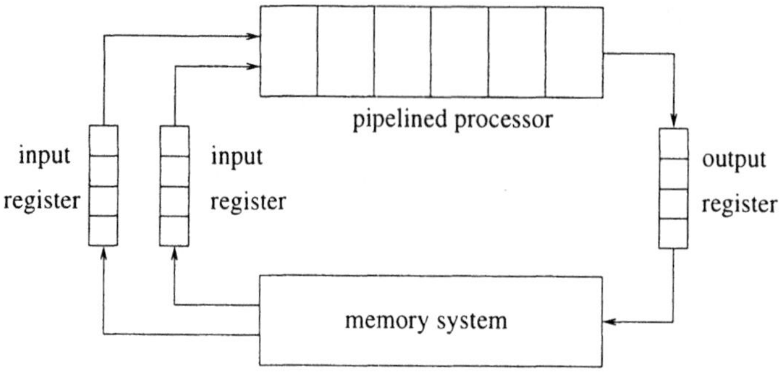

Figure 8.1. The pipeline machine model

What We Have

High-performance computers are also called "supercomputer." Some of them have multiple scalar processors, some have pipeline processors. A number of classification schemes have been used. Flynn taxonomy [52] has proven to be useful. This classification is based on the manipulation method of instruction and data streams: single stream vs. multiple streams. Therefore, four classes are defined as SISD (Single Instruction stream and Single Data stream), SIMD, MISD, and MIMD. SISD machines are the conventional computers that contain one CPU and execute one instruction stream sequentially. MISD makes no sense to some people but could mean pipeline machines to some others when the data items receive multiple operations along the pipeline stages [48]. Some researchers consider pipeline computers as "shared memory SIMD" [44]. Figure 8.1 gives a general machine configuration of a pipeline machine. Some examples of such computers are Cray systems, CDC Cyber 205, and Fujitsu VPP5000 series. Pipeline computers can naturally take advantage of the sequential-operation parallelism. A large number of pipeline PRIP implementations have been reported in the literature.

Multiprocessor computers are classified into SIMD and MIMD. They can be further divided into groups according scalar/array instruction and scalar/array execution [55]. They can also be further classified from the storage organization point of view. Some parallel machines use a shared memory system with multiple CPUs sharing the same address space. The user does not need to be aware of the physical data location. Some other parallel computers employ a distributed memory system and each CPU has a local storage unit. An interconnection network supports data exchange between the CPUs. The user must know where the data are stored explicitly.

A distributed-memory SIMD (DM-SIMD) computer usually has a large number of simple and identical processing elements (PEs). All PEs

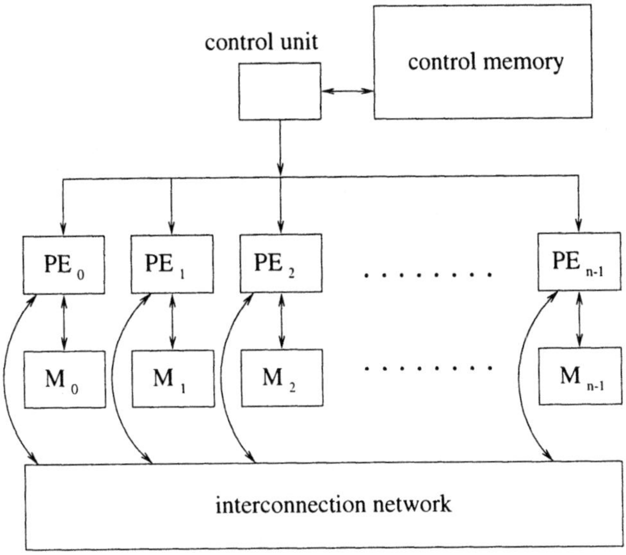

Figure 8.2. The DM-SIMD machine model

execute the same instruction on their own data items in lock-step. The number of processors can be up to 65,536 (e.g., in the CM-2 machine). The basic structure of a DM-SIMD computer is presented in Figure 8.2. This type of computer is also called the *array processor*, and it is most suitable for low-level image processing as it can naturally take advantage of pixel parallelism and neighborhood parallelism. Example machines of this type are MasPar MP-1, MP-2, CPP DAP Gamma II and the Alenia Quadrics [44].

MIMD machines have multiple processors that execute different instruction streams concurrently on different data streams. The number of processors can be as small as two or four, and can also be up to thousands. Each processor is usually more complex and more powerful than those of the SIMD computers, and the local memory units are large enough to hold individual instruction sequences. If there is only one memory address space used by all processors and the knowledge of the physical data location is of no concern to the user, this machine is considered to have a shared memory. Figure 8.3 gives a general machine architecture of SM-MIMD. The DM-MIMD model is depicted in Figure 8.4. Accessing the memory unit directly associated to each processor is much faster than communicating from memories attached to other processors by message-passing through the interconnection network. The programs are usually designed to minimize remote data exchange. Distributed-memory MIMD (DM-MIMD) is definitely the fastest growing member of

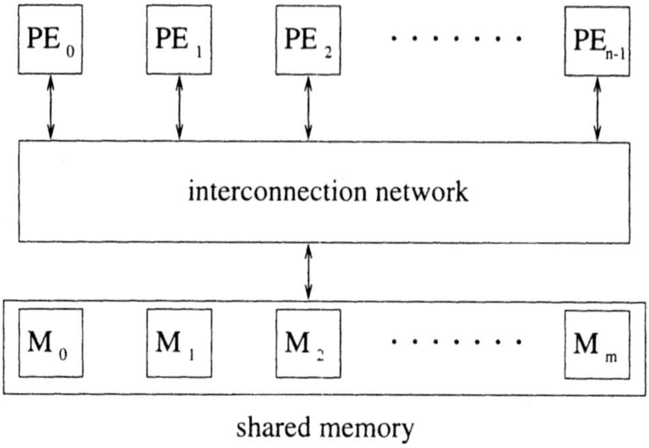

Figure 8.3. SM-MIMD machine models

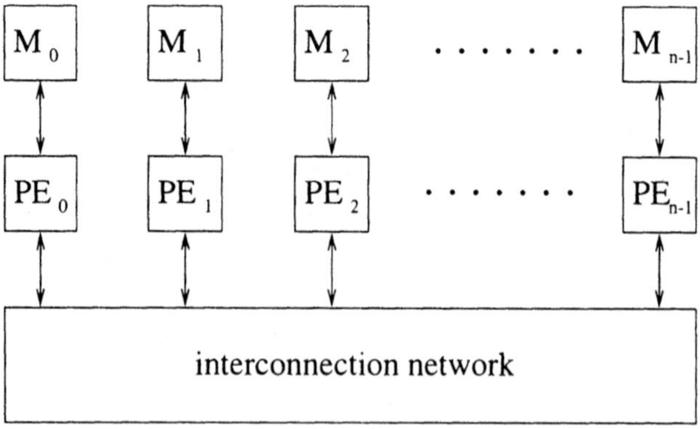

Figure 8.4. DM-MIMD machine models

the supercomputer family. The majority of the recent supercomputers belong to this category.

Some machines can work as SIMD or MIMD. For example, the Thinking Machines Corporation's CM-5 is a typical DM-MIMD computer that can also operate in a SPMD (single-program, multiple data) mode.

Both SIMD and MIMD machines employ interconnection networks to link the processors and memories for data exchange. A great number of interconnection networks have been proposed and built. Commonly used network types include the following:

- The *bus* is the simplest network that connects every processors and memory units together. It can be readily assembled from existing technologies, but its bandwidth is limited. Each node (processor or memory module) has only one link to the bus. Sitting on the other extreme of the network connectivity is the *crossbar* that is a grid of logic gates providing direct connection between any pair of processors or memory units. A one-stage crossbar can connect a small number of nodes, say, 64 of them. To connect more nodes, a multi-stage crossbar is often used where the crossbars at level one connect to a crossbar of level two. This multi-level or multi-stage crossbar has a logarithmic complexity, and a few thousand nodes are linked together with only a few switching steps. This interconnection network is popular among the current DM-MIMD computers, such as the Sun E1000 Starfire introduced in 1997, Hitachi SR8000 system in 1998, and the Compaq AlphaServer SC Series in 1999.

- The *Omega network* is a multistage shuffle-exchange that employs a set of switch boxes each can perform exchange and broadcasting. The control scheme is distributed and its routing algorithm provides a unique connection path from every input to every output. The connection complexity is $n \log n$ for n nodes, which makes it an attractive choice when the number of processors gets large. This network is used on the IBM RS/6000 SP (introduced in 1999). A butterfly network, similar to Omega, is used on the BBN TC2000.

- The *mesh* network, also called torus, is a 2-D or 3-D grid. Image processing and many other large-scale physical simulations can be naturally mapped on this topology. In this network, each node has a fixed number of direct links regardless the total number of nodes. Array processors, such as Thinking Machines' CM-1, CM-2, and the Quadrics Apemille (1999), use a mesh connection. Some DM-MIMD computers also use it, such as the Fujitsu AP3000 (1996) and the Tera/Cray T3E (1997). A pure mesh network does not have explicit global connection links. Different modifications have been proposed, such as the "enhanced mcsh" which includes a bus along the rows and columns of a mesh [49, 54].

- A *hypercube network* connects each of the 2^n nodes to n nearest neighbors. That is, each node is directly linked to another node if the binary expressions of their node indices are off by exactly one bit. The number of steps to transmit data from any node to any other node is at most n. One reason for the popularity of the hypercube is the fact that one can embed and simulated many other networks, including rings, trees, and meshes on the cube machine. The cube network is used in CM-1, CM-2, and the RISC-based DM-MIMD SGI Origin 2000 series, introduced in 1996.
- The *wormhole routing* make the physical interconnection and actual network topology less important. When a message is sent from one node to another, a header message establishes a direct link and the actual data transfer can be carried out without interrupting the nodes along the path. This way, the communication time does not depend on the link distance. However, multiple messages cannot use the same path. The waiting and re-routing may also take time. A large amount of regular data exchange, as often encountered in low-level PRIP computations, can still make a full use of a powerful physical interconnection like hypercube or mesh.

Some example interconnection networks are presented in Figures 8.5, 8.6, 8.7 and 8.8 The Omega network shown in the figure happens to be performing a circular shift (downwards rotation)

$$i \longrightarrow (i+1) \bmod 8. \tag{8-1}$$

Table 8.1 list a number of well-known supercomputers. More complete lists can be seen on the Internet [19, 24, 34, 40, 44].

Both the SIMD and MIMD machines have been used for PRIP tasks. The data communication patterns and the routing skills in SIMD can be similar to those in MIMD. Later chapters deal with the storage issues for IAP data on a multiprocessor system, and present a number of routing schemes for parallel computers.

What We Need

Many machines at research institutes provide free computer time for academic research, which gives a PRIP programmer a great deal of freedom in using more powerful and more computation-intensive algorithms.

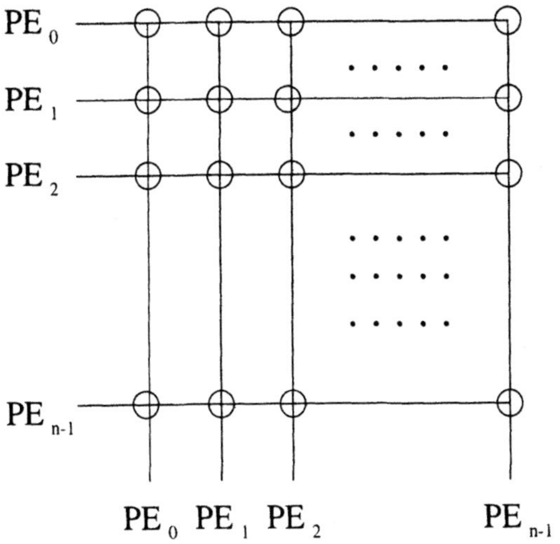

Figure 8.5. Crossbar network

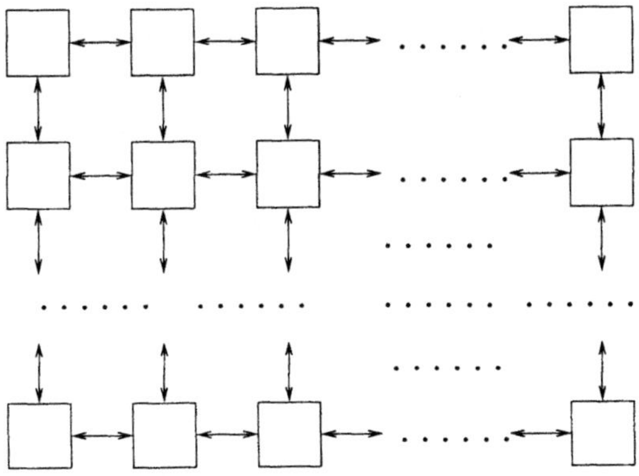

Figure 8.6. 2-D mesh network

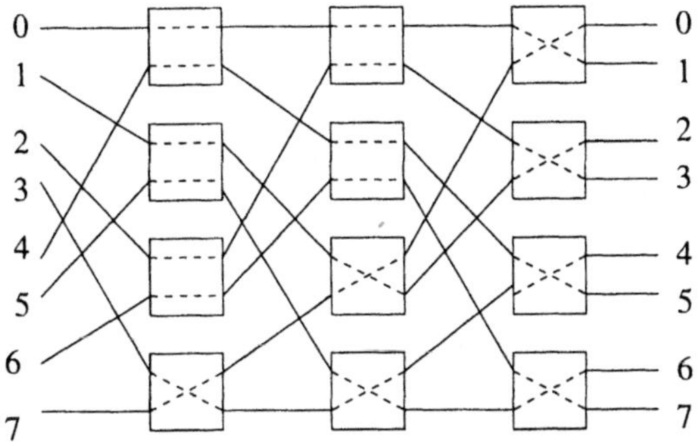

Figure 8.7. Omega network

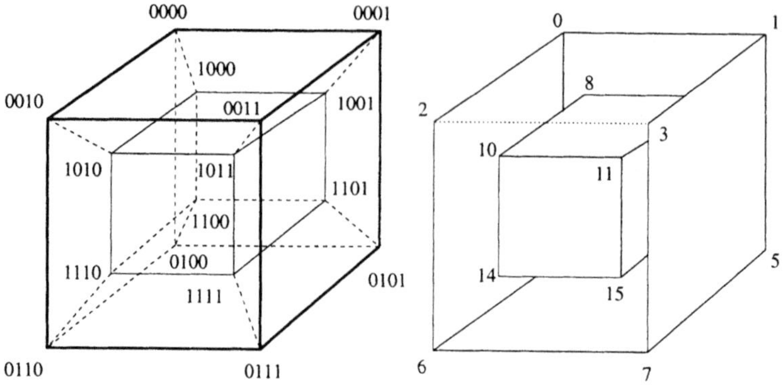

Figure 8.8. Hypercube network

However, the remote access can still be troublesome. The special requirement in using each machine, including possible rewriting parts of the code, presents a burden. The computation speedup provided by remote machines may be offset by the network communication delays and interruptions. Software tools on specialized computer architectures may still be limited. Solving the above problems may greatly facilitate the PRIP programmer in attacking applications of a much larger scale.

Table 8.1. Parallel and vector computer examples

Type	Machine	Network	Year
Processor array	Thinking Machines' CM-2	mesh, cube	1987-1991
Processor array	MasPar MP-1, MP-2	X-Net	1990-1996
Processor array	Quadrics Apemille	3-D mesh	1999-
SM multi-vector	Tera/Cray SV1	crossbar	1998-
DM multi-vector	NEC SX-5	Multi-stage crossbar	1998-
SM MIMD	BBN TC2000	butterfly	-1990
DM MIMD	Thinking Machine CM-5	fat tree	1991-
DM MIMD	HP Exemplar V2600	ring	1999-
DM MIMD	IBM RS/6000 SP	omega	1999-
DM MIMD	Tera/Cray T3E	3-D torus	1997-
DM MIMD	SGI Origin 2000 series	crossbar, cube	1996-
DM MIMD	Hitachi SR8000 system	crossbar	1998-

8.4 Image and Multimedia Databases on the Internet

Commercial Image Collections

Many commercial image databases exist on the Internet for various customers. For example, *Wieck Photo DataBase* [13] provides media photos and graphics on the business from Fortune 500 companies, such as detailed pictures of inside and outside of cars for automobile manufacturers, travel and leisure images for vacation destinations. Although the full access to the database is limited to registered news media, public viewing of the images in low-resolution, non-downloadable form is possible. *Commwais* [36] provides a collection of artworks. Several long listings of artists and their artworks can be used to locate anyone's favorite [10, 17, 33]. Poster databases for different purposes can also be found [20]. To serve special regional interests, the Prince of Wales Northern Heritage Centre of the Northwest Territories (Canada) lists 20,000 photographs of the area [42]. Low-resolution images and simple descriptions are presented with a detailed price list and on-line ordering instructions.

Free Image Collections for General Use

Many people put their family photos, especially the photos of children, on their Web pages. These pictures provide a rich source of portraits that could be easily used for informal testing by PRIP algorithm designers working on face recognition or image segmentation. One can also find a large number of landscape images posted on the Internet [26], which can be useful for PRIP researchers in the field of object recognition or color analysis.

The entertainment industry has a wide selection of on-line multimedia databases for movies, theater performances, TV shows, and celebrities. For example, *The Imperial Database* [7] has collections of text, sound and image files for "Star Wars", "Jurassic Park", "Friends", etc.

Museums and historical organizations have prepared very impressive multimedia databases on the Internet to promote culture understanding and academic study. One typical example is [39] where *The Minnesota Historical Society* has made available a wide range of objects and materials chronicling Minnesota's history. Each section has a general overview in the form of text description and sample images. Their collection includes art works, maps, movie films, museum collections, and thousands of artifacts at 23 historic sites. The database also contains current photographs: thousands of portraits of people, rural and urban, at work and at leisure, as well as thousands of landscape views depict the state's geography. Over one thousand posters for different purposes are also included. This multimedia database provides a simple but effective search tool.

Free Image Collections for Special Purposes

Many multimedia databases are available for special interest groups and special topic studies. For example, *EIKON Image Database* [6] provides digital resources for teaching and research in the field of Biblical studies. An archive of the solar surface at different wavelengths is available at [11]. A taxonomy of Japanese ants with colorful images can be found at [1].

Image Databases with Retrieval Software Tools

IBM's QBIC system is available for download with a free 90 day trial license [43]. The package includes a sample image collection and image search engine. The search engine supports a content-based image retrieval using image properties, such as color, texture and shape of objects. Excalibur [32] (recently changed name to Convera [22]) provides another powerful document indexing and retrieval system. A number of major multimedia database retrieval systems are provided by academic research groups, such as the Visual Computing Laboratory at UCSD, led by Prof. Ramesh C. Jain [12] and the group in the Department of Computer Science and Information Technology at the University of Florence, led by Prof. Alberto Del Bimbo [30].

To support medical image analysis, *BrainWeb* [18] provides a Simulated Brain Database (SBD) which contains realistic images produced by an MRI simulator. These images give a researcher a "ground truth" for evaluating their image analysis methods, which can be quite useful for the neuroimaging community. For both normal and multiple sclerosis (MS) anatomical models, full 3-D data volumes have been simulated and can be viewed and downloaded. The user can specify the modality, slice thickness, noise level, etc.

8.5 Conclusion

The Internet has made the hardware and software computational resources available for the PRIP communities world-wide. The tremendous number of image databases can be on the fingertips of any PRIP programmer. To make a full use of the rich resources becomes critically important in IAP data management and PRIP technology research and development. A careful investigation and in-depth design can take a full advantage of this rich resource on the Internet.

References

[1] http://ant.edb.miyakyo-u.ac.jp/Taxo_E/F80903.html.

[2] http://bersoft.com/bimagem/index.htm.

[3] http://documents.cfar.umd.edu/.

[4] http://documents.cfar.umd.edu/imageproc/.

[5] http://dolphin.wmin.ac.uk/filter_design.html.

[6] http://eikon.divinity.yale.edu/.

[7] http://membrane.com/ dan/index.html.

[8] http://research.microsoft.com/ zhang/Calib.

[9] http://support.intel.com/support/performancetools/libraries/ipl/.

[10] http://the-artists.org/.

[11] http://umbra.nascom.nasa.gov/images/latest.html.

[12] http://vision.ucsd.edu/ jain/.

[13] http://wieck.com/public/.

[14] http://www-dsp.rice.edu/splib.

[15] http://www.aai.com.

[16] http://www.alacron.com/index.htm.

[17] http://www.artwin.com/.

[18] http://www.bic.mni.mcgill.ca/brainweb.

[19] http://www.cacr.caltech.edu/resources/index.html.

[20] http://www.chisholm-poster.com/chisholm/CoverR.html.

[21] http://www.clemex.com.

[22] http://www.convera.com/.

[23] http://www.coreco.com/corecodefault.html.

[24] http://www.cs.cmu.edu/ scandal/resources.html.

[25] http://www.cs.cmu.edu/afs/cs/project/cil/ftp/html/v-source.html.

[26] http://www.cs.ualberta.ca/ kenw/photos.html.

[27] *http://www.cs.wright.edu/ agoshtas/skinseg.html.*

[28] *http://www.cygraph.demon.co.uk/.*

[29] *http://www.datacube.com/.*

[30] *http://www.dsi.unifi.it/ delbimbo/.*

[31] *http://www.euresys.com/SoftwareTools/eVision.htm.*

[32] *http://www.excalib.com/.*

[33] *http://www.fine-art.com/artist/.*

[34] *http://www.geocities.com/Athens/6270/superp.html.*

[35] *http://www.inf.ufes.br/ thomas/home/tooldiag.html.*

[36] *http://www.lib.colum.edu/commwais.html.*

[37] *http://www.lizardtech.com/company/index.html.*

[38] *http://www.matrox.com/imgweb/genesism.htm.*

[39] *http://www.mnhs.org/library/collections/index.html.*

[40] *http://www.netlib.org/benchmark/top500.html.*

[41] *http://www.ph.tn.tudelft.nl/PRInfo/hardware/msg00006.html.*

[42] *http://www.pwnhc.learnnet.nt.ca/.*

[43] *http://wwwqbic.almaden.ibm.com.*

[44] *http://www.top500.org/ORSC/2000/overview00.html.*

[45] *http://www.virtual-microscope.com/fairfield/frames.htm.*

[46] *http://www.vysor.com.*

[47] *South China Morning Post, April 28, 2001.*

[48] G. Almasi and A. Gottlieb. *Highly Parallel Computing.* Benamin/Cummings, 1994.

[49] K. Bondalapati and Viktor K. Prasanna. Reconfigurable meshes: Theory and practice. In *Proc. of Reconfigurable Architectures Workshop, International Parallel Processing Symposium*, 1997.

[50] H.M. Deitel, P.J. Deitel, and T.R. Nieto. *Internet & World Wide Web – How to Program.* Prentice Hall, 2000.

[51] A. Zomaya (editor). *Parallel and Distributed Computing Handbook.* McGraw-Hill, 1996.

[52] M.J. Flynn. Some computer organizations and their effectiveness. *IEEE Transactions on Computing*, C-21:948–960, 1972.

[53] K. Hwang. *Advance Computer Architecture: Parallelism, Scalability, Programmability.* McGraw-Hill, 1993.

[54] K. Hwang, H.M. Alnuweiri, V. Prasanna Kumar, and D. Kim. Orthogonal multiprocessor sharing memory with an enhanced mesh for integrated image.

[55] D. Kuck. *The structure of computers and computaitons.* John Wiley, 1978.

Chapter 9

PARALLEL PROCESSING FOR IMAGE RESTORATION

In the practical transmission of block-based coding image, bit errors may occur, which often results in lost block. Error concealment is a widely used technique to conquer the transmission error. Chapter 6 has proved that Best Neighborhood Matching (BNM) algorithm is a very good error concealment approach in terms of restored image quality [1]. However, all kinds of these concealment algorithms (including BNM) are computation intensive, which restricts their real applications on large-scale image restoration or image sequence restoration. In this chapter, we propose an improved fast implementation method, named Jump and look all round Best Neighborhood Matching (JBNM) algorithm. JBNM is defined and some experimental results are given in Section 9.2. To speed-up our algorithm again, a parallel JBNM is proposed in Section 9.3. Section 9.4 shows some experimental results and performance analysis related to our parallel algorithm. We make a conclusion in Section 9.5.

9.1 Introduction

Block-based techniques are adopted by most existing image and video compression standards, such as JPEG [2], H.261 [3], and MPEG [4]. In a block-based coding system, variable length coding is usually used. So, the encoded bit stream is vulnerable to transmission error. Loss of a single bit often results in loss of a whole block and even may cause consecutive block losses.

Error concealment is a widely used technique to conquer the transmission error. The aim of error concealment is to mask the effect of damaged blocks to construct subjectively acceptable images. Before error concealment, an appropriate transport format must be done to detect damaged blocks. Then, damaged blocks will be restored by spatial correlation property of natural images [1, 5-8], which can be categorized into two layers: One layer is DC and AC coefficients correlation of compressed image blocks [5-8], and the other is block-wise similarity within nature images [1]. For a video sequence, both spatial and temporal correlation properties will be employed in restoration processing.

In Chapter 6, it show that Best Neighborhood Matching (BNM) algorithm may be a very good error concealment algorithm in terms of both objective and subjective image quality [1]. The reason lies on that both neighboring and remote pixel information are used in image restoration. However, lots of error concealment algorithms like BNM are computation intensive, which restricts their real applications on large-scale image restoration or image sequence restoration. In this chapter, we develop an improved algorithm, JBNM (*Jump and look all round Best Neighborhood Matching*), to solve this problem after carefully studying the circuitous continuation of images. In our algorithm, eyes' intelligence of human beings is simulated. When a person searches a right part for replacing damaged part in quick style, a *jump and look all round* algorithm is used. In other words, one searches a good part in the rough style, and he looks carefully in round when an approximate block is found. Furthermore, a parallel JBNM (PJBNM) working on a cluster of workstations is then developed, which can achieve a high performance.

9.2 JBNM Algorithm

Searching Policies

The information in any image has correlation, especially within a search range for a damaged block. So the match function, MSE_M, for a local window and candidate windows within a search range is a continuous-liked function. If a candidate window has a great difference with the local window, all closed candidate windows to it will have a little bit chance to get the better matching. Therefore, we can restore damaged blocks by simulating eyes' intelligence of human beings. When a person searches a right part for replacing damaged part in quick style, a *jump and look all round* algorithm is used. In other words, one searches a good part in the rough style, and he looks carefully in round when an approximate block is found. Our improved BNM can be described in the following:

In JBNM algorithm, there are two kinds of search styles: one is called as "jump search", and the other as "look all round search". Therefore, our algorithm is defined as *Jump and look all round* BNM (i.e., JBNM), where a search procedure begins with "jump search". For a certain damaged block, the first remote window is formed at the upper-left corner of the search range. If the remote window is a candidate window, the MSE_M will be calculated. Otherwise, if the remote window contains damaged pixels, what we should do is to skip it and go on forming another remote window. In our JBNM algorithm, the second remote windows are formed in J_s (>1) pixel steps (i.e., after J_s pixels in column or below J_s pixels in row from the previous remote window).

When a best one is obtained in all compared candidate windows, it will start to "look all round search". Firstly, a small search range is formed through extending the edge of the best candidate window from top, bottom, left and right. Each direction is extended with J_s -1 pixels. So the small search range, called S', is defined by $((J_s -1)\times 2+N)\times((J_s -1)\times 2+N)$ pixels. In the small search range, remote windows are formed in one pixel step as a careful search procedure. After the searching in a small search range, "jump search" and "look all round search" will go on in turn until the bottom-right of the whole search range. At last the best candidate window is obtained. Based on above searching procedure, "jump and look all round search ", can be described as follow:

```
For ( y=S.start; y<S.end; y+=Js) /*S.start and S.end mean the start and the
                                      end point of S, respectively. */
    { Form a remote windows ry , where y is the start position of ry ;
     If ( ry is a candidate window)
      { Calculate MSEM for the local window l and ry;
      If ( ry is a best one in all compared candidate windows)
        { Update the best matching MSEM with the MSEM for ry and l, then
                  choose ry as the best matching window;
         /*now a small search range will be formed, and looking all round
                         search will begin*/
          For ( m=S'.start; m< S'.end; m+=1)
           If ( rm is a candidate window)
             { Calculate MSEM for l and rm;
             If ( rm is a best one in all compared candidate windows)
               Update the best matching MSEM and choose rm as the best
                              matching window;
             }
        } /*end of If (ry is a best one in all compared candidate windows) */
      } /* end of If (ry is a candidate window) */
    } /* end of for (y=S.start; y<S.end; y+=Js) */
```

The remote windows are formed in J_s pixel step in the jump style. So, the number of the candidate windows could be greatly reduced when J_s increases gradually. Then, the number of the candidate windows, which determines computation complexity, will be cut down. However, the small searching range will become large with the increasing of J_s. For example, $J_s = 4$, the small range is 16×16 pixels and $J_s = 8$, the small range is 24×24 pixels. As a result, the number of remote windows formed in the small search range in one step will increase with J_s going up. The whole number of the remote windows also will go up when the J_s goes beyond some scale. In our experiment results, the scale is defined as 7. Another important thing is that the quality of restored images will drop with J_s going up. As a result, we must choose a right J_s to keep the quality of restored image. Meanwhile, the processing time can be reduced greatly. From our experimental results, the step $J_s = 4$ is a right choice.

Simulation Results

In our experiment, we use the following parameters. The damage blocks are isolated and distributed randomly. The sizes of a local window, *l*, and a remote window, *r*, are fixed to be 10×10 pixels. A lost block with 8x8 pixels locates at the center of a local window. So, the matching part of the local window is one pixel wide boundary round the lost block. The candidate windows are selected from an 80x80 square region (what we regard as the search range, *S*) with the local window locating at its center. When a damage block is close to the image boundaries, the 80x80 searching range may exceed the image boundaries. In such a case, we move the searching range into the image until its boundary reaches the image boundary. The candidate window, whose boundary pixels can match the neighborhood of a lost block best, becomes a winning candidate window. For the luminance transformations, the 1-order matching are used. The jump step $J_s = 4$ is finally determined according to our experimental results.

The proposed JBNM has been tested on some standard gray level images with complex textures and fine details. Figure 9.1 shows comparison of the subjective concealment results by BNM and JBNM. The original image "Barb" is shown in Figure 9.1(a), and the damaged image in Figure 9.1(b), with a block loss rate of 10%, which is randomly generated to simulate the block loss scenario. The concealed image by BNM and the restored image by JBNM are shown in Figures 9.1(c-d), respectively. To observe more clearly, the results of an enlarged comparison of "Barb" are shown in Figures 9.2(a-d). Furthermore, the results of restored image "Baboon" are given in Figures 9.3(a-d). From these results, we can see that the visual quality of the restored images is very good even when the areas contain a lot of detail information.

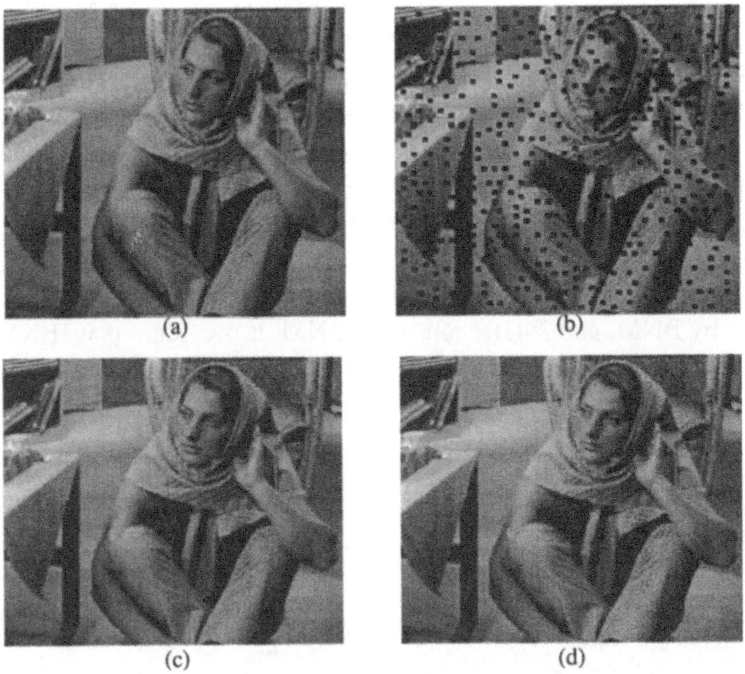

Figure 9.1. Comparison of the concealment results with the loss radio of 10%. (a) Original image "Barb" with 512 by 512 pixels and 8 bits per pixel, (b) Damaged image "Barb", PSNR=16.39dB, (c) Restored image by BNM, PSNR=37.1, and (d) Restored image by JBNM, PSNR=36.75

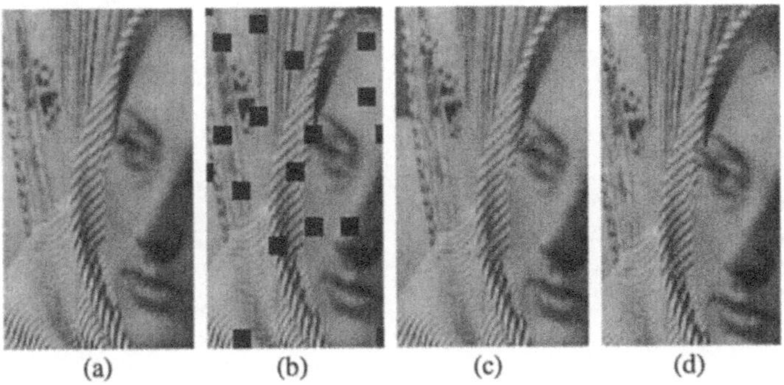

Figure 9.2. Illustration of the concealment results of one enlarged area for image "Barb". (a) Original part, (b) Damaged part with the loss radio of 10%, (c) Restored "Barb" by BNM, and (d) Restored "Barb" by the proposed JBNM

Figure 9.4(a) shows some comparisons of the objective quality of image restoration, *PSNR*, and Figure 9.4(b) indicates the processing time for

"Barb" with block loss rates ranging from 2.5%-15.0% by BNM and JBNM, respectively. For easy comparison, *PSNR* without any concealment is also provided in Figure 9.4(a), where "Ncon" means the PSNR without any concealment process. It is clear that the PSNR values obtained by BNM and JBNM are almost the same and they are much higher than that without concealment process. From Figure 9.4(b) we can know that the processing time by JBNM is only about 1/6 of that by BNM. For example, at a loss rate of 10%, the PSNR is about 16.39dB without any concealment, 37.1dB by BNM, and 36.75 dB by our JBNM, and the processing time is 14.17 (second) by BNM, and 2.41(second) by JBNM. It is evident that JBNM is an efficient image restoration algorithm.

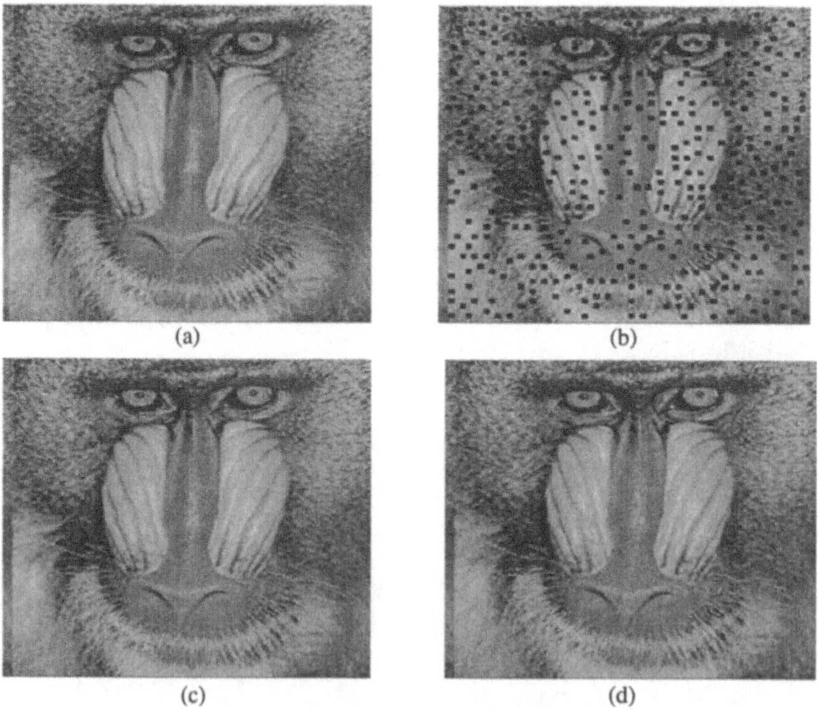

Figure 9.3. Illustration of the concealment results of another image "Baboon". (a) Original image "baboon" with 512 by 512 pixels, (b) Damaged image "Baboon" with a block loss rate of 10%, (c) Reconstructed image "Baboon" by BNM, and (d) Reconstructed image "Baboon" by JBNM

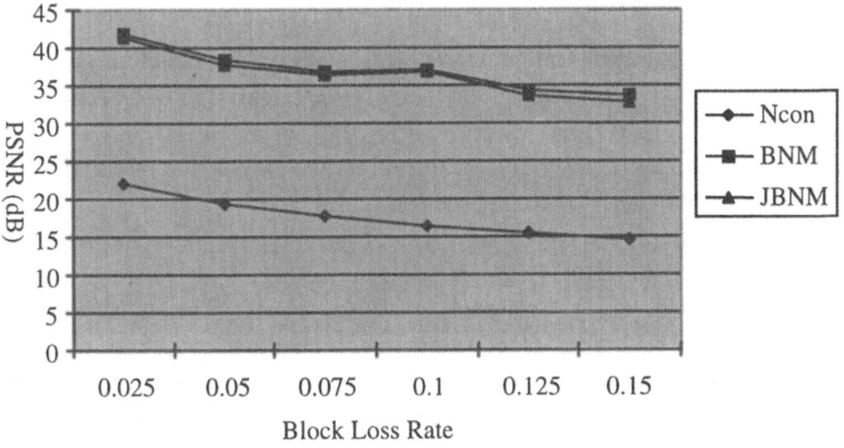

(a)

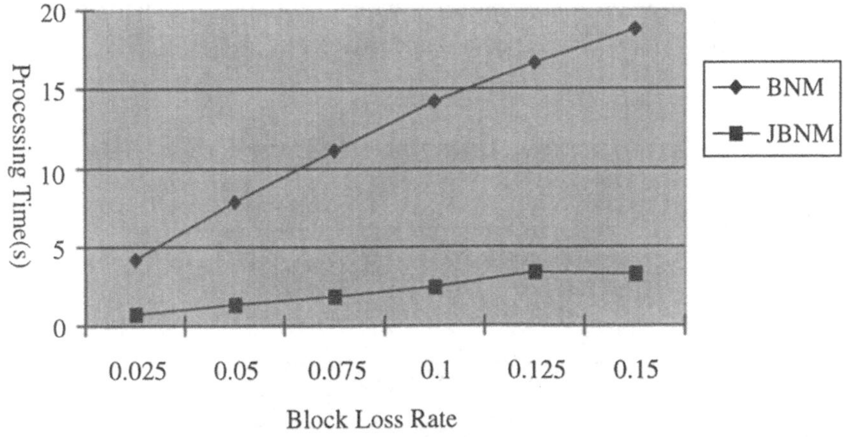

(b)

Figure 9.4. PSNR and processing time comparison for "Barb" with block loss rates range from 2.5-15.0 by BNM and JBNM respectively, for easy comparison, PSNR without any concealment also provided. (a) PSNR, (b) Processing time

The above experiments are simulated on a computer with multiple nodes each with a 300MHZ PowerPc 604e processor and 256MB local memory. These nodes are connected through a 100Mbps switched Ethernet. Here, only one node is used. In the following parallel processing, multiple nodes will be involved in.

9.3 Parallel Computation

Distributed and parallel computer systems have become efficient computing systems to solve computing intensively applications. To reduce the processing time and meet the requirements of both large-scale image restoration and real-time image restoration, we develop a parallel JBNM algorithm (called PJBNM) in this section.

Generally, there are two main types of parallelism, data parallelism and task parallelism. In JBNM, the whole processing is to repeat five steps mentioned in Chapter 6 for each damaged block. The most excessive computing of JBNM is to select a best match candidate window in a search range, which requires a great deal of comparison and computation. Fortunately, the search range is a limited range. In our experiment, the search range is 80×80. This shows that the computing data has locality. Moreover, the processing for each damaged block is independent. Therefore, JBNM is adapted for data parallelism on cluster system. In data parallelism, data partition is a very important issue, which influences the performance of a parallel algorithm, such as speedup and efficiency

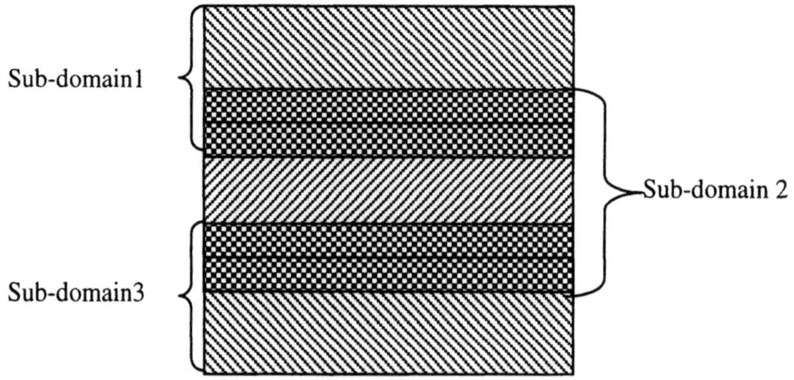

Figure 9.5. An illustration of stripe region overlap technique for data partition, which a file is divided into three sub-domains

Data Distribution Strategies

In PJBNM, if the divided region can guarantee the right search range, irrelative data partition can be reached. This means that there will be no communication in the parallel computing processing. In our parallel algorithm, we use stripe region overlap technique to realize irrelative data partition as Figure 9.5. Therefore, each processor can process a sub-domain data independently. In this way, the correction of parallel algorithm can be guaranteed and a good load balancing is obtained.

Another important thing is how computing nodes get the corresponding sub-domain data. PJBNM is an I/O intensive application. For such applications, the I/O subsystem represents a significant obstacle in the way of achieving good performance. High I/O performance dependents on three aspects. The first is parallel I/O hardware, the second is I/O software like parallel file system, the last is related to I/O strategy in real application, such as I/O pattern. At present, massively parallel architectures do provide high performance parallel I/O hardware. I/O software and I/O strategics are primary factors. Here we put our emphasis on I/O strategies.

In a general architecture of cluster, control node has a great capability for storage. Each processor has a small hard-disk to store local data or files. A master is a processor, which an executable parallel program is submitted to. Other processors involved in the same parallel program are called slaves. In parallel processing, there are three kinds of file locating styles: (1) The file is stored on a control node; (2) Each processor has a file copy; and (3) The file is stored on one of the processors.

In general, files only locate on the control node, i.e. in style one. So, we will discuss the first case more carefully. In fact, there are still two strategies of data distributions. *Strategy (a)* - Each processor opens the same file and reads sub-domain data of the file in parallel. We call this strategy "Parallel Reading from Control node" (*PRC*), and the distributing time of *PRC* is defined as *Tpr*. *Strategy (b)* - The master processor opens the file and reads the whole data, then distributes the sub-domain data to each processor. We call this strategy "Master Reading a file then Distributing it" (*MRD*), and the distributing time is defined as *Tmr*

$$Tpr = \mathrm{Max}\,(Tr(i)+Ts(i)), \qquad (i=0,\ldots,n) \tag{9-1}$$

$$Tmr = Tw+Tu+Tv, \tag{9-2}$$

where n is the number of computing nodes, which are involved in reading operation. Also, Tr(i) is represented as the time of reading sub-domain data from the hard disk of the control node to its sending buffer (i - reading request from processor i); $Ts(i)$ as the time of transferring the data from the sending buffer of the control node to the receiving buffer of processor i; Tw as the time of reading whole file from the hard disk of the control node to its sending buffer; Tu as the time of transferring the whole file from the sending buffer of the control node to the receiving buffer of the master; and Tv as the time of transferring sub-domain data from the master to each processor.

There are some overlapping between $Tr(i)$ and $Ts(j)$ when i is not equal to j in *Strategy (a)*. And there is little overlap among *Tw, Tu, and Tv*. This indicates that I/O performance in *Strategy (a)* will be higher than that in *Strategy (b)*. We have also made tests about above two strategies of data distribution. Based on our tests, it shows that *Strategy (a)* can achieve higher I/O performance than *Strategy (b)*. Therefore, *Strategy (a)* is used in our PJBNM.

Communication Optimization

The communication latency is the major overhead and has great influence on the performance of parallel algorithms. It is mentioned above that there will be no communication in the parallel computation processing due to our good data partition. But the local results achieved by each processor are needed to gather together. To reduce the communication and improve the performance, a "key position" technique in PJBNM is used. In parallel processing, each process only records the key positions of damage windows and the chosen candidate windows. After completing all the sub-domain processing, slave processes transfer the key positions to the master. At last, not each process but master does image restoration according to key positions. This technique can reduce the communication greatly.

PJBNM Outline

```
Step 1: Generate n processes;
    /* The following is done in parallel. Single Program Multiple Data
           is adopted */
Step 2: Each process gets its sub-domain file data in PRC strategy.
Step 3: While (not complete the sub-domain processing).
        { If (the block is a damaged one)
          { Extract the damaged block as a local window, l, and form a
                searching range, S;
            Do jumping and looking all round search;
            Record the key position;
          }
        }
Step 4: For (i=0;i<n-1;i++)
            If ( proid<>0 )    /* proid!=0 means the process is a slave
                                      process*/
                Send the key positions to process with proid=0;
            else { proid==0}  /* proid==0 means the process is the master
                                      process */
                Receive the key positions
Step 5: If (proid==0)
                Restore the damaged block with the good block according to
                 the key positions.
```

Step 6: If (proid==0)
 Saving the restored image.
End

9.4 Experimental Results and Analysis

In PJBNM, experimental parameters are the same as that in JBNM. For data partition, we first divide an image averagely in row. Then, we extend 40 rows as an overlap region if the boundary of a sub-domain is not the boundary of the whole image. The sizes of testing images are 512x512 pixels (256 gray levels), 1024x1024, and 2048x2048, respectively. In parallel processing, images with different sizes will be tested by the different number of computing nodes. For example, the number of processors for images with 512x512 pixels is in range from 1 to 4, and for images with 2048x2048 is ranging from 1 to 16.

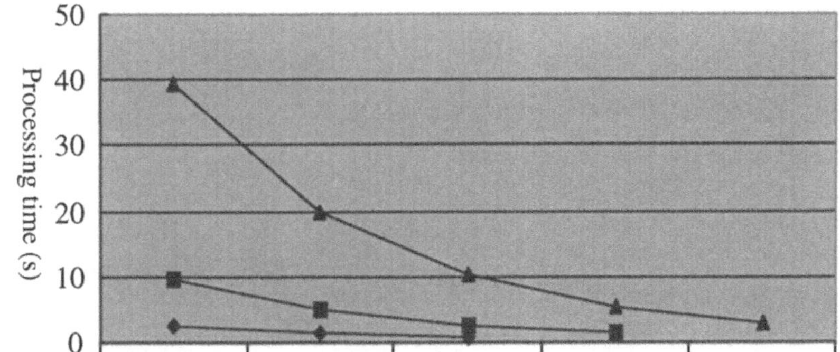

	1 PS	2 PS	4 PS	8 PS	16 PS
—◆— 512	2.41	1.32	0.69		
—■— 1024	9.62	4.87	2.53	1.34	
—▲— 2048	39.43	20.02	10.18	5.23	2.91

Figure 9.6. Comparisons of computational time by PJBNM for 512x512 pixels' image, 1024x1024 pixels' image, 2048x2048 pixels' image. "PS" means the number of processors

According to above parameter, PJBNM is still implemented on Dawning 2000-Ⅰ cluster system. The code of our parallel algorithm is written in *c* language and MPI (Message Passing Interface). The code has portability on various High Performance Computer platforms. Figure 9.6 shows the computational time by PJBNM. It is obvious that the computational time reduces greatly with the number of processors increasing. For example, it takes 2.41 (second) for restoring a 512x512 pixels image when only one processor is used. And it only takes 0.69 (second) for restoring the same image when four processors are used.

Two parameters: Parallel Speedup (S_p) and Efficiency (E_p), are two important criteria used in evaluating parallel algorithms. Speedup can be defined as

$$S_p = T_s / T_p, \quad (9\text{-}3)$$

where T_s is the serial runtime of the best serial algorithm for solving a problem and T_p is the time taken on a parallel system with *p processors*. Speedup is used to evaluate effectiveness of parallel algorithms. Efficiency is defined as

$$E_p = S_p / p, \quad (9\text{-}4)$$

where p is amount of processors. Efficiency can be used to evaluate the scalability of parallel algorithms [9].

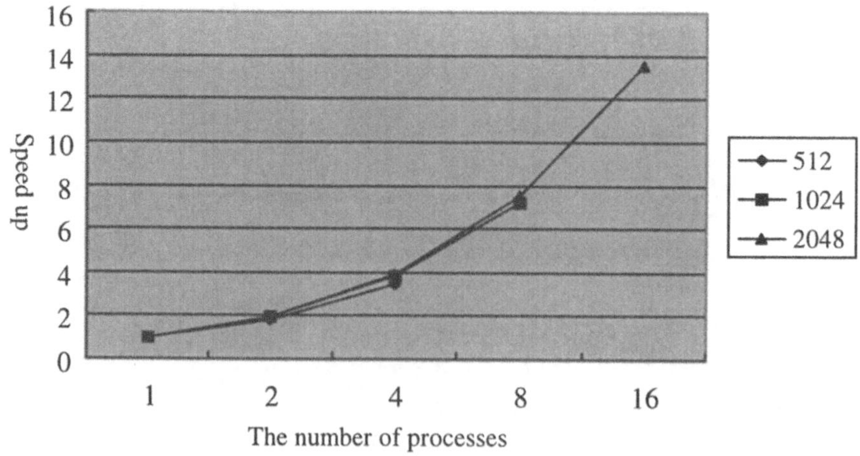

Figure 9.7. Speedup results of PJBNM for 512x512 pixels' image, 1024x1024 pixels' image, 2048x2048 pixels' image

Figure 9.7 shows the speedup of PJBNM. As it is shown that the speedup of PJBNM is very good. It is nearly linear. For example, the speedup is 3.49 when a 512x512 image is disposed by 4 processors. The speedup is 7.18 if a 1024×1024 image is restored by 8 processors; Other result is 13.55 if an image with 2048×2048 pixels is restored by 16 processors. The high efficiency of PJBNM is given in Figure 9.8. The efficiency has some declination with the number of processors increasing. The reason lies that the ratio between the computation and communication decreases, when the processor nodes increase. But on the whole, the efficiency keeps above 0.8.

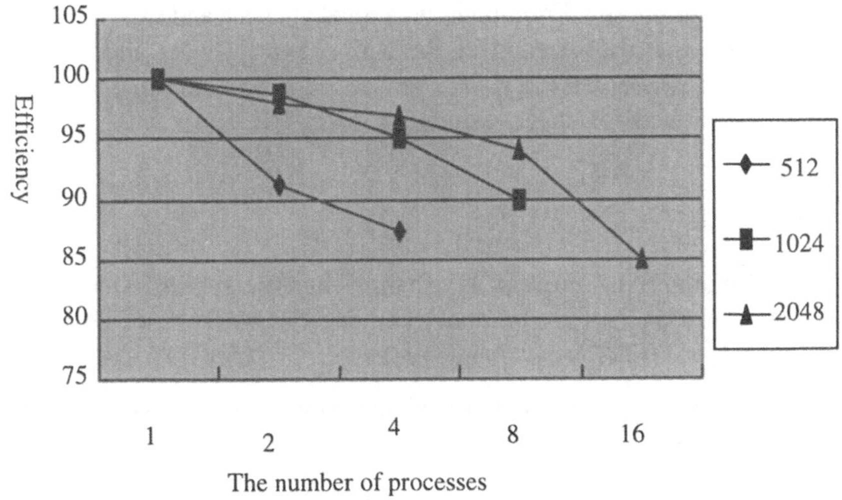

Figure 9.8. Efficiency results of PJBNM for 512×512 pixels' image, 1024×1024 pixels' image, 2048×2048 pixels' image

Scalability is another important metric, which is used to evaluate how problem sizes and processors influence the performance of parallel algorithms [9]. If the efficiency is approximately invariable as the problem sizes and processors increase, a parallel algorithm is scalable. In Figure 9.8, it is shown that the efficiency of PJBNM is very good and does not vary greatly. When we double the image side length and the problem size scales by 4, the corresponding execution times can be obtained. This means that our PJBNM is scalable.

So, when PJBNM is used for large-scale image restoration, the high performance can be reached. The experimental results also show that real-time image restoration application may be realized on cluster system.

The peak signal-to-noise ratio (PSNR) is still used to give a quantitative evaluation on the quality of the reconstructed image. Based on the methods in our PJBNM, the restored image quality of PJBNM is the same as that of JBNM.

9.5 Conclusion

In this chapter, an improved Best Neighborhood Matching algorithm, JBNM, is developed. By using this algorithm, the computing time can be reduced to 1/6 of the original BNM. In order to meet the requirements of both large-scale and real-time image restoration applications, a parallel JBNM algorithm is proposed. From both theoretical analysis and experiment results, it is shown that the speedup of PJBNM is nearly linear and efficiency is above 0.8. PJBNM can effectively reduce the processing time and provide a new efficient way for image restoration.

References

[1] Z. Wang, Y.L. Yu, and D. Zhang, "Best neighborhood matching: an information loss restoration technique for block–based image coding systems," *IEEE Trans. Image processing*, 7:1056-1061, July 1998.

[2] G. Walleye, "The JPEG still picture compression standard," *Commun. ACM*, 34:30-44, Apr. 1991.

[3] M. Liou, "Overview of the p×64 kbit/s video coding standard," *Commun. ACM*, 34:59-63, Apr. 1991.

[4] D.L. Gall, "MPEG: A video compression standard for multi-media applications," *Commun. ACM*, 34:46-58, Apr. 1991.

[5] X. Lee, Y.Q. Zhang, and A.Leon-Garcia, "Information loss recovery for block-based image coding techniques—A fuzzy logic approach," *IEEE Trans. Image processing*, 4:259-273, Mar. 1995.

[6] S.S. Hemami and T.H.Y. Meng, "Transform coded image reconstruction exploiting interblock correlation," *IEEE Trans. Image processing*, 4:1023-1027, July 1995.

[7] H. Sun and W. Kwok, "Concealment of damaged block transform coded images using projections onto convex sets," *IEEE Trans. Image Processing*. 4:470-477, Apr. 1995.

[8] W.M. Lam and A.R. Reibman, "An error concealment algorithm for image subject to channel errors," *IEEE Trans. Image Processing,* 4:533-542, May 1995.

[9] X.F. Wu, *Performance Evaluation, Prediction and Visualization of Parallel system*. Kluwer Academic Publishers, Boston/Dordrecht/ London, 1999.

Chapter 10

IMAGE STORAGE MANAGEMENT ON PARALLEL COMPUTERS

In this chapter, we will discuss some techniques for the design of parallel memory systems. Some background information for parallel memory systems will be introduced in Section 10.1. Linear skewing schemes are described in Section 10.2. Section 10.3 introduces XOR schemes. Some concluding remarks are given in Section 10.4.

10.1 Introduction

In parallel and supercomputer systems, parallel memory systems are usually provided in order that the memory bandwidth is matched with the processing speed of the powerful processing elements. A parallel memory system consists of a number of memory modules (memory banks). This design is for the purpose that as many memory words as the number of memory modules can be accessed simultaneously. This is especially necessary, and effective, for parallel image processing as well as scientific and engineering computations. There are a number of memory locations in each module. Each memory module has a unique module number. When a data element is needed to be accessed from the parallel memory system the actual memory module number and location within the module needs to be generated. We call a location within a memory module the displacement within a module or local address, or simply call it an address when no confusion will be caused. Thus the physical address of a data element consists of two parts, i.e. memory module number and displacement (or local address).

In the above design, although we have got a number of memory modules that can be accessed in parallel, we may not really obtain a bandwidth as multiple times big as the bandwidth of a single memory module when we access some data structures in real application programs. For example, a 4 by 4 matrix is stored in a parallel memory system with four modules as shown in Figure 10.1. This corresponds to a scheme where the elements of the matrix are arranged in row-major order and the memory modules arranged with low order interleaving. Suppose that each memory module can provide one element in each cycle. Although the system has the ability to provide four data elements in a memory cycle, we need four cycles when we want to access the four elements of any column since the four elements of any column are stored in the same memory module. We will say that conflict occurs in the parallel access in this case. Also, we need two cycles to access a 2 by 2 block of a[0,0], a[0,1], a[1,0], and a[1,1], since they are stored in two different modules and we can only access two elements in each cycle. If the modules are arranged with high order interleaving, four elements of any column can be accessed in each cycle, but four elements of any row will need four cycles to be accessed. Thus, a critical issue in parallel memory system design is how to distribute the elements of a data structure such that as many as possible data elements can really be accessed in parallel without conflict. In the following context, we will call any parallel memory scheme a skewing scheme, no matter it distributes the data elements by skewing or scrambling using other methods.

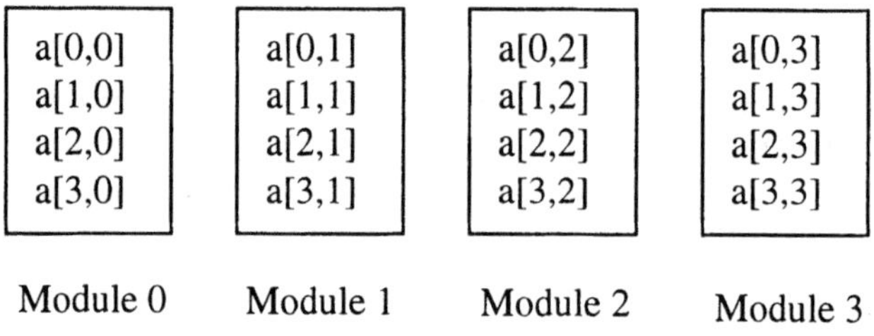

Figure 10.1. A distribution of a 4 by 4 matrix in 4 memory modules

Let the parallel memory system consist of M memory modules numbered from 0 to M-1, each memory module consist of D locations from 0 to D-1, and the logical address space of a data structure be L. Thus a skewing scheme needs to have two functions, i.e. skewing function s, which decides a data element will be stored in which memory module, and addressing function f, which decides a data element will be stored in which memory location in the memory module. Thus a skewing function is a mapping from L to $\{0, 1, \ldots, M\text{-}1\}$, and an addressing function f is a mapping from L to $\{0, 1, \ldots, D\text{-}1\}$ such that for any two logical addresses $x1$ and $x2$, $x1, x2 \in L$ and $x1 \neq x2$, if $s(x1)=s(x2)$ then $f(x1) \neq f(x2)$. Notice that the addressing function also has some effect on memory space utilization and the implementation complexity, this will be seen after we discuss the scheme based on the Chinese Remainder Theorem. It is obvious that addressing function does not affect the parallel accessibility of a parallel memory system. Because the key issue of a skewing scheme is how to distribute data in the memory modules which is decided by the skewing function, we will simply call a skewing function a skewing scheme when no confusion will be caused.

Some key issues must be considered in the design of parallel memory schemes. The first issue is the power of the scheme, i.e. how many "patterns" can be accessed in parallel in such a system. Note that patterns here are also called templates in literature, which are subsets of elements of a data structure. The second issue is simplicity of the design, which mainly includes implementation of the memory module number computation and local address computation. The third issue is the implementation of the data alignment requirements, i.e. simplicity of arranging the accessed data elements into some desired order. While the first issue is about the functionality of a parallel memory scheme, the second and the third are implementation issues.

10.2 Linear Parallel Memory Systems

Linear parallel memory schemes are firstly introduced by P. Budnik and D. Kuck in [1], and further formalized by D. Lawrie in [2], and extensive theoretical results are given by H. Wijshoff in [3]. We will first introduce some basic results in [1-3], then we will introduce a parallel memory system based on the Chinese Remainder Theorem.

Theoretical Results for Linear Parallel Systems

A data structure, matrix, is most frequently used in scientific and engineering computation, especially in image processing. We will discuss skewing schemes mainly for 2-dimensional arrays. The ideas can be easily extended to higher dimensional arrays.

Definition 10. 1 A linear skewing scheme is defined by $s(i, j)=a*i+b*j \bmod M$.

Using a linear skewing scheme $s(i, j)=a*i+b*j \bmod M$ means that the element on the ith row and jth column will be stored in the memory module numbered $s(i, j)$. Given a particular a and b, a linear skewing scheme is called an (a, b) skewing scheme. In *linear* skewing schemes, the *skew* is defined to be the distance measured in columns that each array row has been shifted relative to the row above it.

Definition 10. 2 A d-ordered p-vector is a vector of p elements of an array, and each pair of two successive elements of the vector are stored in memory modules $d \bmod M$ apart.

For example, any column of an $N \times N$ matrix stored using a linear skewing scheme $s(i, j)=a*i+b*j \bmod M$ is an a-ordered N-vector, any row is a b-ordered N-vector, a forward diagonal is an $(a+b)$-ordered N-vector, and a backward diagonal is an $(a-b)$-ordered N-vector.

Theorem 10.1 The necessary and sufficient condition for a d-ordered p-vector to be accessed in *one* memory cycle without conflict is $p \leq M/GCD(d, M)$.

Proof: Let the greatest common divisor of d and M be $GCD(d, M)=g$. Let $d=g*x$ and $M=g*y$. The ith element and the jth element of a p-vector will be stored in memory modules $(j-i)*d=(j-i)*g*x \bmod M$ apart.

When $p>M/g$, one can always find j and i such that $(j-i)=y$. Then $(j-i)*g=y*g=M$, and $(j-i)*d=(j-i)*g*x=0 \bmod M$. This means that the ith and the jth elements are stored in the same memory module, thus they can not be accessed in one memory cycle without conflict.

When $p \leq M/g$, we prove that for any j and i, $j-i<p$, we have $(j-i) \neq 0 \bmod M$.

Suppose that there are i and j such that $(j-i)<p$ and $(j-i)*d=0 \bmod M$. Thus we have $(j-i)*d=c*M$ where c is an integer. Then we have

$$(j-i)*g*x=c*g*y, \tag{10-1}$$

$$(j-i)*x=c*y, \text{ and} \tag{10-2}$$

$$y=((j-i)/c)*x. \tag{10-3}$$

Since $p \neq M/g$, $(j-i)<y$. Thus x can be factored as $x=c*x'$ since the product $((j-i)/c)*x$ must be an integer (i.e. y). Furthermore, we know $x>c$ since $(j-i)<y$. Therefore y and x have a common devisor $x'>1$. Thus M and d have a common divisor $g'=g*x'>g$. This contradicts to $GCD(d, M)=g$.

Thus there does not exist such a pair of i and j that $(j-i)<p$ and $(j-i)*d=0 \bmod M$. This means that no two elements in the p-vector are stored in a single memory module. Therefore all the p elements can be accessed in one memory cycle without conflict. ■

Theorem 10.1 provides a bound for the length of a d-ordered vector which can be accessed in one memory cycle without conflict in a linearly skewed parallel memory system with M modules. Also it can be considered as a bound of the minimal number of memory modules in a linearly skewed parallel memory system for a d-ordered p-vector to be accessible in *one* memory cycle without conflict. One may make trade-off between the number of simultaneously accessible data elements and the number of memory modules in a system design. Multiple fetch may be needed for some long vector in some system where a large number of memory modules are not available. The following theorem is from [3] for the bound of the number of memory modules for a *d*-ordered *p*-vector to be accessible in *r* memory cycles without conflict.

Theorem 10.2 A *d*-ordered *p*-vector can be accessible in *r* memory cycles without conflict if and only if $M \geq \left(\left\lfloor \frac{p-1}{r} \right\rfloor + 1 \right) GCD(d, M)$.

Theorems 10.1 and 10.2 provide the reason why a prime number of memory modules are desired -- if *M* is prime *d* can be any number (except a multiple of *M*) such that *GCD*(*d*, *M*)=1 and the memory system can be accessed in its full bandwidth.

The frequently used data templates—rows, columns, and diagonals (forward and backward)-- can be described by *d*-ordered *p*-vector, as shown above. Theorem 10.1 can then be used to design a linear skewing for them. The template of square blocks is also a very important data template in real applications, but it is difficult to use the idea of *d*-ordered *p*-vector to describe such a template.

The following observation is from P. Budnic and D. Kuck for blocks. Notice that in the description of the following theorem an *x* by *y* area means an area of *x* rows and *y* columns.

Theorem 10.3 With an (*S*, 1) skewing scheme, the elements in a rectangular area of $\lfloor M / S \rfloor \times S$ can be accessed in one memory cycle without conflict.

Proof: Suppose that a matrix *A* is stored by an (*S*, 1) skewing scheme. For any two elements $a(i, j)$ and $a(i', j')$ in a rectangular area of $\lfloor M / S \rfloor \times S$, $a(i, j)$ will be stored in module $s(i, j) = S*i + j \mod M$ and $a(i', j')$ will be stored in module $s(i', j') = S*i' + j' \mod M$. Thus $s(i, j) - s(i', j') = S*(i - i') - (j - j') \mod M$.

If the two elements are in the same row, i.e. $i = i'$, we know that $s(i,j) - s(i',j') = j - j' \neq 0$ since $j \neq j'$.

Suppose that the two elements are in different rows, i.e. $i \neq i'$. We know that $|j - j'| < S$ since the two elements in the same area of $\lfloor M / S \rfloor \times S$. But we always have $|S*(i - i')| \geq S$ since $i \neq i'$. Thus we also have $s(i,j) - s(i',j') \neq 0$.■

P. Budnic and D. Kuck give a skewing schemes in [1], where $M = 2^{2L} + 1$ memory modules or $M = 2^{2L+1} - 1$ modules are used with skew of 2^L, i.e. $s(i, j) = 2^L * i + j$. Frequently used *M*-vectors of rows, columns, forward and backward diagonals, and blocks can be accessed in one memory cycle without conflict.

The Parallel Memory System Based on the Chinese Remainder Theorem

A prime memory system for BSP is introduced in [4]. The prime memory system uses two equations for the computation of an element (i, j) of an two dimensional $I \times J$ array:

$$f(i, j)=[j*I+i+base] \bmod M, \tag{10-4}$$

and

$$g(i, j)=[j*I+i+base]/P\ . \tag{10-5}$$

Equation (10-4) is for the computation of the memory module number, and Equation (10-5) is for the local address. In the above equations, M is the number of memory modules, which is a prime number. P is the number of processors, which is the greatest complete power of two less than M. One modulo M operation for the generation of the memory module number is needed, and one division by P is needed for the generation of local address. In this scheme, some memory location will be left unused because of the local address generation equation. These unused memory locations are called "holes". The number of holes in each row is M-P in general. Indexing equations and hardware mechanism is introduced for a solution of this problem.

We now introduce a parallel memory system, which also uses a prime number of memory modules. A merit of the system introduced here is that it does not leave "holes" for the usage of memory locations. Another merit is that only a modular operation of a complete power of two is needed for the computation of the local address in a memory module, which is easy to be implemented than a integer divide operation.

Theorem 10.4 The Chinese Remainder Theorem

Given two sets of integers $\{a_1, a_2, \cdots, a_k\}$ and $\{b_1, b_2, \cdots, b_k\}$, where any two integers in $\{a_1, a_2, \cdots, a_k\}$ are relatively prime to each other. For the following k simultaneous equations, $b_i = x \bmod a_i$, $(1 \le i \le k)$, where x is an integer unknown, x has one and only one solution modulo n, and the unique solution of x satisfies

$$x = \sum_{i=1}^{k} b_i \times c_i \times \prod_{j=1(j \ne i)}^{k} a_j \bmod n, \tag{10-6}$$

where $n = \prod_{j=1}^{k} a_j$, and $c_1, c_2, \cdots, c_k$ are k constants satisfying

$$\sum_{i=1}^{k} c_i \times \prod_{j=1(j \neq i)}^{k} a_i = 1 \bmod n . \quad (10\text{-}7)$$

Different descriptions and proof of the Chinese Remainder Theorem can be found elsewhere. For the purpose of development of a parallel memory system, we concern more about the existence and uniqueness of the solution of x rather than how to obtain the solution of x.

Any high dimensional data structure will be stored in a one-dimensional memory address space in its implementation. For example, the element on row i and column j of an $I \times J$ matrix may be stored in memory location $a=base+i*J+j$, or ($a=base+j*I+i$), which will be called the logical address of the element. Let a data element with logical address a be stored in memory module m, and its local address (displacement in module m) be d.

The parallel memory system based on the Chinese Remainder Theorem (PCRT scheme) is as follows: Let the number of memory modules in the system be M, and each memory module have L locations, where L is a complete power of two, and M is a prime number. Logical address a is mapped to $\{m, d\}$, where $m=a \bmod M$, and $d=a \bmod L$.

From the above definition we can see that the address computation for the location in a memory module only needs an operation of modulo L, and it is very simple since L is a complete power of two. Another advantage of this scheme is that the mapping between the whole logical address space and the memory location space is one to one, thus no memory space is wasted.

Theorem 10.5 In scheme PCRT, each logical address a maps to one and only one memory location $\{m, d\}$, also each memory location maps to one and only one logical address a.

Proof: It is clear that each logical address a maps to one and only one memory location $\{m, d\}$ since $m=a \bmod M$, and $d=a \bmod L$.

For the mapping from $\{m, d\}$ to a, observing that M, the number of memory modules, and L, the number of locations in each memory module, are relatively prime, we know that a has one and only one solution for each $\{m, d\}$ (from the Chinese Remainder Theorem). Thus each memory location in any memory module maps to one and only one logical address. ■

Note here that the restriction that the number of memory modules in the system is prime is in fact not necessary. It is sufficient that the number of memory modules is an odd number as well as the number of locations in a module is a complete power of two (this is the general case in memory system design). We propose the number of memory modules is prime because of convenience of implementation, since a number of algorithms for the implementation of prime modular operation have been proposed, especially for the prime numbers of the form $M = P = 2^t + 1$ and $M = P = 2^t - 1$. Also more *P*-vectors may be accessed in parallel without conflict if *P* is prime.

From Theorem 10.5 we are sure that the PCRT scheme will not leave "holes" for the usage of the memory modules since each physical memory location maps to a logical address. An example for *M*=5 and *L*=8 is shown in Figure 10.2.

d \ m	0	1	2	3	4
0	0	16	32	8	24
1	25	1	17	33	9
2	10	26	2	18	34
3	35	11	27	3	19
4	20	36	10	28	4
5	5	21	37	13	29
6	30	6	22	38	14
7	15	31	7	23	39

Figure 10.2. The PCRT scheme for P=5 and L=8

It is obvious that any row or any column of an *N*×*N* matrix can be accessed in parallel without memory conflict provided that *N* is not a multiple of *M*. It can not be guaranteed that blocks and diagonals are accessed in parallel since there no particular skew is applied in the parallel scheme based on the Chinese Remainder Theorem. In order that more patterns can be accessed in parallel without memory conflict, appropriate skewing is needed. The idea of using the Chinese Remainder Theorem may be used in combination with the techniques presented in [1, 2] so that desired patterns can be accessed in parallel while no "hole" will exist in the memory modules, and the computation of the local address will be simplified.

10.3 XOR Storage Schemes

In XOR schemes, the address (the memory module number of a matrix element) generation uses only bitwise Exclusive-OR (XOR) operation. Frailong et al formalized such a kind of method to design parallel memory system in 1985, some special XOR scheme had been proposed and used before 1985, though. In comparison with linear skewing schemes, especially to the schemes using prime number operations, XOR schemes have the merit that address generation is simple since only bitwise XOR operations are needed. Bitwise XOR operations only need XOR gates for their hardware implementation. Thus their implementation are fast and simple. Another merit of the XOR schemes over the schemes using prime numbers is that the data alignment is easier to be implemented. This is because the data alignment requirements for XOR schemes can generally be described by Linear Complement permutations (LC permutations), even Bit Permute Complement permutations (BPC permutations, which is a subset of LC permutations while it is a simpler subset than general LC permutations). Implementation of data alignment requirements will be discussed in detail in Chapter 12.

Suppose that an $N \times N$ matrix X is to be processed on a system with N memory modules, where $N = 2^n$, and n is a positive integer. We use an $N \times N$ matrix to describe a skewing scheme: element $x_{i,j}$ of X is stored in memory module $m_{i,j}$. Matrix M is called the *mapping matrix*. For example, a 4×4 matrix X is stored by the mapping matrix M shown in Figure 10.3, we say that $x_{3,3}$ is stored in memory module 0, $x_{2,2}$ is stored in Memory Module 3.

General description of an XOR scheme is as the following. Let $i = i_{n-1}i_{n-2}\cdots i_0$, $j = j_{n-1}j_{n-2}\cdots j_0$, and $m_{i,j} = m_{i,j,n-1}m_{i,j,n-2}\cdots m_{i,j,0}$ be the binary representation of i, j, and $m_{i,j}$ respectively. Any XOR scheme can be described by the following equation:

$$m^{\tau}{}_{i,j} = (A \times i^{\tau}) + (B \times j^{\tau}) \tag{10-8}$$

where $m^{\tau}{}_{i,j}$, i^{τ}, and j^{τ} are the transpositions of $m_{i,j}$, i, and j respectively; A and B are $n \times n$ matrices with their elements being only "1" or "0", and the operations "×" and "+" are carried out over GF(2). Thus "+" is only a bitwise Exclusive-OR ($\oplus$), and we will use $\oplus$ for this operation hereafter. We will use $m_{i,j} = (A \times i) \oplus (B \times j)$ to denote $m^{\tau}{}_{i,j} = (A \times i^{\tau}) +$

$(B \times j^{\tau})$ in the following text when no confusion will arise. The memory module number where an data element is stored in XOR scheme is decided by the matrices A and B in Equation (10-8), we will call matrices A and B *generation matrices* for an XOR scheme. The data patterns (templates) of N elements in an $N \times N$ matrix can be described by n column vectors of the generation matrices A and B in an XOR scheme. We will see how these n column vectors are used to define the data patterns and to prove features of an XOR scheme.

i \ j	0	1	2	3
0	0	1	2	3
1	2	3	0	1
2	3	2	1	0
3	1	0	3	2

Figure 10.3. A 4×4 mapping matrix M

We will use matrix E to denote the identity matrix. We denote column k of matrix A (B) as $a_{*,k}$ ($b_{*,k}$), for $0 \le k \le n-1$. Note that when we express an $n \times n$ matrix A (or B), $a_{n-1,n-1}$ (or $b_{n-1,n-1}$) is the top-left element, and $a_{0,0}$ (or $b_{0,0}$), the bottom-right element.

The EE Parallel Storage Scheme

We introduce an XOR storage scheme in this section. The name of the scheme is Exchange and Expansion (EE, for short). Its intuitive explanation will be given first, then it will be described by giving its generation matrices in the general form of XOR scheme. Intuitively, the EE scheme works as follows:

Let the elements in the first row of M be numbered from 0 to N-1. The second row is formed by exchanging the first and the second halves of the first row, the next two rows are created from the first two rows by cutting the first two rows into quarters and exchanging the first and second quarters and the third and fourth, and so on, the lower half matrix is formed by exchanging $N/2$ two adjacent columns of the up half matrix ($N/2$ rows). The resulting matrix is our mapping matrix M. This expansion process is shown in Figure 10.4 for $N=8$.

In this storage scheme, the elements of a matrix are stored according to their row index in any memory module, i.e. element $x_{i,j}$ is stored in memory module $m_{i,j}$, and its displacement in the module is i. This means that the local address in any memory module does not need computation, rather only the memory module number $m_{i,j}$ needs to be computed. Therefore address generation in the scheme refers only to the memory module number computation when an element is to be accessed.

Let $br(i)$ be the bit-reversal function of integer i, and let $\oplus$ be the bitwise Exclusive-OR operation. Given the indices of an element $x_{i,j}$, $m_{i,j}$ is computed by the following equation:

(1)

0	1	2	3	4	5	6	7

(2)

0	1	2	3	4	5	6	7
4	5	6	7	0	1	2	3

(3)

0	1	2	3	4	5	6	7
4	5	6	7	0	1	2	3
2	3	0	1	6	7	4	5
6	7	4	5	2	3	0	1

(4)

0	1	2	3	4	5	6	7
4	5	6	7	0	1	2	3
2	3	0	1	6	7	4	5
6	7	4	5	2	3	0	1
1	0	3	2	5	4	7	6
5	4	7	6	1	0	3	2
3	2	1	0	7	6	5	4
7	6	5	4	3	2	1	0

Figure 10.4. The exchange-expansion process for $N=8$

$$m_{i,j} = br(i) \oplus j . \tag{10-9}$$

In terms of XOR-schemes, the scheme can be expressed as

$$m_{i,j} = (R \times i) \oplus (E \times j) , \tag{10-10}$$

where matrix R is such that all the elements on its backward diagonal, and only these elements, are 1.

Observing that in step k in the Exchange-Expansion process the position of $m_{i,j}$ is exchanged with a position 2^{n-k} distant to it in its row, it is not difficult to see that Equation (10-10) does implement the idea of Exchange-Expansion. A mapping matrix generated by Equation (10-10) for $N=16$ is given in Figure 10.5.

We now prove that in the EE scheme, for any integers P and Q ($PQ=N$), a continuous area of $P \times Q$ in matrix X can be accessed simultaneously in one memory cycle. Rows and columns are special cases of $P \times Q$ blocks with $P=1$ or $Q=1$. We will also prove that the simultaneously accessible blocks can shift along vertical and horizontal stripes in EE scheme. In addition we will prove that N points scattered over the matrix plane, partial-row-pairs, and partial-column-pairs, are accessible in parallel. These features are important in various parallel algorithms [1, 4-8]. Some continuous areas which are simultaneously accessible are shown in Figure 10.5.

0	**1**	**2**	**3**	**4**	**5**	**6**	**7**	**8**	**9**	**10**	**11**	**10**	**13**	**14**	**15**
8	**9**	**10**	**11**	**10**	**13**	**14**	15	0	1	2	3	4	5	6	**7**
4	**5**	**6**	**7**	**0**	**1**	**2**	**3**	10	13	14	15	8	9	10	**11**
10	13	14	15	8	9	10	11	4	5	6	7	0	1	2	**3**
2	3	0	1	6	7	4	5	10	11	8	9	14	15	10	**13**
10	11	8	9	14	15	10	13	2	3	0	1	6	7	4	**5**
6	7	4	5	2	3	0	1	14	15	10	13	10	11	8	**9**
14	15	10	13	10	11	8	9	6	7	4	5	2	3	0	**1**
1	0	3	2	5	4	7	6	9	8	11	10	13	10	**15**	**14**
9	8	11	10	13	10	15	14	1	0	3	2	5	4	**7**	**6**
5	4	7	6	1	0	3	2	13	10	15	14	9	8	**11**	**10**
13	**10**	**15**	**14**	9	8	11	10	5	4	7	6	1	0	**3**	**2**
3	**2**	**1**	**0**	**7**	6	5	4	11	10	9	8	15	14	**13**	**10**
11	**10**	**9**	**8**	**15**	14	13	10	3	2	1	0	7	6	**5**	**4**
7	**6**	**5**	**4**	**3**	2	1	0	15	14	13	10	11	10	**9**	**8**
15	**14**	**13**	**10**	**11**	10	9	8	7	6	5	4	3	2	**1**	**0**

Figure 10.5. A 16×16 mapping matrix for the EE scheme

For a given integer pair (k, l), $0 \le k, l \le N-1$, a continuous PQ-block of X is expressed as $BLK(P,Q:k,l) = \{x_{k+a,l+b} \mid 0 \le a \le P-1, 0 \le b \le Q-1\}$. We call ($k$, l) the *positioning point* of the continuous PQ-block. A PQ-block consists of $P \times Q$ elements, and $x_{k,l}$ is the top-left element of the block.

Definition 10.3 A main *PQ*-block (MBLK(*P,Q:k,l*)) of matrix *X* is a continuous *PQ*-block with $(k = 0 \bmod P) \wedge (l = 0 \bmod Q)$.

Theorem 10.6 With the memory module number generation scheme given by Equation (10-10), the *N* elements of any main *PQ*-block of *X* can be accessed in one memory cycle.

Proof: We need only to prove that all the elements in a main *PQ*-block are stored in different memory modules, that is to say that we need to prove $m_{i,j} = m_{i',j'}$ if and only if *i*=*i'* and *j*=*j'* since $x_{i,j}$ and $x_{i',j'}$ are stored in memory module $m_{i,j}$ and $m_{i',j'}$ respectively. Because *PQ*=*N*, we can express *P* as $P = 2^p$, *Q* as $Q = 2^q$, and *p*+*q*=*n*.

Let $m_{i,j}$, $m_{i',j'} \in$ MBLK(*P,Q:k,l*). From Equation (10-10) we have $m_{i,j} = (i_0 \cdots i_{p-1} i_p \cdots i_{n-1}) \oplus (j_{n-1} \cdots j_q j_{q-1} \cdots j_0)$ and $m_{i',j'} = (i'_0 \cdots i'_{p-1} i'_p \cdots i'_{n-1}) \oplus (j'_{n-1} \cdots j'_q j'_{q-1} \cdots j'_0)$. Because $m_{i,j}$ and $m_{i',j'}$ are in the same main *PQ*-block, we know $i_{n-1} \cdots i_p = i'_{n-1} \cdots i'_p$ and $j_{n-1} \cdots j_q = j'_{n-1} \cdots j'_q$.

Considering *p*+*q*=*n*, we have

$$m_{i,j} \oplus m_{i'j'} = (i_0 \oplus i'_0) \cdots (i_{p-1} \oplus i'_{p-1})(j_{q-1} \oplus j'_{q-1}) \cdots (j_0 \oplus j'_0) \quad (10\text{-}11)$$

From Equation (10-11), we know that $m_{i,j} = m_{i',j'}$ if and only if *i*=*i'* and *j*=*j'*.

■

A main (1×*N*)-block is a row; a main (*N*×1)-block is a column; a main $\sqrt{N} \times \sqrt{N}$-block is an $\sqrt{N} \times \sqrt{N}$ square (when *N* is an even power of two). Thus according to Theorem 10.6, all the above desired subsets of a matrix investigated by a number of researchers can be accessed simultaneously in the EE scheme. Furthermore, the theorem guarantees that any one row, two adjacent half rows, four adjacent one fourth rows, ⋯ , one column, can be accessed simultaneously in one memory cycle. The "shape" of the desired subset is variable.

Definition 10.4 A shifted *PQ*-block (SHBLK(*P,Q:k,l*)) of matrix *X* is a continuous *PQ*-block with $(k = 0 \bmod P) \vee (l = 0 \bmod Q)$.

Shifted blocks are such blocks that their shape are the same as main blocks with their positioning points are shifted vertically or horizontally. We have the following stronger theorem for the scheme.

Theorem 10.7 Any shifted *PQ*-block SHBLK(*P,Q:k,l*) can be accessed simultaneously in one memory cycle.

Its proof is omitted here. This theorem says that not only are the shapes of simultaneously accessible blocks variable, but also the position of the blocks are circularly changeable along horizontal strips of width *P*, or vertical strips of width *Q*. For example, in Figure 10.5, the 4×4 block on the bottom left of the 16×16 matrix can be accessed in one memory cycle. When it is shifted up by one position, or shifted to the right by one position, the resulting block can still be accessed in one memory cycle.

It is impossible to propose a skewing scheme such that a block of *N* elements at any arbitrary position can be accessed in one memory cycle without memory conflict [7]. From Theorem 10.7 we have the following corollary for EE scheme:

Corollary 10.1 Any block of *N* elements at any arbitrary position can be accessed in at most two memory cycles.

Note that the blocks in the corollary are not only allowed to have arbitrary shapes (rectangles), but also allowed to start at arbitrary position. This feature is more important for associative cache systems, which will be seen in Chapter 11.

In image processing, not only do the adjacent image points in the continuous blocks need to be accessed simultaneously, but also some scattered image points need to be accessed simultaneously. We will call them *scattered blocks* (they are also called *points at the same positions* in some literature).

Definition 10.5 Given integers *a* and *b*, $0 \le a \le P-1$, and $0 \le b \le Q-1$, a scattered *PQ*-block (SCBLK(*P,Q:a,b*)) is defined as the set consisting of all the elements $x_{i,j}$ with *i=a mod P* and *j=b mod Q*:

$$\text{SCBLK}(P,Q{:}a,b)=\{x_{i,j} \mid (i = a \bmod P) \wedge (j = b \bmod Q)\}.$$

Theorem 10.8 With the memory module number generation scheme of Equation (10-5), any scattered *PQ*-block SCBLK(*P,Q:a,b*) can be accessed in one memory cycle.

With Definition 10.5, this theorem can be proved similarly as the proof of Theorem 10.6. Its proof is omitted here.

Notice that the scattered *PQ*-blocks here are flexible combinations of *N* elements. The sets of elements at the same positions not only include the elements at the same positions in each main $\sqrt{N} \times \sqrt{N}$ squares, scattered *PQ*-blocks here can be the elements at the same positions in main *PQ*-blocks with *different shapes.*

Folded lines, partial-row-pairs, and partial-column-pairs are useful patterns for image processing. An upper fold line is the set of elements $\{x_{0,k}, x_{1,k}, \cdots, x_{k-1,k}, x_{k,k+1}, x_{k,k+2}, \cdots, x_{k,N-1}\}$. A lower fold line is the set of elements $\{x_{k,0}, x_{k,1}, \cdots, x_{k,k-1}, x_{k+1,k}, x_{k+2,k}, \cdots, x_{N-1,k}\}$. Storage scheme EE cannot guarantee conflict-free access to the fold lines. For the partial pairs, EE has the following feature.

Definition 10.6 For $0 \le k \le N-1$, a partial-row-pair(*k*) of matrix *X* is the set of elements PRP(*k*)=$\{x_{k,0}, x_{k,1}, \cdots, x_{k,k-1}, x_{N-1-k,0}, x_{N-1-k,1}, \cdots, x_{N-1-k,N-1-k-1}\}$.

Definition 10.7 For $0 \le k \le N-1$, a partial-column-pair(*k*) of matrix *X* is the set of elements PCP(*k*)=$\{x_{0,k}, x_{1,k}, \cdots, x_{k-1,k}, x_{0,N-1-k}, x_{1,N-1-k}, \cdots,$ $x_{N-1-k-1,N-1-k}\}$.

Lemma 10.8 $\forall\, i,j$, we have $m_{i,j} = m_{N-1-i,N-1-j}$, where $0 \le i,j \le N-1$.

Theorem 10.9 Any PRP(*k*), where $0 \le k \le N-1$, can be accessed in one memory cycle.

Similar to the above, we have the following theorem.

Theorem 10.10 Any PCP(*k*), where $0 \le k \le N-1$, can be accessed in one memory cycle.

The MG Scheme and EE-MG Scheme

A scheme is proposed in [9] where the Gray code is used, but with that scheme, the important data patterns, forward and backward diagonals can not be accessed in parallel without memory conflict. With a slight modification to that scheme, we will introduce a scheme called Modified Gray scheme (MG scheme, in short), with which the diagonals can be accessed in one memory cycle without conflict. We will also discuss the combination of EE and MG schemes so that an EE-MG scheme is formed and new features will be observed.

The Modified Gray scheme is expressed by the following equation:

$$m_{i,j} = i \oplus (G \times j) \tag{10-12}$$

where the generation matrix *G* has the form that $g_{n-1,n-1} = g_{n-1,1} = g_{n-1,0} = 1$, and $g_{k,k} = g_{k,k+1} = 1$ for $0 \le k \le n\text{-}2$, and the remaining elements of *G* are all 0.

For example, the generation matrix $G_{5\times5}$ is as the following (recall that $g_{n-1,n-1}$ is the top-left element):

$$G_{5\times5} = \begin{pmatrix} 1\,0\,0\,1\,1 \\ 1\,1\,0\,0\,0 \\ 0\,1\,1\,0\,0 \\ 0\,0\,1\,1\,0 \\ 0\,0\,0\,1\,1 \end{pmatrix}$$

In fact $G\times j$ would be the Gray code of j for $0\leq j\leq N\text{-}1$ if $g_{n-1,0}$ and $g_{n-1,1}$ were not 1. It is for this reason that the skewing scheme is named MG (for *Modified Gray*) scheme. It can be seen that matrix G is nonsingular. The mapping matrix of 16×16 for the MG scheme is shown in Figure 10.6.

Let us discuss some features of the MG scheme.

Theorem 10.11 In the MG scheme, any row and any column can be accessed simultaneously in one memory cycle.

Proof: The theorem is obviously true for any column. It is also true for any row since $G_{n\times n}$ is nonsingular for any n. ■

Theorem 10.12 In scheme MG, the forward diagonal can be accessed in one memory cycle.

Proof: We now prove that any two elements on the diagonal are stored in different memory modules according to the MG scheme. Let $x_{i,i}$ be in module $m_{i,i}$ and $x_{j,j}$ be in $m_{j,j}$. Let E be the identity matrix and the kth column of E be denoted as $e_{*,k}$.

We have $m_{i,i} \oplus m_{j,j} = (i \oplus (G \times i)) \oplus (j \oplus (G \oplus j)) = (E \oplus G) \times (i \oplus j)$. Let us denote $C = (E \oplus G)$. From a simple calculation we know that the matrix C contains n column vectors of $e_{*,n-1}$, $e_{*,n-2}, \ldots, e_{*,1}$, and $(e_{*,0} \oplus e_{*,n-1})$. These n column vectors are independent. Thus matrix C is nonsingular. So, $m_{i,i} = m_{j,j}$ if and only if i=j. This is to say that any two elements on the diagonal will be in different memory modules according to the MG scheme. ■

0	9	11	2	6	15	13	4	10	5	7	14	10	3	1	8
1	8	10	3	7	14	10	5	13	4	6	15	11	2	0	9
2	11	9	0	4	13	15	6	14	7	5	10	8	1	3	10
3	10	8	1	5	10	14	7	15	6	4	13	9	0	2	11
4	13	15	6	2	11	9	0	8	1	3	10	14	7	5	10
5	10	14	7	3	10	8	1	9	0	2	11	15	6	4	13
6	15	13	4	0	9	11	2	10	3	1	8	10	5	7	14
7	14	10	5	1	8	10	3	11	2	0	9	13	4	6	15
8	1	3	10	14	7	5	10	4	13	15	6	2	11	9	0
9	0	2	11	15	6	4	13	5	10	14	7	3	10	8	1
10	3	1	8	10	5	7	14	6	15	13	4	0	9	11	2
11	2	0	9	13	4	6	15	7	14	10	5	1	8	10	3
10	5	7	14	10	3	1	8	0	9	11	2	6	15	13	4
13	4	6	15	11	2	0	9	1	8	10	3	7	14	10	5
14	7	5	10	8	1	3	10	2	11	9	0	4	13	15	6
15	6	4	13	9	0	2	11	3	10	8	1	5	10	14	7

Figure 10.6. The MG scheme for N=16

Similarly to Theorem 10.12, we have

Theorem 10.13 In scheme MG, the backward diagonal can be accessed in one memory cycle.
We now investigate combination of the schemes EE and MG, which will be formed as a new storage scheme. We will see some features of the new scheme. We will describe how to adapt different XOR schemes in one system.

The new scheme is a combination of EE and MG, and is called EE-MG scheme, which is expressed by the following equation:

$$m_{i,j} = (R \times i) \oplus (G \times j) \tag{10-13}$$

The mapping matrix for $N=16$ is give in Figure 10.7. One can check that the scheme guarantees that rows, columns, various main blocks of N elements (MBLK($P,Q:k,l$), where $PQ=N$) can be accessed simultaneously in one memory cycle; it guarantees that any diagonal can be accessed in one memory cycle; it also guarantees that all the scattered PQ-blocks SCBLK($P,Q:a,b$) are accessible in one memory cycle except $P=N/2$. We omit the proofs of the above features here.

This scheme has the additional feature that chessboard patterns of N elements in various areas can be accessed in one memory cycle. We now restate the definitions for red and black chess boards and some results given by Frailong et al in [10].

Definition 10.8 The *Red Chessboard* RC(*n, c*) consists of the elements $x_{i,j}$ in a rectangle of size $2^c \times 2^{n+1-c}$ such that the sum of the indices *i* and *j* of $x_{i,j}$ is even. The *Black Chessboard* BC(*n, c*) consists of the rest elements in the rectangle.

According to [10], the red chessboard RC(*n, c*) based at (0, 0) is accessible in one memory cycle if and only if the *n* column-vectors in matrices *A* and *B* in Equation (10-8). ($a_{*,0} \oplus b_{*,0}$), $b_{*,1}$, $b_{*,2}$, ..., $b_{*,c-1}$, $a_{*,1}$, $a_{*,2}$, ..., $a_{*,n-c}$ are linearly independent.

If the red chessboard RC(*n, c*) can be accessed in parallel, then the black chessboard BC(*n, c*) can also be accessed in parallel under the same condition. The scheme given in [11] guarantees conflict-free access to RC(*n*,1), RC(*n, n*), RC(*n, n/2*) and RC(*n, n/2*+1) when *n* is even.

In fact, the EE scheme guarantees RC(*n*,1) and RC(*n, n*) to be accessible in parallel for *n* being any integer. The scheme EE-MG expressed by Equation (10-10) has the following stronger feature.

0	9	11	2	6	15	13	4	10	5	7	14	10	3	1	8
8	1	3	10	14	7	5	10	4	13	15	6	2	11	9	0
4	13	15	6	2	11	9	0	8	1	3	10	14	7	5	0
10	5	7	14	10	3	1	8	0	9	11	2	6	15	13	4
2	11	9	0	4	13	15	6	14	7	5	10	8	1	3	10
10	3	1	8	10	5	7	14	6	15	13	4	0	9	11	2
6	15	13	4	0	9	11	2	10	3	1	8	10	5	7	14
14	7	5	10	8	1	3	10	2	11	9	0	4	13	15	6
1	8	10	3	7	14	10	5	13	4	6	15	11	2	0	9
9	0	2	11	15	6	4	13	5	10	14	7	3	10	8	1
5	10	14	7	3	10	8	1	9	0	2	11	15	6	4	13
13	4	6	15	11	2	0	9	1	8	10	3	7	14	10	5
3	10	8	1	5	10	14	7	15	6	4	13	9	0	2	11
11	2	0	9	13	4	6	15	7	14	10	5	1	8	10	3
7	14	10	5	1	8	10	3	11	2	0	9	13	4	6	15
15	6	4	13	9	0	2	11	3	10	8	1	5	10	14	7

Figure 10.7. The EE-MG scheme for N=16

Theorem 10.14 In scheme EE-MG, for any integer *n* and *c*, $1<c<n$, RC(*n, c*) (also BC(*n, c*)) can be accessed in one memory cycle.

Proof: For any *n* and *c*, $1<c<n$, from Equations (10-12) and (10-14) we have

$$\begin{cases} r_{*,0} + g_{*,0} = e_{*,0}, \\ g_{*,1} = e_{*,n-1} + e_{*,1} + e_{*,0}, \\ g_{*,k} = e_{*,k} + e_{*,k-1}, & \text{for} \quad 2 \le k \le c-1, \\ r_{*,k} = e_{*,n-1-k}, & \text{for} \quad 1 \le k \le n-c. \end{cases} \tag{10-14}$$

		11		6		13		12		7		10		1	
	1		10		7		12		13		6		11		0
4		15		2		9		8		3		14		5	
	5		14		3		8		9		2		15		4
2		9		4		15		14		5		8		3	
	3		8		5		14		15		4		9		2
6		13		0		11		10		1		12		7	
	7		12		1		10		11		0		13		6
1		10		7		12		13		6		11		0	
	0		11		6		13		12		7		10		1
5		14		3		8		9		2		15		4	
	4		15		2		9		8		3		14		5
3		8		5		14		15		4		9		2	
	2		9		4		15		14		5		8		3
7		12		1		10		11		0		13		6	
	6		13		0		11		10		1		12		7

Figure 10.8. The red chess boards RC(4,3)

Thus given n column-vectors $(r_{*,0} \oplus g_{*,0})$, $g_{*,1}$, $g_{*,2}$, ..., $g_{*,c-1}$, $r_{*,1}$, $r_{*,2}$, ..., $r_{*,n-c}$, one can always add $r_{*,n-c}$ to $g_{*,c-1}$ generating $e_{*,c-2}$, add this to $g_{*,c-2}$ and $e_{*,c-3}$ is generated, ... , add $e_{*,1}$ and $e_{*,0}$ to $g_{*,1}$ so that $e_{*,n-1}$ is generated. Therefore we can get n column-vectors $e_{*,0}$ through $e_{*,n-1}$, which are obviously linearly independent.

Thus we know that for any c, $1<c<n$, the n column-vectors $(r_{*,0} \oplus g_{*,0})$, $g_{*,1}$, $g_{*,2}$, ..., $g_{*,c-1}$, $r_{*,1}$, $r_{*,2}$, ..., $r_{*,n-c}$ are linearly independent. ■

From the above we can see that functionally this scheme is very powerful. The red chess boards RC(4, 3) are shown in Figure 10.8.

The Adaptive Parallel Storage System

Memory module number calculation needs to be carried out at run time, so that it should be implemented it in hardware. Theoretically, one can design a number of memory module number generation mechanisms in hardware such that when a different data pattern is needed a different mechanism is selected to generate the memory module numbers. However, it is preferable that the least number of mechanisms are used to cover the most useful data patterns, and that switch between different mechanisms is simple.

We have introduced a powerful skewing scheme EE-MG above. Although EE-MG Scheme can cover the largest set of the useful data patterns, there are still some data patterns that cannot be covered by the EE-MG scheme itself, but can be covered by scheme EE and scheme MG. From the process for developing EE-MG it can be seen that it is easy to combine these schemes into one system: the only thing needs to do is to inhibit the functions R, or G, or R and G, when generating the memory module numbers.

From Equations (10-10), (10-12), and (10-13) we can see that the three schemes employ very simple memory module number calculations. They involve only the Exclusive-OR operation, which can be easily implemented in hardware, and can be completed in constant time. Note that in the general case the product of an $n \times n$ matrix (A or B) and an n-vector (i or j where $0 \leq i, j \leq N-1$) cannot be completed in constant time, because any *one* bit of the result (the kth bit of the memory module number) depends on two n-bit vectors (i or j and $a_{k,*}$ or $b_{k,*}$). In the schemes EE, MG, and EE-MG, however, only one, two, or three "1" s exist in any row of any matrix, thus the memory module number calculation functions here can be completed in constant time. Furthermore, it is easy to synthesize the three schemes in one system. Only two bits are needed to select the desired scheme in the application algorithms. Let's call the two bits the *scheme selection register*, and "01" be for scheme EE, "10" for scheme MG, and "11" for scheme EE-MG. The pattern "00" can be used for implementing the scheme $m_{i,j} = i \oplus j$, which is first stated in [11] and used in STARAN, thus all the simultaneously accessible patterns in the STARAN scheme can all be retained in one system. When the system is used for a particular algorithm, one only needs to set the "scheme selection register" to a particular value. The structure of the mechanism to implement the memory module calculation is pictured in Figure 10.9. We call this adaptive scheme as EE*MG.

From Figure 10.9 we can see that memory module generation can be completed in constant time because only a constant number of bits are involved for generating any bit of i' or j' (one bit for any bit of i', three bits for j'_{n-1}, and two bits for any other bit of j'). The hardware needed is only $\lceil n/2 \rceil$ two by two switches and n Exclusive-OR gates, and a 2-bit register (the scheme selection register). Complexity of the hardware needed for memory module generation is $O(n)$ because the fixed connections between the bits of i and i' (or j and j'). In order to use these schemes, what is needed is only the address generation mechanism in the part of hardware, and to set the two bits of the scheme selection register in the part of software. It is efficient in terms of both hardware, speed and the number of data patterns that can be accessed simultaneously.

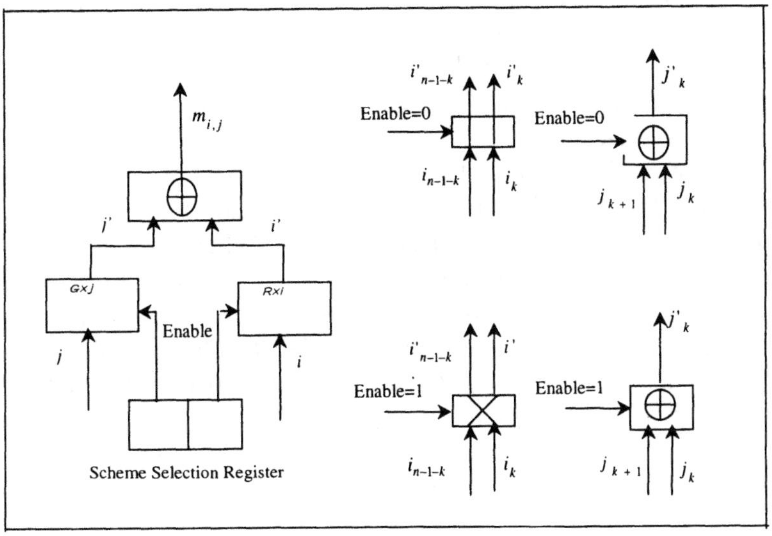

Figure 10.9. The adaptive system

Processing Different Sized Arrays on Large Systems

With the rapid advance in hardware technology, massively parallel processing systems are available. A large number of processing elements and memory modules --- hundreds, even thousands --- are employed in such a system. In practice, the number of processing elements may not be the same as the size of the matrix being processed.

Let X be a matrix of $N \times N$ to be processed on a system with W memory modules and W processing elements. Let $U = W/N$.

Processing large matrices on small systems has been discussed in literatures. If $W \leq N$, it is simple to use several $((N/W)^2)$ mapping matrix planes to tessellate the plane of the array of $N \times N$ to be processed. This will not lower the utilization of the system resources. When $W>N$, if we produce an $N \times N$ mapping matrix, and still only N elements (e.g. one row, or one column) can be accessed in parallel, the resources of the system are no longer being fully utilized. Our goal here is to access $U \times N$ $(=W)$ elements of matrix X simultaneously in one memory cycle. We can see that both scheme EE and scheme MG naturally satisfy this requirement.

With scheme EE or scheme MG, it is easy to deal with the case of $W>N$ One can simply use a part of the mapping matrix of $W \times W$ (for example, the most convenient is the top left part of $N \times N$) to be the mapping matrix of $N \times N$. This implies that for different sized matrices we need only a single mapping matrix of $W \times W$ on a system of size W, thus only a single mechanism for address generation is needed, which is independent of the size of the matrix to be processed. All the characteristics listed in the previous sections are retained except the scattered blocks, because we do not have $P \times Q = W$ points scattered over a $W \times W$ plane on the $N \times N$ plane if $W>N$. Other $P \times Q$ (here $P \times Q = W$) subarrays can be accessed simultaneously in one memory cycle.

Let's consider the top left part (16×16) of a 64×64 mapping matrix of scheme EE for example. Suppose a 16×16 array is to be processed on a system with 64 PEs and memory modules. When this part is to be the mapping matrix of 16×16, any four rows (64 elements) can be accessed simultaneously in one memory cycle, also any four main blocks or shifted blocks can be accessed in one memory cycle, etc. One may also check to see that the benefit can also be obtained if the top left part of Figure 10.7 (the scheme of EE-MG) is used as the mapping matrix of a 8×8 matrix.

Note that this feature is not generally true with other skewing schemes. In general, for the schemes which do not satisfy the above feature, one may partition the memory modules (also the processors) into groups, and use some skewing schemes hierarchically: generate the group number, then generate the memory module number in the group. The following condition must hold: if the group numbers for any two elements are the same, their memory module numbers in the group must be different so that memory conflicts are avoided. This can be done by using some skewing scheme recursively, but then different sized matrices require different connections of the n bits of i and i', as well as j and j', in the address generation mechanism.

10.4 Conclusion and Discussion

Parallel memory systems are used in parallel and supercomputer systems in order to provide high memory bandwidth. Matrix manipulation operations are used intensively in parallel image processing, pattern recognition, raster-graphics, as well as scientific and engineering computations, where some data patterns need to be accessed simultaneously. Because of regularity of the frequently used data patterns, simultaneous access to data elements of a data template often causes memory conflicts. Memory conflicts result in degradation of effective memory bandwidth. Parallel storage schemes are needed in order to allow data elements to be accessed simultaneously without memory conflict. Key issues in parallel storage scheme design include functionality of the scheme, simplicity for implementation of memory module computation and local address computation, and simplicity for implementation of the data alignment requirements. While we have discussed the first two issues in this chapter, the third issue will be discussed in Chapter 14. It is possible to combine several desired scheme into one parallel memory system in practice, we also discussed an adaptive parallel storage system which combines some parallel schemes and with powerful functionality and appropriate complexity.

Data access patterns can be described by *d*-ordered *p*-vectors in linear schemes and can be characterized by *n* vectors in the generation matrices in XOR schemes. We introduced such descriptions in the definitions of the data access patterns and in the proofs of the features of parallel memory schemes. We introduced some XOR schemes, named EE scheme, and MG scheme. The introduced schemes have merits that they can cover most frequently used data access patterns in application algorithms in image processing and pattern recognition, signal processing, and scientific and engineering computations. It is simple to implement the EE and MG schemes -- only constant levels of XOR gates are needed to implement memory modules number computation. Also, we discussed the feasibility of combining EE and MG schemes into one parallel memory system.

Parallel memory schemes have been investigated extensively by researchers. Budnik and Kuck [1] develop a skewing scheme where a prime number of memory modules are used. Their scheme allows parallel access to rows, columns, diagonals, backward diagonals, and square blocks. Theoretical foundation is estiblished for linear skewing systems in [1] and [2]. Lawrie and Vora present a design of memory systems based on the use of a prime number of memory modules in [4]. Lawrie presents a scheme in [2] where rows, columns, diagonals, backward diagonals, and square blocks can be accessed in parallel. In this scheme, for an $N \times N$ matrix, $2N$ memory modules are needed, and N must be an even power of two. It is easier to implement the data alignment requirements than a system using a prime number of memory modules. Extensive theoretical results for linear and periodical skewing systems are presented in [12] and [3]. Voorhis and Morrin focus their attention on skewing schemes particularly for image processing in [5]. The schemes allow simultaneous access to not only squares blocks, but also $1 \times PQ$, $PQ \times 1$ and $P \times Q$ subarrays, where P and Q are given as design parameters. The system allows access to some combinations of $1 \times PQ$, $PQ \times 1$

and $P\times Q$ subarrays when PQ memory modules are used, and all these subarrays can be accessed simultaneously when the number of memory modules is larger than PQ. Their schemes are flexible in that the accessible elements can be of different shapes provided that the parameters P and Q are given before designing the system. Park gives an efficient design for simultaneous access to $1\times PQ$, $PQ\times 1$ and $P\times Q$ subarrays in [13]. Only $PQ+1$ memory modules are used in the system. Some theoretical results for conflict-free access to rectangular blocks are given in [14]. Gao proposed the parallel memory scheme based on the Chinese Remainder Theorem in [15], and its implementation issue is discussed in [16].

XOR memory systems are an important class of parallel memory systems. XOR schemes have the merits over linear schemes in its simplicity of address computation (memory module number generation) and its simplicity of data alignment requirement implementation.

The memory system in STARAN used a scheme to store a matrix, where the element on the ith row and jth column is stored in memory module $i \oplus j$ [4]. This can be seen as an XOR scheme used for parallel memory system design, where both matrix A and B in Equation (10-8) are taken as the identical matrix. Frailong et al present a general description for XOR-schemes, and given the name for this important class, in [10]. Also an XOR scheme is constructed in [15], where rows, columns, various blocks, and chess boards can be accessed in parallel. Balakrishnan et al. present a skewing scheme in [17], and Lee proposes a scheme in [18]. Lee proposes a scheme in [6], where rows, columns, square blocks, and points at the same positions in different blocks can be simultaneously accessed. Lee and Aboelaze present a scheme in [19]. Kim and Kumar propose a scheme where rows, columns, diagonals, square blocks, and points at the same position in different blocks can be simultaneously accessed [7]. Raghavendra and Boppana [20] present a general description method (bit linear permutation, *blip*) for skewing schemes. The blip schemes can be viewed as special cases of the XOR Schemes with matrix A being the identity matrix. They extended their blip schemes to *Clip* schemes for the description of skewing schemes for arbitrary sized systems [21]. They construct a special blip (clip) scheme Γ_n , where rows, columns, diagonals, and square blocks can be accessed simultaneously. Norton and Melton propose skewing scheme for access to strides based on linear transformation [22]. Schemes which can be applied to a system of size N, where N is any power of two, and rows, columns, diagonals, squares, and some rectangles can be accessed simultaneously are developed in [9, 23-25]. A scheme is developed in [26] where patterns with strides of complete powers of two can be access in parallel in addition to various blocks. Harper III and Linebarger propose a skewing scheme for strides in vector access based on row rotation and a pipelined architecture

[27]. Harper III also propose skewing schemes for strides, blocks, and FFT accesses based on linear transformation, and propose dynamic use of the skewing schemes [28, 29]. Automatic generation of skewing schemes in connection with network implementation of the permutations required for data alignment is discussed in [30, 31].

References

[1] P. Budnik and D.J. Kuck, The Organization and Use of Parallel Memories, *IEEE Trans. on Computers*, C-20(10):1566-1569, Dec.1971.

[2] D.K. Lawrie, Access and Alignment of Data in Array Processors, *IEEE Trans. on Computers*, C-24(10):1145-1155, Dec.1975.

[3] Harry A.G. Wijshoff, *Data Organization in Parallel Computers,* Kluwer Academic Publishers, Boston, 1989.

[4] D.H. Lawrie and C.R. Vora, The Prime Memory System for Array Access, *IEEE Trans. on Computers*, C-31(5):435-442, May 1982.

[5] D.V. Voorhis and T.H. Morrin, Memory Systems for Image Processing, *IEEE Trans. on Computers*, C-27(2):113-105. February 1978.

[6] D. Lee, *A Multiple-processor Architecture for Image Processing*, Ph.D Thesis, Department of Computing Science, University of Alberta, Edmonton, Alberta, Canada, 1987.

[7] K. Kim and V.K.P. Kumar, Parallel Memory Systems for Image Processing, *Proc. of the 1989 Conference on Computer vision and Pattern Recognition (CVPR'89)*:654–659, 1989

[8] X. Li, Parallel Algorithms for Hierarchical Clustering and Cluster Validity, *IEEE Trans. Pattern Aanl. and Mach. Intell.* 10(11):1088-1092, Nov. 1990.

[9] Z. Liu, X. Li, and J. You, On Storage Schemes for Parallel Array Access, *Proc. of the 1992 ACM International Conference on Supercomputing*, 282-291, 1992.

[10] J.M. Frailong and W. Jalby and J. Lenfant, XOR-Schemes: A Flexible Data Organization in Parallel Memories, *Proc. of the 1985 International Conference on Parallel Processing,* 276 – 283, Aug. 1985.

[11] K. Batcher, The Multidimentional Access Memory in STARAN. *IEEE Transactions on Computers*, C-26(2):174-177, February 1977.

[12] H.D. Shapiro, Theoretical Limitations on the Efficient Use of Parallel

Memories, *IEEE Trans. on Computers*, C-27(5):421-428, May 1978.

[13] J.W. Park, A Efficient Memory System for Image Processing, *IEEE Trans. on Computers*, C-35(7):669-674. July 1986.

[14] C.J. Colbourn and K. Heinrich, Conflict –free Access to Parallel Memories, *Journal of Parallel and Distributed Computing*, 14(2): 193-200, February, 1992.

[15] Q. Gao, The Chinese Remainder Theorem and the Prime Memory System, in *Proceedings of the 20th International Symposium on Computer Architecture, San Diego, USA*: 337-340. 1993.

[16] Q. Gao and Z. Liu, A Prime number Memory System Based on Chinese Remainder Theorem, *Computer Research and Development*, 32(5):1-7, (in Chinese) 1994.

[17] M. Balakrishnan and R. Jain and C.S. Raghavendra, On Array Storage For Conflict-free Memory Access For Parallel Processors, *Proc. of the 1988 International Conference on Parallel Processing*, I:103-107, Aug.1988.

[18] D. Lee, On Access and Alignment of Data in a Parallel Processor, *Information Processing Letters*, 33(1):11-14, Oct.1989.

[19] D. Lee and M. Aboelaze, An Efficient Method for Distributing Data in Hypercube Computers, *Proc. of the 5th Distributed Memory Conference*: 858-866. April 1990.

[20] C.S. Raghavendra and R. Boppana, On Methods for Fast and Efficient Parallel Memory Access, *Proc. of the 1990 International Conference on Parallel Processing,* 76–83, Aug. 1990.

[21] R. Boppana and C.S. Raghavendra, Efficient Storage Schemes for Arbitrary Square Matrices in Parallel Processors with Shuffle-Exchange Networks, *In Proceedings of the 1991 International Conference on Parallel Processing,* I:365-368, Aug. 1991.

[22] A. Norton and E. Melton, A Class of Boolean Linear Transformations for Conflict-free Power-of-Two Stride Access, *Proc. of the International Conference on Parallel Processing,* 247-254. Aug. 1987.

[23] Z. Liu and X. Li, *Routing Linear Complement Permutations on Synchronous Hypercubes*, Technical Report 92-01, Department of Computing Science, University of Alberta, Edmonton, Alberta, Canada, T6G 2H1, 1992.

[24] Z. Liu, X. Li, and J. You, An Adaptive Memory System for Image Processing, *Proc. of the Vision Interface'92*, 1992.

[25] Z. Liu and X. Li, XOR Storage Schemes for Frequently Used Data Patterns, *Journal of Parallel and Distributed Computing*, 25:162-173. 1995.

[26] E. Li and Z. Liu, LR: An Efficient Parallel Storage Scheme, *Science in China (Series E)*, 28(2):1-7 (in Chinese) , February 1998.

[27] D. Harper III, Address Transformation to Increase Memory Performance, *Proc. of 1989 International Conference on Parallel Processing*, 237-241, Aug. 1989.

[28] D. Harper III and D. Linebarger, A Dynamic Storage Scheme for Conflict-free Vector Access, *Proc. of the 16th International Symposium on Computer Architecture*, 72-77, 1989.

[29] D. Harper III, Block, Multistride Vector, and FFT Accesses in Parallel Memory Systems, *IEEE Trans. on Parallel and Distributed Systems*, 2(1):43-51, January 1991.

[30] M.A. Al-Mouhamed and S.S. Seiden, A Heuristic Storage for Minimizing Access Time of Arbitrary Data Patterns, *IEEE Transactions on Distributed Systems*, 8(4): 441-447, 1997.

[31] M.A. Al-Mouhamed and S.S. Seiden, Minimization of Memory and Network Contention for Accessing Arbitrary Data Patterns in SIMD systems, *IEEE Transactions on Computers*, 45(6):757-762, 1996.

[32] R. Boppana and C.S. Raghavendra, On Self Routing in Benes and Shuffle-Exchange Networks, *Proc. of the 1988 International Conference on Parallel Processing*, I:196-200, Aug.1988.

[33] R. Boppana and C.S. Raghavendra, Optimal Self-Routing of Linear-Complement Permutations in Hypercubes, *Proc. of the 5th Distributed Memory Computing Conference*,800-808, April, 1990.

[34] B. Chor, C.E. Leiserson, and R.L. Revist, An Application of Number Theory to the Organization of Raster-Graphics Memory. In *Proc. of the 23rd Annual Symposiem on Foundation of Computer Science*, 92-99, 1982 .

[35] Q. Gao and Z. Liu, A Class of Skewing Schemes for Conflict-free Memory Accesses, *Science in China (Series A)*, 24(10):1099-1107 (in Chinese), Oct. 1994.

[36] R. Gonzalez and P. Wintz, *Digital Image Processing*, Addison-Wesley, Reading, MA, 1987.

[37] Z. Liu, J. You, and X. Li, A Parallel Storage Scheme and Its Implementation Issues, *Proc. of the 6th International Parallel*

Processing Symposium, 550-557, March 1992.

[38] Z. Liu and J. You, An Implementation of a Non-linear Skewing Scheme, *Information Processing Letters*, 42(4):209-215, June 1992.

[39] A. Sengupta and K. Zemoudeh, Self-Routing Algorithms for Strongly Regular Multistage Interconnection Networks, *Journal of Parallel and Distributed Computing*, 14(2):187-192, February 1992.

[40] K. Zemoudeh and A. Sengupta, Routing Frequently Used Bijections on Hypercube, *Proc. of the 5th Distributed Memory Computing Conference*, 824-832, April 1990.

Chapter 11

DATA MANAGEMENT FOR SEQUENTIAL COMPUTER SYSTEMS

As the advances in hardware technology, the gap between fast CPU and the slow memory system is increased severely also in sequential computer systems. Hierarchical memory systems are used in sequential computers to bridge the gap. Cache is a widely used mechanism in the memory hierarchy. But it has been found that cache performance is not satisfying for many important application algorithms since its hit ratio is very low for many frequently data access patterns due to conflict use of the cache lines. This problem shares some similarity with the problem of memory module access conflict in parallel memory systems discussed in Chapter 10. In addition, some special issue (data reuse rate) need to be considerate in cache systems. We will discuss the cache line conflict problem and some techniques to solve it in this chapter.

11.1 Introduction

The computation power of microprocessors has increased dramatically, but the increase in processor speed has not been accompanied by a similar increase in memory speed [13, 21]. While the single microprocessor has obtained more than 100-fold speed-up since 1980, the access times of DRAMs have decreased only by a factor of 3. Presently a single CPU can process several hundred million operations per second, even billion operations per second, the access time of DRAM is still several tens nanoseconds. The speed gap between CPU and main memory increases by 40 percent per year. As a result, CPU could spend half of its time waiting for data from memory [14]. To "feed" the fast central processor, hierarchical memory structures are used. As the top level of the memory hierarchy, cache plays a critical role in system speedup [12, 21]. First level cache has been used in microprocessor on the same chip with CPU, and second level cache has usually been used even in PC systems. Nowadays, a big percentage of chip area is used for on-chip cache (first level cache) of size (e.g 64KB). The off-chip cache (level 2 cache) of size 256KB to 4MB is 5 to 10 times faster than the main memory. For example, in MIPS R8000, the data cache (capacity 1 - 4MB) access speed is 2×64 bits/cycle, while the main memory speed is only 128 bytes/53 cycles [23]. Generally speaking, each DRAM access takes 20-30 ns, which accessing SRAM takes only 5-6 ns.

A conceptual structure of cache is pictured in Figure 11.1. Cache memory can be organized in fully associative, set associative, or direct mapped manner. In set associative cache, the cache memory consists of several banks. We only pictured one bank in Figure 11.1. Cache memory consists of a number of cache lines or sets. Usually the number of cache lines is a complete power of two. Each cache line is further divided into a number of bytes. In traditional design, the cache line is numbered using a segment of the address register as shown in the figure. This indicates the fixed mapping between the main memory address and the cache line number. Programmer cannot directly control in which line a data element will be stored because of the fixed mapping. We only pictured the data path for reading data from cache. Also, we omitted some fields for cache management such as the field for validity of a line and the field for dirty line recording.

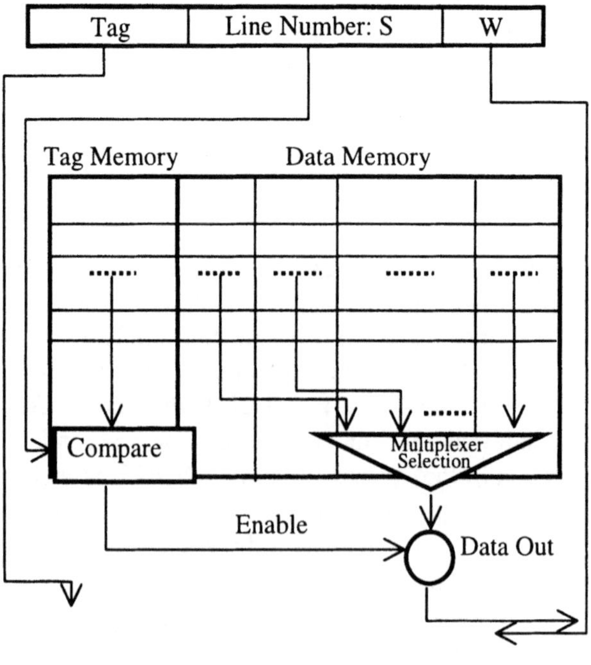

Figure 11.1. Cache structure

When the data element that is to be accessed is not in the cache memory, a cache miss occurs, otherwise the access has a cache hit. There are three kinds of cache misses. The first is compulsory miss. Compulsory miss is caused when the first time a data element in the main memory is accessed. The second is capacity miss, which is caused because the data elements need to be accessed during the program execution can not all be contained in cache memory due to the capacity of the cache memory. The third is conflict miss, which occurs in set associative or direct mapped cache because too many data elements needed in the execution of the program are mapped into one cache line. A data element of a data access pattern is accessed from main memory to the cache and used, then it remains in the cache. After that, another data element is required and accessed from main memory to the cache. The new data element may need to be put in the same cache line with the previously used data element. Thus a cache line conflict occurs, and the previously used data element is deleted from the cache. When the previously used data element needs to be reused later on, it has to be accessed from main memory again, this makes the cache ineffective.

The effectiveness of cache systems is based on the locality of the accessed data. Only when the data reuse rate is high and the reused data is physically located in the cache, the cache can have positive effect. Data locality depends mainly on application algorithms, precisely, on the data access patterns of the application algorithms. Unfortunately, many data access patterns cannot satisfy the locality requirement, although the data reuse rate can be logically very high.

Let us see an example. Suppose that a 16×16 matrix is stored in a row-major order in main memory, and the size of a direct mapped cache is 16. If a column of the matrix is to be accessed (in C language), all these 16 elements will fight for one cache line. To reduce the miss rate, one can increase the cache by 100% and make it 2-way associative. The miss rate is lower, but the cache efficiency is still 1/16. To completely avoid conflict misses in this case, one needs to make the cache 16 times larger, and increase the associativity to 16. This is of course not feasible since the theoretical analysis indicates that more than 4-way associativity has a low performance-cost ratio. This example demonstrates that merely increasing the cache size cannot efficiently reduce conflict misses. Cache efficiency is also an important consideration. Because the cache addressing is handled by hardware, and transparent to the programmer, to utilize cache capacity is especially challenging.

An application programmer should realize that not the entire cache is usable. Hardware architecture designers should also be aware of that merely increasing cache size and employing prefetch cannot completely solve the problem of conflict miss. We will analyze some image processing and pattern recognition algorithms and introduce some software as well as hardware techniques to reduce conflict misses.

11.2 Reuse Ratio Analysis

Data organization and memory access problems have been studied extensively for numerical analysis in scientific and engineering computations. Numerous methods have been proposed to solve the memory access bottleneck problems. On the other hand, it is well known that pattern recognition and image processing (PRIP) often require heavy computation and large matrices. As in numerical analysis, heavy computation and the memory access is a bottleneck in many useful PRIP algorithms. Besides increasing memory bandwidth, increasing cache hit ratio is also a critical issue. For example, the linear algebra algorithms with higher data reuse ratio can often have a higher cache hit ratio. Some PRIP algorithms, such as FFT, Jacobi method for eigen computation, also have a relatively high data reuse ratio. Some other algorithms, such as matrix-vector multiplication and Hough transforms, have a relatively low data reuse ratio, hence cannot achieve high cache efficiency easily. Some cache optimization methods can still be used though. We now study several PRIP algorithms from the following three aspects: computation complexity, main memory size requirement, and main memory access requirement. We examine the frequently used matrices and their data reuse ratio, and partition the PRIP algorithms into three classes according to their memory access feature, and list some example algorithms in each class.

We use ϕ_{comp} for the number of computation steps, ϕ_{size} for the size of the matrices, ϕ_{reuse} for the number of times the elements of a certain array will be accessed. When ϕ_{comp} is too large, the algorithm is mainly numerical computation carried in CPU and the memory access speed problem is not serious. Most PRIP algorithms do not belong to this category. When $\phi_{comp} \approx \phi_{size}$, i.e., each array element is fetched once and only involved in a couple of steps of computation, then cache would be of no use because of the low data reuse ratio. When ϕ_{reuse} is reasonably high, improving cache utilization will be helpful.

To simplify further discussion, the following variables and their ranges are given below. To maintain some of the physical meaning of the matrices, the variable names used in this section are tied to PRIP terminology.

Table 11.1. Variables in PRIP

	Indices	Maximum Value
image	iR, iC	N=256, 512, ... 4096, or 240×300, 480×600
filter	ir, ic	n=3,5,7,9; (-1,0,1); (-3..3), n^2 <100
gray level	IG	G=256
features	IF	M∈{2,3, ···, 2^{14}}
patterns	IP	P∈{100, ···, 2^{15}}
clusters	K	N_c∈{ 4, 5, ···, 100}

Algorithms With Almost No Data Reuse

In some PRIP algorithms, the computation complexity is about the same as memory access complexity, therefore, the data reuse ratio is low and the cache may not be expected to provide a significant speedup. Because the sizes of many images are a power of 2, there could be a significant amount of conflict misses.

1) Histogram Creation

An example of this kind of algorithms is histogram creation. Generating the grayscale histogram is a common pre-processing procedure.

```
For(iG){
    histo(iG)=0;
}
for(iR){
    for (iC){
        iG=image(iR,iC);
        histo(iG)++;
    }
}
```

For this algorithm, ϕ_{comp} = N^2+G and ϕ_{size} =N^2+G. The order that the elements of matrix "image" being accessed is irrelevant, either by row or by column. There are many PRIP algorithms have the similar memory access pattern, such as thresholding and moment computations [9]. The order matrix element access should match the order in which they are stored in memory. The above pseudo code is for the row-major storage, such as in C. If Fortran is used, the loops should be exchanged. This is also true for the following algorithms. Similar analysis can also be applicable to the histogram equalization algorithm, which involves one scan of the array histo and one scan of the image. In this algorithm both ϕ_{comp} and ϕ_{size} also equal N^2+G.

2) Stochastic Relaxation as a Matrix Vector Multiplication

Suppose there are N_r regions in the image to be labeled and there are N_l possible labels, then the labeling of all regions can be represented by a long column vector $\vec{L}$ of size $N=N_rN_l$, and the constraint relation can be written as a square matrix C of size N×N, and the relaxation labeling process is a sequence of iterative multiplication of C and $\vec{L}$: $\vec{L}^{(t+1)} = C*\vec{L}^{(t)}$. Written in a pseudo code form, it is:

```
Repeat until stable{
    for (irow=1;irow<=N;irow++){
        tmp = 0;
        for (icol=1;icol<=N;icol++){
            tmp += C(irow, icol) * L_old(icol);
        }
        L_new(irow) = tmp;
    }
}
```

Here, $\phi_{comp} = 2N^2$ and $\phi_{size} = N^2$. This is a general numerical analysis problem of matrix-vector multiplication. Previous experiments of our group indicate that array padding and loop unrolling can speed up the general matrix-vector multiplication by 20 to 50 percent. Because of iterative nature of the relation computation, this technique can provide more significant improvement than a regular matrix-vector multiplication.

3) Hierarchical Clustering (Johnson's Algorithm)

In exploratory data analysis, hierarchical clustering algorithms are commonly used. After each merge of clusters, two rows and two columns of the proximity matrix prox should be modified [10]. The data access patterns of the algorithm are shown below.

```
For each level of the hierarchy{
    find a pair of clusters with minimum distance;
    for (iP1){
        prox(iP1,*);
    }
    for (iP2){
        prox(*,iP2);
    }
}
```

Both ϕ_{comp} and ϕ_{size} equal to P^2 . If the matrix is stored in the row-major order, the column access may cause cache conflict. The column-major storage will cause problem for row access. Therefore, cache address mapping or row/column padding can be used to improve cache utilization. Also important, the order in which the matrix elements are accessed should match the order in which they are stored in memory.

Algorithms With Data Reuse Ratio Independent of Matrix Size

This section discusses several PRIP algorithms in which the elements of a large matrix are reused and the reuse ratio does not depend on the size of that matrix.

1) Filtering

Filtering operation is the most frequently used operation in image processing. It is also called windowing, template matching, or convolution. Wavelet transform can be implemented as a filtering operation followed by sampling. Basic morphological operations, such as erosion and dilation, and the combined operations, such as opening, closing, hit-and-miss transform, can also be implemented as filtering. Different applications of filtering employ different windows and different arithmetic or logic computations, but the memory access patterns are essentially the same. Parallel thinning algorithms useful for character recognition can also be implemented as iterative filtering. The following algorithm is the simplest template matching.

```
For (iR){
    for (iC){
        tmp = 0;
        for (ir){
            for (ic){
                tmp += filter(ir, ic) * image_in(iR+ir, iC+ic);
            }
        }
        image_out(iR, iC) = tmp;
    }
}
```

A simple complexity analysis gives the following results in Table11.2: Since the window is usually small, one can store it completely in cache and no conflict miss will occur. If the window is as small as 3x3 or 5x5, the window is written in the program code. When the window is large, FFT may be considered.

2) Partional Clustering

Partional clustering is frequently used in preliminary data analysis, and is often included in general statistical software packages. Usually, the number of pattern vectors involved is in the order of hundreds or thousands. In image compression, vector quantization can be viewed as a partional clustering. For example, for the case of 4×4 subimages, M=16, $P=2^{3+6+6}=2^{15}$, and the number of clusters N_c is between 64 and 256.

```
Repeat until stable{
    for (iP){
        min=BIG;
        for (k=1;k<= Nc;k++){
            r = 0;
            for (iF){
                r += (patt(iP,iF)-cent(k,iF))**2;
            }
            if (r<min){
                min=r;
                k1=k;
            }
        }
        label(iP)=k1;
    }
    for k{
        for (iF){
            cent(k,iF) = 0;
            number = 0;
            for (iP){
                if (label(iP)==k){
                    number++;
                    cent(k,iF) += patt(iP,iF);
                }
            }
            cent(k,iF) = cent(k,iF)/number;
        }
    }
```

The reuse ratio is shown in Table 11.2. Since the matrix cent is small and can fit in cache completely, and each row of matrix patt needs to be fetched only twice, this algorithm will be relatively efficient from cache performance point of view. The order of the loops in the second half of the algorithm is very important. Using loop k as the outermost one is conceptually simpler and could be the order used by straightforward PRIP programmers, but it will cause a great deal of cache misses.

Table 11.2. Reuse ratio for filtering & partitional clustering

ϕ_{comp}	ϕ_{size}	ϕ_{reuse}	Access Pattern
$2N^2n^2$	N^2+n^2 $\approx N^2$	Image_in n^2:10...100	subimage
$PN_c(3M+1)+PN_cM$ $\approx 4N_cPM$	$PM+N_cM$ $\approx PM$	(patt) N_c: 64...256	row

Algorithms With Data Reuse Ratio Dependent on Matrix Size

In pattern analysis, the computation of distances between pattern vectors is the foundation for many other algorithms, such as clustering, nearest neighbor classification, and feature selection. Many variations of nearest neighbor rule have been proposed to simplify the distance computation. Prototypes of training patterns and triangular inequality have been used. After all, we still need to compute distances between a number of training patterns and a number of testing patterns. Let use P_1 and P_2 for the number of training and testing patterns involved. Consider the case that $P_1, P_2 \in \{2^7, \cdots, 2^{10}\}$, and $2<M<2^6$ where M is the number of features. If we use P^2 to represent P_1P_2, $\phi_{comp} \approx 3P^2M$, $\phi_{size} \approx P^2+2PM$. The elements of matrix *train* are reused P_2 times. Similarly, matrix *test* will be reused P_1 times.

Nearest neighbor rule or any other classification rule can be used in feature selection. One way for selecting k features is to perform classification using individual features. Usually, $2<k<2^4$. In this case, the data reuse ratio would be k times higher.

The generation of a covariance matrix [7] has a relatively high data reuse rate P which is the number of vector samples.

Consider a population of random vectors of the form $\vec{x} = \begin{bmatrix} x_1 \\ x_2 \\ \vdots \\ x_M \end{bmatrix}$. The mean vector of this population is $\overrightarrow{m_x} = E\{\vec{x}\}$. The covariance matrix of this vector population is defined as $C = E\{(\vec{x} - \vec{m}_x)(\vec{x} - \vec{m}_x)^t\}$. For P vector samples, C can be approximated by

$$C = \frac{1}{P}k = \sum_{k=1}^{P} \overrightarrow{x_k}\overrightarrow{x_k^t} - \overrightarrow{m_x}\overrightarrow{m_x^t} \quad . \tag{11-1}$$

If we only consider the vector multiplication part, the algorithm can be given as below.

```
Initialize cov;
for (iP=1;iP<= P;iP++){
        for (iF1=1;iF1<=M-1;iF1++){
              for (iF2=iF1+1;iF2<=M;iF2++){
                    r = patt(iP, iF1) * patt(iP, iF2);
                    cov(iF1, iF2) += r;
                    cov(iF2, iF1) += r;
              }
        }
}
```

ϕ_{reuse} is P for the above computation. Following the covariance matrix generation, eigen vectors can be calculated. The Jacobi algorithm is commonly used. The cache optimization for Jacobi algorithm will be given later on.

There are a number of PRIP algorithms using a similar tree structure, such as consistent labeling procedures and model-based matching algorithms [9], have the similar situation, that is, the data reuse ratio depends on the matrix size, but the major matrix is small enough to fit in cache entirely. Address mapping or row/column padding may be used to avoid conflicts, but "blocking" is not necessary.

11.3 Performance Improvement from Cache Optimization

This section suggests some simple software method to improve some PRIP algorithms from the memory access point of view. We use more general variables and array names here, such as A, B, C, i, j, and k.

Covariance Matrix Generation

Consider a case of computing covariance matrix of several thousand face images. The input is a set of $N=2^{12}$ small square matrices, each of size $2^7 \times 2^7$. These images together form, conceptually, a pattern matrix A of $N \times M$ where $M=2^{14}$. The output of the algorithm is a covariance matrix C of $M \times M$. From matrix C, eigenfaces can be computed. In face recognition, millions of new faces are processed, and new face images can be used to accumulatively update the eigenface basis using the same procedures. Each element of A occupies a byte, and an element of C occupies a word (4 bytes). Neither A nor C can fit in cache entirely, considering a cache of size 512 KB, which is 2^{19} bytes or 2^{17} words.

If we divide matrix A into M/m blocks of size N×m, assuming M is a multiple of m for simplicity here, each A element will be accessed M/m times. The total number of cache hits is approximately $h = (2Nm)(2m) + 4m^2N = 8Nm^2$, which is maximized when m takes the largest possible value, with the constraint of $2Nm + 4m^2 *4 < 2^{19}$. That is, $2^{13}m+2^4m^2 < 2^{19}$, $m^2+2^9m < 2^{15}$, i.e., m=32. Assuming that 128 consecutive bytes are fetched from the main memory together (2^7 elements of A and 2^5 elements of C), 2^{28} memory visits are needed instead of 2^{35}, resulting in a 100-fold improvement.

Jacobi Algorithm

A preliminary investigation of cache optimization for Jacobi algorithm is given in [4]. The main part of Jacobi algorithm is as follows [4]:

```
I. Initialization;
II. For k = 1,2,... until converge do
   for (p=0; p<n-1;p++)
     for (q=p+1;q<n;q++) {
       if (fabs(A[p][q]) > thresh){
        1) compute the rotation angle;
        2) rotate upper triangular part of p & q-th row and columns of array A:
           No. 1. for (j=0; j<p;j++)
                  ROTATE(A,j,p,j,q);
           No. 2. for (j=p+1;j<q;j++)
                  ROTATE(A,p,j,j,q);
           No. 3. for (j=q+1;j<n;j++)
                  ROTATE(A,p,j,q,j);
        3) rotate p & q-th columns of eigenvector array Vec:
           No. 4. for (j=0;j<n;j++)
                  ROTATE(Vec,j,p,j,q);
     }
   }
III. Compute the eigenvalues and output the results.
```

Here, ROTATE(a,i,j,k,l) is defined as: # define ROTATE(a,i,j,k,l):

```
g=a[i][j];
h=a[k][l];
a[i][j]=g-s*(h+g*tau);
a[k][l]=h+s*(g-h*tau).
```

where s and tau are two scalars related to the rotation angle.

There are high cache conflict rates in steps No.1, No.2 and No.4. We apply "soft cache" technique [4, 13]: copying uncontinuous data elements into small continuous memory locations which can be repeatedly used in the computation. The p-th column of A is copied into a 1-d array SCA[*], and the p-th column of Vec is copied into another 1-d array SCV[*]. Thus, the rotations are done on SCA[*] in step No. 1, and on SCV[*] in step No. 4. After the rotations, SCA and SCV should be copied back to suitable places of matrix A or Vec.

We tested it on a Pentium 133M PC with an 8 KB level-1 cache and line length of 32B. Two dense matrices (Arrays 1 and 2) and a tridiagonal matrix (Array 3) are used for each matrix size n.Tables 1, 2 and 3 give the speedup ($S_p=T_1/T_2$) results where T_1 is the time of the original Jacobi method, and T_2 is the time using "soft cache" technique.

Table 11.3. Speed-up for Jacobi method ($n = 2^m$)

n	64	128	256	512
Array 1	1.275	1.3935	1.5044	1.468
Array 2	1.273	1.3362	1.5011	1.2966
Array 3	1.3333	1.3915	1.5098	1.4705

Table 11.4. Speed-up for Jacobi method ($n \neq 2^m$)

n	80	100	200	400
Array 1	1.2635	1.2835	1.294	1.3066
Array 2	1.2652	1.2865	1.2908	1.2128
Array 3	1.2857	1.2867	1.2940	1.3102

Table 11.5. Speed-up for Jacobi method (n is a prime number)

n	53	89	179	427
Array 1	1.1205	1.2425	1.2915	1.2774
Array 2	1.1429	1.2469	1.2867	1.1925
Array 3	1.125	1.2662	1.2939	1.2791

The improvements for the above three cases are 27% - 50%, 21% - 31%, and 12% - 29%. This example shows that a very simple program transformation can have significant effect on its performance.

Hough Transform

Parameter space computation is heavily involved in PRIP algorithms. For example, Hough transform is commonly used in detecting object with a known (possibly analytically) shape, such as a straight line, a circle, or a parabola. In real implementations, the Hough space is usually built on top of the input image. One can define the Hough space of a circle to be three dimensional, in which x and y correspond to the image pixel locations, and r corresponds to the circle radius. In other words, the Hough space is many images "overlay" on each other. We consider a Hough transform for detecting circles $(x-i)^2+(y-j)^2 = r^2$. We only discuss the "standard Hough transform" , but the principle can be easily applied to other versions of Hough transform (randomized, adaptive, etc). We use a 2-D matrix *edge* for the co-ordinates of edge points. Element edge[0][k]} and edge[1][k]} give the x and y co-ordinates of the k-th edge point in the image. Each *imageln* element can be either an edge or not an edge. If we deal with r in the same way as x and y, a 3-D *hough* matrix is used, and the kernel of general Hough transform is:

```
for (k=0; k<n; k++) {
    x = edge[0][k];
    y = edge[1][k];
    for (i=0; i<width; i++) {
        for (r=rmin; r<rmax; r++) {
            t=sqrt(r*r-(x-i)*(x-i));
            j1 = y-t; j2 = y+t;
            if (j1>0 && j1<height)
                hough[i,j1,r]++;
            if (j2>0 && j2<height)
                hough[i,j2,r]++;
        }
    }
}
```

The declaration of this matrix (as hough[width][height][r]) or as hough[height][width][r] is critical and should receive more attention. One can either make i-loop the outer loop (called "choice 1"), or make the j-loop ($0 \leq j<height$) the outer loop, and for every r, compute corresponding i (called choice 2).

An experiment is conducted on a MIPS R4,000 (150 Mhz) based computer. The main architecture features of the computer are:

- main memory size: 384 Mbytes, 2-way interleaved
- Instruction cache size: 16 Kbytes
- Data cache size: 16 Kbytes
- Secondary unified instruction/data cache size: 1 Mbyte

The codes were written in C language (Version IRIX C 7.2.1), and the operation system is IRIX 6.5.

When width≈height, choice 1 and choice 2 has little difference in performance. The larger the difference between width and hight, the larger the difference between the performance of the above two choices. When width is between 120 and 480, height is around 1000, the ratio of the computation time ranges from 1.39 to 1.06.

If r only takes a few possible values, one can define the *hough* array as 2-D and eliminate the "for (r=..)" line above.

We applied "loop unrolling" and the test results are given in Table 4. In the table, Time1 is the running time of the original algorithm (in 1.0e-2 * second). Time2 is the running time of the program with loop unrolling (in 1.0e-2 * second).

Table 11.6. Results for the cases where *hough* is 2-D

Width	Height	R	Time 1	Time 2	Time 1/Time 2
500	500	100	6.55	5.59	1.17
1000	1000	100	13.93	11.85	1.18
1000	2000	100	22.79	20.61	1.15
1000	4000	100	33.73	31.66	1.07
2000	1000	100	23.42	19.04	1.23
4000	1000	100	42.27	33.28	1.27
4000	3000	100	93.76	84.86	1.15

The general improvement is between 7% and 27%.

11.4 XOR Cache Mapping

Since the mapping from main memory address to the cache line number is traditionally by using a segment of the main memory address, accesses to the data elements in many frequently used data patterns cause cache line conflicts. One of a promising way to solve this problem is to scramble the data in the cache. This can be done in hardware using some mechanism to change the mapping. The most important consideration is the simplicity of mechanism since it needs to be implemented in hardware. Also we need to consider the functionality of the mapping such that cache miss ratio will be decreased significantly for as many as possible frequently used regular data patterns. We introduce a technique to improve cache performance which distributes the data elements of data structure (arrays and matrices) in some certain scrambled way such that cache hit ratio is largely increased and the computation of the system is sped up. The proposed scheme has been implemented. Experimental results show that 30 to 60 percent speed up can be obtained using the proposed technique (even with partial implementation on the second level cache). The proposed cache mapping technique with its implementation and the experimental results are introduced in this section.

EE and LR Functions for Data Caches

Since a basic consideration is the simplicity of hardware implementation of the new mapping function, XOR mapping is a feasible candidate for the mapping function. Our idea is to use some XOR functions to map the main memory address into cache line number such that the mapping for the frequently used data patterns will be as evenly as possible. Also, the mapping should not have negative effect on those data patterns that are already distributed evenly using traditional mapping.

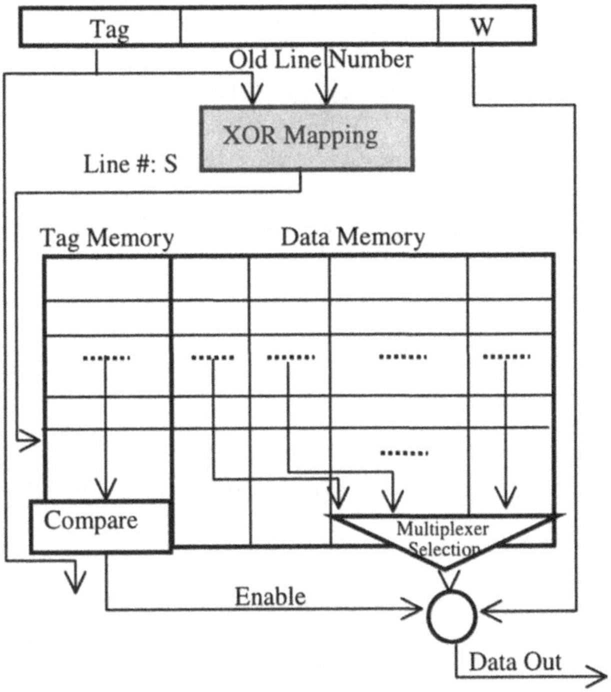

Figure 11.2. Cache structure with XOR mapping

Suppose that a cache consists of $N = 2^n$ cache lines, a cache line consists of 2^w bytes, and that the size of the main memory is $M = 2^m$ bytes. The address of a data element is A. Then the cache line number where the data element will be stored is expressed by the n bits (from bit w to bit $w+n-1$) of address A in traditional design. In the XOR mapping, a cache line number is generated by using a bitwise Exclusive-OR of the traditional cache line number field (or a part of it) and the tag field (or a part of it) of main memory address A. The structure of a cache using XOR functions for cache address mapping is expressed in Figure 11.2.

EE scheme is the most simple one in its hardware implementation. It needs only one stage of XOR gates to implement. Also, it is powerful in that it can cover most of the frequently used data patterns as we have seen in Chapter 12. The following feature of EE especially useful for a cache with associativity of two, and important for blocked matrix manipulation and image processing.

Theorem 11.1 For a set associative cache with associativity equal to or greater than two, EE scheme can guarantee that N elements of a square or rectangular blocks located at any position of an N×N matrix can be stored in the N cache lines simultaneously without conflict.

Proof: This is true because of Corollary 10.1. ■

Although EE scheme can cover most frequently used data patterns, it can not cover the access of strides of complete powers of 2, which is an important access pattern frequently used in signal processing (e.g. in FFT computation). An XOR scheme named LR is designed for parallel memory system in [16]. In addition to covering most frequently used data patterns LR can also cover access of strides of complete powers of 2. LR scheme can be described as follows. In Equation (10-8), an identical matrix E is also used for matrix B, but another matrix H is used for matrix A, where H is expressed by Equation (11-2):

$$h_{i,j} = \begin{cases} 1, & \text{when} \quad (j = n-1-i) or ((j = i) and (\lceil n/2 \rceil \le i \le n-1)), \\ 0, & \text{otherwise.} \end{cases} \tag{11-2}$$

Intuitively, H is a matrix where all the elements on its back diagonal and all the elements on the lower half part of its diagonal are 1s while other elements of H are 0s.

In addition to rows, columns, square or rectangular blocks, and scattered blocks of N elements, LR scheme can also cover vectors of strides of any complete power of 2.

Theorem 11.2 Vectors of N elements with strides of any complete power of two can be stored in an LR mapped cache without conflict.

One may refer to [16, 21] for the proof of the above features. Also, LR is simple to implement in that it needs at most two levels of XOR gates which is obvious from Equation (11-2).

An Experimental PC System Using EE Mapping -- The PEACE Machine

In order to observe the effect on cache hit ratio of using EE mapping, simulations were carried out for cache systems [6, 15]. Results show that cache hit ratio can be significantly increased for various algorithms frequently used in real applications, and that it does not have negative effect for the applications where cache hit ratio has been good when traditional cache mapping method is used. In order to observe real speed up measured by the execution time of application programs, experimental computer system is designed and implemented. The experimental system is a Pentium PC, called PEACE. EE mapping is implemented by using PAL chips for the mapping of second level cache in the PEACE machine. The first level cache is usually implemented on the same chip with CPU (on chip cache). Thus it is difficult for our group to change its mapping circuit in the chip. Thanks to the simplicity of the EE scheme, it can be implemented in the second level cache system. In an "ideal" design, EE function may be designed in the bus interface for the second level cache (82437FX family controller). But it is still difficult for our group since we can change nothing in the chip of 82437FX. Thus separate PAL chips are used to implement the EE function for second level cache. Structure of the PEACE machine is shown in Figure 11.3.

Some considerations for the design of PEACE are introduced briefly. 82437FX controller is connected to the Pentium processor bus, it is also connected the Pentium processor to the PCI bus so that the Pentium processor can access all the resources on PCI. In addition to control logic for the L2 cache in 82437FX, there are also main memory interface, PCI interface, and other functional circuits in 82437FX. If additional logic is added outside 82437FX for address mapping, we have to guarantee correct access to the main memory and other devices connected to the PCI and ISA buses in the system. Also, some times 82437FX needs to send address signals to the Pentium processor. Thus logic is needed to realize the inverse of EE function. It is easy to see that the inverse of EE is also simple in that only one stage of XOR gates is needed.

The chip 82437FX not only is used to control the second level cache but also is used for the management of the main memory. In the system, some pins of the bus have different functions in different cycles --- for rows or columns addresses of the main memory. Furthermore, the system is a virtual memory system, and we have to guarantee correct functioning of the paging system. Addition of the EE (and inverse EE also, as explained above) logic must not violate the pre-decided features of the virtual memory management system. Thus EE function (and its inverse) can only realized partially on some bits of address for L2 cache.

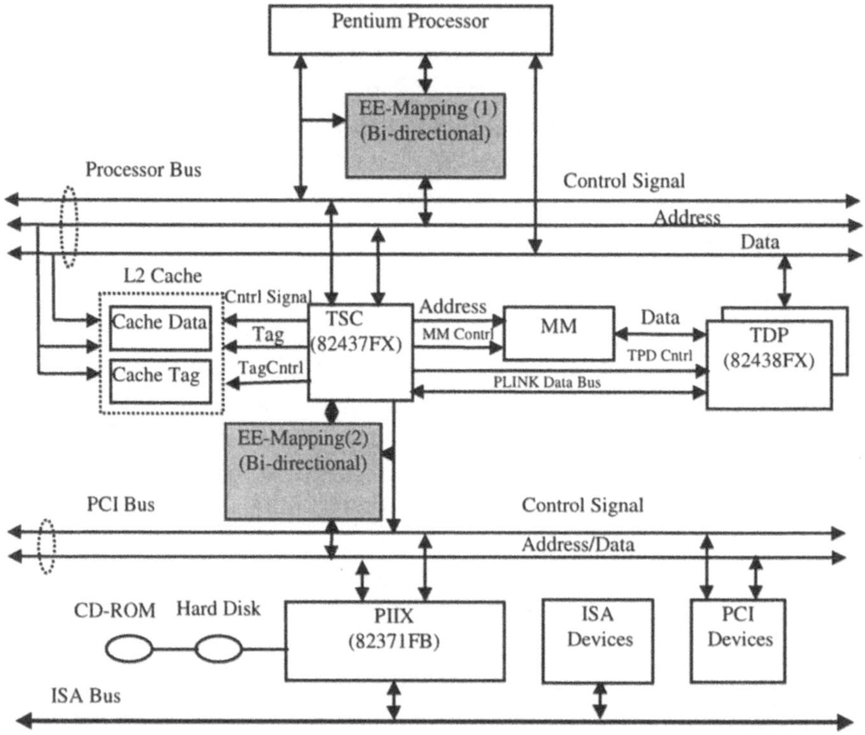

Figure 11.3. A pentium system with EE mapping for L2 cache

In the system, the page size is 4k bytes, and the pins SA[11~0] are for the address within a page. The size of the main memory is 32M bytes. SA[23~18] and SA[11~6] are used as inputs of the EE function to generate RA[11~6] as the output. Although EE mapping is only partially applied to the L2 cache, experimental results show a significant speed-up.

Logic circuits are designed for the devices connected to the ISA bus with considerations similar to the above. Also, the PEACE machine is designed mainly to test the effectiveness of XOR mapping for the second level cache. We want to compare the execution times of the programs executed on a machine with EE address mapping for the L2 cache and the times executed on the same hardware and software environments except that EE mapping is not used. Thus control logic is used to enable or disable EE functioning.

Experimental Results

Experiments were carried out to test speed-up of the PEACE machine. Each program was executed on the machine when EE mapping was used and when EE mapping was not used on L2 cache. Experimental programs include kernel algorithms frequently used in scientific and engineering computations, image processing and pattern recognition, and signal processing, as well as some general programs where data access pattern is random (irregular or stochastic "patterns"). Results show that 30 to 60 percent speed-ups can be obtained for the algorithms with regular data access patterns even with a partial implementation on L2 cache. Applying EE mapping does not have negative effect for programs with irregular data accesses or regular accesses where cache hit ratio is already high with traditional mapping.

(1) Matrix Product

Matrix product computation is used widely in scientific and engineering computations. Frequently used algorithms for matrix product include "inner product method", "mid product method", and "outer product method". Also, "block method" is widely used for its high data reuse ratio. Because data access patterns are different in the above methods, the cached data reuse ratio is different. Thus the real execution times of the above methods are different. Experiments were carried out for the above methods using EE mapping and without EE mapping. Results are shown in Table 11.7. 30~60 percent speed-up has been obtained.

(2) Matrix inversion

Matrix inversion is also frequently used in scientific and engineering computations. The kernel of the algorithm is a repeatedly executed two level loops, such as

```
for (k=0; k<m; k++)
    ...
    for (i=0; i<m; i++)
        for(j=0; j<m; j++)
            a[i][j]=pr[i]*pc[j].
```

The order of the loop variants has effect on the execution speed. When EE mapping is used, the execution speed can be increased by 46 percent. The results are show in Table 11.8.

Solving Liner Systems of Equations with LU Decomposition. The kernel is a repeatedly executed two level loop. 30 percent speed up can be obtained using EE mapping. Results are shown in Table 11.9.

(3) Eigen Computation with Jacobi Method
Around 40 percent speed up has been obtained on PEACE machine with using EE mapping. Results are shown in Table 11.10.

(4) Partial Differential Equations
Standard five-point format on a square area was used. Traditional method is SOR algorithm. Red-black is a popular method for parallel computation. Diagonal method is also often used. The above methods are logically equivalent from the point of view of convergence speed. But due to the difference of their data access patterns, their real execution speeds are quite different. 11~31 percent speed up has been obtained on PEACE machine using EE mapping. The Results are shown in Table 11.11.

Table 11.7. Matrix multiplication

	L2 Cache						(N×M)
	T1	T2	T1/T2	T3	T1/T3	T2/T3	
(i,k,j)	696.79	680.14	1.024	676.36	1.030	1.006	1024x1024
(k,j,i)	1107.74	1032.16	1.073	760.88	1.456	1.357	(Double
(j,i,k)	1579.60	1589.39	0.994	991.97	1.592	1.602	Precision)

Table 11.8. Matrix inversion

	L2 Cache						N×M
	T1	T2	T1/T2	T3	T1/T3	T2/T3	
j Major	1421.42	1367.55	1.039	1367.31	1.040	1.000	1024x 1024
i Major	331.59	354.33	0.936	243.10	1.364	1.458	512x 4096

(5) FFT
For an FFT of size $N = 2^k$, the computation consists k stages, the stride in the ith stage is $\delta = 2^{i-1}$. This is a main reason for the conflict miss. 30

percent speed up has been obtained on PEACE machine with EE mapping. The results are shown in Table 11.12 and 11.13.

The following results were obtained by running the corresponding programs on the PEACE machine. In the table, T1 is the time on the PEACE machine without L2 cache, T2 is the time on the PEACE machine with L2 cache using traditional mapping, and T3 is the time on the PEACE machine with L2 cache using EE mapping. T1/T2 shows the effect of using L2 cache. T2/T3 shows the effect of using EE mapping.

Table 11.9. System of linear equations with LU decomposition

	L2 Cache						(N×M)
	T1	T2	T1/T2	T3	T1/T3	T2/T3	
LSLU	53.94	52.79	1.028	37.95	1.421	1.391	512x512
	434.02	437.29	0.993	304.89	1.424	1.424	1024x1024

Table 11.10. Eigen computation with Jacobi

	L2 Cache						(Double Precision)
	T1	T2	T1/T2	T3	T1/T3	T2/T3	
Jacobi	22.19	22.84	0.972	15.93	1.393	1.434	128×512
	179.17	185.26	0.967	130.06	1.378	1.424	256×512
	1442.2	1495.78	0.964	1081.76	1.333	1.383	512×512

Table 11.11. Partial differential equations

	L2 Cache						N×M
	T1	T2	T1/T2	T3	T1/T3	T2/T3	
5 point	1.71	1.64	1.043	1.32	1.295	1.240	33x32,769
Red-Black	1.59	1.65	0.964	1.26	1.262	1.310	
Diagonal	2.86	2.42	1.182	2.14	1.336	1.131	
5 point	4.95	4.78	1.036	4.78	1.036	1.000	50x30,000
Red-Black	5.60	5.16	1.085	5.22	1.073	0.989	
Diagonal	10.60	8.95	1.184	8.90	1.191	1.006	

Table 11.12. FFT (One Dimensional)

	L2 Cache						N
	T1	T2	T1/T2	T3	T1/T3	T2/T3	
FFT1D	70.74	13.96	0.933	10.71	1.216	1.304	131,072
	147.75	29.38	0.935	22.25	1.235	1.321	262,144
	307.91	61.64	0.933	46.36	1.240	1.326	524,288

Table 11.13. FFT (Two Dimensional)

	L2 Cache						N×M
	T1	T2	T1/T2	T3	T1/T3	T2/T3	
FFT2D	7.97	1.10	1.045	0.72	1.597	1.528	64x4096
	16.97	2.36	1.072	1.59	1.591	1.484	128x4096
	36.63	5.33	1.051	3.52	1.591	1.514	256x4096

For the programs where data access pattern is serial or random, the data reuse rate is already good when using traditional cache design, the execution speeds are of little difference between the cases with and without EE mapping.

11.5 Conclusion

Data organization and memory access problems have been studied extensively for numerical analysis in scientific and engineering computations. Numerous methods have been proposed to solve the memory access bottleneck problems. As in numerical analysis, many useful pattern recognition and image processing (PRIP) algorithms suffer from heavy computation and the memory access is a bottleneck. Besides increasing memory bandwidth, increasing cache hit ratio is an important issue to improve the performance of the application programs. Cache line conflict miss is a main source for cache miss [6, 8, 13-15, 26, 28, 29]. A PRIP application programmer should realize that not the entire cache is usable. Hardware architecture designers should also be aware of that merely increasing cache size and employing prefetch cannot completely solve the problem of conflict miss.

We study several PRIP algorithms from the following three aspects: computation complexity, main memory size requirement, and main memory access requirement. We examine the frequently used matrices and their data reuse ratio, classify the frequently used PRIP algorithms into three categories according their memory access features, and discuss bottlenecks and possible solutions from software and hardware side.

On the software side, various program transformations are applied to increase the data reuse ratio and to reduce the miss ratio of cache [5, 12, 14, 24]. Miss ratio can be reduced by either changing the locations of data structures (e.g. merging arrays, padding and aligning structures, packing structures and arrays) or modifying the order in which data structures are referenced (e.g. loop interchange, loop fusion, blocking structure, and reversed execution of parallel loops) [23, 25]. Matrix blocking and row/column padding are very effective. Some of those techniques were originally used for vector machines.

On the hardware side, besides increasing the cache size and using prefetch, various techniques have been proposed to avoid cache line conflict misses [6, 8, 11, 15, 21, 22, 27-29]. A simple XOR mapping method was used in the TLB system design [2]. An XOR function is used for address mapping between main memory and cache to reduce miss ratio, especially for the access stride of complete powers of two [22]. Victim cache is proposed in [11], where a small fully associative cache is used to store the removed data from direct mapped cache such that they may not be needed to read from main memory again when they are used later on. Column associative cache is proposed where different functions are automatically applied for address mapping for different sets when conflicts occur [1]. Two way skewed associative cache is described in [27]. In two way skewed associative cache, different functions are used to map memory addresses to different cache banks in set associative cache. Interesting design technique for two way associative mapping functions is presented. Cache miss ratio is reduced in comparison with the traditional two-way associative cache. A technique named one's complement cache is proposed in [28, 29]. In one's complement cache, a cache with a prime number of lines is used, and a prime number module function is used to map the main memory address to the cache line number. The computation of the cache line number can be carried out in parallel with the main memory address in RISC machine so that additional time for cache line number generation is not necessary. Simulation results show that cache miss ratio is decreased significantly in one's complement cache [29]. Extensive simulations are carried out to evaluate effectiveness of XOR mapping schemes for cache memories [8]. Hardware implementation and experimental results for speed up are seldom presented in literature (to our knowledge).

A simple while powerful XOR mapped cache system with its hardware implementation is introduced in this chapter. A basic consideration in designing the scheme is the simplicity for its hardware implementation. The mapping function needs only one (EE mapping) or two levels (LR mapping) of XOR gates to implement. Another feature of the scheme is that the designing is application-oriented. Most data access patterns frequently used in various application algorithms are investigated and integrated into an uniformed system. Experimental results are presented by the speed up of the real execution time. Extensive simulations had been carried out to evaluate the benefits measured by cache hit ratio before the real hardware experimental computer system PEACE machine was implemented, though. Experiment results show that significant speed up can be obtained for frequently used algorithms with EE mapping even only implemented in second level cache system. The introduced technique can be used by chip designers to design CPU chips where more than the above speed up can be obtained, it can also be used by chip designers to design a memory system controller chip where the design can be simpler than the implementation here. It can also be used by system designers to design PC systems or workstations.

References

[1] A. Agarwal, S.D. Pudar, Column-Associative Caches: A Technique for Reducing the Miss Rate of Direct-Mapped Caches, *Proceedings of the International Symposium on Computer Architecture*, 179-190, 1993.

[2] J.M Felman, C.T Retter, Computer Architecture, *A Designer Text Based on Genetic RISC*, McGraw-Hill Inc. New York, 1994.

[3] J.M Frailong, W.Jalby, and J.Lenfant, XOR Schemes: A Flexible Data Organization in Parallel Memories, *Proceedings of the 1985 International Conference on Parallel Processing*, Aug, 276-283, 1985.

[4] Q. Gan, Hierarchical memory and high performance computation, *Master Thesis, Institute of Computing Technology*, Chinese Academy of Sciences, June 1997.

[5] D. Gannon, W. Jalby, and K. Gallivan, Strategies for cache and local memory management by global program transformation, *Journal of Parallel and Distributed Computing*,5:587-616, 1988.

[6] Y. Gao, *Vector Cache with Skewing*, MS Thesis, Institute of Computing Technology, Chinese Academy of Sciences, Beijing, China, May, 1994.

[7] R. Gonzalez and R. Woods, *Digital image processing*, Addison-Welsley, 1993.

[8] A. Gonzalez, M. Valero, N. Topham, and J. Parcerisa, On the Effectiveness of XOR-Mapping Schemes for Cache Memories, *UPC*, Spain, Report Number: UPC-CEPBA-1996-14.

[9] R. Haralick and L. Shapiro, *Computer and robot vision*, Addison-Wesley, 1993.

[10] A. Jain and R. Dubes, *Algorithms for clustering data*, Prentice Hall, 1988.

[11] N. Jouppi, Improving Direct-Mapped Cache Performance by the Addition of a Small Fully-Associative Cache and Prefetch Buffers, *Proceedings of the International Symposium on Computer Architecture*, 364-373,1990.

[12] K. Hwang, *Advanced Computer Architecture,* MeGraw-Hill, Inc., 1993.

[13] M.S.Lam, E.E RothBerg, and M.E.Wolf, The Cache Performance and Optimization of Blocked Algorithms, *Proceedings of ASPLOS'91*, 63-74,1991.

[14] A. Lebeck and D. Wood, Cache Profiling and the SPEC Benchmarks: A Case Study, *Computer*, 27(10):15-26,October 1994.

[15] H. Li, *Performance Analysis of Cache with XOR Mapping*, MS Thesis, Institute of Computing Technology, Chinese Academy of Sciences, Beijing, China, May, 1995.

[16] E. Li and Z. Liu, LR: An Efficient Scheme for Parallel Memory Systems, *Science in China (Series E)*, 28(2):1-7, February 1998.

[17] Z. Liu, X.Li and J.You, An Adaptive Memory System for Image Processing, *Proceedings of Vision Interface'92*, 163-168, 1992.

[18] Z. Liu and H. Li, Parallel and Hierarchical Memory Systems, *Proceedings of the 8th National Conference on Storage Systems*, Xi'an, China, 1-10, October 1994.

[19] Z. Liu and X.Li, XOR Storage Schemes for Frequently Used Data Patterns, *Journal of Parallel and Distributed Processing*, 25:162-173 1995.

[20] Z. Liu, E. Li, and X. Qiao, XOR Mapping Technique for Data Caches, *China Patent #97120245.1,* Pending, Nov. 6, 1997.

[21] S.A. Mckee et. al., Smarter memory: improving bandwidth for streamed references, *IEEE Computer*,54-63, July, 1998.

[22] E.A. Melton et al, Mechanism for the Randomization of Cache Access Utilizing a Bit-Matrix Multiplication of Cache Addresses, *US Patent 5,133,061*, July 21, 1992.

[23] SGI Inc., *Power Challenge Technical Report*, 1996.

[24] J.K. Peir et. al., Techniques to enhance cache performance across parallel program sections, *Proc. of the Int. Conf. on Parallel Processing*, CRC Press Inc., I: 12-19, Aug., 1993.

[25] X.Z. Qiao, Cache performance and algorithm optimization, *Proc. of HPC Asia'97,* IEEE Press, 2:12-17, May 1997.

[26] X. Qiao et al, Cache Optimization in Scientific Computations, *Proceedings of the 1999 ACM Symposium on Applied Computing*, 548-552, February 28 --- March 2, 1999.

[27] A. Seznec, A Case for Two-Way Skewed Associative Caches, *Proceddings of the 20th International Symposium on Computer Architecture*, 169-178, 1993.

[28] Q.Yang, Performance of Cache Memories for Vector Computers, *Journal of Parallel and Distributed Computing*, 19:163-178, 1993.

[29] Q.Yang *Introducing a Conflict-free Cache Design, in Practical Aspects of Parallel Computing*, (ed. By L.Tao and T.Li), International Academic Publishers, 19-33, 1995.

Chapter 12

PERMUTATION ROUTING FOR INTERCONNECTION NETWORK

Interconnection networks provide communication facility for parallel processing systems. In distributed memory systems, processors exchange messages through interconnection networks. In shared memory systems, processors access data from parallel memory system through interconnection networks. In order to reduce communication overhead (both hardware overhead and time overhead), interconnection networks and corresponding routing techniques have been the key issues in the research of parallel and distributed processing systems. Interconnection networks with connection complexity of $O(N\log_2 N)$ make a good tradeoff between the cost of hardware and the delay of message transmission. This kind of networks includes multistage interconnected networks (MINs), which are referred to as *dynamic* networks, and hypercube, which is referred to as a kind of *static* or *point to point* connected network. Hypercube is an important network for its topological features. We will introduce some permutation routing algorithms for hypercubes. The algorithms introduced in this chapter have a common feature that they can avoid conflicts in the message transmission process. Also they are simple for their implementation.

12.1 Introduction

In communication networks, messages can be transmitted in packet switched mode, circuit switched mode, and wormhole mode. Conflicts in message transmission process have important effects on hardware implementation and communication speed.

In a packet switched mode, a whole message packet is maintained as an entity. In a routing step it is forwarded one *link* along the path from its source to its destination. A *link* in a network is also called an *edge* in a graph. For a routing algorithm in packet switched mode, if a node is to hold more than one message at any time, we say that a network conflict occurs on the node. If a routing algorithm can guarantee that no network conflict occurs, no buffer is needed for the transmission, and no computation for arbitration is needed to "select" a messages to send.

In circuit switched mode, a complete path needs to be established dedicatedly for a message packet from its source to its destination. Any link on this path cannot be used by any other packet during the transmission process of this packet.

In a wormhole routing mode, a packet is partitioned into a number of flits, which are units for routing. In a routing step, a flit can be forwarded one link along its path, and contiguous flits of a packet are always on the same or adjacent nodes along their path.

For a routing algorithm in circuit switched and wormhole routing mode, if more than one message is to be sent on one edge, we say that a *network conflict* occurs *on the edge.* Note that when no edge is shared by two paths we say that the two paths are independent to each other. The number of messages needing to use an edge is also referred to as *congestion* of the edge in literature [1]. The maximum congestion of the edges in the network is called the *congestion* of the routing algorithm. We say that a routing algorithm is conflict-free in a circuit switched or wormhole routing mode if its congestion is only one. A conflict-free algorithm makes the transmission efficient in terms of both communication time and hardware.

On the other hand, simplicity of a routing algorithm also has important effect on required hardware and communication time. We say that a routing algorithm is *oblivious* if the path for a packet is decided before routing, and in routing time it does not need to know the routing for other message packets in the system, nor does it need to remember the routing history for itself. An oblivious routing algorithm is simple to be implemented since a node (a source or intermediate) routes a message packet on it based solely on the destination address of the packet (and the address of the current node, of course).

We will introduce three routing algorithms for some frequently permutations on hypercubes. We will focus our discussion on conflict avoidance of the routing algorithms.

12.2. Two-Stage Routing for BPC Permutations

Some Definitions

An n dimensional hypercube has $N=2^n$ nodes. There is a link (edge) between Node i and j if there is one and only one k such that $i_k \neq j_k$, where $0 \leq i,j \leq N-1$, $0 \leq k \leq n-1$, and $i_{n-1}i_{n-2}\cdots i_0$ and $j_{n-1}j_{n-2}\cdots j_0$ are binary representations of integer i and j. We also call the link the kth dimensional link.

If the communication takes the form that one PE sends a message to only one PE, and no more than one PE sends message to any one PE, it is called a *permutation*. Permutation is an important kind of communications. There are N messages communicated in a permutation. We will express a permutation as $P=\{(S,D)|\ 0 \leqslant S,D \leqslant N\text{-}1\}$, where S is the source address of a message, and D is its destination address. We express S and D in their binary forms $s_{n\text{-}1}s_{n\text{-}2}\cdots s_0$ and $d_{n\text{-}1}d_{n\text{-}2}\cdots d_0$. In a permutation, each S and D appears only once.

A BPC (Bit Permute Complement) permutation is a permutation that the bits in the binary representations of the destinations are resulted from permuting the bits in the binary representations of their sources, with some bits being (possibly) complemented.

Definition 12.1 A BPC permutation of N numbers can be defined by an *n-tuple*

$$F=(f'_{n\text{-}1}, f'_{n\text{-}2}, \cdots, f'_0), \tag{12-1}$$

where $(f'_{n\text{-}1}, f'_{n\text{-}2}, \cdots, f'_0)$ is a permutation of (n-1, n-2, $\cdots$, 0), and $f_i=|f'_i|$ for $0 \leqslant i \leqslant n\text{-}1$, such that

$$d_i = \begin{cases} s_{f_i} & \text{if} \quad f_i' \geq 0, \\ \overline{s_{f_i}} & \text{if} \quad f_i' < 0. \end{cases} \tag{12-2}$$

Note that we distinguish +0 and –0 here, and we consider –0<0 in the above definition, the same as in [2].

For example, with a 3-tuple F=(-0, -1, 2), the relation between any source and its destination in the permutation is $d_2 = \overline{s_0}$, $d_1 = \overline{s_1}$, and $d_0 = s_2$. This means that, for example, the message on Node 6 (110_2) is to be sent to Node 5 (101_2) since $d_2 d_1 d_0 = \overline{s_0}\,\overline{s_1}\, s_2 = \overline{0}\overline{1}1 = 101$.

Any permutation can be expressed by "cycles". A cycle of length t ($1 \leqslant t \leqslant n$) is an ordered set ($v_1$, v_2, $\cdots$, v_t) where $f_{v_1} = v_2, f_{v_2} = v_3, \cdots, f_{v_t} = v_1$. In a cycle ($v_1$, v_2, $\cdots$, v_t) if v_i=max{v_1, v_2, $\cdots$, v_t }, $1 \leqslant i \leqslant t$, we say that v_i is the top dimension of the cycle. We use *TOPSET* to denote the set of the top dimensions of a given permutation.

For example, consider n=5. The perfect shuffle permutation can be described by $F=(f_4, f_3, f_2, f_1, f_0)$=(3, 2, 1, 0, 4), which has one cycle (3, 2, 1, 0, 4) and the *TOPSET*={4}. The bit reversal permutation can be described by $F=(f_4, f_3, f_2, f_1, f_0)$=(0, 1, 2, 3, 4), which has three cycles (0, 4), (1, 3), and (2) and TOPSET={4, 3, 2}.

A Two-Stage Routing Algorithm

Definition 12.2 If a node is connected to Node S through the ith dimensional link in a hypercube, we refer to the node as the ith *imagery node* of Node S, and denote it as Node $IMG^{(i)}(S)$, where $0 \leqslant S \leqslant N\text{-}1$, and $0 \leqslant i \leqslant n\text{-}1$.

For example, in a 4-cube, $IMG^{(1)}(3)=1$, and $IMG^{(3)}(3)=11$. The well-known naive hypercube routing algorithm works as follows: The n dimensions of the hypercube are used sequentially, usually in a low to high (ascending) or high to low (descending) order. On dimension k, if the kth bit of the destination address of the packet is different from the kth bit of current node address, the packet is sent to the current node's neighboring node through the kth dimensional link.

Not all the permutations can be passed without conflict by the naive routing algorithm. However, we can show that if a permutation satisfies some condition, it can be passed through hypercube in n steps without conflict using the naive routing algorithm.

Definition 12.3 A *Complete Residue System modulo m* (*CRS mod m*) is a set of integers which contains exactly one representative of each residue class *modulo m*.

In the following, we denote an integer B, $0 \leqslant B \leqslant N\text{-}1$, as $B = \sum_{i=0}^{n-1} b_i \times 2^i$, where b_i is the ith bit value (0 or 1) of the binary representation of B.

We define *Virtual Modular* operation, which will be used for describing the passable condition of permutations through hypercubes.

Definition 12.4 Virtual Modular Operation *VMOD*:

$$VMOD_{(k_1,k_2,\cdots,k_l)}(B) = \sum b_i \times 2^{i-\alpha_i}, \tag{12-3}$$

where $i \in \{0,1,\cdots,n\text{-}1\}\text{-}\{k_1,k_2,\cdots,k_l\}$, $0 \leqslant k_1,k_2,\cdots,k_l \leqslant n\text{-}1$, and

$$\delta_i = \| \{k \mid (k \in \{k_1,k_2,\cdots,k_l\}) \wedge (k<i)\} \|, \tag{12-4}$$

and $\|S\|$ is the cardinality of set S.

The result of the virtual modular operation is an integer obtained from dropping the bits on the dimensions $k_1,k_2,\cdots,k_l$. For example, $B=39=100111_2$, $VMOD_{(1)}(B)=10011_2=19$, and $VMOD_{(1,3)}(B) = 1011_2 = 11$. Note that in the following context we will mainly use the virtual modular operation of the form $VMOD_{(k-1,k-2,\cdots,0)}(B) = b_{n-1}b_{n-2}\cdots b_k$, and denote it as $VMOD^{(k)}$ without indicating which k bits are dropped when no confusion will arise.

A hypercube can be partitioned into a number of subcubes. A k-subcube of an n dimensional hypercube consists of 2^{n-k} nodes such that for any Node A and B in the same subcube we have $a_{k-1}a_{k-2} \cdots a_0 = b_{k-1}b_{k-2} \cdots b_0$, where $1 \leqslant k \leqslant n-1$.

Let $\{D\}$ be the set of all the destination addresses of the packets in any k-subcube of a hypercube. We have the following condition for the naive routing.

Theorem 12.1 A permutation is passable in n steps without conflict by the naive routing algorithm in a high to low order if and only if : for any k such that $0 \leqslant k \leqslant n-1$, $\{\ VMOD^{(k)}(D)\}$ constitute a *CRS mod* 2^{n-k} .

Using the topological similarity between hypercube and the Ω^{-1} network, the theorem can be proved similarly to the passability condition for the Ω^{-1} network in [3], and this theorem is a special case of Theorem 1 in [4]. The proof is omitted here.

Permutations that satisfy the above condition are very limited. In the case that a permutation does not satisfy the above condition, it may be rearranged in some way into an intermediate permutation which satisfies the above permutation and then route the intermediate permutation using the naive routing algorithm. We will give a rearrangement algorithm for BPC permutations so that any BPC permutation will be realized through hypercube without conflict. The rearrangement algorithm is called BPC-Partition. In the following algorithm, D is the destination address of the packet on node S in any step.

```
Algorithm BPC-Partition;
{
    /* The nodes do the following in parallel. */
    For{j=0;j<=n-2;j++}{
        IF ((j is not in TOPSET) && (d_j=1))
            send the packet to IMG^(j)(S);
    }
}
```

The above algorithm is a genetic description of the rearrangement process for any BPC permutation. Usually the special form for specific class of BPC permutations is known in the real application programs. For example, the perfect shuffle and bit reversal permutations are used in FFT computations. Thus for any specific BPC permutation the TOPSET is always known before run time. Therefore, the TOPSET information can be incorporated into a specific form of the above algorithm description so that there is no need to decide whether a dimension is a top dimension at run time. For example, for the perfect shuffle and its variants (shuffle with some bits being complemented) the routing process for the rearrangement can be described as

```
For{j=0;j<=n-2;j++}{
    IF (d_j=1) send the packet to IMG^(j)(S);
}
```

For the bit reversal permutations and its variants, the routing process can be described as:

```
For{j=0;j<=⌊n/2⌋-1;j++}{
    IF (d_j=1) send the packet to IMG^(j)(S);
}
```

We will prove that any BPC permutation will become a permutation after the rearrangement algorithm and the resulted permutation satisfies the passable condition given in Theorem 12.1. Thus the complete routing algorithm for BPC permutations is very simple: First, rearrange the BPC permutation using the algorithm BPC-Partition; Second, routing the intermediate permutation using the naïve hypercube routing algorithm with the n dimensions being used in a descending order.

An example is given in Figure 12.1 for a 8 node hypercube. In the example, the permutation is a bit reversal with every bit being complemented. There are two cycles of the dimensions: (1) and (0, 2), thus *TOPSET*={1, 2}. In the figure, a column of numbers is shown alongside each node. The first number is the serial number of the node (the source of the message packet), and the second number is the destination address of the packet. The rest numbers in the column are a sequence of destination addresses of the packets on the node in each routing step. Part (a) shows how the original permutation are rearranged into an intermediate permutation passable by Algorithm BPC-Partition in one step, and Part (b) shows that the intermediate permutation passed through hypercube by the naive routing algorithm in three steps.

We now prove correctness of the two stage routing algorithm for BPC permutations on hypercubes. We need to prove three facts. First the BPC-Partition routing is conflict-free; the second, the intermediate distribution is really a permutation; the third, the intermediate permutation satisfies the passable condition given by Theorem 12.1.

In the following we refer to the destination address of any message packet as a number for simplicity. We will denote the node that a packet whose destination address is D resides on at Step i by $S^{(i)}$. In packet switched routing, both naïve routing algorithm and the BPC-Partition algorithm use the n dimensions of a hypercube in a predetermined order, thus no conflict will arise for the use of the links. So when we say conflict we just mean conflict on nodes, i.e. when a packet is to remain on a node while another packet is to be sent to the same node in some step.

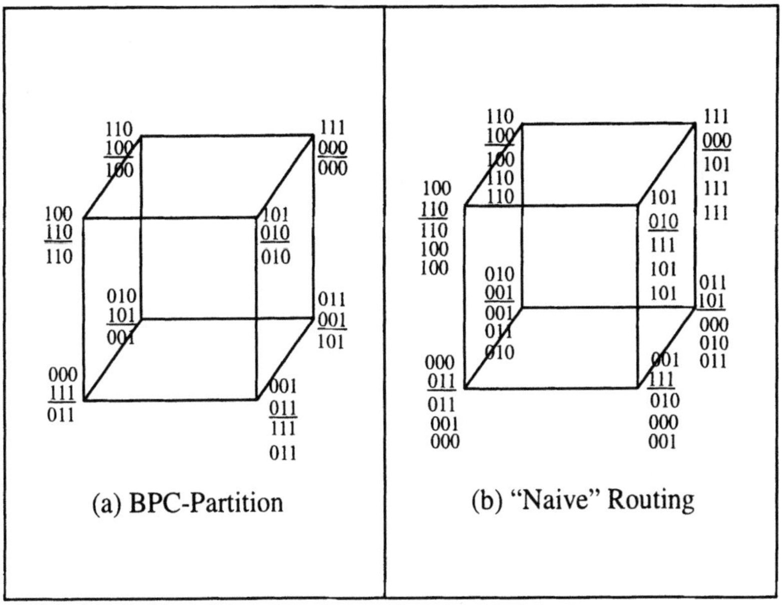

Figure 12.1. Two-Stage routing for BPC permutation

We now introduce some additional notations for the proof of correctness of the algorithm. We denote f_{f_i} as f_i^2 (f_i^1 means f_i), and $f_{f^k{}_i}$ as f_i^{k+1}, where k is an integer. We use $s^*_{f_i}$ to denote s_{f_i} (if $f_i' \geq 0$) or $\overline{s_{f_i}}$ (if $f_i' < 0$). When we say "at Step i" we mean "at the beginning of Step i".

Given a BPC permutation described by $F=(f'_{n-1}, f'_{n-2}, \cdots, f'_0)$, D can be represented as

$$D = d_{n-1}d_{n-2}\cdots d_0 = s^{(0)*}_{f_{n-1}} s^{(0)*}_{f_{n-2}} \cdots s^{(0)*}_{f_0}. \tag{12-5}$$

Algorithm BPC-Partition skips over all the top dimensions, and transmits the packets only on the non-top dimensions. The following is obvious from the description of the algorithm: at Step 0, D is on Node $s^{(0)}_{n-1}s^{(0)}_{n-2}\cdots s^{(0)}_0$.

At Step 1, D will be on node

$$\begin{cases} s^{(1)}_{n-1}s^{(1)}_{n-2}\cdots s^{(1)}_0 = s^{(0)}_{n-1}s^{(0)}_{n-2}\cdots s^{(0)}_0 (s^{(0)}_0 \oplus s^{(0)*}_{f_0}), & \text{if} \quad 0 \notin TOPSET, \\ s^{(1)}_{n-1}s^{(1)}_{n-2}\cdots s^{(1)}_0 = s^{(0)}_{n-1}s^{(0)}_{n-2}\cdots s^{(0)}_0, & \text{if} \quad 0 \in TOPSET. \end{cases} \tag{12-6}$$

At Step 2, D will be on node

$$\begin{cases} s_{n-1}^{(2)} s_{n-2}^{(2)} \cdots s_0^{(2)} = s_{n-1}^{(1)} s_{n-2}^{(1)} \cdots s_2^{(1)} (s_1^{(1)} \oplus s_{f_1}^{(0)*}) s_0^{(1)}, & \text{if} \quad 0 \notin TOPSET, \\ s_{n-1}^{(2)} s_{n-2}^{(2)} \cdots s_0^{(2)} = s_{n-1}^{(1)} s_{n-2}^{(1)} \cdots s_0^{(1)}, & \text{if} \quad 0 \in TOPSET. \end{cases} \tag{12-7}$$

Repeatedly reasoning as the above, we have the following lemma.

Lemma 12.1 The stability of substrings in the source address:
At Step j in the Algorithm BPC-Partition, the number, D, is on Node $S^{(j)} = s_{n-1}^{(j)} s_{n-2}^{(j)} \cdots s_0^{(j)}$, with

$$\begin{cases} s_k^{(j)} = s_k^{(0)}, & \text{if} \quad (k \in TOPSET) \vee (j \le k \le n-1), \\ s_k^{(j)} = s_k^{(0)} \oplus s_{f_k}^{(0)*}, & \text{if} \quad (k \notin TOPSET) \wedge (0 \le k \le j-1), \\ s_k^{(x)} = s_k^{(y)}, & \text{for} \quad (0 \le k \le j-2) \wedge (k+1 \le x, y \le j). \end{cases} \tag{12-8}$$

Suppose that D and D' were on $S^{(0)}$ and $S'^{(0)}$ respectively at Step 0, and they are on $S^{(j)}$ and $S'^{(j)}$ respectively on Step j. Because $S^{(j)}$ and $S'^{(j)}$ are connected by one jth dimensional link, we have

$$\begin{cases} s_k^{(j)} = s'^{(j)}_k, & \text{if} \quad k \ne j, \\ s_j^{(j)} \ne s'^{(j)}_j. \end{cases} \tag{12-9}$$

Theorem 12.2 Let D and D' be the two numbers on the two nodes connected by a jth dimensional link at Step j. We have:

$$\begin{cases} d_j = d'_j & \text{if} \quad j \notin TOPSET, \\ d_j \ne d'_j & \text{if} \quad j \in TOPSET. \end{cases} \tag{12-10}$$

Proof:

Case 1: j does not belong to TOPSET

Because j is not a top dimension, we are sure that $j \ne f_j$. Thus we only have the following two cases.

Subcase (1), $f_j > j$. According to Lemma 12.1 we know $s_{f_j}^{(j)} = s_{f_j}^{(0)}$ and $s'^{(j)}_{f_j} = s'^{(0)}_{f_j}$. From Equation (12-9) we know $s_{f_j}^{(j)} = s'^{(j)}_{f_j}$. Thus we have $s_{f_j}^{(0)} = s'^{(0)}_{f_j}$. Therefore

$$s_{f_j}^{(0)*} = s'^{(0)*}_{f_j}, \text{ i.e. } d_j = d'_j. \tag{12-11}$$

Subcase (2), $f_j<j$. From Lemma 12.1 we can get

$$\begin{cases} s_{f_j}^{(j)} = s_{f_j}^{(0)} \oplus s_{f_j^2}^{(0)*}, \\ s'^{(j)}_{f_j} = s'^{(0)}_{f_j} \oplus s'^{(0)*}_{f_j^2}. \end{cases} \quad (12\text{-}12)$$

It can be rewritten as

$$\begin{cases} s_{f_j}^{(j)} = s_{f_j}^{(j)} \oplus s_{f_j^2}^{(0)*}, \\ s'^{(j)}_{f_j} = s'^{(j)}_{f_j} \oplus s'^{(0)*}_{f_j^2}. \end{cases} \quad (12\text{-}13)$$

If $f_j^2 > j$, according Lemma 12.1 we have

$$\begin{cases} s_{f_j^2}^{(j)} = s_{f_j^2}^{(0)*}, \\ s'^{(j)}_{f_j^2} = s'^{(0)*}_{f_j^2}. \end{cases} \quad (12\text{-}14)$$

From Equations (12-9) and (12-14) we have $s_{f_j^2}^{(0)} = s'^{(0)}_{f_j^2}$, and then we have

$$s_{f_j^2}^{(0)*} = s'^{(0)*}_{f_j^2}. \quad (12\text{-}15)$$

Because of Equation (12-9), we have

$$s_{f_j}^{(j)} = s'^{(j)}_{f_j}. \quad (12\text{-}16)$$

From Equations (12-13), (12-15), and (12-16), we have $s_{f_j}^{(0)} = s'^{(0)}_{f_j}$, thus

$$s_{f_j}^{(0)*} = s'^{(0)*}_{f_j}, \text{ i.e. } d_j = d'_j. \quad (12\text{-}17)$$

If $f_j^2 < j$, the above reasoning process goes on repeatedly. Because the dimensions lower than j will be exhausted by the above reasoning process, eventually we will get a number t such that
$f_j^k < j$ for $1 \le k \le t-1$, but $f_j^t > j$, and that

$$\begin{cases} s_{f_j}^{(0)} = s_{f_j}^{(j)} \oplus s_{f_j^2}^{(j)} \oplus \cdots \oplus s_{f_j^{t-1}}^{(j)} \oplus s_{f_j^t}^{(0)*}, \\ s'^{(j)}_{f_j} = s'^{(j)}_{f_j} \oplus s'^{(j)}_{f_j^2} \oplus \cdots \oplus s'^{(j)}_{f_j^{t-1}} \oplus s'^{(0)*}_{f_j^t}. \end{cases} \quad (12\text{-}18)$$

Since $f_j^2 < j$, for $1 \le k \le t-1$, and $f_j^t > j$, together with Equation (12-9), we have

$$s^{(j)}_{f^k_j} = s'^{(j)}_{f^k_j} \text{ for } 1 \le k \le t-1 \text{, and } s^{(0)}_{f^t_j} = s'^{(0)}_{f^t_j}. \tag{12-19}$$

Thus we have $s^{(0)}_{f_j} = s'^{(0)}_{f_j}$, and hence

$$s^{(0)*}_{f_j} = s'^{(0)*}_{f_j}, \text{ i.e. } d_j = d'_j. \tag{12-20}$$

Case 2: j belongs to TOPSET. We have two subcases: $f_j = j$ and $f_j \ne j$.

Subcase (1), $f_j = j$. In this case , from Lemma 12.1, we have

$$d_j = s^{(0)}_{f_j} = s^{(0)}_j = s^{(j)}_j \text{, and } d'_j = s'^{(0)}_{f_j} = s'^{(0)}_j = s'^{(j)}_j. \tag{12-21}$$

From Equation (12-9), we know that $s^{(j)}_j \ne s'^{(j)}_j$, and so $s^{(j)*}_j \ne s'^{(j)*}_j$. Thus we have $d_j \ne d'_j$.

Subcase (2), $f_j \ne j$. Because j is a top dimension, we only have $f_j<j$. Thus we know

$$\begin{cases} s^{(0)}_{f_j} = s^{(j)}_{f_j} \oplus s^{(0)*}_{f^2_j}, \\ s'^{(0)}_{f_j} = s'^{(j)}_{f_j} \oplus s'^{(0)*}_{f^2_j}. \end{cases} \tag{12-22}$$

Similar to the reasoning process for the case that j does not belong to *TOPSET* (similar to its subcase (2), but here we can only have $f^2<j, f^3<j,\cdots$, because j is a top dimension), we will obtain a t, such that $f^t_j = j$ (since j is a top dimension of a cycle, which will be exhausted with such a number t), and that

$$\begin{cases} s^{(0)}_{f_j} = s^{(j)}_{f_j} \oplus s^{(j)}_{f^2_j} \oplus \cdots \oplus s^{(j)}_{f^{t-1}_j} \oplus s^{(0)*}_{f^t_j}, \\ s'^{(0)}_{f_j} = s'^{(j)}_{f_j} \oplus s'^{(j)}_{f^2_j} \oplus \cdots \oplus s'^{(j)}_{f^{t-1}_j} \oplus s'^{(0)*}_{f^2_j}. \end{cases} \tag{12-23}$$

i.e.

$$\begin{cases} s^{(0)}_{f_j} = s^{(j)}_{f_j} \oplus s^{(j)}_{f^2_j} \oplus \cdots \oplus s^{(j)}_{f^{t-1}_j} \oplus s^{(0)*}_{j}, \\ s'^{(0)}_{f_j} = s'^{(j)}_{f_j} \oplus s'^{(j)}_{f^2_j} \oplus \cdots \oplus s'^{(j)}_{f^{t-1}_j} \oplus s'^{(0)*}_{j}. \end{cases} \tag{12-24}$$

From Equation (12-9) we have

$$\begin{cases} s^{(j)}_{f_j} = s'^{(j)}_{f_j}, \\ s^{(j)}_{f_j^2} = s'^{(j)}_{f_j^2}, \\ \quad \cdots\cdots \\ s^{(j)}_{f_j^{t-1}} = s'^{(j)}_{f_j^{t-1}}, \\ s^{(0)}_{j} \neq s'^{(0)}_{j}. \end{cases} \tag{12-25}$$

From Equations (12-24) and (12-25), we have $s^{(0)}_{f_j} \neq s'^{(0)}_{f_j}$, and hence $s^{(0)*}_{f_j} \neq s'^{(0)*}_{f_j}$, i.e., $d_j \neq d'_j$. ■

For example, in Figure 12.1, at the beginning (Step 0) number D (D=111_2) is on Node 0 and number D' (D'=011_2) is on Node 1, we have d_0=d'_0=1 (0 does not belong to *TOPSET*). At Step 1, number D (D=011_2) is on Node 0 and number D' (D'=001_2) is on Node 2, we have $d_1 \neq d'_1$ (1 belongs to *TOPSET*).

Theorem 12.2 expresses the relationship between the destination addresses of the two message packets on the neighboring nodes connected by the *j*th dimensional link, which guarantees no conflict will occur in the transmission process on the algorithm BPC-Partition.

Theorem 12.3 No conflict will occur at any step in the transmission process of Algorithm BPC Partition.

Proof: At any Step *j*, $0 \leqslant j \leqslant n$-2,

1), If *j* belongs to *TOPSET*, no transmission occurs between any neighboring nodes. Thus no conflict can occur.

2), If *j* does not belong to *TOPSET*, according Theorem 12.2, the number *D* on any Node *S* and number *D'* on its *j*th neighboring Node *S'* have the relation of d_j=d'_j. Thus if *D* is to be sent from *S* to *S'*, *D'* is also to be sent from *S'* to *S* (in the case that d_j=d'_j=1), no conflict will occur. If *D* is to remain on Node *S*, *D'* is also to remain on *S'* (in the case that d_j=d'_j=0), no conflict will occur either. ■

For example, in Figure 12.1, in Step 0, the number 7 is sent from Node 0 to Node 1 while 3 is sent from Node 1 to Node 0; also, 6 remains on Node 4 while 2 remains on Node 5. No conflict occurs.

Theorem 12.4 Let *D* and *D'* be two numbers on Node *S* and *S'* respectively at Step *j*.

If $d_{n-1} \cdots d_{j+1}=d'_{n-1} \cdots d'_{j+1}$ and $d_j \neq d'_j$, then we have

$$\begin{cases} s_j^{(j)} = s'^{(j)}_j, & \text{if} \quad j \notin TOPSET, \\ s_j^{(j)} \neq s'^{(j)}_j, & \text{if} \quad i \in TOPSET. \end{cases} \tag{12-26}$$

It can be proved similarly to Theorem 12.2.

Theorem 12.5 After the transmission process of Algorithm BPC-Partition, any BPC permutation will become a permutation passable on hypercube by the naive routing algorithm using the n dimensions in a high-to-low order.

Proof: Since no conflict occurs in the transmission process of BPC-Partition, each node holds one and only one number after BPC-Partition. Thus the resulted distribution of the packets is *really a permutation*. We need only to prove that the resulted permutation satisfies the passable condition of Theorem 12.1.

Let a k-subcube($c_{k-1}, c_{k-2}, \ldots, c_0$) be a subcube consisting of the nodes with their 0th, ..., (k-1)th bits being $c_0, \ldots, c_{k-2}$, and c_{k-1} respectively, where c_i is 1 or 0. For example, the 2-cube(1,0) in a 4 dimensional hypercube is the subcube consisting the Nodes 1, 5, 9, 13, i.e. the nodes with form of xx01.

At Step 0: Consider any two numbers D and D' with $d_i=d'_i$, for $i>0$, but $d_0 \neq d'_0$. Suppose that D is on Node S and D' is on Node S' respectively. *Note that here S and S' are not necessarily connected by a 0th dimensional link.*

If 0 does not belong to *TOPSET*, from Theorem 12.4 we know that $s_0=s'_0$. It means that both D and D' are in the same 1-subcube(s_0). According to Algorithm BPC-Partition, if $d_0=0$ and $d'_0=1$, D will remain in 1-subcube(s_0) and D' will be sent to 1-subcube($\overline{s_0}$). If $d'_0=0$ and $d_0=1$, D' will remain in 1-subcube(s_0) and D will be sent to 1-subcube($\overline{s_0}$).

If 0 belongs to *TOPSET*, from Theorem 12.4 we know that $s_0 \neq s'_0$. This means that D and D' are in two different 1-subcubes. According to Algorithm BPC-Partition, no transmission occurs in this case, and D and D' will remain in the two different 1-subcubes (i.e. 1-subcube(s_0) and 1-subcube($\overline{s_0}$)).

For example, in the left part of Figure 12.1, consider the two numbers $d_2d_1d_0$=111 and $d'_2d'_1d'_0$=110 which are on Node 0 and Node 4 respectively. Node 0 and Node 4 are in the same 1-subcube (0) since 0 does not belong to *TOPSET*. In the first Step D=111 (d_0=1) is sent to Node 1, which is in another 1-subcube, while D'=110 (d'_0=0) remains on Node 4.

Because at Step 0 the N numbers constitute a *CRS mod* 2^n, after Step 0 the N numbers, under $VMOD^{(1)}$, in the two 1-subcubes constitute two *CRSs mod* 2^{n-1} .

For example, after the first Step in Figure 12.1, the numbers in 1-subcube(0) are {011, 001, 100, 110}. Under $VMOD^{(1)}$ they are {01, 00, 10, 11}, which constitute a *CRS mod* 2^{3-1}. The numbers in 1-subcube(1) are {111, 101, 000, 010} (under $VMOD^{(1)}$ they are {11, 10, 00, 01}), which also constitute a *CRS mod* 2^{3-1}.

Suppose that after Step *j*-1 , all the numbers under $VMOD^{(j)}$ in any *j*-subcube constitute a *CRS mod* 2^{n-j} .

At Step *j*, in any *j*-subcube(c_{j-1}, c_{j-2}, ...,c_0), where c_k is 0 or 1, for $0 \leqslant k \leqslant j-1$, consider the two numbers *D* and *D'* with $d_i=d'_i$, for $i>j$, but $d_j \neq d'_j$. Note that because the numbers, under $VMOD^{(j)}$, in any *j*-subcube constitute a *CRS mod* 2^{n-j} we are sure that there are two and only two such numbers in any *j*-subcube.

If *j* does not belong to *TOPSET*, from Theorem 12.4 we know that $s_j=s'_j$. It means that both *D* and *D'* are in the same (*j*+1)-subcube(s_j, c_{j-1}, c_{j-2}, ...,c_0). According to Algorithm BPC-Partition, if $d_0=0$ and $d'_0=1$, D will remain in (*j*+*1*)-subcube(s_j , c_{j-1}, c_{j-2}, ...,c_0) and *D'* will be sent to (*j*+1)-subcube($\overline{s_j}$, c_{j-1}, c_{j-2}, ...,c_0). If $d'_0=0$ and $d_0=1$, *D'* will remain in (*j*+1)-subcube(s_j, c_{j-1}, c_{j-2}, ...,c_0) and *D* will be sent to (*j*+1)-subcube($\overline{s_j}$, c_{j-1}, c_{j-2}, ...,c_0) .

If *j* belongs to *TOPSET*, from Theorem 12.4 we know that $s_j \neq s'_j$. This means that *D* and *D'* are in two different (*j*+1)-subcubes. According to Algorithm BPC-Partition, no transmission occurs in this case, and *D* and *D'* will remain in the two different (*j*+1)-subcubes (i.e. (*j*+1)-subcube(s_j, c_{j-1}, c_{j-2}, ...,c_0) and (*j*+1)-subcube($\overline{s_j}$, c_{j-1}, c_{j-2}, ...,c_0)).

Thus after Step *j* , the numbers, under $VMOD^{(j+1)}$, in any (*j*+1)-subcube constitute a *CRSs mod* $2^{n-(j+1)}$.

In Figure 12.1, the algorithm skips over dimension 1 since 1 belongs to *TOPSET*. The numbers in any 2-subcube(c_1, c_0) (i.e. two nodes connected by a link on dimension 2) constitute a *CRS mod* 2^{3-2} (under $VMOD^{(2)}$). For example the two numbers on Node 1 and 5 are 111 and 010, and {$VMOD^{(2)}$(111), $VMOD^{(2)}$(010)}={1, 0}, which constitute a *CRS mod* 2^{3-2}. ■

Due to Theorem 12.5, we can use Algorithm BPC-Partition to rearrange any BPC permutation into a permutation passable on hypercube in at most *n*-1 steps, and then use the naïve routing algorithm to realize the resulted permutation in at most *n* steps. In such a two stage routing manner, any BPC permutation can be realized in at most *2n*-1 steps. Some specific BPC permutations can be realized using the two stage routing method in a certain number of steps less than 2*n*-1. For example, one can show that a perfect shuffle permutation can be realized in $2n$-1 steps, but a bit reversal permutation can be realized in $2n-\lfloor n/2 \rfloor-1$ steps, and a vector reversal permutation can be realized in n steps.

Realizing Multiple Permutations Simultaneously

Let us see how to use the above two stage routing scheme to realize multiple BPC permutations simultaneously in a conflict-free style.

In the above scheme, the n dimensions are used in a strictly high-to-low order. We now generalize the theorems to allow any sequence of dimensions to be used if the sequence satisfies some condition.

A subscript mapping scheme $M(n\text{-}1, n\text{-}2, ..., 0)=(v_{n-1}, v_{n-2}, ..., v_0)$ is a mapping such that $(v_{n-1}, v_{n-2}, ..., v_0)$ is a permutation of $\{n\text{-}1, n\text{-}2, ..., 0\}$, and that if the kth dimension is used in the naïve routing then the v_kth dimension is used under the subscript mapping scheme. A subscript mapping is called shift mapping if $v_i=k+i \bmod n$ or $v_i=k-i \bmod n$, where $0 \leqslant k \leqslant n\text{-}1$. The shift mapping schemes are in "circularly sequential orders" from high to low or low to high. For example, the mapping $M(5, 4, 3, 2, 1, 0)=(2, 1, 0, 5, 4, 3)$ is a shift mapping. The following theorem shows that the BPC-Partition works under any shift subscript mapping for any BPC permutations. However, one should notice that a BPC permutation may have different dimensions in *TOPSET*.

Theorem 12.6 Under any shift mapping scheme, Algorithm BPC-Partition arranges any BPC permutation into a passable permutation.

Theorem 12.6 can be proved similarly as Theorem 12.5.Theorem 12.6 makes it possible to pass n independent BPC permutations simultaneously. We can choose n different shift mapping schemes such that at any time one and only one dimension is used by any scheme. The following table illustrates this manner for the case of n=4.

Table 12.1. Realize multiple permutations simultaneously

Dimensions used by Different Permutations in Different Steps							
Permut.	Step 1	Step 2	Step 3	Step 4	Step 5	Step 6	Step 7
0	0	1	2	3	2	1	0
1	1	2	3	0	3	2	1
2	2	3	0	1	0	3	2
3	3	0	1	2	1	0	3

From the above we can see that each of the n permutations uses the links on one and only one dimension in any step, thus no conflict occurs on the use of the dimensional links between different permutations. Also, according to Theorem 12.3 no conflict occurs on any node within each permutation. Therefore n BPC permutations can be realized simultaneously in $2n$-1 steps without conflict. In this way, on synchronous hypercube systems (e.g. like the Connect Machine) all the dimensional links are kept busy in every dimension cycle, and n permutations can be realized in two "machine cycles" (as $2n$ "steps" here). Thus the bandwidth can be fully utilized.

Theorem 12.6 also has an impact on the required width of the links of a hypercube network. Consider the task of transmitting one permutation packets and suppose that each packet contains $n*b$ bytes. Dimensional links of $n*b$ bytes wide are needed if we want to finish a transmission in one step. By partitioning a packet into n segments with b bytes of each one can transmit the n segments using the above method. Thus links of b bytes wide one each dimension are needed. The cost of a hypercube system can be reduced in this way.

12.3 Routing LC Permutations on MIMD Hypercubes

Linear complement permutations are an important class of permutations that are frequently used in various parallel computation tasks. They are recognized and called LC permutations in [5]. BPC-permutations [2, 6] are a subset of LC-permutations. The usefulness of BPC-permutation are described in [2, 6]. In addition, the importance of LC-permutations is that data alignment requirements in many non-linear parallel storage schemes, as XOR-schemes described in Chapter 12, are LC-permutations. Since they are frequently used as kernel communication tasks in many application programs, like numerical analysis, image processing, scientific and engineering computations, the efficiency of their realization has important effect on the efficiency of whole computation.

A linear permutation is a permutation that any destination address of a message can be expressed as $D^{\tau}=T\times S^{\tau}$, where D is the destination, S is the source (in binary representation of n bits), and T is a $n\times n$ nonsingular matrix.

Definition 12.5 A permutation is a linear-complement (LC) permutation if and only if it can be expressed as $P'=\{(S,D\oplus C)|0\leqslant S,D,C\leqslant N\text{-}1\}$, where $P=\{(S,D)|0\leqslant S,D\leqslant N\text{-}1\}$ is a linear permutation.

Let $D^{\tau}=(T\times S^{\tau})\oplus C$. Since matrix T is a nonsingular matrix, it has a nonsingular inversion matrix R. We will call matrix T and its inversion matrix R the *transformation matrices*, since they transform source (destination) addresses into destination (source) addresses. We will express

$D^\tau = T\times S^\tau$ as $D=T\times S$ when no confusion will arise. We use t_k (r_k) to denote the kth row of T (R). We use matrix E to denote the identity matrix, and e_k is the kth row of E.

We call all the permutations that have the same transformation matrix T (but different constant modifier C) a *type* of LC permutations. We will see that the constant modifier C does not affect the routing sequence with respect to conflicts (it only has effect on the transmission paths of the individual messages).

We introduce an algorithm to avoid conflict in a way that in addition to exchange messages along one dimension in some steps, we find two dimensions in some steps along which the messages are transmitted circularly such that each node holds one and only one message at each step. The routing algorithm realizes any LC-permutations in n steps, but the time to forward the messages by one step is only one Exclusive-OR gate's delay, since only one bit in the destination address of the packet is tested at each routing step. Thus the gate-level delay of an LC-permutation is only n. The algorithm is completely distributed as each node decides where to send its message independently, no central control is necessary in the system and no additional communication is needed between the neighboring nodes for routing. It may not be called "self-routing" because it needs precomputation. However it is different from traditional non-self-routing in that the precomputation is not for any individual permutation but for a set of permutations which have a common form, and in the routing process any node routes its message based solely on the destination address of its own message. The precomputation can be carried out before run-time. The algorithm can be realized simply by a shift register in each node.

In order to describe the idea easily, we assume that the algorithm works dimension by dimension from dimension n-1 down to dimension 0. In fact, it does not necessarily use the n dimensions in this order in its implementation.

Intuitively, the algorithm works as follows. In each step, step k, for $1\leqslant k\leqslant n$, we are to make the (n-k)th bits of the destination addresses the same as the node addresses so that all the messages will arrive at their destinations in at most n steps. However, conflicts may occur in some steps if the nodes transmit the messages only along the links on one dimension (the (n-k)th dimension). If conflict will not occur, each two nodes connected by the (n-k)th dimension will exchange their message (may or may not, based on the (n-k)th bits of the destination addresses of the two messages). We call this transmission *exchange*. If conflict will occur, the algorithm will look for another dimension, dimension b, to coordinate with the (n-k)th dimension, and each four nodes connected by the (n-k)th and the bth dimension will transmit the messages circularly along the loop formed by the links of these two dimensions. We call this transmission *circulation*. In this way, conflict will be avoided, and the goal of making the (n-k)th bit of the destination addresses the same as the node addresses will also be achieved. We call dimension b the *detour* dimension of dimension n-k. This transmission process looks similar to playing with a Rubick's cube in some sense. (It is more flexible than playing with a Rubick's cube in that each small "cube" turns around separately rather than a whole layer of small cubes turns around.)

Note that here the "circulation" in the system are formed automatically while each node only tests one bit of its own message without knowing any information about the messages on its neighboring nodes, thus no additional communication is needed among the four neighboring nodes. Which kind of transmissions (exchange or circulation) will be needed in each step? Which dimension will be used coordinately with a dimension if circulation is needed? All these can be determined before run-time for LC-permutations by examining their transformation matrices.

For example, in the first step, if $t_{n-1,n-1}=1$ and $d_{n-1} \neq s_{n-1}$, then send the packet from S to $IMG^{(n-1)}(S)$, otherwise no action happens; if $t_{n-1,n-1}=0$, we find an element $t_{n-1,b}$ in T such that $t_{n-1,b}=1$ (we are sure that such an element exists, and we call dimension b the detour dimension of n-1), in this case if $d_{n-1} \neq s_{n-1}$, then send the packet from S to $IMG^{(n-1)}(S)$, else send the packet to $IMG^{(b)}(S)$. After one step, the transformation matrix will be updated accordingly. Then the algorithm transmits the packets according to $t_{n-2,n-2}$. The above process repeats n times.

The following algorithm determines which kind of transmissions is needed in each step, and which dimension will be used as a detour dimension of a dimension if circulation is needed in the corresponding step.

A vector of size n---*detour*---is used to record the above information. The algorithm puts the detour dimension of dimension k in *detour*[k]. If dimension k does not need a detour dimension, the algorithm just set *detour*[k] to n (just for the description, naturally there is not a dimension n in an n-cube), and exchange operation will be carried out on this dimension at communication time, otherwise circulation will be carried out along the dimension and its detour dimension.

```
Algorithm DetourFinding;
/* Find a detour dimension for each dimension. */
/* T, R: transformation matrices, R=T^1.
r_k: the kth row of R
e_k: the kth row of the identity matrix.
detour[n-1:0]: the detour array. */
{
    for(k=n-1;k>=0;k--){
        if (_k,k=1)
```

```
                detour[k]=n;
            r_k=e_k;
            /* Modify R using Equation 12-21. */
        else
                Find b such that b<k and t_{k,b}=1;
        detour[k]=b;
        r_b=r_b⊕r_k⊕e_k;
        r_k=e_k;
        /* Modify R using Equation(12-39). */
        T:=R^-1;  /* Modify T according to R. */
    }
}
```

Any LC-permutation used in a special parallel computation is known before the application algorithm is running. For example, in the XOR skewing schemes [7-12], data alignment requirements for all the N rows of a $N \times N$ matrix have the same transformation $n \times n$ matrix (but for any two different rows they are different permutations). In image processing, an image array may be stored using a certain skewing scheme. Once the skewing scheme is decided, the transformation matrix is known. Thus Algorithm DetourFinding can be carried out to generate vector detour before run-time. At run-time, when the elements of the image array need to be accessed and aligned, a register in each node is set to vector *detour*, and is used for routing the permutation to align data. The routing algorithm is as follows:

```
Algorithm ExCir-Routing;
{
    for(k=n-1;k>=0;k--){
        if (d_k≠s_k )
            send D to IMG^(k)(S);
        else
            send D to IMG^(detour[k])(S);
    }
}
```

Recall that when the dimension k does not need a detour dimension, *detour*[k]=n, and $IMG^{(n)}(S)$ is Node S itself, thus send D to $IMG^{(detour[k])}(S)$ in this case means "do nothing" (the message packet D just remains in the same node). We will see that, if *detour*[k]=n the only possible transmission in Algorithm ExCir-Routing in Step k is an exchange, otherwise it is a circulation.

An example is shown in Figure 12.2. The permutation is D=$T \times S$ ⊕

(0000). The transformation matrices are:

$$T = \begin{pmatrix} 0 & 0 & 1 & 1 \\ 0 & 0 & 0 & 1 \\ 1 & 0 & 0 & 0 \\ 0 & 1 & 0 & 0 \end{pmatrix}, \quad \text{and} \quad R = \begin{pmatrix} 0 & 0 & 1 & 0 \\ 0 & 0 & 0 & 1 \\ 1 & 1 & 0 & 0 \\ 0 & 1 & 0 & 0 \end{pmatrix}.$$

The vector *detour* found by Algorithm Detour Finding is (1044).

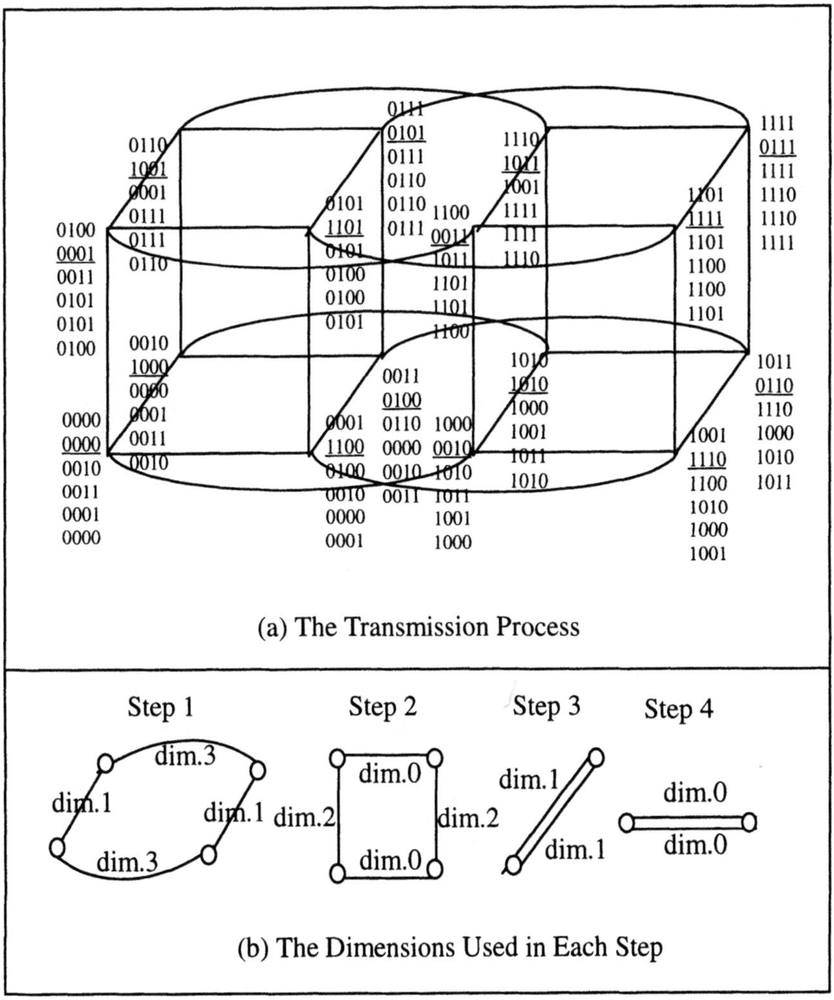

(a) The Transmission Process

(b) The Dimensions Used in Each Step

Figure 12.2. ExCir-routing process

Thus , at run-time, the permutation will be routed by Algorithm ExCir-Routing as follows:

Step 1, Transmit the packets circularly along dimensions 3 and 1;

Step 2, Transmit the packets circularly along dimensions 2 and 0;

Step 3, Transmit the packets along dimension 1;

Step 4, Transmit the packets along dimension 0.

Part (a) of Figure 12.2 shows the transmission process. A column of numbers is shown beside each node. The first number is the node number; the second one (underlined) is the destination address of the message, and can also be thought of the id of the message. Each of the following numbers indicates that the message with that id has arrived at the node in each step. After four steps all the packets arrive at their destinations. One can see that no conflict occurs as each node has one and only one number at any step.

From Part (b) of Figure 12.2 we can see that although each node routes based only on one bit of its own message without knowing any information about its neighboring nodes, circulation along dimensions 3 and 1 is formed in Step 1, and along dimensions 2 and 0 in Step 2; and exchanges happen on dimension 1 in Step 3, and on dimension 0 in Step 4.

We now prove the correctness of the above routing algorithm by induction.

Lemma 12.2 In the transmission process of ExCir-Routing, no conflict will occur in the first step.

Proof: At the first step, only two cases are possible: $t_{n-1,n-1}=1$ or $t_{n-1,n-1}=0$.

Case 1: $t_{n-1,n-1}=1$.

In this case, transmission can only take place between two nodes connected by the (n-1)th dimensional link. Consider any two nodes connected by an (n-1)th dimensional link and the two packets on them. Let the two nodes be S and S', and the two packets be D and D' correspondingly.

Because of the hypercube connection topology, we know

$$\begin{cases} s'_{n-1} \neq s_{n-1}, \\ s'_k = s_k, \quad \text{for} \quad k \neq n-1. \end{cases} \tag{12-27}$$

According to the transformation matrix T, we have

$$\begin{cases} d_{n-1} = s_{n-1} + \sum_{k=0}^{n-2} t_{n-1,k} \times s_k + c_{n-1} \\ d'_{n-1} = s'_{n-1} + \sum_{k=0}^{n-2} t_{n-1,k} \times s'_k + c_{n-1} \end{cases} \tag{12-28}$$

Because of Equations (12-27) and (12-28), we have

$$d'_{n-1} \neq d_{n-1} \; . \tag{12-29}$$

According to Equations (12-27) and (12-29) we know only two cases could be possible: the first, $d_{n-1}=s_{n-1}$ and $d'_{n-1}=s'_{n-1}$, so no transmission will occur between the two nodes; the second, $d_{n-1} \neq s_{n-1}$ and $d'_{n-1} \neq s'_{n-1}$, so D will be sent from S to S' while D' will be sent from S' to S. No conflict occurs in either case. After the transmission, we have $d_{n-1} = s_{n-1}$ on every node.

Case 2: $t_{n-1,n-1}=0$.

Because T is nonsingular and $t_{n-1,n-1}=0$ we are sure there is a non-zero element in the $(n-1)$th row, i.e. we can find an element $t_{n-1,b}$ such that $b<n-1$ and $t_{n-1,b}=1$. Thus we have *detour*$[n-1]=b$ according to Algorithm DetourFinding. According to the routing algorithm, transmissions can only take place along dimensions n-1 and b.

Consider any four nodes connected by the four links on dimensions n-1 and b and the four messages on them. Let the four nodes be S_0, S_1, S_2, and S_3, and the destinations of the four messages be D_0, D_1, D_2, and D_3 respectively. Without loss of generality, let $S_1=IMG^{(n-1)}(S_0)$, $S_3=IMG^{(n-1)}(S_2)$, $S_2=IMG^{(b)}(S_0)$, and $S_3=IMG^{(b)}(S_1)$.

So we have

$$\begin{cases} s_{0,n-1} \neq s_{1,n-1}, \\ s_{2,n-1} \neq s_{3,n-1}, \\ s_{0,n-1} = s_{2,n-1}, \\ s_{1,n-1} = s_{3,n-1}. \end{cases} \tag{12-30}$$

Similar to Equation(12-29), we have

$$\begin{cases} d_{0,n-1} = d_{1,n-1}, \\ d_{2,n-1} = d_{3,n-1}, \\ d_{0,n-1} \neq d_{2,n-1}, \\ d_{1,n-1} \neq d_{3,n-1}. \end{cases} \tag{12-31}$$

According to Equations (12-30) and (12-31), we could only have the following two subcases:

Subcase 1: $d_{0,n-1}=s_{0,n-1}$ (so $d_{1,n-1} \neq s_{1,n-1}$, $d_{2,n-1} \neq s_{2,n-1}$, and $d_{3,n-1}=s_{3,n-1}$).

In this case D_0 will be sent from S_0 to S_2, D_1 from S_1 to S_0, D_3 from S_3 to S_1, and D_2 from S_2 to S_3.

Subcase 2: $d_{0,n-1} \neq s_{0,n-1}$ (so $d_{1,n-1}=s_{1,n-1}$, $d_{2,n-1}=s_{2,n-1}$, and $d_{3,n-1} \neq s_{3,n-1}$).

In this case the messages are sent along the loop as above, except that the direction of the circulation is reversed.

The above configuration is shown in Figure 12.3.

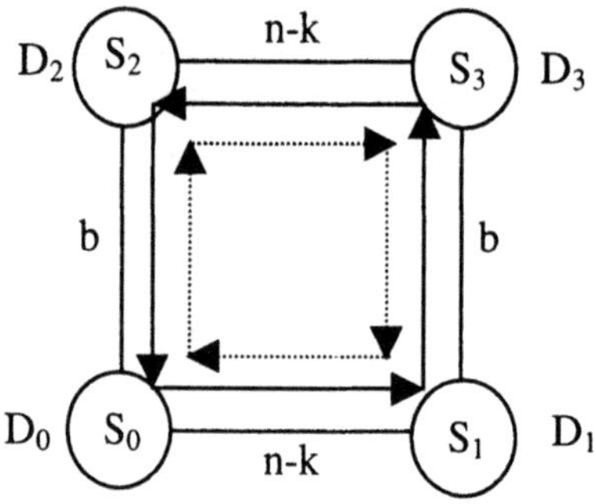

Figure 12.3. A well-formed loop

We say the four nodes and the four links on the two dimensions constitute a *well-formed loop* for the the four packets in the above case. In any subcase, all the messages are transmitted circularly along the well-formed loops, so no conflict occurs.

After the transmission, we also have $d_{n-1}=s_{n-1}$ on every node. ■

From the above we can see that two types of transmission may occur in the routing process. The first (when $t_{n-1,n-1}=1$), each pair of two neighboring nodes connected by the (n-1)th dimension (may or may not) exchange their messages. We call this type of transmission *exchange operation.*

The second (when $t_{n-1,n-1}=0$), the four neighboring nodes connected by the (n-1)th and bth links transmit their messages along the well-formed loop. We call this type of transmission *circulation operation*. The novelty of this algorithm is to use the two types of transmissions on hypercube to avoid conflict.

Refer to Figure 12.2, at the first step, each four nodes connected by dimension 3 and dimension 1 constitute a well-formed loop. For example, message 5 (0101) is transmitted from Node 7 (0111) to Node 5 (0101), message 13 from Node 5 to Node 13, message 15 from Node 13 to Node 15, message 7 from Node 15 to Node 7. We have $d_3=s_3$ on every node after the transmission.

Let's see what the relation between the destination addresses and the node address will be after the first step. Suppose that a message D is on Node S at the beginning, and on S' after the transmission (note that here S' will not necessarily be the $(n-1)$th neighbor of S).

From the proof of the above theorem, after the first step, regardless of exchange or circulation, we have

$$s'_{n-1}=d_{n-1} \tag{12-32}$$

There are two cases possible for the relations between the other bits.

First, when the first step is exchange. We know that in this case S' is the $(n-1)$th neighbor of S, thus the two bits of S and S' on any dimension, except the $(n-1)$th dimension, are all the same.

So that we can express the relation between D and S' as $s'_k=\sum_{j=0}^{n-1} r_{k,j}\times d_j \oplus c_k$ for $0\leqslant k\leqslant n-2$. From this expression and Equation (12-32) we can express the relation between S' and D as $S'=R'\times D\oplus C'$, where $c'_{n-1}=0$, the other bits of C' are the same as that of C, and

$$\begin{cases} r'_{n-1}=e_{n-1}, \\ r'_j=r_j, \quad \text{for} \quad j\neq n-1. \end{cases} \tag{12-33}$$

Secondly, the first step is circulation. Because transmission can only occur along the $(n-1)$th and the bth dimensions, we know the two bits of S and S' are all the same except on these two dimensions.

According to the algorithm, whether or not the message should be transmitted along dimension b is determined by d_{n-1}: if and only if $d_{n-1}=s_{n-1}$ it will be transmitted along dimension b, so that we have $s'_b=s_b\oplus \overline{(d_{n-1}\oplus s_{n-1})}$. That is $s'_b=s_b\oplus(d_{n-1}\oplus s_{n-1})+1=(\bar{r}_{n-1,n-1}\oplus r_{b,n-1})\times d_{n-1}$ $+(r_{n-1,n-2}\oplus r_{b,n-2})\times d_{n-2}+\cdots+(r_{n-1,0}\oplus r_{b,0})\times d_0+c_b+c_{n-1}+1$. Thus the relation between S' and D can be expressed as $S'=R'\times D\oplus C'$, where $c'_{n-1}=0$ and $c'_b=c_b+c_{n-1}+1$, and the other bits of C' are the same as those of C, and

$$\begin{cases} r'_{n-1}=e_{n-1}, \\ r'_b=r_b\oplus r_{n-1}\oplus e_{n-1}, \\ r'_j=r_j, \quad \text{for} \quad j\notin\{n-1,b\}. \end{cases} \tag{12-34}$$

Because of Lemma 12.2 we know each node holds one and only one message after the first step, so that the mapping between the node addresses and the destination addresses is one-to-one mapping. Thus we know that R' is a nonsingular matrix in any case.

Lemma 12.3 Suppose that an n by n nonsingular matrix T has the form of

$$\left[\begin{array}{c|c} A & B \\ \hline C & D \end{array}\right]$$

where A is a $k\times k$ identity matrix, B is a $k\times(n\text{-}k)$ matrix with all its elements being 0, and D is an $(n\text{-}k)\times(n\text{-}k)$ matrix, and $1\leqslant k\leqslant n\text{-}1$. Then there is at least one element $t_{n\text{-}k\text{-}1,b}$ such that $b\leqslant n\text{-}k\text{-}1$ and $t_{n\text{-}k\text{-}1,b}=1$ (i.e. the first row of submatrix D contains at least one non-zero element).

Proof: Suppose that such an element does not exist. Because A is a $k\times k$ identity matrix and B has its all elements being zero, we can find x rows in T, $t_{u_1}, t_{u_2}, \cdots t_{u_x}$, where $1\leqslant x\leqslant k$ and $\{u_1, u_2, \cdots u_x\}\subseteq\{n-1, n-2, \cdots n-k\}$, such that $t_{u_1}, t_{u_2}, \cdots t_{u_x}$ and $t_{n\text{-}k\text{-}1}$ are linearly dependent. That means that T is singular. This is a contradiction to the condition given in the lemma (T is nonsingular). ∎

From the above we can see that after the first step we have $d_{n\text{-}1}=s_{n\text{-}1}$, $S=R\times D\oplus C$, R is nonsingular, and C is a constant. Suppose that after the (k-1)th step, $1\leqslant k\leqslant n$, we have

$$d_{n\text{-}1}\cdots d_{n\text{-}k+1}=s_{n\text{-}1}\cdots s_{n\text{-}k+1} \tag{12-35}$$

and $S=(R\times D)\oplus C$, where R is a nonsingular matrix and C is a constant. We prove the following lemma.

Lemma 12.4 Firstly, at Step k , $1\leqslant k\leqslant n$, no conflict will occur. Secondly, after Step k, we have $d_{n\text{-}1}\cdots d_{n\text{-}k}=s_{n\text{-}1}\cdots s_{n\text{-}k}$, and it is still an LC-permutation, which can be expressed as $S=(R\times D)\oplus C$, so that the algorithm can proceed.

Proof**:** If an $n\times n$ matrix is nonsingular, it has an inverse matrix. Let T be the inversion matrix of R at Step k. From Equation (12-35) we know R has the form of

$$R=\begin{pmatrix} 1 & 0 & \cdots & 0 & 0 & \cdots & 0 \\ 0 & 1 & \cdots & 0 & 0 & \cdots & 0 \\ \cdots & & \cdots & & & \cdots & \\ 0 & 0 & \cdots & 1 & 0 & \cdots & 0 \\ r_{n-k,n-1} & r_{n-k,n-2} & \cdots & & r_{n-k,n-k} & \cdots & r_{n-k,0} \\ \cdots & & \cdots & & & \cdots & \\ r_{0,n-1} & r_{0,n-2} & \cdots & & r_{0,n-k} & \cdots & r_{0,0} \end{pmatrix}$$

i.e.

$$\begin{cases} s_i = d_i, & \text{for} \quad n-k+1 \le i \le n-1 \\ s_i = \sum_{j=0}^{n-1} r_{i,j} \times d_j \oplus c_i, & \text{for} \quad 0 \le i \le n-k. \end{cases} \tag{12-36}$$

Thus we know T has the form of

$$\left(\begin{array}{c|c} \mathrm{A} & \mathrm{B} \\ \hline \mathrm{C} & \mathrm{D} \end{array}\right)$$

where A is a $(k\text{-}1)\times(k\text{-}1)$ identity matrix, B is a $(k\text{-}1)\times(n\text{-}k\text{+}1)$ matrix with all its elements being 0, and D is an $(n\text{-}k\text{+}1)\times(n\text{-}k\text{+}1)$ matrix.

According to Lemma 12.3, we have $t_{n-k,n-k}=1$ or we can find b, such that $b \leqslant n\text{-}k\text{-}1$ and $t_{n-k,b}=1$. Therefore the algorithm can proceed at Step k. This is why in Algorithm DetourFinding we can always find b such that $b<k$ and $t_{k,b}=1$. Notice that the dimension used in Step k is $n\text{-}k$.

We have the following two cases:

Case 1: $t_{n-k,n-k}=1$.

Similar to the case of the first step, we know exchange operation will occur on dimension $n\text{-}k$, no conflict will occur, and after the kth step we have $S'=(R'\times D)\oplus C'$, where $c'_{n-k}=0$, the other bits of C' are the same as that of C, and

$$\begin{cases} r'_{n-k} = e_{n-k}, \\ r'_j = r_j, \text{for} \quad j \ne n-k. \end{cases} \tag{12-37}$$

Case 2: $t_{n-k,n-k}=0$.

According to the above, we can find b such that $b \leqslant n\text{-}k\text{-}1$ and $t_{n-k,b}=1$. Similar to the first step, we know that each four nodes connected by the (n-

k)th and the bth dimension constitute a well-formed loop, and circulation operation will be carried out along the well-formed loops, so that no conflict occurs.

Suppose a packet D has been sent from Node S to S' in this step, we have $s'_{n-k}=d_{n-k}$, $s'_b = s_b \oplus (d_{n-k} \oplus s_{n-k})$ and $s'_i=s_i$ for all $i \notin \{n-k,b\}$. Thus s'_b can be expressed as:

$$\begin{aligned} s'_b &= s_b \oplus d_{n-k} \oplus s_{n-k} + 1 \\ &= (r_{n-k,n-1} \oplus r_{b,n-1}) \times d_{n-1} + \cdots + (r_{n-k,n-k+1} \oplus r_{b,n-k+1}) \times d_{n-k+1} \\ &\quad + (\overline{r}_{n-k,n-k} \oplus r_{b,n-k}) \times d_{n-k} + (r_{n-k,n-k-1} \oplus r_{b,n-k-1}) \times d_{n-k-1} \\ &\quad + \cdots + (r_{n-k,0} \oplus r_{b,0}) \times d_0 + c_b + c_{n-k} + 1. \end{aligned} \tag{12-38}$$

Therefore the relation between the destination and the nodes can be expressed as $S'=(R'\times D)\oplus C'$, where $c'_{n-k}=0$ and $c'_b=c_b+c_{n-k}+1$, the other bits of C' are the same as those of C, and

$$\begin{cases} r'_{n-k} = e_{n-k}, \\ r'_b = r_b \oplus r_{n-k} \oplus e_{n-k}, \\ r'_j = r_j, \qquad \text{for} \quad j \notin \{n-k,b\}. \end{cases} \tag{12-39}$$

Because the transmission is conflict-free in any case, each node holds one and only message after the kth Step. Thus we know R' is still nonsingular as the mapping between the node addresses and the destination addresses is one-to-one mapping. ■

Theorem 12.7 The algorithm ExCir-Routing can realize any LC-permutation in n steps without conflict.

Proof: From Lemmas 12.2 and 12.4, we can see, by induction, that no conflict occurs at any step, and after the kth Step we always have $d_{n-1}\cdots d_{n-k}=s_{n-1}\cdots s_{n-k}$,. Thus after n steps any packet D will be on Node S such that $D=S$. This means all the messages arrive at their destinations after n steps. ■

We now analyze the complexity of the routing algorithm. It is clear that the routing algorithm itself is completed in n steps, and only one comparison of two bits is needed in each step.

In the precomputation algorithm, Algorithm DetourFinding, the most complex part of computation is the modification of the transformation matrix T in each step (in fact it is enough to modify one row in each step). This includes an inversion of an $(n-k)\times$ $(n-k)$ matrix on GF(2) in Step k. We present an algorithm for $n \times n$ matrix inversion on GF(2) with the time complexity (bit-level) of its sequential version being $O(n^2)$ in the worst case, or $O(n)$ in the best case. Time complexity of its parallel version is $O(n)$. Thus time complexity (bit-level) of Algorithm DetourFinding is $O(n^3)$ in the worst case, or $O(n^2)$ in the best case, when done sequentially; and $O(n^2)$ when done in parallel. Because all the operations (+ and ×) are carried out in GF(2), matrix inversion is much simpler than matrix inversion in the real field in general. It is not a difficult job even by hand to generate a detour array for systems with thousands of PEs .

It is important that the precomputation is carried out once for a type of permutations, and the transformation matrix of the permutations going to be used in applications are known before run-time, so that the precomputation can be carried before run-time.

Some mechanisms in hardware and software are needed for the implementation of the routing scheme. As we stated before, the result of the precomputation is the *detour* vector, which has *n* elements. In the hypercube system a register can be provided in each node, and is set to *detour* at some stage of the application program. The register shifts $\lceil \log_2 n \rceil$ (one element of the *detour* vector) in each routing step to control the transmission. The routing process does not need the central control processor of the hypercube system to take care, and it does not need to interrupt the work of the processing element in the nodes either. It is simple enough to separate the routing function from the processing element in each node, such that the processing element can be more concentrated on computation rather than taking care of communication. In this way, hardware design of the hypercube nodes can be simplified, since the routing process only needs an Exclusive-OR gate of two bits and a shift register.

In the software part, the shift register can be set directly by the programmer, or by a "smart" compiler that detects the patterns of the permutations and determines the going-to-be values of the shift register at compile-time. The choice is a matter of a tradeoff between the programmer and the system. It is suitable that the programmer states the patterns of the permutations and the compiler determines the setting of the register. This is not difficult to either the programmer or the compiler, since usually the programmer knows the patterns of the permutations (e.g. FFT requires shuffle and bit-reversal), while the compiler knows the details of the system.

The algorithm requires that the messages in different nodes to be sent along two different dimensions at some steps. This ability is supported on MIMD systems [13], but today's commercially available SIMD hypercube systems do not exploit this potential (to our knowledge).

From the above we can see that it is not difficult to give new designs to adapt this algorithm on both MIMD as well as SIMD hypercube systems so that frequently used permutations can be realized more efficiently.

In fact the n dimensions are not necessarily used from n-1 to 0. Because of the symmetric feature of the hypercube topology, any ordering for the use of the n dimensions is applicable as well as the principle underlying the routing algorithm is followed.

12.4 Setting up *N* independent Paths for LC-Permutations

The algorithm presented in Section 12.3 works in a packet switched mode. We now introduce an algorithm for routing LC permutations in circuit switched or wormhole routing mode on hypercubes, which can set up N independent paths while only one bit-comparison is needed in each routing step. First, an algorithm is presented which can find an ordered sequence of the n dimensions of the hypercube for any type of LC permutations without knowing the particular permutation itself (thus it can be carried out off-line for any type of LC permutations). When this ordered sequence of dimensions is used in communication time to route the individual packets, N independent paths will be set up simultaneously without any conflict on the use of the edges.

The algorithm is inspired by the algorithms in [6, 14, 15] and the algorithm presented in Section 12.3. It seems that if some order of dimensions can be found off-line, then the paths for the N packets can be determined before run time. The routing itself can be done in an oblivious manner. The idea is that we use some imaginary dimension such that if the packets were transmitted along that dimension (in addition to other dimension) then the transformation between the current nodes where the packets reside and the destinations will always be expressed by a nonsingular matrix. Thus the sequence of the use of the n dimensions can be decided only using the transformation matrix, without resorting to the permutation itself (thus the sequence can be pre-decided off-line). This reasoning process is similar to the routing process presented in Section 12.3, but no circulation operation is really executed in the routing process of the algorithm presented in this section. Also, we notice that the transmission path of a packet may not be the same as the path that the packet is transmitted in the process in ExCir-Routing, although the Algorithm Sequencing presented below looks similar to Algorithm Detour Finding in Section 12.3.

We refer to the destination address of a packet on Node S as D at any step. Let $D=(T\times S)\oplus C$, and R be the inverse matrix of T. Thus it can also be expressed as $S=(R\times D)\oplus C'$ where C' is also a constant.

The following algorithm, Algorithm Sequencing, is used to find out an order for the use of the n dimensions before run time. In communication time, any packet will match one bit of its destination address and the node address. Only difference between the routing here and the naive routing is that the routing algorithm here will use the order generated by the Sequencing algorithm, rather than the simple descending or ascending order in naive routing algorithm.

```
Algorithm Sequencing;
/* T, R: transformation matrices, where R=T^-1.
Selected: the set of dimensions selected so far.
Seq[1:n]: an array for the ordered sequence.
aux: a variable used to record the "imaginary" dimension.
This is only used for modifying the transformation matrices,
and for the proof of the correctness of the routing algorithm,
it has nothing to do with the real routing process. */
{
    k=n-1;
    Selected={ };
    aux=n;
    for(j=1;j<n+1;j++){
        Seq[j]=k;
        Selected=Selected+{k};
        if (t_{k,k}=1){
            if (k=aux)
                aux=n;
            r_k=e_k;
            /* Modify R according to Equation (12-43). */
        }
        else{
            if (aux=n)
                Find a such that t_{k,a}=1, and aux=a;
            r_aux =r_aux ⊕ r_k ⊕ e_k;
            r_k=e_k;
            /* Modify R according to Equation (12-46)1. */
        }
        T=R^-1;
        /* Modify T according to R. */
        if (aux=n)
            Pick up an unselected dimension b;
        else
            Find b such that t_{b,a}=1;
        k=b;
    }
}
```

The above algorithm takes dimension n-1 as the first dimension to be used. Actually, any dimension can be taken as the first one to be used without affecting the validity of the algorithm because of the symmetry of the problem in hand. The above algorithm generates an ordered sequence for the use of the n dimensions, any packet in a permutation will travel the n dimensions (if necessary) in that order. The routing algorithm itself in communication time will be extremely simple --- only one bit-comparison is needed in each step:

"FOR k:=1 TO n DO IF $d_{Seq[k]} \neq s_{Seq[k]}$, THEN send the packet along dimension Seq[k]."

We give an example in Figure 12.4. In the Figure, the first number on each node is the node number, and the second number (the underlined) is the destination address of the packet issued by the node. The permutation is the same as the one given in Figure 12.2.

The ordered dimension sequence generated by Algorithm Sequencing is (3, 1, 2, 0). Note that because there is not a "dimension n" in an n-dimensional hypercube, whenever we say "n is the imaginary dimension aux" we mean "no such an imaginary dimension aux is needed". The transmission paths which are set up automatically in communication time have been shown. On each link of each path there is a square that represents the message packet transmitted along the link, and its destination address is shown in the square. A path (for the packet from 6 to 9) has been highlighted by bold lines. From the figure we can see that no edge is shared between any two packets, thus N paths are set up automatically while each packet is routed independently. Also, all the packets are transmitted along the shortest paths. Notice that the path a packet travels may not be the same as the one in Section 12.3. We can see that Packet 9 (1001) travels through 6, 14, 12, 8, to 9 in Figure 12.3, but it travels through 6, 14, 10, 8, to 9 in Figure 12.2.

Validity of the routing algorithm here can be proved similarly to that of the Algorithm ExCir-Routing in Section 12.3. The difference is that two packets may reside on one node while no packet resides on some nodes in the routing process here. Therefore we need to discuss what the relation will be between the destination address of a packet and the current node address in the proof here.

It is easy to see that any packet arrives at its destination correctly after the routing, because any packet just simply matches one bit of its destination address with the node in each step of the routing process. We will prove that no edge will be shared by any two packets in the routing process. In order to prove this, it is enough to prove that whenever two packets meet on any node in their transmission, they will be transmitted from the node along different dimensions. It is equivalent to say that only one packet can arrive at any node through a link on any one dimension.

In the following, we just simply call it Packet D, if the destination of a packet is D, $0 \leqslant D \leqslant N\text{-}1$.

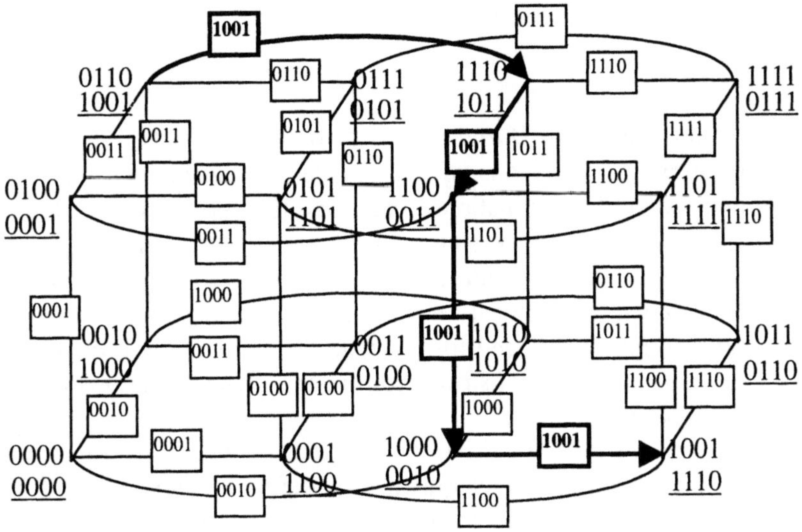

Figure 12.4. A permutation $D=(T\times S)\oplus(0000)$

We are discussing the routing in circuit switched or wormhole mode, but we describe the process in the following proof as if it was in a packet switched mode, so that we can catch n snapshots in the routing process, each of which corresponds to a step in packet switched routing mode. In the Algorithm Sequencing, the matrices T and R are modified in each iteration. Let's $T^{(k)}$ and $R^{(k)}$ be the matrices after the kth modification. Thus $T^{(0)}$ and $R^{(0)}$ are the original transformation matrices.

We say that dimension k is an *active dimension* in a step if packets can only be actually transmitted along this dimension in the step. We first prove that each modification of the matrices T and R represents a snapshot of the distribution of the packets on the nodes.

In the first step, dimension n-1 is to be used as the active dimension.

Case 1, $t^{(0)}_{n-1,n-1}=1$. From a simple analysis (similar to the first step for ExCir-Routing) we know that the relation between the destination D and its *new node address* S can be expressed as: $s_{n-1}=d_{n-1}$ and $s_j = r^{(0)}_{j,*}\times D + c'_j$. That is

$$S = R^{(1)}\times D + C'^{(1)}, \tag{12-40}$$

where $r_{n-1}^{(1)} = e_{n-1}$, $c_{n-1}^{'(1)} = 0$, and $r_j^{(1)} = r_j^{(0)}$, $c_j^{'(1)} = c_j^{'(0)}$, for $j \neq n-1$.

Also we are sure that $R^{(1)}$ is nonsingular because the mapping is one to one. Thus there is a matrix $T^{(1)}$ which is the inversion of $R^{(1)}$.

Case 2, $t_{n-1,n-1}^{(0)}$ =0. In this case, we have

$$d_{n-1} + d_{n-1}^{'} = t_{n-1,n-1}^{(0)} \times (s_{n-1} + s_{n-1}^{'}) = 0\,. \tag{12-41}$$

Thus we know that both *D and D'* will be on one of the two nodes (*S* or *S'*) after this step since only one of them is transmitted in this step. Then the mapping between the destination address and the current node could also be expressed by the same expression using $R^{(1)}$ as in Equation (12-40). But this time, we are sure that *R* would be singular since two packets would match one node number. There would not exist an inversion matrix of $R^{(1)}$, and it would be difficult to proceed to select the following active dimensions by only manipulating the transformation matrix without knowing the real permutation before run time.

The key idea here is how to find a nonsingular transformation matrix after each step such that we can always predefine the next active dimension before run time only by using the transformation matrix.

Imagine that if the packets were routed along two dimensions (dimension *n*-1 and a dimension aux) as in the case that a circulation operation is executed in the Algorithm ExCir-Routing, we could also get a distribution that each node held only one packet. We can obtain that after the first step the relation between D and S can be expressed by $S = R^{(1)} \times D + C'^{(1)}$, where $r_{n-1}^{(1)} = e_{n-1}$, $r_a^{(1)} = e_{n-1} \oplus r_{n-1}^{(0)} \oplus r_a^{(0)}$, and $r_j^{(1)} = r_j^{(0)}$, for $j \neq a$ and $j \neq n-1$. Since the mapping could be expressed as above and it was one to one if routed circularly, we are sure that $R^{(1)}$ is nonsingular, and it has an inversion $T^{(1)}$, and the reasoning process can proceed.

But we do not actually transmit packets circularly. From the above analysis we are sure of the following: (1) A node can have two packets or zero packets; and (2) Packet *D* on a Node *S* can be expressed as $D = T^{(1)} \times S + C^{(1)}$, or $D = T^{(1)} \times S'' + C^{(1)}$, where *S"* is the node connected to S on dimension aux.

Theorem 12.8 A packet *D* is on Node *S* or *S''* after the *j*th dimension in the ordered sequence is used for routing, where $D = T^{(j)} \times S + C^{(j)}$, and *S''* is a neighbor of *S* on dimension aux.

Proof: It is true for j=0 since $D = T^{(0)} \times S + C^{(0)}$. Suppose that it is true when *j=u,* we prove it is true for *j=u*+1, where $0 \leqslant u \leqslant n-1$.

Suppose that the active dimension in Step u is k, and the Algorithm Sequencing finds that the next active dimension is b.

Case 1, $t_{b,b}^{(u)} = 1$.

Consider the two packets D and D' on the two nodes S and S' respectively, where S and S' are connected by a link on dimension b. It is easy to see that $d_b \neq d'_b$ since $d_b + d'_b = t_{b,b} \times (s_b + s'_b) + 0 = 1$. Thus, in Step u+1, if D will be sent to S' then D' will be sent to S, or both of them will not be sent. Therefore, after Step u+1 the relation between a packet D and the node number S will be that only s_b and d_b become the same, the other bits remain the same as before. This is expressed by

$$s_b = d_b \text{, and } s_j = r_j^{(u)} \times D + c'^{(u)}_j \text{, for } j \neq b. \tag{12-42}$$

This means that after Step u+1 we have $S = (R^{(u+1)} \times D) \oplus C'^{(u+1)}$, where $c_b'^{(u+1)} = 0$, the other bits of $c'^{(u+1)}$ are the same as that of $C'^{(u)}$, and

$$r_b^{(u+1)} = e_b \text{, and } r_j^{(u+1)} = r_j^{(u)} \text{, for } j \neq b. \tag{12-43}$$

The algorithm does appropriately modify the transformation matrix R in accordance with Equation (12-43) in this case (see line 13).

Case 2, $t_{b,b}^{(u)} = 0$.

It is easy to see that $d_b = d'_b$. Let's consider the two packets, D and D'', mapped by Node S and Node S'', where S and S'' are two nodes connected by a link on dimension aux. D and D'' may be really on S and S'' respectively, or they may be actually on one of S and S''. Let aux=a.

Subcase 1, D and D'' are really on Nodes S and S'' respectively, i.e. the mapping is really one to one, similar to the original distribution. Since $d_b + d_b'' = t_{b,a}^{(u)} \times (s_b + s_b'') + 0 = 1$, we know only one of them is to be transmitted on dimension b. Similar to the argument in the first step, if we imagine only the packet whose bit b has not been the same as bit b of its node would be transmitted on dimension b, otherwise it would be transmitted on dimension a, then transmission of the four packets on the four nodes connected by the links on dimension b and dimension a would form a circle. Consequently, each node would hold only one packet, and all the nodes would match its bit b, and the packets, and only those packets, whose bit b has been matched, would be sent on dimension a (i.e. only s_a would change).

If we denote that a packet D is on Node $S^{(old)}$ before this circular transmission, and it is on Node $S^{(new)}$ after this transmission, then we have

$$s_a^{(new)} + s_a^{(old)} = s_b^{(old)} + d_b + 1. \tag{12-44}$$

$$s_a^{(new)} = s_a^{(old)} + s_b^{(old)} + d_b + 1 = (r_a^{(u)} \times D + c'^{(u)}_a) + (r_b^{(u)} \times D + c'^{(u)}_b) + (e_b \times D) + 1. \quad (12\text{-}45)$$

That is after Step $u+1$ we have packet D on Node S where

$$\begin{cases} s_b = d_b, \\ s_a = (e_b + r_a^{(u)} + r_b^{(u)}) \times D + c'^{(u)}_a + c'^{(u)}_b + 1, \text{ and} \\ s_j = r_j^{(u)} \times D + c'^{(u)}_j, \text{ for } j \neq a \text{ and } j \neq b. \end{cases} \quad (12\text{-}46)$$

The relation between the destination addresses and the nodes can be expressed as $S = R^{(u+1)} \times D + C'^{(u+1)}$, where $c'^{(u+1)}_b = 0$ and $c'^{(u+1)}_a = c'^{(u)}_a + c'^{(u)}_b + 1$, the other bits of $C'^{(u+1)}$ are the same as those of $C'^{(u)}$, and

$$\begin{cases} r_b^{(u+1)} = e_b, \\ r_a^{(u+1)} = e_b \oplus r_a^{(u)} \oplus r_b^{(u)}, \text{ and} \\ r_j^{(u+1)} = r_j^{(u)}, \text{ for } j \neq a \text{ and } j \neq b. \end{cases} \quad (12\text{-}47)$$

Subcase 2, D and D'' are actually on one Node, S or S'', similar to the distribution that when $t_{n-1,n-1}^{(0)} = 0$ but after they are transmitted on dimension n-1.

$$d_b + d_b'' = (\sum_{j=0}^{n-1} t_{b,j}^{(u)} \times S + c_b^{(u)}) + (\sum_{j=0}^{n-1} t_{b,j}^{(u)} \times S'' + c_b^{(u)}) = t_{b,a}^{(u)} \times (s_a + s_a'') + 0 = 1 \times 1 + 0 = 1.$$

(12-48)

Thus we are sure that only one of them will be sent on dimension b, and that no conflict will occur on the use of the links on this dimension. However, the key problem here is how to modify the transformation matrix such that our reasoning process can proceed. Notice that it will not be correct to use Equation (12-43) to modify matrix R although packets are only transmitted on dimension b.

Let's consider another two Nodes X and X'' in addition to the two nodes S and S'', where X and X'' are also connected on dimension a, X and S, and X'' and S'', are connected on dimension b, as shown in Figure 12.5.

Suppose that packets Y, Y'', D, and D'' are on Nodes X, X'', S, and S'' respectively by the imagination. Actually we may have the following two real situations.

Situation 1, D and D'' are on Node S, while Y and Y'' are on Node X.

From the above we already know that only one of the two packets D and D'' will be transmitted on dimension b, similarly we know only one of Y and Y'' will be transmitted on dimension b.

Since $d_b + y_b = (\sum_{j=0}^{n-1} t_{b,j}^{(u)} \times S + c_b^{(u)}) + (\sum_{j=0}^{n-1} t_{b,j}^{(u)} \times X + c_b^{(u)}) = t_{b,b}^{(u)} \times (s_b + x_b) + 0 = 0 \times 1 + 0 = 0$, we know that only one of D and Y will be transmitted on dimension b. Similarly we know that only one of D'' and Y'' will be transmitted on dimension b.

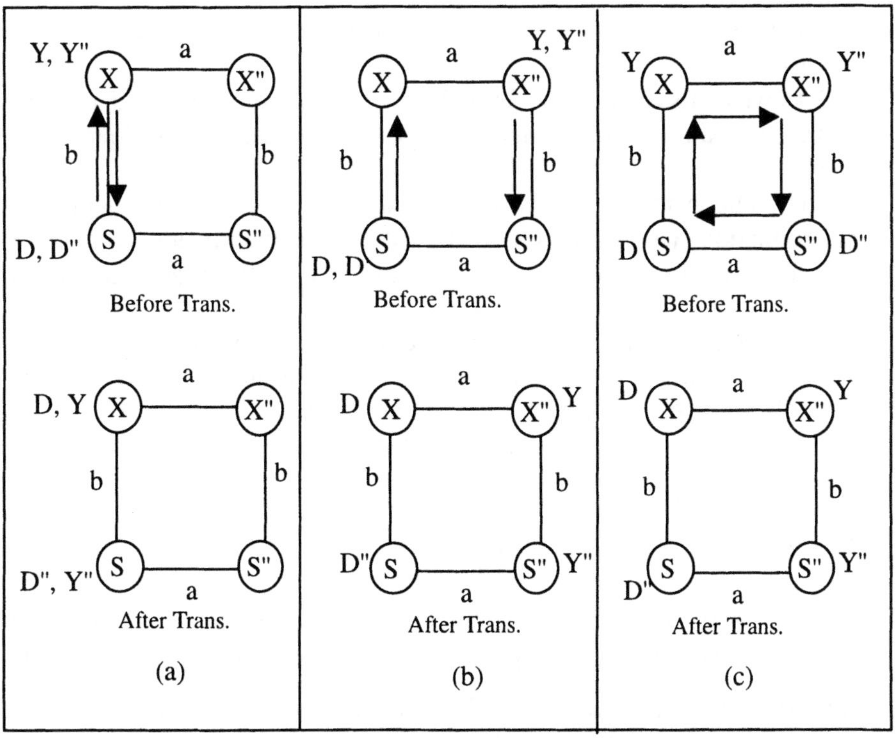

Figure 12.5. Different distributions

Combining the above analysis for D, D'', Y, and Y'', without lose of generality, suppose that D and Y'' will be transmitted. The resulted distribution after Step u+1 will be that D and Y will be on Node X while D'' and Y'' will be on Node S.

This is shown in Figure 12.5(a), and is the same as the imaginary transmission that D and Y'' are transmitted on dimension b while D'' and Y are transmitted on dimension a, as shown in Figure 12.5(c).

Situation 2, D and D'' are on Node S, while Y and Y'' are on Node X''.

The same as in Situation 1, only one of D and D'' can be transmitted on dimension b, and only one of Y and Y'' can be transmitted on dimension b. Also, only one of D and Y can be transmitted on dimension b, and only one of D'' and Y'' can be transmitted on dimension b. Again, suppose that D and Y'' are transmitted on dimension b in accordance with situation 1 above.

After D and Y'' are transmitted on dimension b, the resulted distribution after Step u+1 will be that D'', D, Y, and Y" are on Nodes S, X, X'', and S'' respectively. This is shown in Figure 12.5(b), and is also the same as the imaginary transmission shown in Figure 12.5(c). The same as in subcase 1, the mapping of the destinations and the nodes will be expressed by Equation (12-46)1.

As we can see from line 21 and line 22 that the algorithm does modify the transformation matrix R appropriately in accordance with Equation (12-46)1.

The above reasoning shows that Algorithm Sequencing modifies the transformation matrices correctly such that each modification represents a snapshot of the mapping between the destination and the node addresses. ■

Notice that in the above proof we did not give a detailed transformation between $C^{(u)}$and $C'^{(u)}$ in each step for two reasons. First, it is simple. Secondly, it does not affect the routing sequence for the use of the n dimensions no matter what a particular constant modifier is in each step.

Theorem 12.9 After the transmission using the sequence of the dimensions any packet arrives at its destination.

Proof: After the routing the mapping is expressed by $D = E \times S \oplus C^{(n)}$ and $c_j^{(n)} = 0$ for $0 \leqslant j \leqslant n$-1. Also, there is not an unused dimension n that D is mapped by the nth neighbor of S. Thus we are sure that each node holds only one packet and the node is exactly the destination of the packet. ■

Theorem 12.10 The algorithm Sequencing is valid in that aux and b can always be found in any step.

Proof: It is similar to Lemma 12.4 from Lemma 12.3. ■

In fact in the sequence finding process, whenever an active dimension is found which is the same as the last imaginary dimension (i.e. k=aux in line 11 of Algorithm Sequencing), we find a "cycle" of dimensions. If the number of dimensions in the cycle is m , and the dimensions are $i_1, i_2, \cdots, i_m$, then all the numbers of $d_{i_1} d_{i_2} \cdots d_{i_m}$ constitute a complete residue system module 2^m. This cycle is similar in the form to a cycle in Bit-Permute for BPC permutations. Although this cycle does not behave like a cycle in Bit-Permute function for BPC-permutations where the cycle maps a source address exactly to a destination, we can use this kind of cycles as an order for the purpose of routing.

The above theorem guarantees that the modification of the transformation matrices in Algorithm Sequencing represents "exactly to some extent" the mapping between the packets and the nodes. Thus a path is predetermined for any packet. In circuit switched mode, a path is set up for a packet, and is kept on the whole transmission process of the packet. In the following, we prove that the paths set up for the *N* packets are independent to each other when the paths are chosen according to the order for the use of the dimensions generated by Algorithm Sequencing.

Theorem 12.11 No edge will be shared by any two paths while the packets are routed independently using the *n* dimensions with the order generated by Algorithm Sequencing.

Proof: Let's call a path for a packet *D* path *D*. We prove that when two paths *D* and *D'* meet at Node *S*, they never meet on any Node *S'* where *S'* is a neighbor of *S* on any dimension.

Suppose that packets *D* and *D'* arrive at Node *S* from the neighbors of S on dimension *k* and *k'*, and suppose Seq[*x*]=k, and Seq[*x'*]=*k'*. Then we have

Case 1:

$$\begin{cases} D = T^{(x)} \times S \oplus C^{(x)}, \\ D' = T^{(x')} \times S \oplus C^{(x')}. \end{cases} \tag{12-49}$$

If $S \neq 0$, only when $x \neq x'$ Equation (12-46)2 can be true. Thus we know that $k \neq k'$. This means that *D* and *D'* arrive at this node from different dimensional links (or, arrive at this node in different steps when routed in packet switched mode). But if *S=0*, and *x=x'*, then *D=D'*.

The above situation means that only one packet can arrive at a node from any dimensional link, thus only one path can use an edge on any one dimension.

Case 2:

$$\begin{cases} D = T^{(x)} \times S \oplus C^{(x)}, \\ D' = T^{(x')} \times S'' \oplus C^{(x')}. \end{cases} \tag{12-50}$$

In this equation S'' is the neighbor of S on some dimension a. If $x=x'$, then we know that D' had already been on Node S before the time D was coming from dimension k (k=Seq[x]). It is only our imagination that D' was sent to S'' through dimension a while D was sent to S through dimension k in Step x.

This also means that only one packet can arrive at a node from a link on any dimension.

The above means that no two paths can share any edge, and N independent paths are set up for the N packets when the packets are routed independently using the n dimensions in the order generated by the Sequencing algorithm. ■

Algorithm Sequencing finds an order for the use of the $\log_2 N$ dimensions of a hypercube with N nodes. When this order is used, N *independent* paths will be established for LC permutations, while only one comparison of two bits is needed in each routing step. The order is decided without knowing a particular permutation. The N independent paths are all shortest paths. In circuit switched and wormhole routing mode, this can guarantee that no contention can occur for the use of any link. The main advantage of this method is that it does not need arbitration computation in routing time to decide which packet should go through which link, and any LC permutation can be realized *in one pass*. Because no contention will occur in the routing process, no policy is needed to solve contention, and no buffer is needed to hold any packet temporarily, the hardware design of the router can be simplified.

12.5 Conclusion

We discussed some routing algorithms for frequently used permutations on hypercubes. We focus our attention on avoidance of network conflicts in the transmission process of the messages. Two kinds of network conflicts are recognized, i.e. conflicts on the nodes and conflicts on the edges. Conflicts in the message transmission have a major effect on the hardware requirement and communication speed. If a routing algorithm cannot avoid conflicts, buffers are needed to store messages temporarily during transmission. Although the buffer space itself in each node seems not a big issue, computation is needed to select one message to send when there are more than one message in a node. Thus each routing step takes longer time, and more complicated control logic is needed for routing. Conflict-free routing algorithms have some merits. First, no buffering is needed. Second, no "selection" process is needed in the routing process. Thus conflict-free algorithms are superior in both hardware complexity and routing speed.

LC permutations are frequently used in image processing and pattern recognition, signal processing, and other scientific and engineering computations. BPC permutations are subset of LC permutations. The well-known important permutations such as matrix transpose, perfect shuffle, unshuffle, bit reversal, are special forms of BPC permutations. A great deal of research effort have been made on routing LC and BPC permutations since their importance to real applications.

Lenfant recognizes five families of frequently used (FUB) permutations in [16]. Nassimi and Sahni recognize a larger set of frequently used permutations, BPC (Bit-Permute-Complement) permutations. BPC-permutations include FUB as a subset. Algorithms have been given to realize BPC permutations in [6, 17-21]. The algorithm presented in [17] can realize BPC permutations on Mesh-connected parallel computers. The algorithm given in [19] can realize BPC permutations in $2\log_2 N$ steps on π network. Using the algorithm given in [18], BPC permutations can be realized in $2\log_2 N$ -1 steps on Benes network. The algorithm presented in [20] can realize BPC permutations in $2\log_2 N$ -1 steps on perfect shuffle network. The algorithm given in [6] can realize BPC permutations in $\log_2$N *unit routes* on hypercube. A fault tolerant routing algorithm has been given in [21] which can realize BPC permutations in $2\log_2 N$ -1 steps on a generalized class of MINs. An algorithm has been given in [22] for the realization of BP permutations. Linear complement permutations are recognized and called LC permutations in [5]. Since they are frequently used as kernel communication tasks in many application programs, like numerical analysis, image processing, scientific and engineering computations, the efficiency of their realization has important effect on the efficiency of whole computation. A great deal of research effort has been made on efficient realization of them [2, 5, 6, 14, 15, 22-29] on hypercubes and multistage networks.

We have described three routing algorithms in this chapter. The three algorithms use three techniques to avoid conflicts in the routing process. The first algorithm introduced in Section 12.2 use two stages to transmit the messages. The first stage is to rearrange a BPC permutation into some intermediate permutation which is passable through hypercube in n steps. The second stage is to pass the intermediate permutation simply using the naïve routing algorithm. The original BPC permutation is realized in two routing stages without any conflict in any stage. The whole process needs $2n$-1 routing steps. This idea of two stage routing is also applicable to realize LC permutations to avoid conflict, but then some simple precomputation will be needed for LC permutations. The second algorithm introduced in Section 12.3 realizes any LC permutation in n steps working in a packet switched mode. Deferent from traditional routing algorithms where only one kind of transmission (exchange) is used, the algorithm uses two kinds of transmissions: exchange and circulation. Conflicts are avoided in the transmission process in a way that in addition to exchange messages along one dimension in some steps, we find two dimensions in some steps along which the messages are transmitted circularly. The idea is similar to that if some traffic jams at some places are predictable, then some vehicles detour in advance so that traffic can go smoothly everywhere, and all the tourists can arrive at their destinations on the scheduled time. Working in circuit switched or wormhole routing mode, the third algorithm introduced in Section 12.4 uses a strategy that the n dimensions of the hypercube are rearranged into some order for their application in real routing process. The order is used by any message packet in the transmission process, then N independent paths will be established for the N message packets, no conflict will occur in the whole routing process, and any LC permutation can be realized in one pass. In any routing step of the above three algorithms, each individual node determines along which dimension to send its message, only a comparison of two bits is needed. The routing process is distributed, no central control is needed, and no additional communication between the neighboring nodes are needed for routing. Thus the routing is simple and fast.

Although the three algorithms are presented for BPC and LC permutations separately, any algorithm can be applied for any kind of permutations since BPC is a subset of LC permutations. The deference is that BPC permutations can be given in a form of "cycles" of the n dimensions and the usage of the n dimensions in routing process can be immediately known. For LC permutations, precomputation is needed for using the above three routing strategies. The precomputation is for each type of LC permutations (in terms of their transformation matrices of $n \times n$) rather than for each individual permutation itself. Furthermore, the types of the permutations used in various application programs are known before run-time. In general they have been known after the application algorithms are developed. Thus the precomputation can be carried out before run-time.

References

[1] F.T. Leighton, *Introduction to Parallel Algorithms and Architectures*, Arrays Trees Hypercubes, Morgan Caufmann Publishers, San Mateo, California, 1992.

[2] D. Nassimi and S. Sahni, A Self Routing Benes Network and Parallel Permutation Algorithms, *IEEE Trans. on Computers*, C-30(5):332-340, May 1981.

[3] K.Y. Lee, On the Rearrangeability of $2\log_2 N$-1 Stage Permutation Networks, *IEEE Trans. on Computers*, C-34(5):412-425, May 1985.

[4] Z. Liu and J. You, *Routing Algorithms for Hypercube*, Technical Report, TR90-26, 1990, Department of Computing Science, University of Alberta, Edmonton, Alberta, Canada T6G 2H1.

[5] R. Boppana and C.S. Raghavendra, On Self Routing in Benes and Shuffle-Exchange Networks, *Proc. of the 1988 International Conference on Parallel Processing*, I:196-200, Aug. 1988.

[6] D. Nassimi and S. Sahni, Optimal BPC Permutations on a Cube Connected SIMD Computer, *IEEE Trans. on Computers*, C-31(4):338-341, April, 1982.

[7] J.M. Frailong and W. Jalby and J. Lenfant, XOR-Schemes: A Flexible Data Organization in Parallel Memories, *Proc. of the 1985 International Conference on Parallel Processing*, 276-283, Aug. 1985.

[8] D. Lee, *A Multiple-processor Architecture for Image Processing*, Ph.D Thesis, Department of Computing Science, University of Alberta, Edmonton, Alberta, Canada, 1987.

[9] D. Lee, On Access and Alignment of Data in a Parallel Processor, *Information Processing Letters*, 33(1):11-14, Oct.1989.

[10] K. Kim and V.K.P. Kumar, Parallel Memory Systems for Image Processing, *Proc. of the 1989 Conference on Computer vision and Pattern Recognition (CVPR'89),* 654 –659, 1989.

[11] C.S. Raghavendra and R. Boppana, On Methods for Fast and Efficient Parallel Memory Access, *Proc. of the 1990 International Conference on Parallel Processing*, 76 – 83, Aug. 1990.

[12] Z. Liu, X. Li, and J. You, On Storage Schemes for Parallel Array Access, *Proc. of the 1992 ACM International Conference on Supercomputing*, 282-291, 1992.

[13] S. Ranka and S. Sahni, Hypercube Algorithms with Applications to Image Processing and Pattern Recognition, *Springer-Verlag, New York*, 1990.

[14] R. Boppana and C.S. Raghavendra, Optimal Self-Routing of Linear-Complement Permutations in Hypercubes, *Proc. of the 5th Distributed Memory Computing Conference*, 800-808, April, 1990.

[15] K. Zemoudeh and A. Sengupta, Routing Frequently Used Bijections on Hypercube, *Proc. of the 5th Distributed Memory Computing Conference*, 824-832, April, 1990.

[16] J. Lenfant, Parallel Permutations of Data: A Benes Network Control Algorithm for Frequently Used Permutations, *IEEE Trans. on Computers, C-27(7)*: 637-647, July 1978.

[17] D. Nassimi and S. Sahni, An Optimal Routing Algorithm for Mesh-

connected Parallel Computers, *J. ACM*, 27(1)6-29, Jan. 1980.

[18] D. Nassimi, A Fault-Tolerant Routing Algorithm for BPC Permutations on Multistage Interconnection Networks, *Proc. of the 1989 International Conference on Parallel Processing*, I:278-287, Aug. 1989.

[19] P.C. Yew and D.H. Lawrie, An Easily Controlled Network for Frequently Used Permutations, *IEEE Trans. on Computers*, C-30(4):296-298, April 1981.

[20] S.T. Huang and S.K. Tripathi, Self-Routing Technique in Perfect-Shuffle Networks Using Control Tags, *IEEE Trans. on Computers*, C-37(2):251-256, Feb. 1988.

[21] D. Nassimi, A Fault-Tolerant Routing Algorithm for BPC Permutations on Multistage Interconnection Networks, *Proc. of the 1989 International Conference on Parallel Processing*, I:278-287, Aug. 1989.

[22] C.S. Raghavendra and M. A. Sridhar, Optimal Routing of Bit-Permutes on Hypercube Machines, *Proc. of the 1990 International Conference on Parallel Processing*, I:286-290, Aug. 1990.

[23] C. Ho and S. Johnsson, Optimal Algorithms for Stable Dimension Permutations on Boolean Cubes, *Proc. of the Third Conference on Hypercube Concurrent Computers and Applications*, 725-736, Jan. 1988.

[24] A. Sengupta and K. Zemoudeh, Self-Routing Algorithms for Strongly Regular Multistage Interconnection Networks, *Journal of Parallel and Distributed Computing*, 14(2):187-192, Feb. 1992.

[25] Z. Liu, J. You and X. Li, Conflict-free Routing on Hypercubes, *Proc. of the 1992 International Conference on Computer and Information*, 153-158 (IEEE Version), May 1992.

[26] Z. Liu, and J. You, Conflict-free Routing for BPC-permutations on Synchronous Hypercubes, *Parallel Computing*, 19(3):323-342, 1993.

[27] Z. Liu and D. Zhang, Oblivious Routing for LC Permutations on Hypercubes, *Parallel Computing*, 25:445-460, 1999.

[28] X. Shen, Optimal Realization of Any BPC Permutation on k-Extra-Stage Omega Networks, *IEEE Trans. Computers*, 44(5): 714-719, May 1995.

[29] Q. Hu, X. Shen, and W. Liang, Optimaly Routing LC Permutations on k-Extra-Stage Cube-Type Networks, *IEEE Trans. on Computers*. 45(1):97-103, January 1996.

[30] S. Abraham and K. Padmanabhan, Reliability of the Hypercube, *Proc. of the 1988 International conference on Parallel Processing*, I:90-94, Aug.1988.

[31] V.E. Benes, Mathematical Theory of Connecting Networks and Telephone Traffic, *Academic Press, New York*, 1965.

[32] P.Y. Chen and D.H. Lawrie and P.C. Yew and D.A. Padua, Interconnection Networks Using Shuffles, *Computer*, 14(12):55-63, Dec. 1981.

[33] Q.F. Stout, Special Issue on Algorithms for Hypercube Computers --- Guest Editor's Introduction, *Journal of Parallel and Distributed Computing*, 8(4):301-302, April 1990.

[34] T. Szymanski, On the Permutation Capability of a Circuit-Switched Hypercube, *Proc. of the 1989 International Conference on Parallel Processing*, I:103-110, Aug. 1989.

Chapter 13

COMPRESSION CODING FOR IAP DATA

This chapter deals with an important issue in IAP data management for Internet PRIP computations: compression coding. Because of the large data volume and the need for fast transmission (sometimes almost real-time), compression coding is critical. The introduction section gives an overview on the motivation ("why") and the general approaches ("how") to IAP data compression. As an example for the spatial- domain methods, Section 13.2 presents two improvements to the reconstruction phase of a quadtree compression algorithm. Section 13.3 discusses a vector quantization scheme that works for a transform-domain compression algorithm. The data structures used in those compression algorithms, a quadtree and a wavelet coefficient tree, are closely related to an encryption coding method discussed in Chapter 16.

13.1 Introduction

The rapid growth of multimedia applications on the Internet demands for high quality images/videos in large quantities, thus requires efficient compression coding algorithms. PRIP processing involves an enormous amount of data. A still gray-level image requires 50 KB to 1 MB of storage. A color picture is of size up to 5 MB. To transmit a sequence of images can put a heavy burden on the communication network. For example, a slow-motion video with ten frames per second and 176×120 pixels per frame needs 5 Mbps for the uncompressed form. A broadcast video with 30 frames/second and $720 \times 480 \times 24$ resolution requires about 250 Mbps transmission for the uncompressed signal. Current image and video compression technique can bring down the above requirements to below 20 Kbps and 10 Mbps, respectively. Compression coding has become a necessary part of any useful storage and transmission system for IAP data.

While the pressing need from the large data volume of PRIP computation makes compression necessary, the existence of a significant amount

Figure 13.1. An image with large smooth areas

of data redundancy makes compression possible. In any non-random still image, there is a strong correlation between pixels. Neighboring pixels in a homogeneous region are almost identical, as can be seen in Figure 13.1. In a video, consecutive image frames may have many pixels unchanged. If the camera is relatively stationary, there would be only a number of objects moving from one position to the next. With motion compensation of the objects, the next frame can be very similar to the previous one.

The above *inter-pixel redundancy* and *inter-frame redundancy* exist in most IAP data. Another type of redundancy is the *coding redundancy* that directly relates to the labeling convention of recording the colors or gray-levels of a pixel. Employing code-words with a shorter length for more frequently appearing values can result in a smaller storage for the whole image. Suppose that among 100 pixels there are 70 pixels with gray-level L1, 20 pixels with L2, and 10 with L3. Instead using 8-bits per pixel, we represent L1 with a one bit symbol 0, L2 and L3 with 2-bit symbols 10 and 11, the total signal size would be 70+60 instead of 800 bits.

The third type of redundancy is called *psychovisual redundancy.* Human eyes are sensitive to different types of errors in different parts of an image. Usually, intensity variations are more easily perceived in a smooth area than a "busy" area, because the human eyes search for distinguishing features (edges, lines and points) and the brain constantly grouping pixels into shapes that relate to certain prior knowledge. That is, we are doing image analysis at the same time as image processing. Consequently, a great deal of minor intensity differences are being ignored by a human observer. Therefore, using fewer colors or gray levels is possible.

To reduce those three kinds of redundancy, a compression coding procedure takes three basic steps: *mapping*, *approximation* or *quantization*, and *symbol encoding* [12]. They may be combined into one or two steps in some algorithms. A mapper intends to transform the original pixel values into another set of numbers that are more independent of each other, thus the inter-pixel and inter-frame redundancy can be reduced. The symbol encoder aims at the coding redundancy, and the quantizer is for reducing the psychovisual redundancy. If no approximation or quantization involved, the compression is said to be *reversible* or *lossless*, and the original data can bc recovered perfectly, but the compression ratio is rarely beyond 3 to 10. A *lossy* compression employs some kinds of approximation and permanently losses information of the original data, but can achieve 20 fold or more compression. For certain images and videos, the compression ratio may even reach hundreds or thousands. A number of *near-lossless* compression schemes yield 10-20 fold size reduction and only the last bit of each pixel may be lost.

Table 13.1. Examples of the first generations image compression coding

"Mappers"	Spatial-domain (predictive coding run-length coding, quadtree) Transform-domain (DCT, wavelet)	reduce interpixel redundancy
"Quantizer"	scalar quantization vector quantization	reduce psychovisual redundancy
"Symbol encoder"	Huffman coding Arithmetic coding LZ coding	reduce coding redundancy

There are hundreds of compression methods proposed in the literature. From the application point of view, the methods can be classified as for sound (1-D signal), for image (2-D signal), either binary, gray-level or color, and for video (2.5-D signal). Some authors classify compression schemes by generations. The pixel-based schemes that code pixel values are called the first generation techniques. The second generation methods conduct a image segmentation and then code the location and properties of each region. The third generation compression schemes are model-based, mostly for videos, especially for video conferencing. Usually, a wire-frame model is used to represent objects such as a human face. This method results in several thousand fold of reduction in bandwidth requirement. The fourth generation (knowledge-based) and fifth generation (semantic-based) methods have not been commonly used. They employ higher-level PRIP techniques for specific IAP data. For example, pattern recognition algorithms are used to recognize and reproduce facial expressions. Table 13.1 presents a typical taxonomy of the first generation image compression methods.

LZ coding takes advantage of the repeating symbols in the source. Huffman coding uses variable-length code words symbols of different frequencies. Arithmetic coding converts a sequence of symbols into a progressively smaller interval of real numbers between 0 and 1. A run-length encoding simply record the number of consecutive pixels with the same (or similar) value, mapping the original pixel values into a sequence of "runs". Predictive coding uses a predictor $x'(i,j)$ for the true pixel value $x(i,j)$ and record only the prediction error $e(i,j) = x(i,j) - x'(i,j)$. A linear predictor $x'(i,j)$ is a round- off version of a linear combination of several neighboring pixels previously encountered in a scan. For $\{x(i,j) \mid i > 0 \text{ and } j > 0\}$, a typical linear predictor is

$$x'(i,j) = \text{round}\left(c_1 x(i-1, j-1) + c_2 x(i-1, j) + c_3 x(i, j-1)\right) \tag{13-1}$$

for some real valued coefficients c_1, c_2, and c_3. The resulting error values have a histogram with a peak around 0, which facilitates a variable-length symbol encoding or arithmetic coding.

A spatial-domain compression algorithm directly deals with the pixel values, and the transform-domain methods convert the pixel values to a set of coefficients. Generally speaking, transform-domain techniques are more powerful than spatial-domain methods. However, the lower computational complexity of spatial-domain algorithms still encourage a certain amount of further examination. Section 13.2 is on quadtree compression, one of the simplest spatial-domain methods. A quadtree is a rooted tree in which every node has zero or four children. The reconstruction phase of quadtree compression is very important in removing blockiness and other artifacts inherent to the quadtree coding.

Fourier-transform, Discrete Cosine Transform (DCT), KL-transform and wavelet transforms have been used to convert the pixel values into a set of coefficients before quantization and symbol encoding take place. Many wavelet coding algorithms produce significantly better results than DCT. Direct vector quantization of the pixels can be viewed as a mapping and an approximation combined together. It treats sub-images (usually 4×4) as vectors and records the index of a similar vector in a vector codebook. The transform coefficients can also be grouped into vectors and approximated using vector quantization. Section 13.3 gives details of a vector quantization method used in a wavelet compression algorithm.

There exist many formats of image compression coding standards. One common format for binary image coding is JBIG (Joint Bilevel Imaging Group) that uses run- length encoding as the mapper and Huffman

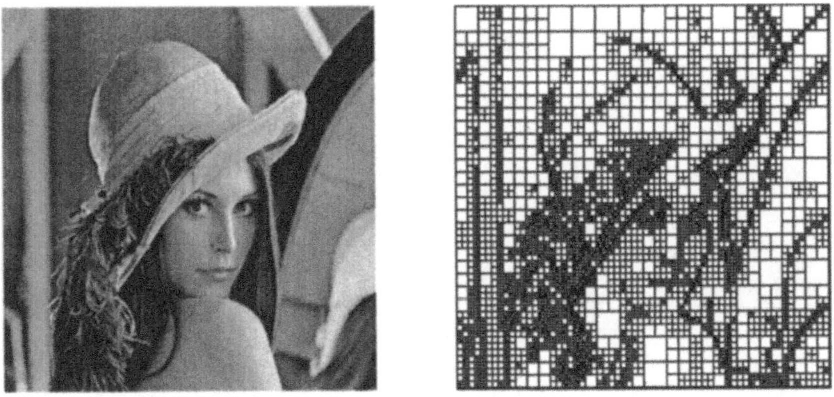

(a) Original image (b) Quadtree decomposition

Figure 13.2. Quadtree decomposition of an image

coding at the end. For grayscale images, LZW is used in a number of popular lossless coding standards, such as TIF (Tagged Image Format), GIF (Graphics Interchange Format) and its later version PNG (Portable Network Graphics). The DCT-based JPEG (Joint Photographic Expert Group) is the most frequently used lossy compression method that employs DCT, DPCM (Differential Pulse Code Modulation), run-length encoding and entropy symbol encoding. JPEG-2000, however, uses Discrete Wavelet Transform, scalar quantization, and arithmetic coding.

13.2 Quadtree Compression and an Improved Reconstruction Phase

One of the simplest compression schemes is the quadtree decomposition method. Quadtree is based on an iterative decomposition of an image into four quarters. One quadtree decomposition example is given in Figure 13.2. The criterion for stopping/continuing the division is some form of homogeneity test applied to the subimage in question. Equivalently, an iterative merging process can also generate a quadtree. The average numbers of operations per pixel for two spatial-domain methods are compared with those of the DCT-based JPEG coding in Table 13.2. "SR" refers to a modified version of the quadtree method proposed by Shusterman and Feder [37]. "SR" stands for "single filter and reconstruction threshold" [18, 20]. Because of the varying tree structure, the number of operations required for each leaf node decreases at lower bit rates. The table presents two bit rates: 0.16 bits-per-pixel (bpp) and 0.80 bpp.

Table 13.2. Average numbers of operations per pixel

	JPEG	SR (.16)	SR(.80)	MPAT (.78)
compress:				
shift	0	0.36	0.50	0.05
+	7.25	2.48	3.13	3.77
*	1.25	0.03	0.16	0
/	1	0	0	0
decompress:				
shift	0	0.03	0.16	0.15
+	7.25	6.69	6.82	2.06
*	2.25	3.00	3.00	0

An even simpler spatial-domain approach is to consider the pixels as a one-dimensional array, and then apply some approximation technique to the 1-D sequence. That method does not make a full use of the 2-D inter-pixel dependency. The average numbers of operations per pixel for such a 1-D algorithm "MPAT" [25] at a rate of 0.78 bpp are also given in Table 13.2.

Quadtrees and quadtree-like data structures have been used for a variety of applications. Many papers are written on quadtree's properties and its usefulness [15, 41, 32, 5, 31, 24], and on its efficiency in storage [30, 11, 13, 16, 35, 10, 14]. Quadtree's good performance for low bit rates encourages active research in its use in image compression [38, 39, 40]. Because of the nature of the quadtree subimage division, the reconstructed images often look "blocky". The decompression phase usually includes a filtering process to "smooth" out the artifacts. In this section, we outline two improvements over the reconstruction method proposed by Shusterman and Feder [37]. A brief description of the quadtree algorithm of [37] is given below.

For an $N \times N$ image (where $N = 2^n$), the quadtree contains up to $n + 1$ levels. The levels can be numbered starting from the leaves or from the root. In this chapter, let the leaves be level 0 in order to be consistent to the related papers. The quadtree node at level i with co-ordinates (j, k) is denoted $x_i(j, k)$. The children of such a node (if any), in the order of NW-NE-SE-SW, would be

$$x_{i-1}(2j, 2k),\ x_{i-1}(2j, 2k+1),\ x_{i-1}(2j+1, 2k+1),\ x_{i-1}(2j+1, 2k) \tag{13-2}$$

as shown in Figure 13.3.

Consider a bottom-up approach for the quadtree generation. Starting from individual pixels, each group of 2×2 pixels can be merged into

<table>
<tr><td>$x_i(j-1, k-1)$</td><td colspan="2">$x_i(j-1, k)$</td><td>$x_i(j-1, k+1)$</td></tr>
<tr><td rowspan="2">$x_i(j, k-1)$</td><td>$x_{i-1}(2j, 2k)$</td><td>$x_{i-1}(2j, 2k+1)$</td><td rowspan="2">$x_i(j, k+1)$</td></tr>
<tr><td>$x_{i-1}(2j+1, 2k)$</td><td>$x_{i-1}(2j+1, 2k+1)$</td></tr>
<tr><td>$x_i(j+1, k-1)$</td><td colspan="2">$x_i(j-1, k)$</td><td>$x_i(j+1, k+1)$</td></tr>
</table>

Figure 13.3. Node $x_i(j, k)$, its 8-neighbors and its children

one "parent" node and the average gray-level of the four "children" are used as the value of the parent node:

$$x_i(j, k) = \frac{1}{4} \sum_{l=0}^{1} \sum_{m=0}^{1} x_{i-1}(2j + l, 2k + m). \tag{13-3}$$

A subimage of 2×2 nodes at level $i - 1$ of the tree should be merged if

$$\bigcap_{l,m=0}^{1} |x_i(j, k) - x_{i-1}(2j + l, 2k + m)| \leq T_i. \tag{13-4}$$

The value of the threshold T_i is not static throughout the quadtree. It decreases as i increases. Merging siblings at higher levels of a tree can potentially cause greater distortion in the resulting image because of the increasing size of the area represented by higher-level nodes. An optimal solution for choosing $T - i$ value is very expensive. An "acceptable sub-optimal solution" is presented in [37], in which an "initial decomposition threshold", T_1, is given for the first level, and the threshold decreases by a factor of two each time the level is incremented. At level i, for $2 \leq i \leq n$,

$$T_i = 2^{1-i} T_1. \tag{13-5}$$

The reconstructed image using a quadtree method often looks blocky, as each leaf in the quadtree represents a square region with a single intensity value. Shusterman and Feder [37] recommend a reconstruction filter, described by Strobach [38], which propagates the values of the quadtree leaves down to the pixel level. The filter is a 3×3 mask:

$$F = \begin{pmatrix} 0.0285 & 0.1519 & -0.0285 \\ 0.1519 & 0.9787 & -0.1357 \\ -0.0285 & -0.1357 & 0.0159 \end{pmatrix}. \tag{13-6}$$

A rotated version of the filter F is placed over the leaf at $x_i(j,k)$ and its 8-neighbors (forming a 3×3 matrix $X_i(j,k)$), and the four children nodes are calculated. Using two rotation operators, R_0 and R_1,

$$R_0 = \begin{pmatrix} 1 & 0 & 0 \\ 0 & 1 & 0 \\ 0 & 0 & 1 \end{pmatrix}, \quad R_1 = \begin{pmatrix} 0 & 0 & 1 \\ 0 & 1 & 0 \\ 1 & 0 & 0 \end{pmatrix}, \tag{13-7}$$

the four rotated version of the filter would be $R_l \, F \, R_m$ for $i, m = 0$ and 1, and $x_{i-1}(2j + l, 2k + m)$ would be the result of applying $R_l F R_m$ to the neighborhood of $x_i(j,k)$, $X_i(j,k)$.

Suppose we have the following values in $X_i(j,k)$:

$$X_i(j,k) = \begin{pmatrix} 200 & 190 & 190 \\ 195 & 185 & 80 \\ 195 & 160 & 50 \end{pmatrix}. \tag{13-8}$$

The resulting values for the four children of the leaf $x_i(j,k)$ will be:

$$\begin{pmatrix} 202 & 175 \\ 200 & 158 \end{pmatrix}. \tag{13-9}$$

The value 202 for $x_{i-1}(2j, 2k)$ looks unreasonable being out of the range of {185, 190, 195, 200}. It seems that the 3×3 filter has over compensated the edge and made the bright side of an edge too bright and the dark side too dark, creating "ghost edges" that extend a short distance from the actual edge. The cause may be the inclusion and influence of the nodes that are neighbors to the parent but not to the child, such as the nodes $x_i(s,t)$ with $s > j$ or $t > k$ in the generation of $x_{i-1}(2j, 2k)$. Figure 13.4(a) shows this "ghost edge" effect in a detailed portion of the reconstructed image "Lena" compressed to 0.42 bpp using the 3×3 filter [38, 37]. The peak signal to noise ratio (PSNR) of the image shown in part(a) is 31.02, and that of the image in part (b) is 31.77.

Based on this belief, a 2×2 filter (that only uses those neighbors at level i bordering on the child) has been proposed to replace the 3×3 one [18, 20]. The 2×2 filter only takes into account the parent node and three of the parent's neighbors in the calculation of the child node value. An illustration of 3×3 and 2×2 filters is given in Figure 13.5.

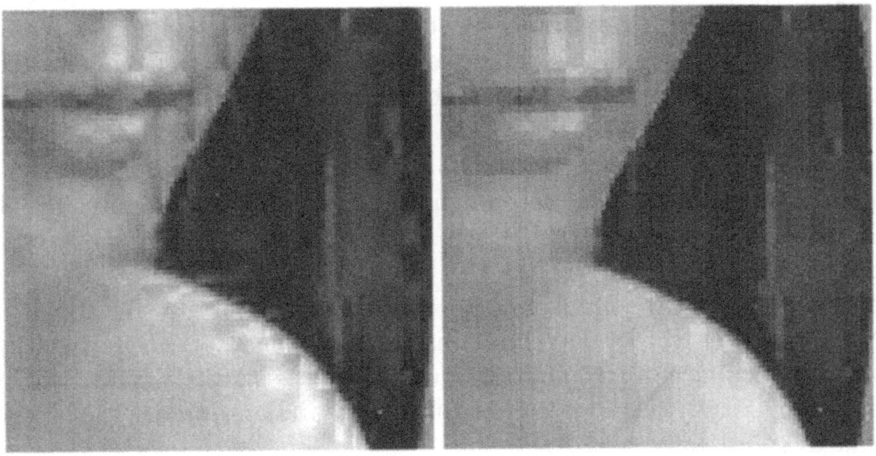

(a) (b)

Figure 13.4. "Ghost edge effect" in quadtree reconstruction using 3×3 filter and 2×2 filters

<table>
<tr><td>$x_i(j-1,k-1)$
*</td><td colspan="2">$x_i(j-1,k)$
*</td><td>$x_i(j-1,k+1)$</td></tr>
<tr><td rowspan="2">$x_i(j,k-1)$
*</td><td>$x_{i-1}(2j,2k)$</td><td>$x_{i-1}(2j,2k+1)$</td><td rowspan="2">$x_i(j,k+1)$</td></tr>
<tr><td>$x_{i-1}(2j+1,2k)$</td><td>$x_{i-1}(2j+1,2k+1)$</td></tr>
<tr><td>$x_i(j+1,k-1)$</td><td colspan="2">$x_i(j-1,k)$</td><td>$x_i(j+1,k+1)$</td></tr>
</table>

Figure 13.5. An illustration of 3×3 and 2×2 filters. The 3×3 filter uses all eight neighbors of the parent node, while the 2×2 filter uses three neighbors marked by "*" in the calculation of $x_{i-1}(2j, 2k)$

Actually, an optimal 3×3 filter could perform better than any 2×2 one. The decision of using 2×2 is based on its computation speed, which enhances the computational simplicity of the quadtree algorithm. An iterative search procedure was performed on a set of 15 images of different types, including several standard test images such as Lena and Goldhill, as well as other portraits, outdoor scenes, and satellite images. Two choices have been tested. The first choice uses a distinct filter for each level of the quadtree, as the nodes at different levels affect different sizes of image areas. The second choice uses a single 2×2 filter for all levels. The search criterion is the mean squared error (MSE), as was done by Strobach to calculate the values of his 3×3 mask [38]. The result using multiple filters, one for each level, generates a slightly lower MSE. However, the second choice, using one single filter, is often able to smooth out much of the blockiness, and sometimes gives a more visually appealing result. The single filter that was found to optimize the 15 test images is presented as follows:

$$F' = \begin{pmatrix} 0 & 0.13 & 0 \\ 0.13 & 0.74 & 0 \\ 0 & 0 & 0 \end{pmatrix}. \tag{13-10}$$

A comparison example between multiple and single filters is given in Figure 13.6. This illustrates a case where the MSE/PSNR is not the best measure of image quality. To some people, part (b) is the more visually appealing image because of its smoothness, even though the PSNR would seem to indicate otherwise. It should be noted that part (b) contains some noticeable "bleeding" artifacts in the shoulder area which are a result of the reconstruction process's inability to distinguish between regions. This shortcoming will be discussed and dealt with below.

In image enhancement and reconstruction, selective averaging techniques estimate the nature of the neighborhood and select the best subset of neighbors to compute the average, thus avoiding averaging across edges. Edge preserving smoothing [26] tries to search for a homogeneous neighborhood around each pixel and averages on that neighborhood only. Half-neighborhood method [34] partitions the neighbors of each pixel into two groups. The absolute difference between the group averages are compared to a threshold. Several similar methods are also used to protect edges in the image enhancement process [9, 28, 21]. In reconstructing an image from a quadtree representation, the existing reconstruction process will attempt to smooth the areas around it, which may lead to "bleeding'" of dark regions onto light regions, and vice versa. A simple solution is to introduce a *reconstruction threshold*, which prevents this from oc-

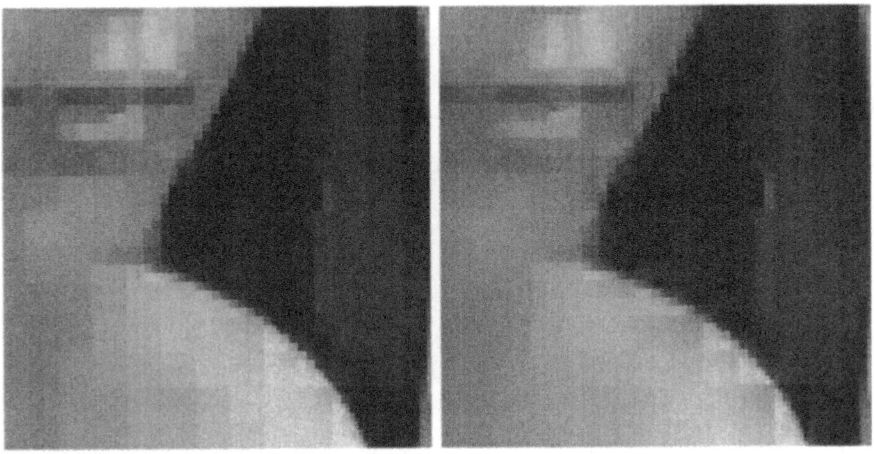

(a) (b)

Figure 13.6. A comparison of the two new filter schemes, using the Lena image compressed to 0.2 bpp: (a) result of using the multiple filters, PSNR=29.17; (b) result of using the new single filter, PSNR=28.63

curring. When the difference between a leaf and its neighbor is below a certain threshold, we proceed with the reconstruction as previously described. Otherwise, that neighbor is ignored. Figure 13.7(a) is an image with many sharp edges, thus is used to illustrate the bleeding effects. The error image (difference between the original and reconstructed image) without reconstruction threshold is shown in part (b). The error image in the case of using a reconstruction threshold is in part (c). The use of a reconstruction threshold seems to improve the images compressed at higher bit rates and the images with sharp edges. However, it does not contribute visually or numerically (in terms of MSE) for the reconstructed image with multiple filters used for different levels of the tree.

After designing the filters and the reconstruction threshold, the modified quadtree compression algorithm is tested on a wide range of grayscale test images. The numerical fidelity criterion is the commonly used peak signal-to-noise ratio (PSNR)

$$\mathrm{PSNR} = 10\log_{10}\left(\frac{A^2}{\mathrm{MSE}}\right) \quad dB \tag{13-11}$$

where A is the maximum input signal value (it is 255 here, as in Equation (7-17)) and MSE is the mean squared error between the original image and the reconstructed version. A number of Rate-Distortion curves (here-

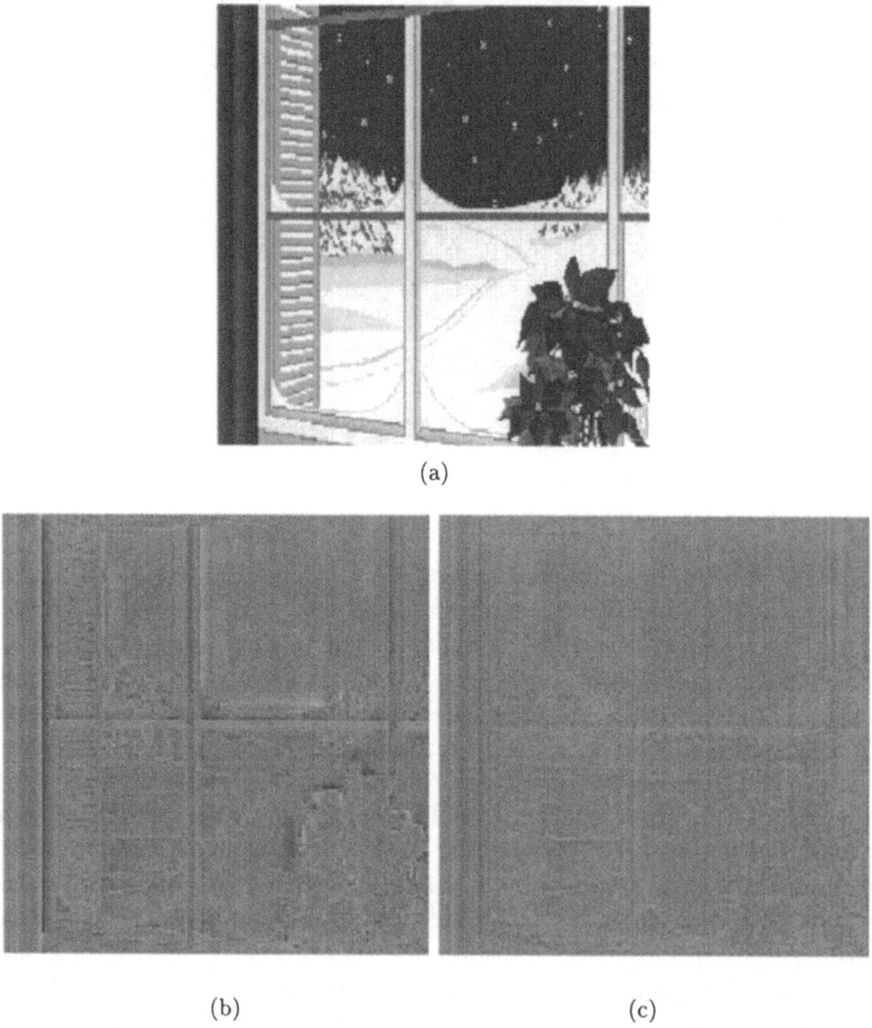

Figure 13.7. "bleeding effect". (a) a test image with many edges, (b) error image when no reconstruction threshold is used, (c) error image when a reconstruction threshold is used

Figure 13.8. Test image "Io"

after referred to as R-D curves) are presented for the original method in [37] (referred to as "SF"), the modified version with multiple filters [17, 19] (referred to as "MF"), single-filter with reconstruction threshold (referred to as "SR"), and the DCT-based JPEG compression. A table summarizing the comparison will also be given. A popular test image, "Io", shown in Figure 13.8, is used with the "Lena" image in the generation of the R-D curves. The "Io" image is more complex than "Lena", thus harder to compress. And it was not a part of the original sample image set used in the filter design. Among many slightly different versions of the "Lena" image, the one from [1] was chosen because it is the same one used in [29].

Figures 13.9 and 13.10 show that the modified quadtree algorithms "MF" and "SR" result in a consistent improvement over "SF" at all bit rates for both images in terms of PSNR. "MF" gives a slightly better PSNR than "SR", but "SR" gives better visual (subjective) results. The comparison between "SR" and JPEG is given in Figures 13.11 and 13.12. "SR" performs better than JPEG at bit rates lower than 0.2 bpp in the case of "Lena", and at 0.35 bpp for "Io". Visually, the JPEG results are quite blocky for bit rates lower than 0.4 bpp, as can be seen in Figure 13.13.

Table 13.3 presents the compression results between "SR" and JPEG for ten other test images . The table contents are (1) the crossing points (in bpp) between the "SR" curve and JPEG curve, and (2) the improvement in PSNR of "SR" over JPEG at 0.2 bpp. The complexity of the quadtree algorithms is measured in numbers of operations. At lower bit rates, the tree has a simpler shape and fewer operation steps are required.

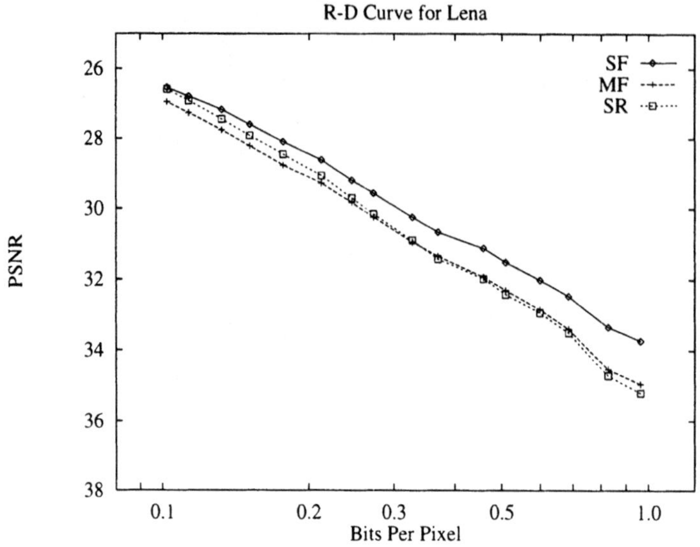

Figure 13.9. Quadtree compression PSNR results for image "Lena"

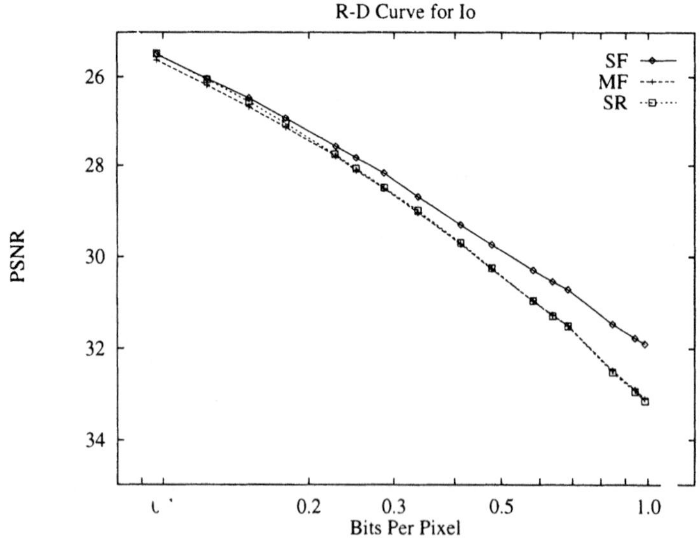

Figure 13.10. Quadtree compression PSNR results for image "Io"

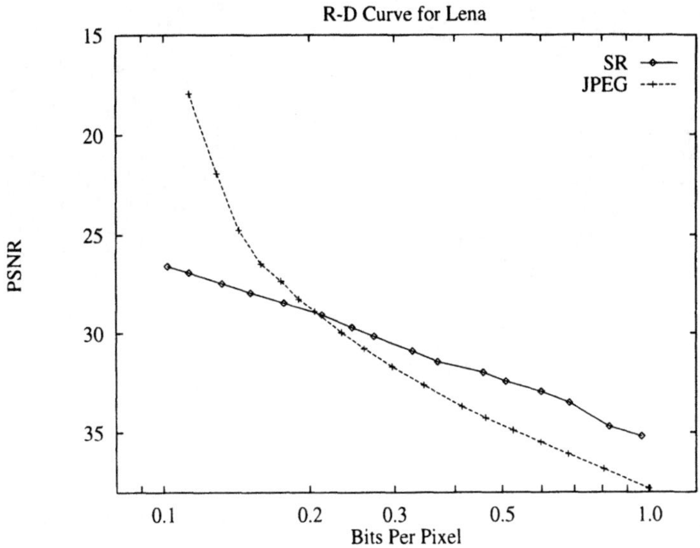

Figure 13.11. "SR" and JPEG PSNR results for image "Lena"

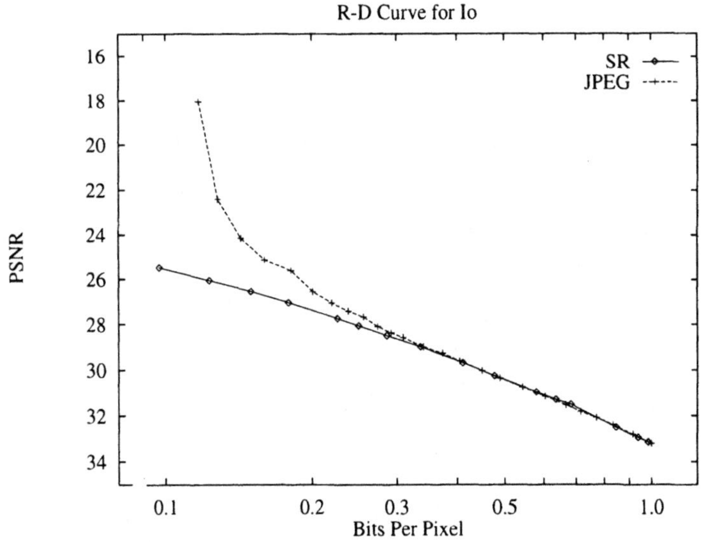

Figure 13.12. "SR" and JPEG PSNR results for image "Io"

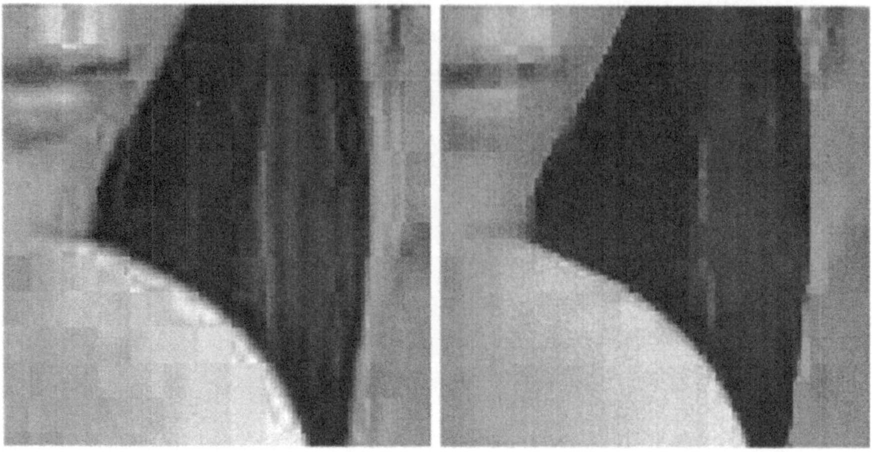

(a) (b)

Figure 13.13. "Lena" image compressed to 0.3 bpp with JPEG and SR

The complexity of JPEG, without the symbol encoder, is based on the fast DCT algorithm described in [27, 3], which requires only 5 multiplications and 29 adds for a 1-D DCT of dimension 8, performed 16 times for each 8×8 block. The quantization of the DCT coefficients requires one division for each pixel. The operation counts are listed in Table 13.2.

Table 13.3. Summary of the R-D curves for ten images compressed by "SR" and JPEG

Image	R-D Intersection	PSNR improvement at 0.2 bpp
Bay	2.26	0.9
Build	3.20	0.8
Carrier	0.27	0.9
Earth	0.26	0.9
Flower	0.28	1.8
Fruit	0.27	1.0
Monalisa	0.29	1.0
Pfeifer	0.26	1.2
Street	0.30	0.5
Sunset	0.25	1.6

In summary, an improved version of Shusterman and Feder's method [37, 18, 20] is presented. It requires fewer operations for the compression phase and outperforms JPEG at low bit rates. The algorithm "SR" employs a 2×2 filter and a reconstruction threshold. It provides faster computation and a better PSNR measurement than the original quadtree method at all bit rates for all test images. Subjectively, "SR" provides a better image quality than both the original quadtree method and the modified version with multiple 2×2 filters. The blockiness and "ghost-edge" effects are reduced.

13.3 Wavelet Compression and Vector Quantization

Wavelet multi-resolution decomposition schemes have been shown in many cases to be a powerful means of image compression [2, 36, 33, 8, 42, 7, 4, 29]. Some algorithms use vector codebooks and optimal bit allocation for different subbands [2]. The EZW [36] and SPIHT [29] algorithms base their coding on a tree structure of the coefficients, and utilize a prediction of the coefficient significance. A combination of EZW with vector quantization was reported in [33]. This section describes a lattice vector quantization scheme working with SPIHT. The formation of the vector codebook and the timing of the vector coding are discussed in detail. This method, named *ModLVQ* [17, 18], gives better results in representing fine details of an image, thus out-performs SPIHT on "busy" images (which are more difficult to compress using any method).

Wavelet Pyramid and Coefficient Significance Prediction

In most wavelet compression algorithms, the lowpass and highpass wavelet filters are applied to the rows and columns of the image, decomposing the image into four "subbands", and then applied iteratively to the low frequency components, as shown in Figure 13.14. The accuracy of the coefficients directly affects the quality of the compression result. That is, the mean squared error (MSE) of the reconstructed image is closely related to the MSE of the quantized coefficients themselves. If G denotes the original image data and W represents the wavelet coefficients, then

$$(1-\epsilon)\|W\|^2 \leq \|G\|^2 \leq (1+\epsilon)\|W\|^2. \tag{13-12}$$

Since ϵ is usually a small number, we have $MSE(G) \approx MSE(W)$. An immediate conclusion of the above observation is that an image compression algorithm should give precedence to the coefficients with a large magnitude. Another desirable property of the wavelet transform is that the coefficients of different subbands are related, as far as the "significance" is concerned. Among the high subbands at different iterations, there exist a certain similarity or dependency. Each coefficient in a high frequency subband corresponds to four coefficients in the next finer resolution level. Shapiro [36] observed that if a coefficient is insignificant (its magnitude smaller than a threshold), then all coefficients of the same

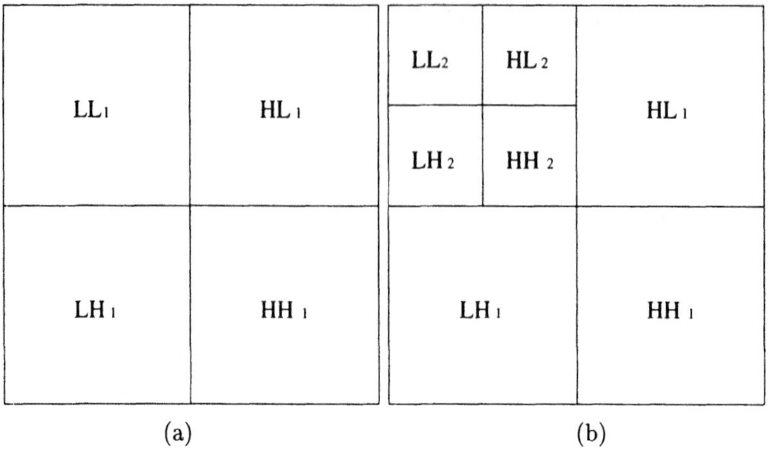

Figure 13.14. Wavelet decomposition of an image

orientation corresponding to the same spatial location at finer levels are *likely* to be insignificant too. That is called the *zerotree* (EZW) assumption, as indicated in Figure 13.15. This similarity relation across wavelet subbands form a "pyramid" that facilitates the prediction of coefficient significance.

Based on the above two properties of the wavelet decomposition, an image compression algorithm needs to give precedence to large coefficients, and it can predict "descendant" coefficients of an insignificant coefficient. Both EZW and SPIHT [29] algorithms do exactly this in a simple fashion.

The EZW algorithm considers all coefficients on the wavelet pyramid in the Z-scan order as shown in Figure 13.16. This ordering insures that the lower resolution coefficients are handled before their higher resolution counterparts. Before scanning the list, the total number of bytes to which the image should be compressed is determined. This *byte budget* will be met exactly by the algorithm, which is a property that neither the spatial-domain methods nor the DCT-based methods can have. An initial threshold, T_0, is determined from the maximum magnitude in the wavelet pyramid, x_m, such that $T_0 = 2^n < x_m \leq 2^{n+1}$. Initially, all coefficients stay in a list called the *dominant list.* Another list, called the *subordinate list*, is empty to begin with. The algorithm goes through several iterations. Each iteration includes one *dominant pass* and one *subordinate pass.* At the end of an iteration, the threshold is reduced to half: $T_i = T_{i-1}/2$. The dominant pass checks the coefficients and updates the dominant list. If the coefficient exceeds the threshold in magnitude,

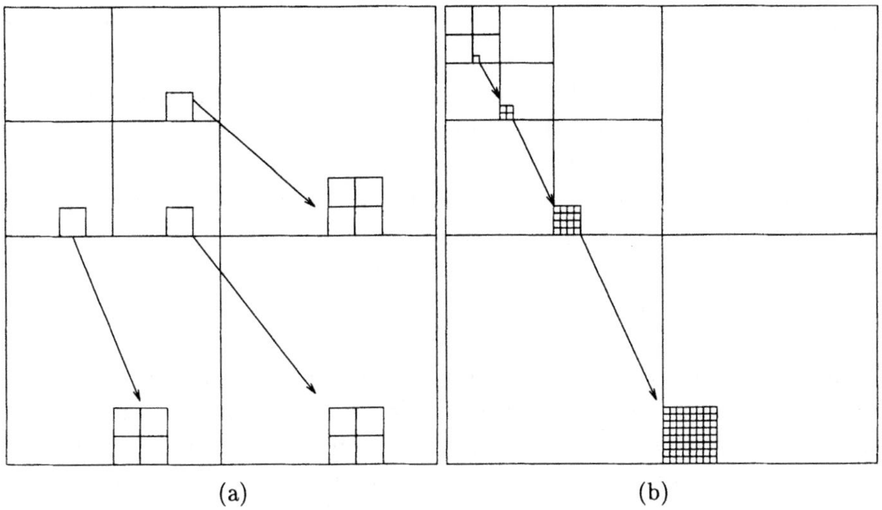

Figure 13.15. Dependencies among high frequency subbands between nodes and immediate children (Part (a)) and between nodes and indirect descendents (Part (b))

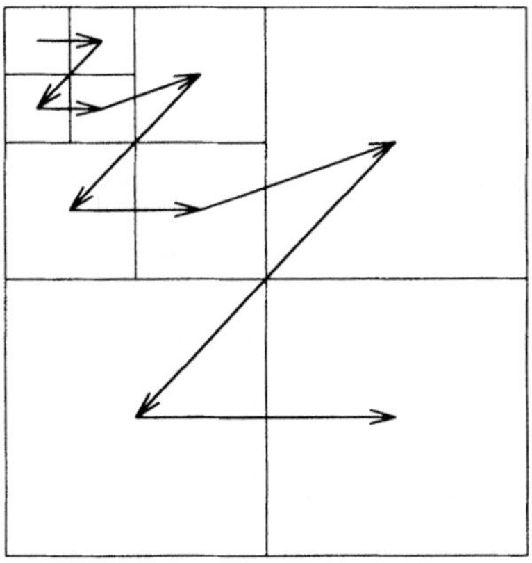

Figure 13.16. Z-scan order of the coefficients in EZW

it is considered significant and a symbol "POS" or "NEG" will be coded depending on the sign of the coefficient. If the coefficient is insignificant, it can be either an isolated zero (some of its descendents being significant) or a zerotree root (all descendents are insignificant). Symbols "IZ" or "ZT" would be used, respectively. The significant coefficient is added to the subordinate list, and a "best guess" of the coefficient magnitude is recorded. Since it is coded within this pass, it must be between T and $2T$. The best guess at this point is $(3/2)T$. The subordinate pass is performed to refine the magnitude of the recorded significant coefficients by comparing the "best guess" provided by the dominant pass with the true magnitude. If the guess was too small, code "1" and add $T/4$ to the guess. If the guess was too big, code "0" and subtract $T/4$ from the guess. This way, the uncertainty interval is reduced to half. The list is then sorted, with the largest coefficient at the front to ensure the larger coefficients get refined before the smaller ones. The loop stops when the threshold has been reduced to 1. The reconstruction of the image from the coded form is simply a reverse. Each coded symbol corresponds to an implicitly known position in the coefficient Z-scan list. Each additional symbol simply adds another piece of information to the wavelet pyramid. Terminating the data stream after n bytes will result in a wavelet pyramid containing n bytes worth of information. This facilitates naturally a progressive transmission and allows a user to compress an image once to suit for many possible bit rates.

The SPIHT algorithm is a variation and more compact version of EZW. Each node of the *spatial orientation tree* corresponds to a pixel (wavelet coefficient) and its direct offsprings correspond to the pixels of the same spatial orientation in the next finer resolution level. The four children form a 2×2 array. The objective of the set partitioning is to make insignificant subsets contain a large number of coefficients and significant subsets contain only one coefficient. For a coefficient $c(i,j)$, three sets are used: $O(i,j)$ contains all offspring of node (i,j), $D(i,j)$ contains all descendents of node (i,j), and $L(i,j) = D(i,j) - O(i,j)$, as shown in Figure 13.17. If at least one coefficient in a set τ exceeds a threshold 2^n, the significance of this set, $S_n(\tau)$, is set to 1. Otherwise, $S_n(\tau) = 0$. To keep track of the order in which the subsets are tested for significance, three lists are used: LIS (list of insignificant sets), LIP (list of insignificant pixels), and LSP (list of significant pixels). Each iteration of the SPIHT algorithm uses a "sorting pass" and a "refinement pass" that are similar to the dominant pass and subordinate pass of EZW, respectively. Instead of using four symbols, only 0s and 1s are output: the comparison results $S_n(i,j)$, $S_n(D(i,j))$, and $S_n(L(i,j))$, as well as the sign of the significant coefficient (plus or minus in order to

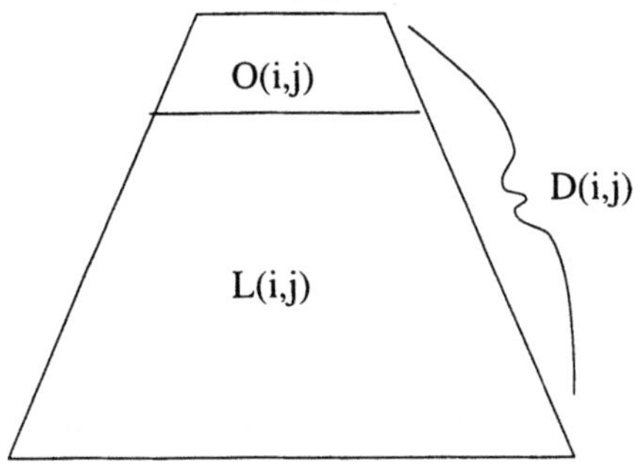

Figure 13.17. Sets defined in the SPIHT algorithm

refine the coefficient). Since only two symbols are used, a straight binary coding can be used avoiding arithmetic coding and the performance is still better than the original EZW. The decoder keeps modifying the three lists (LIS, LIP, and LSP) in exactly the same way as the coder, and the spatial location of each list item is implicitly known. SPIHT algorithm is extremely fast and generates better compression results than all previous variations of EZW. A great deal of research work has been done along the direction of EZW and SPIHT, and most of them compare their results with ZEW and SPIHT.

Lattice Vector Quantization

Sampson *et al.* [33] described a variation of EZW using lattice vector quantization. Wavelet coefficients are grouped into 4, 8 and 16 dimensional vectors and then approximated by vectors of a lattice codebook. The choice of using lattice vectors instead of the well-known LBG scheme [22] is to avoid the heavy computation of creating and searching the codebook. An implicit threshold and unit vectors from the codebook are used. The vectors in the first shell of the the D_4, E_8 and Λ_{16} [23] lattices are used, because they are known to give the best sphere packing properties. Lattice D_4, also called the checkerboard lattice, contains the vectors (u_1, u_2, u_3, u_4) with $\sum u_i = 0 \mod 2$. The first shell contains the 24 vectors with the form $(\pm 1, \pm 1, 0, 0)$. The E_8 lattice contains the vectors in D_8 and those vectors shifted by $\frac{1}{2}$ in all dimensions. The first shell has 240 vectors. The Λ_{16} lattice is also knows as the Barnes-Wall lattice. Its first shell has 4320 vectors which take the form $\frac{1}{\sqrt{2}}(\pm 2^2, 0^{14})$ (480 of them, including all permutations) and $(\pm 1^8, 0^8)$ where the nonzero components are positioned according to the first-order weight 8 Reed-Muller code [6, 23] in addition to having an even number of minus signs. To ensure convergence, the algorithm in [33] multiply the threshold by a real number $a < 1$ instead dividing by 2. Therefore, at step n of the refinement, the approximation to vector $\vec{x}$ is

$$a\vec{x_1} + a^2\vec{x_2} + \ldots + a^n\vec{x_n} \tag{13-13}$$

where x_i is the codebook vector employed at refinement step i, as shown in Figure 13.18.

A Modified Lattice Vector Quantization Scheme

This section describes a modified vector quantization scheme combined with the SPIHT algorithm. The general method can also be applied to other types of wavelet compression.

First, the hierarchical structure of wavelet coefficients is extended to handle vectors instead of only scalars. Figure 13.19 shows the structure with 2×2 squares. The first choice would be the D_4 lattice and the Λ_{16} lattice. One difficulty of using lattice vectors to approximate wavelet

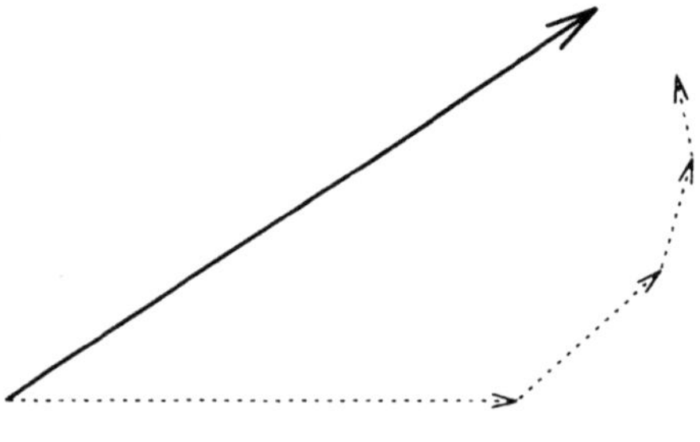

Figure 13.18. Convergence of vectors

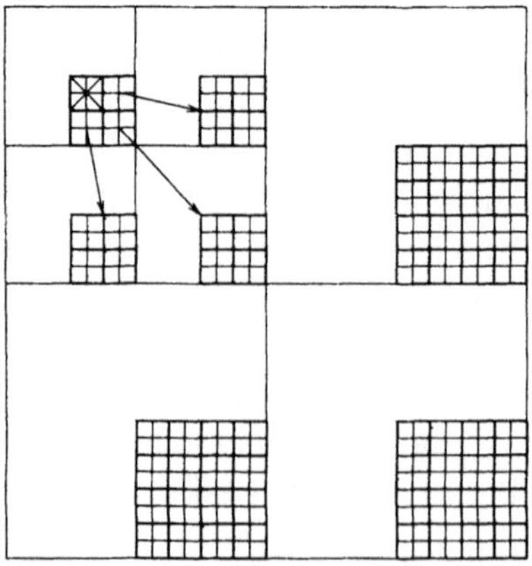

Figure 13.19. Hierarchical structures of vectors

coefficients is the "holes". Although a lattice is regular, it is by no means completely even. Many holes exist in a lattice structure. If a wavelet coefficient vector or a residual vector falls into one of the holes, a poor match will occur and it is possible that it will never converge. For instance, to approximate $\vec{v} = (1, 1, 1, 0.9)$ using the D_4 lattice, $a = 1/2$ and $T = 1$. Since $T \leq ||\vec{v}|| < 2T$, $\vec{v}$ will be coded at this refinement pass. Among all normalized first shell D_4 lattice vectors, the best match is a permutation of $(\frac{1}{\sqrt{2}}, \frac{1}{\sqrt{2}}, 0, 0)$, and the residual will have a magnitude of 1.408 which is greater than the *current* threshold T. The residual will never be reduced to zero. The worst case of a lattice vector quantization is that many wavelet coefficients *regularly* fall into holes and the residuals can be very large.

The normal (Gaussian) distribution of the coefficient magnitude indicates that significant coefficients occur sparsely, therefore, many 2×2 or 4×4 vectors become significant merely because a single *dominant component.* The best match to those vectors would be the permutations of $(\pm 1^1, 0^3)$ and $(\pm 1^1, 0^{15})$. Since $(\pm 2^1, 0^3)$ belong to the second shell of D_4 and only the shape (orientation) of the vectors are used, including the second shell D_4 can solve this problem. There is no vector in the first shell of Λ_{16} which can match $(\pm 1^1, 0^{15})$. The second shell of that lattice consists 61440 vectors, too many to be all included in the codebook. Therefore, a modified set of Λ'_{16} becomes:

- 32 vectors of the form $(\pm 1^1, 0^{15})$,
- 480 vectors of the form $\frac{1}{\sqrt{2}}(\pm 2^2, 0^{14})$,
- 7680 vectors of the form $(\pm 1^8, 0^8)$ where the positions of ± 1 correspond to the nonzero elements of the first-order weight 8 Reed-Muller code. Among them, 3840 vectors have an even number of negatives (forming the standard Barnes-Wall lattice), and the other half have odd number of negatives.

Because of the inclusion of those 3840 "near-lattice" vectors and the 32 non-lattice vectors, Λ'_{16} provides a better coverage for the wavelet coefficient vectors without using an excessively large codebook. Note that the non-lattice vectors can be efficiently tested for matches with input vectors.

During the vector refinement process, the magnitude of each residual vector is compared against the current threshold. If its magnitude is small, it should NOT be coded until next pass. Otherwise, the residual may get bigger, as shown in Figure 13.20.

Choosing a proper time (an optimal pass) to code a given vector is a sensitive issue, and it heavily depends on the match between the given vector $\vec{x}$ and the codebook vector $\vec{c}$ (normalized). And the match between them can be measured by the projection P of $\vec{x}$ on $\vec{c}$, as shown in Figure 13.21. Consider the following four cases:

Case (1): $aT < P < (aT + T)/2$
Case (2): $(aT + T)/2 < P < T$
Case (3): $T < P < (T + T/a)/2$
Case (4): $(T + T/a)/2 < P$

Poor matches are found in cases (1) and (2), while the matches are relatively good in (3) and (4). For case (1), $\vec{x} - aT\vec{c} < \vec{x} - T\vec{c}$, thus $\vec{x}$ should be coded with the same code vector in the *next* refinement pass, as indicated in Figure 13.22(a). For case (4), as shown in Figure 13.22(d), the same codebook vector should be used in the *previous* pass. Only in cases (2) and (3), the actual coding should happen during the current pass. Using the projection length as a criterion to determine the optimal pass to code the given vectors has been proven to be a better choice than using the vector length for the significant test. One problem of this approach is that some vectors with smaller magnitude could be coded before larger ones. Leaving the coding of some significant vectors to the subsequent pass could be risky since the current pass could be

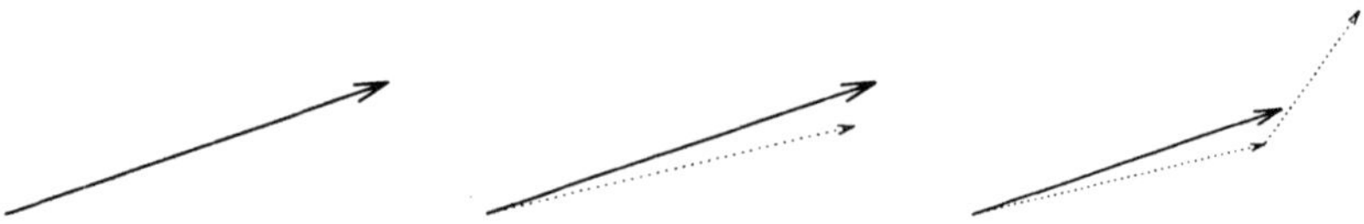

(a) (b) (c)

Figure 13.20. Consequence of coding insignificant vectors: (a) The original vector; (b) The original is matched well by a codevector leaving a small residual; (c) The small residual is vector quantized even though it is insignificant, resulting in a larger residual

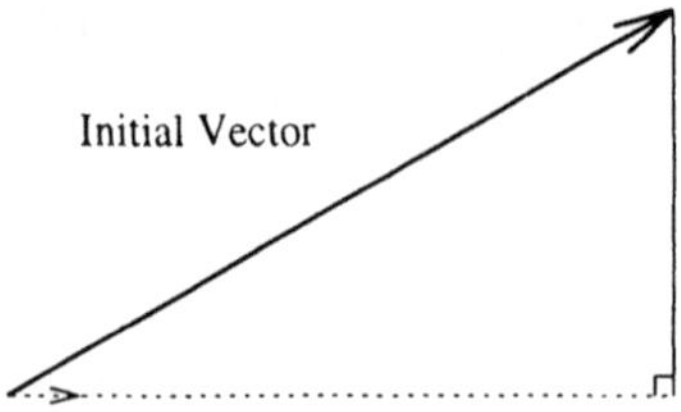

Figure 13.21. Residual Optimization

the final pass. However, the performance improvement out-weighs those shortcomings.

The above modified vector quantization scheme has incorporated with the SPIHT framework and the new algorithm is called *ModLVQ* . The significance test becomes a comparison between the projection of the vectors in a set with the threshold T. This threshold is updated at the end of every iteration: $T \longleftarrow aT$ [17]. The value of a is set to 0.65 here. The vector refinement is done in the sorting pass since the residuals of each quantized vector are placed back into the coefficient array.

13.4 The Performance of the ModLVQ Algorithm

The same set of test images for the quadtree algorithms (discussed in the previous sections) are used for ModLVQ. The individual modifications are tested first. Out of 182 test runs on 28 test images, the addition of codebook vectors with one dominant component of the form $(\pm 1^1, 0^{15})$ result in 0.01 dB PSNR improvement 115 times. The addition of the vectors with the Reed-Muller form and odd number of negative terms

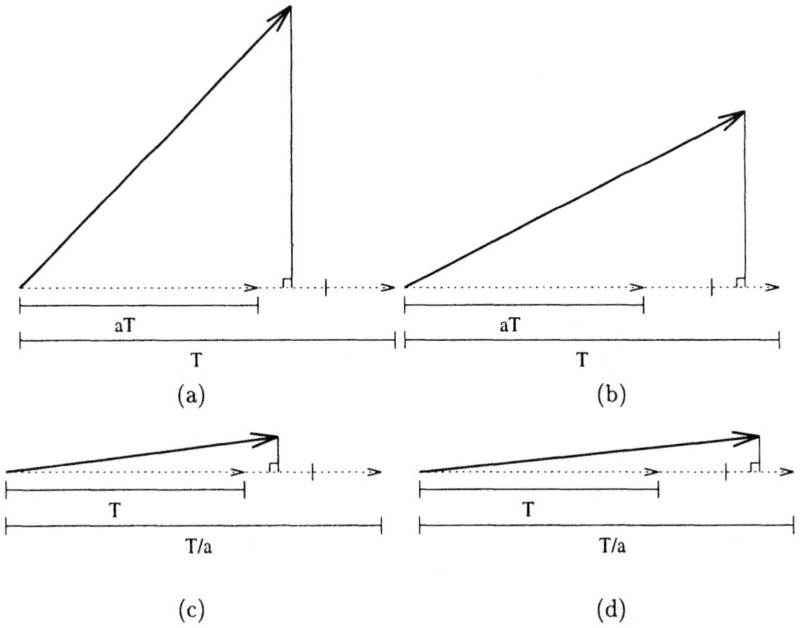

Figure 13.22. Four cases of matching between the given vector and the codebook vector in terms of the projection. (a) and (b) represent poor matches, (c) and (d) represent good matches

give a more pronounced improvement. It wins 124 times and the increase in PSNR can be up to 0.31 dB. The modification to the significance test and the coding pass selection make small changes, more positive than negative, to the results. The overall numerical comparisons are given for four typical images in Tables 13.4 and 13.5

Table 13.4. EZW, SPIHT and *ModLVQ* results (in dB PSNR) for images Lena and Barbara

	Lena image			Barbara image		
bpp	EZW	SPIHT	ModLVQ	EZW	SPIHT	ModLVQ
1	39.55	40.42	40.47	35.14	37.45	37.52
1/2	36.28	37.22	37.02	30.53	32.10	32.50
1/4	33.17	34.12	33.99	26.77	28.13	28.95
1/8	30.23	31.10	30.81	24.03	25.37	26.16
1/16	27.54	28.38	28.20	23.10	23.77	24.20
1/32	25.38	25.97	25.92	21.94	22.71	22.79
1/64	23.63	23.97	24.01	20.75	21.79	21.67
1/128	21.69	22.08	22.17	19.54	20.62	20.62

Table 13.5. SPIHT and *ModLVQ* results (in dB PSNR) for images Io and Mandril

	Io image		Mandrill image	
Bits per pixel	SPIHT	ModLVQ	SPIHT	ModLVQ
1	36.40	36.12	29.17	29.46
1/2	32.90	32.61	25.64	25.78
1/4	30.36	30.08	23.27	23.44
1/8	28.21	28.07	21.72	21.91
1/16	26.42	26.36	20.74	20.82
1/32	25.01	24.95	19.98	20.08
1/64	23.67	23.68	19.57	19.59
1/128	22.41	22.48	19.18	19.18

Image "Io" has a constant background and image "Lena" has some smooth areas. The images "Barbara" and "Mandril" contain more details, i.e., busier. Generally speaking, busy images have more high frequency details, as shown by the wider distribution of the coefficient values in Figure 13.23(b). Because of the large number of significant high frequency coefficients, busy images are more difficult to compress by *any* method, and they generally give lower quality reconstructed images for almost all bit rates. As it turns out, smooth images tend to be better compressed by SPIHT, and the *ModLVQ* algorithm can result in higher quality images for busier images, as indicated in Tables 13.4 and 13.5

In most cases, for busy images, *ModLVQ* reconstructed images are indeed more visually appealing. Figure 13.24 shows a tablecloth portion of the Barbara image compressed to 0.25 bpp by both the SPIHT and *ModLVQ* methods. Apparently, the *ModLVQ* retains more details. Figure 13.25 shows a segment of the Lena image containing part of the hat (above the rim). The compression ratio is also 0.25 bpp for both algorithms. Again, some fine texture is retained by *ModLVQ* but not by SPIHT.

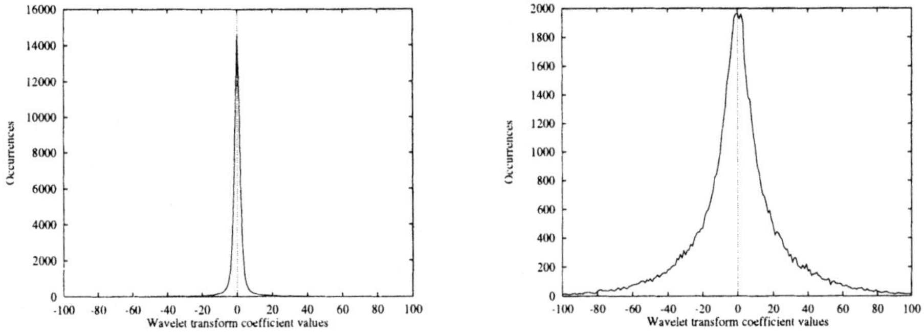

(a) (b)

Figure 13.23. Wavelet coefficient distributions for a smooth image (a) and a busy image (b)

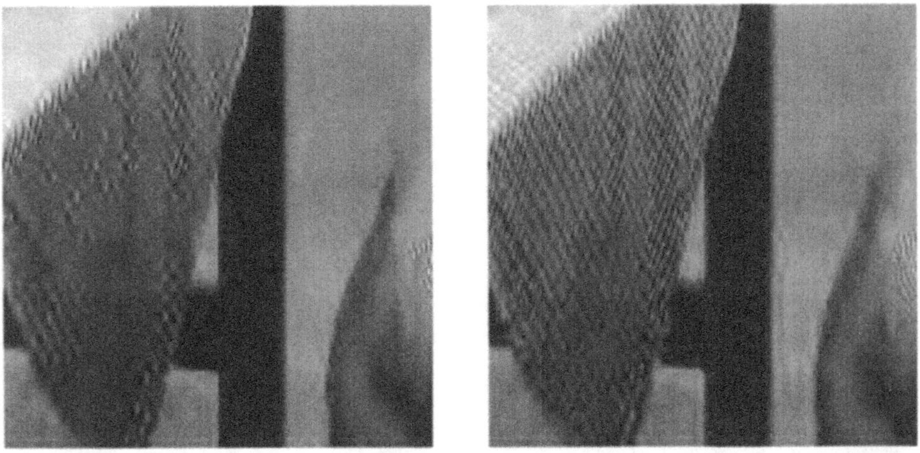

(a) (b)

Figure 13.24. Tablecloth portion of Barbara image: (a) SPIHT results; (b) *ModLVQ* results

13.5 Conclusion

This chapter is about the compression coding of IAP data. After a general discussion on the need and feasibility of compression and a basic framework of compression coding, two examples of image compression algorithms are presented.

One example is an improved version of a quadtree method proposed in [37]. The modifications are on the reconstruction side [20, 17], and the result algorithm shows an improvement in computation speed and image quality , visually and numerically. This quadtree method requires fewer operations than the DCT-based JPEG.

The *ModLVQ* algorithm, based on modifications to SPIHT including the addition of a modified lattice vector codebook, can give better compression results (both visually and numerically) for busy images and busy image portions, possibly because it can code image areas with high number of large wavelet coefficient more efficiently [17].

As expected, wavelet-based algorithms outperform spatial-domain methods at every bit rate for most images, as can be seen in Table 13.6. However, for the images with very few gray-levels, large homogeneous regions and well defined sharp edges, the quadtree-based algorithms can have an advantage over various transform domain methods [17].

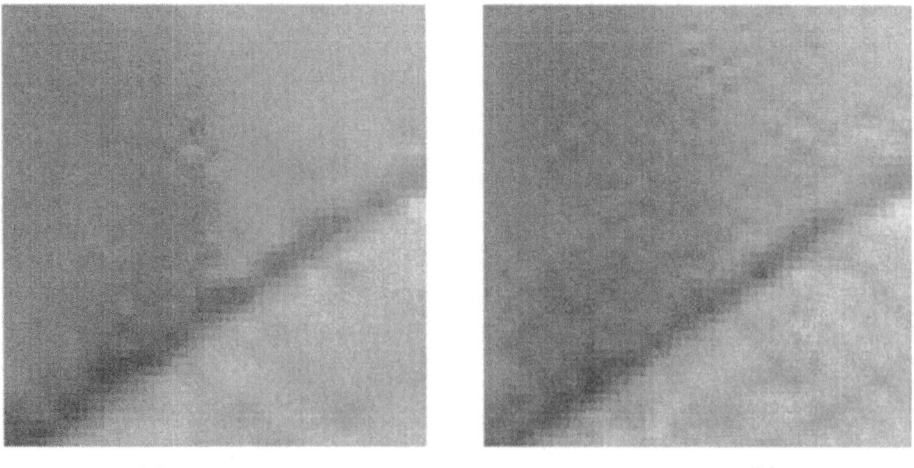

(a) (b)

Figure 13.25. Hat portion of the Lena image: (a) SPIHT result; (b) *ModLVQ* result

Table 13.6. ModLVQ and *SR* on *Lena*

Bits per pixel	ModLVQ	SR
0.964	40.30	35.16
0.501	37.03	32.14
0.271	34.26	29.79
0.154	31.88	27.78
0.102	30.04	26.41
0.074	28.74	25.18
0.036	26.29	23.37
0.017	24.23	21.75

References

[1] *ftp://ipl.rpi.edu.*

[2] M. Antonini, M. Barlaud, P. Mathieu, and I. Daubechies. Image coding using wavelet transform. *IEEE Trans. Image Proc.*, 1(2):205–220, 1992.

[3] Y. Arai, T. Agui, and M. Nakajima. A fast dct-sq scheme for images. *Trans. of the IEICE*, 71(11):1095, 1988.

[4] A. Averbuch, D. Lazar, and M. Israeli. Image compression using wavelet transform and multiresolution decomposition. *IEEE Trans. Image Proc.*, 5(1):4–15, 1996.

[5] Y. Cohen, M. Landy, and M. Pavel. Hierarchical coding of binary images. *IEEE Trans. Pattern Anal. Mach. Intel. PAMI-7.*, pages 284–298, 1985.

[6] J.H. Conway and N.J.A. Sloane. *Sphere Packings, Lattices and Groups.* Springer-Verlag, 1988.

[7] P.C. Cosman, S.M. Perlmutter, and K.O. Perlmutter. Tree-structured vector quantization with significance map for wavelet image coding. *Proceedings Data Compression Conference*, pages 33–41, March 1995.

[8] L.H. Croft and J.A. Robinson. Subband image coding using watershed and watercourse lines of the wavelet transform. *IEEE Trans. Image Proc.*, 3(6):759–771, 1994.

[9] L. Davis and A. Rosenfeld. Noise cleaning by iterated local averaging. *IEEE Trans. Systems, Man and Cyber.*, SMC-8(9):705–710, 1978.

[10] D. Fuhrmann. Quadtree traversal algorithms for pointer-based and depth first representations. *IEEE Trans. Pattern Anal. Mach. Intel. PAMI-10.*, pages 955–960, 1988.

[11] I Gargantini. An effective way to represent quadtrees. *Commun. ACM.*, 25:905–910, 1982.

[12] R. C. Gonzalez and R.E. Woods. *Digital Image Processing*. Addison-Wesley, 1992.

[13] W.I. Grosky and R. Jain. Optimal quadtrees for image segments. *IEEE Trans. Pattern Anal. Mach. Intel. PAMI-5.*, pages 77–83, 1983.

[14] F.C. Holroyd and D.C. Mason. Efficient linear quadtree construction algorithm. *Image and Vision Computing*, pages 218–224, 1990.

[15] G.M. Hunter and K. Steiglitz. Operations on images using quad trees. *IEEE Trans. Pattern Anal. Mach. Intel. PAMI-1.*, pages 145–153, 1979.

[16] L. Jones and S. Iyengar. Space and time efficient virtual quadtrees. *IEEE Trans. Pattern Anal. Mach. Intel. PAMI-6*, pages 244–247, 1984.

[17] J. Knipe. Improved spatial and transform domain compression schemes, Master thesis, University of Alberta, 1996.

[18] J. Knipe and X. Li. A new quadtree decomposition reconstruction method. *Proc. of 13th Int'l Conference on Pattern Recognition*, pages B364–369, 1996.

[19] J. Knipe and X. Li. An improved lattice vector quantization scheme for wavelet compression. *IEEE Trans. Signal Proc.*, 46(1):239–243, 1998.

[20] J. Knipe and X. Li. On the reconstruction of quadtree data. *IEEE Trans. Image Proc.*, 7(12):1653–1660, 1998.

[21] S. Lai, X. Li, and W. Bischof. On techniques for detecting circumscribed masses in mammogrrams. *IEEE Trans. Medical Imaging*, 8(4):377–386, 1990.

[22] Y. Linde, A. Buzo, and R.M. Gray. An algorithm for vector quantizer design. *IEEE Trans. Commun.*, COM-28(1):84–95, 1980.

[23] F.J. MacWilliams and N.J.A. Sloane. *The Theory of Error Correcting Codes*. North-Holland, 1978.

[24] M. Manohar, P. Sudarsana, and S. S. Iyengar. Template quadtrees for representing region and line data present in binary images. *Comput. Vision, Graphics, and Image Proc.*, 51:338–354, 1990.

[25] J. Modayil, H. Cheng, and X. Li. An improved piecewise approximation algorithm for image compression. *Pattern Recognition*, 31(8):1179–1190, Aug 1998.

[26] M. Nagao and T. Matsuyama. Edge preserving smoothing. *Computer Graphics and Image Processing*, 9:394–407, 1979.

[27] W.B. Pennebaker and J.L. Mitchell. *JPEG Still Image Data Compression Standard.* Van Nostrand Reinhold, 1993.

[28] A. Rosenfeld and A. Kak. *Digital Picture Processing.* Academnic, 1982.

[29] A. Said and W.A. Pearlman. A new fast and efficient image codec based on set partitioning in hierarchical trees. *Submitted to IEEE Trans. Circuits and Systems for Video Tech.*, 1995.

[30] H. Samet. An algorithm for converting rasters to quadtrees. *IEEE Trans. Pattern Anal. Mach. Intel. PAMI-3.*, pages 93–95, 1981.

[31] H. Samet and M. Tamminen. Efficient component labelling of images of arbitrary dimension represented by linear bintrees. *IEEE Trans. Pattern Anal. Mach. Intel. PAMI-10*, pages 579–586, 1988.

[32] H. Samet and R.E. Webber. On encoding boundaries with quadtrees. *IEEE Trans. Pattern Anal. Mach. Intel. PAMI-6*, pages 365–369, 1984.

[33] D.G. Sampson, E.A.B. da Silva, and M. Ghanbari. Wavelet transform image coding using lattice vector quantization. *Electronics Letters*, 30(18):1477–1478, 1994.

[34] A. Scher, F.R.D. Velasco, and A. Rosenfeld. Some new image smoothing techniques. *IEEE Trans. Systems, Man and Cyber.*, SMC-10(3):153–158, 1980.

[35] C.A. Shaffer and H. Samet. Optimal quadtree construction algorithms. *Comput. Vision, Graphics and Image Proc.*, 37:402–419, 1987.

[36] J.M. Shapiro. Embedded image coding using zerotrees of wavelet coefficients. *IEEE Trans. Signal Proc.*, 41(12):3445–3462, 1993.

[37] E. Shusterman and M. Feder. Image compression via improved quadtree decomposition. *IEEE Transactions on Image Processing.*, 3(2):207–215, 1994.

[38] Peter Strobach. Tree-structured scene adaptive coder. *IEEE Trans. Commun.*, 38(4):477–486, 1990.

[39] Peter Strobach. Quadtree-structured recursive plane decomposition coding of images. *IEEE Trans. Sig. Proc.*, 39(6):1380–1397, 1991.

[40] G.J. Sullivan and R.L. Baker. Efficient quadtree coding of images and video. *IEEE Transactions on Image Processing*, 3(3):327–331, 1994.

[41] R. Wilson. Quad-tree predictive coding: A new class of image data compression algorithms. *Proc. Int. Conf. Acoustics, Speech and Signal Proc., 29.3.1*, 1984.

[42] A. Zandi, J.D. Allen, E.L. Schwartz, and M. Boliek. Crew: Compression with reversible embedded wavelets. *Proceedings Data Compression Conference*, pages 212–221, March 1995.

Chapter 14

REDUCTION OF BLOCKING EFFECTS AND REMOVAL OF IMPULSE NOISE

In this chapter, we propose a new approach for removing blocking artifacts in the reconstructed block-encoded images. The key of the approach defined in Section 14.2 is using piecewise similarity within different parts of the image as a prior to give reasonable modifications to the block boundary pixels. This makes our approach different from traditional ones which are often developed by applying some kinds of smoothing constraints on local regions. In Section 14.3, the experimental results show that our approach well achieves enhanced decoding for JPEG-decoded images both objectively and subjectively. We also introduce the progressive switching median filter for the removal of impulse noise and its detection using fuzzy techniques in Sections 14.4 and 14.5, respectively.

14.1 Introduction

"Blocking effect" is one of the major disadvantages of block-based image coding techniques. There are two general approaches to reduce blocking effects. In the first approach, the blocking effect is dealt with at the encoding side using overlapping schemes [1, 2]. This kind of methods may lead to an increase in the bit rate or modify the encoding and decoding procedures dramatically. The second approach uses some post-processing techniques at the decoding side. It can improve the visual quality of the reconstructed image without using any extra bits or applying any modification on the encoding or decoding procedures. Due to these advantages, most recently proposed algorithms are conducted by using the second approach [1, 3-6].

Generally speaking, the traditional post-processing techniques, whether they are applied in spatial or transform domain, are implemented by applying some smoothing constraints on the local regions. In this letter, we propose a fundamentally different approach which breaks through the traditional framework in two ways: (1) It is not necessary to apply any smoothing constraint on local regions; (2) It can make use of the information of remote regions. Our approach is developed by employing a special kind of information redundancy — "Piecewise similarity" in natural images. In Jacquin's fractal block coding technique [7], "Block-wise similarity" at different scales had been used to implement the function of image compression. We think such "Block-wise similarity" can be generalized to any shape as "Piecewise similarity" and can also be used at the same scale.

In Section 14.4, we present a new median-based switching filter, called Progressive Switching Median (PSM) filter, where both the impulse detector and the noise filter are applied progressively in iterative manners. The noise pixels processed in the current iteration are used to help the process of the other pixels in the subsequent iterations.

Section 14.5 presents another new algorithm, which can remove impulse noise from corrupted image while preserving details. The algorithm is based on fuzzy impulse detection and fuzzy noise cancellation techniques. Experimental results show that our algorithm is capable of providing significant improvement over many published techniques in terms of both subjective evaluations.

14.2 Blocking Effect Reduction Algorithm

Suppose the image block size is fixed to be $N \times N$. Our algorithm is first applied horizontally to recover vertical boundaries. Let $\boldsymbol{x} = (x_{-N/2}, x_{-N/2+1}, \ldots, x_{-1}, x_0, \ldots, x_{N/2-2}, x_{N/2-1})$ be the vector of the pixel values across the boundary of two blocks in the blocky image, where $x_{-N/2}, x_{-N/2+1}, \ldots, x_{-1}$ and $x_0, \ldots, x_{N/2-2}, x_{N/2-1}$ are two groups of pixels in the same line of the left and right blocks, respectively. The real block boundary is between x_{-1} and x_0. Let $\boldsymbol{y} = (y_{-N/2}, y_{-N/2+1}, \ldots, y_{-1}, y_0, \ldots, y_{N/2-2}, y_{N/2-1})$ be the vector of a line of pixels within one block. Since all the pixels in $\boldsymbol{y}$ are in the same block, we assume $\boldsymbol{y}$ is of good continuity and use the continuity of $\boldsymbol{y}$ to recover the discontinuity of $\boldsymbol{x}$. For a certain $\boldsymbol{x}$, there exist many possible $\boldsymbol{y}$*'s* in the whole image, but we choose only one from them. First, a candidate $\boldsymbol{y}$ should not be very far away from $\boldsymbol{x}$. We restrict it to be within an m pixel wide and n pixel high rectangle region centered about the middle point of $\boldsymbol{x}$. The criterion for the selection of $\boldsymbol{y}$ from these candidate $\boldsymbol{y}$*'s* is how well it can match $\boldsymbol{x}$ through a matching function f. In other words, it should be similar to $\boldsymbol{x}$. This is what we have called "Piecewise similarity". We use a first-order linear function $f(y) = a_0 + a_1 y$ as the matching function and use the Weighted Mean Square Error (WMSE) to evaluate the matching result. WMSE is determined by a weight vector $\boldsymbol{w} =$

($w_{-N/2}$, $w_{-N/2+1}$, ..., w_{-1}, w_0,..., $w_{N/2-2}$, $w_{N/2-1}$) which satisfies the following conditions:0

$$0 \le w_i \le 1 \ (i = -N/2, \cdots, N/2-1), \tag{14-1}$$

$$w_{-k} = w_{k-1} \ \ (k = 1, \cdots, N/2), \tag{14-2}$$

$$\sum_{i=-N/2}^{N/2-1} w_i = 1. \tag{14-3}$$

Then, WMSE can be written as:

$$E = \sum_{i=-N/2}^{N/2-1} w_i [x_i - f(y_i)]^2 = \sum_{i=-N/2}^{N/2-1} w_i [x_i - (a_0 + a_1 y_i)]^2 . \tag{14-4}$$

By solving the equations: $\partial E / \partial a_0 = 0$ and $\partial E / \partial a_1 = 0$, We can obtain the parameters a_0 and a_1:

$$\begin{cases} a_1 = \dfrac{(\sum_{i=-N/2}^{N/2-1} w_i x_i) \cdot (\sum_{i=-N/2}^{N/2-1} w_i y_i) - \sum_{i=-N/2}^{N/2-1} w_i x_i y_i}{(\sum_{i=-N/2}^{N/2-1} w_i y_i)^2 - \sum_{i=-N/2}^{N/2-1} w_i y_i^2} \\ \\ a_0 = \sum_{i=-N/2}^{N/2-1} w_i x_i - a_1 \cdot \sum_{i=-N/2}^{N/2-1} w_i y_i \end{cases} \tag{14-5}$$

Each candidate $\boldsymbol{y}$ will result in an E but only the one with the minimal E is our ultimate choice. The selected $\boldsymbol{y}$, together with $\boldsymbol{x}$, is used to generate the recovered vector $\boldsymbol{x}' = (x'_{-N/2}, x'_{-N/2+1}, \cdots, x'_{-1}, x'_0, \cdots, x'_{N/2-2}, x'_{N/2-1})$. Each x'_i is a linear combination of x_i and $f(y_i)$ which is determined by a weight vector $\boldsymbol{c}$ = ($c_{-N/2}$, $c_{-N/2+1}$, ... , c_{-1}, c_0 , ... , $c_{N/2-2}$, $c_{N/2-1}$), where

$$0 \le c_i \le 1 \ (i = -N/2, \cdots, N/2-1), \tag{14-6}$$

$$c_{-k} = c_{k-1} \ \ (k = 1, \cdots, N/2). \tag{14-7}$$

Then we have,

$$x'_i = [1 - c_i \cdot g(E)] \cdot x_i + c_i \cdot g(E) \cdot f(y_i). \tag{14-8}$$

Here, $g(E)$ is defined as:

$$g(E)=\begin{cases}1-(\frac{1-T_C}{T_E})\cdot E & \text{if } 0 \le E \le T_E \\ 0 & \text{otherwise}\end{cases} \tag{14-9}$$

where T_C and T_E are two parameters used to control the shape of $g(E)$. The goal of using $\boldsymbol{c}$ and $g(E)$ is to provide a tradeoff between modification and maintenance of $\boldsymbol{x}$. $\boldsymbol{c}$ should be selected so that the closer the pixel to the block boundary, the more it is modified, while $g(E)$ is selected so that the better $\boldsymbol{y}$ can match $\boldsymbol{x}$, the more $\boldsymbol{x}$ is modified. In very few special cases where we can not find a $\boldsymbol{y}$ that can match $\boldsymbol{x}$ well, i.e., all $E > T_E$, we just use a simple method to smooth x_{-1} and x_0:

$$x'_{-1} = (1 - p) \cdot x_{-1} + p \cdot x_0 , \tag{14-10}$$

$$x'_0 = p \cdot x_{-1} + (1 - p) \cdot x_0 , \tag{14-11}$$

where $0 < p < 1$ is employed to determine how much the pixel values are smoothed. Our algorithm is first applied to the vertical block boundaries of every line. Then it is applied to the horizontal block boundaries using the same way. For each of the block corner pixels, both of these two procedures will suggest a value. We use the average of these two values as the final result.

14.3 Experimental Results

We use several 8bpp (bits/pixel) gray scale images to test our algorithm. The test images are first coded using JPEG standard at different bit rates, where the JPEG program is from the Independent JPEG Group (IJG) JPEG Release 6a (available at http://www.jcu.edu.au/docs/jpeg). The JPEG decoded images are then subject to our blocking effect reduction algorithm. In our approach, the following control parameters are chosen:

$$N = 8;\ m = 64;\ n = 32;\ T_E = 200;\ T_C = 0.75;\ p = 0.3,$$

$$\boldsymbol{w} = (0.2, 0.15, 0.1, 0.05, 0.05, 0.1, 0.15, 0.2),$$

$$\boldsymbol{c} = (0.25, 0.55, 0.65, 1, 1, 0.65, 0.55, 0.25).$$

Note that the parameters m and n are different. The reason is that the vector $\boldsymbol{x}$ is horizontally located in the image. In such a case, we find experimentally that searching $\boldsymbol{y}$ in a rectangle region with its width larger than its height is more likely to get a good match for $\boldsymbol{x}$. Obviously, when $\boldsymbol{x}$ is vertically located in the image, *m* becomes the height and *n* becomes the width. The same set of parameters is applied to all the test images coded at all tested bit rates. These parameters are optimized for a small number of images such as "Peppers" and Lena", but they also lead to similar restoration results on many other images.

To make our algorithm easily compared with other approaches, the experimental results given in this letter are under the following conditions: (1) The test image is 512×512 image "Lena". (2) Peak Signal-to-Noise Ratio (PSNR) is used as the objective standard to evaluate the post-processing results. (3) The test image is encoded and then decoded using JPEG standard at a relatively large range of bit rates ranging from about 0.15 to 0.45 bpp. The decoding and post-processing results are shown in Table 14.1 and Figure 14.1. By using our blocking effect reduction algorithm, PSNRs are improved by a magnitude of 0.2dB - 0.85dB. Our algorithm achieves relatively good results among those obtained by other approaches such as POCS [4], CLS [4] and Crouse et al.'s method [5] which are also shown in Figure 14.1. Figure 14.2 gives subjective illustrations of the decoding and post-processing results of the enlarged hat region of "Lena". The post-processed image appears enhanced quality from the JPEG decoded image.

Table 14.1. Post-processing results of "Lena" 512 by 512, 8bits/pixel

Bit Rate (bpp)	PSNR (dB) of JPEG Decoded Image	PSNR (dB) of Post-Processed Image
0.175	27.33	28.18
0.219	29.47	30.22
0.246	30.41	31.09
0.310	31.95	32.48
0.365	32.96	33.33
0.415	33.70	33.97

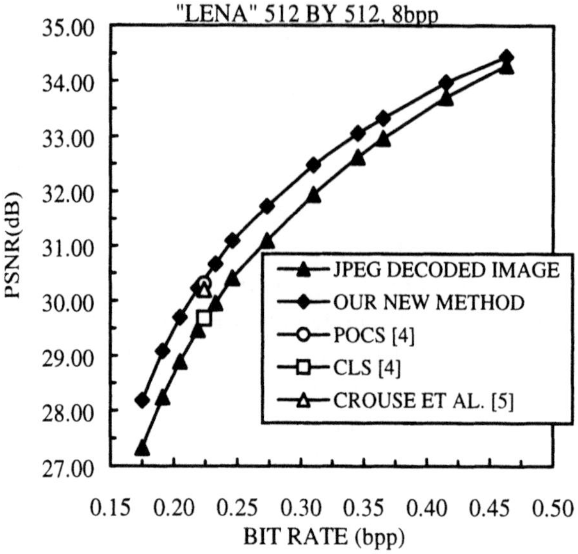

Figure 14.1. Post-processing results for JPEG-decoded image

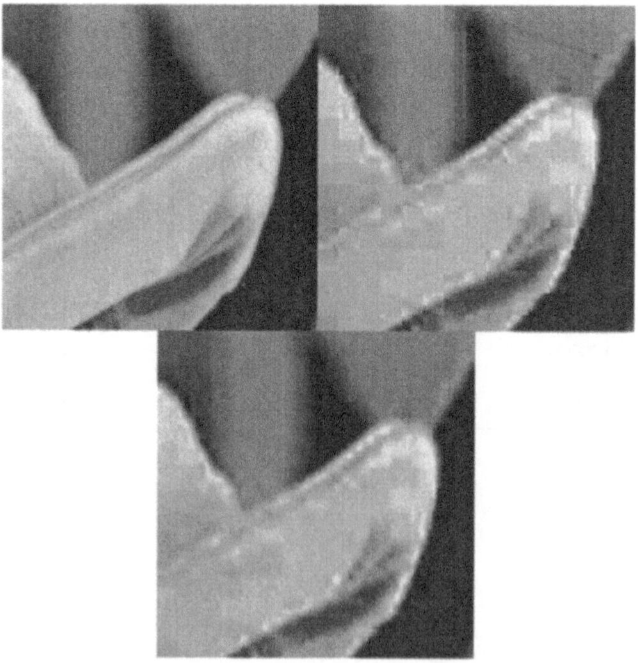

Figure 14.2. Illustration of post-processing result for hat region of "Lena". Top-left: original image; Top-right: JPEG-decoded image, 0.219bpp; Bottom: Post-processed image

14.4 Progressive Switching Median Filter for the Removal of Impulse Noise

Images are often corrupted by impulse noise due to errors generated in noisy sensors or communication channels. It is important to eliminate noise in the images before some subsequent processing, such as edge detection, image segmentation and object recognition. For this purpose, many approaches have been proposed [13]. In the past two decades, median-based filters have attracted much attention because of their simplicity and their capability of preserving image edges [8, 9, 13, 14]. Nevertheless, because the typical median filters are implemented uniformly across the image, they tend to modify both noise pixels and undisturbed good pixels. To avoid the damage of good pixels, the switching scheme is introduced by some recently published works [8, 9, 11, 15, 16], where impulse detection algorithms are employed before filtering and the detection results are used to control whether a pixel should be modified. Figure. 14.3 shows a general framework for such kind of algorithms which had proved to be more effective than uniformly applied methods when the noise pixels are sparsely distributed in the image. However, when the images are very highly corrupted, a large number of impulse pixels may connect into noise blotches. In such cases, many impulses are difficult to detect, thus impossible to be eliminated. In addition, the error will propagate around their neighborhood regions.

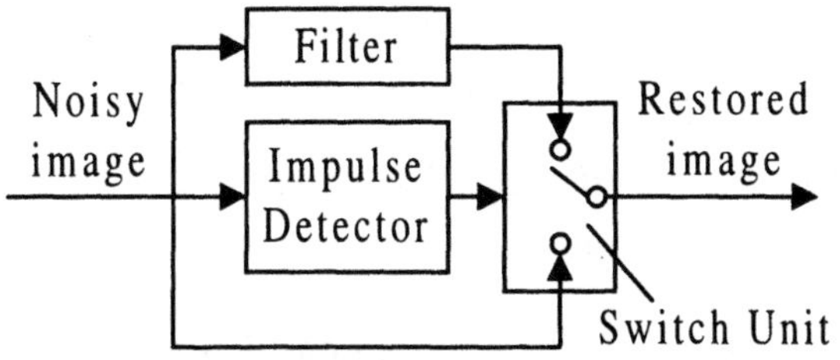

Figure 14.3. A general framework of switching scheme-based image filters

Noise Filtering

Like the impulse detection procedure (see Section 7.2), the noise filtering procedure also generates a gray scale image sequence, $\{\{y_i^{(0)}\}, \{y_i^{(1)}\}, \ldots, \{y_i^{(n)}\}, \ldots\}$, and a binary flag image sequence $\{\{g_i^{(0)}\}, \{g_i^{(1)}\}, \ldots, \{g_i^{(n)}\}, \ldots\}$. In the gray scale image sequence, we still use $y_i^{(0)}$ to denote the pixel value at position i in the noisy image to be filtered and use $y_i^{(n)}$ to represent the pixel value at position i in the image after the n-th iteration. In a binary flag image { $g_i^{(n)}$ }, the value $g_i^{(n)} = 0$ means the pixel ***i*** is good and $g_i^{(n)} = 1$ means it is an impulse that should be filtered. A difference between the impulse detection and noise filtering procedures is that the initial flag image { $g_i^{(0)}$ } of the noise filtering procedure is not a blank image, but the impulse detection result { $f_i^{(N_D)}$ }, i.e., $g_i^{(0)} \equiv f_i^{(N_D)}$.

In the *n*-th iteration (n = 1, 2, ...), for each pixel $y_i^{(n-1)}$, we also first find its median value $m_i^{(n-1)}$ of a $W_F \times W_F$ (W_F is an odd integer and not smaller than 3) window centered about it. However, unlike that in the impulse detection procedure, the median value here is selected from only good pixels with $g_j^{(n-1)} = 0$ in the window. Let M denote the number of all the pixels with $g_j^{(n-1)} = 0$ in the $W_F \times W_F$ window. If M is odd, then

$$m_i^{(n-1)} = \text{Med}\ \{\ y_j^{(n-1)} \mid g_j^{(n-1)} = 0, j \in \Omega_i^{W_F}\ \}. \tag{14-12}$$

If M is even but not 0, then

$$m_i^{(n-1)} = (\text{Med}_L\{\ y_j^{(n-1)} \mid g_j^{(n-1)} = 0, j \in \Omega_i^{W_F}\ \} + \text{Med}_R\{\ y_j^{(n-1)} \mid g_j^{(n-1)} = 0, j \in \Omega_i^{W_F}\ \})/2, \tag{14-13}$$

where Med_L and Med_R denote the left and the right median values, respectively. That is, Med_L is the (M/2)-th largest value and Med_R is the (M/2 + 1)-th largest value of the sorted data. The value of $y_i^{(n)}$ is modified only when the pixel ***i*** is an impulse and M is greater than 0:

$$y_i^{(n)} = \begin{cases} m_i^{(n-1)} & \text{if} \quad g_i^{(n-1)} = 1 \quad \text{and} \quad M > 0 \\ y_i^{(n-1)} & \text{else} \end{cases} \tag{14-14}$$

Once an impulse pixel is modified, it is considered as a good pixel in the subsequent iterations:

$$g_i^{(n)} = \begin{cases} g_i^{(n-1)} & \text{if} \quad y_i^{(n)} = y_i^{(n-1)} \\ 0 & \text{if} \quad y_i^{(n)} = m_i^{(n-1)} \end{cases} \tag{14-15}$$

The procedure stops after the N_F-th iteration when all of the impulse pixels have been modified, i.e.

$$\sum_i g_i^{(N_F)} = 0. \tag{14-16}$$

Then we obtain the image { $y_i^{(N_F)}$ } which is our restored output image.

Implementation and Simulation

In our experiments, the original test images are corrupted with fixed valued salt-pepper impulses, where the corrupted pixels take on the values of either 0 or 255 with equal probability. Mean Square Error (MSE) is used to evaluate the restoration performance. MSE is defined as:

$$\mathrm{MSE} = \frac{1}{N}\sum_{i}(u_i - v_i)^2 \tag{14-17}$$

where N is the total number of pixels in the image, u_i and v_i are the pixel values at position $\boldsymbol{i}$ in the original and the test images, respectively.

To implement the PSM algorithm, four parameters must be predetermined. They are the filtering window size W_F, the impulse detection window size W_D, the impulse detection iteration number N_D and the impulse detection threshold T_D. Our experiments show that almost all the best restoration results are obtained when $W_F = 3$ and $N_D = 3$. In addition, these two parameters are not sensitive to noise rate and image type. Therefore, we simply set both W_F and N_D to be 3. The other two parameters, W_D and T_D, are sensitive to how much the image is corrupted. From Figure 14.4, we can observe that, for image "Bridge", $W_D = 3$ is more suitable for low noise ratio and $W_D = 5$ is better for high noise ratio, with a cross point at about R = 30%. The experiments on some other images give similar conclusion except that the cross point may be a little bit lower or higher such as R = 25% or R = 35%. The influence of T_D is investigated in Figure 14.5. It appears that the best T_D is decreasing with the increase of R. To determine W_D and T_D, we first make a rough estimation on the noise ratio, which again uses the impulse detection measurement of Sun and Neuvo's switch I scheme [8]. Initially, we set

$$N_I = 0\,, \tag{14-18}$$

where N_I is the number of impulses that have been detected. For each pixel x_i, we find the median value of the samples in the 3×3 window centered about it:

$$m_i = \mathrm{Med}\,\{x_j \mid j \in \Omega_i^3\}. \tag{14-19}$$

The difference between m_i and x_i is used to make a decision on whether it is an impulse:

$$\text{if} \quad |m_i - x_i| \geq T_I, \quad \text{then} \quad N_I + 1 \rightarrow N_I\,, \tag{14-20}$$

where the threshold T_I is predefined as 40 in our experiments. After all the pixels in the image have been scanned once, we give an estimation of the noise ratio as:

$$\hat{R} = N_I / N, \tag{14-21}$$

where N is the total number of pixels in the image. Then W_D and T_D are defined according to $\hat{R}$:

$$W_D = \begin{cases} 3 & if \quad \hat{R} \le T_R \\ 5 & if \quad \hat{R} > T_R \end{cases} \tag{14-22}$$

$$T_D = a + b \cdot \hat{R} \ . \tag{14-23}$$

According to our experimental results, we choose T_R, a and b as 25%, 65 and –50, respectively.

Although our parameter pre-selection scheme brings about several new parameters, the restoration results are experimentally less sensitive to them, thus only rough estimations are needed. This is important for the usage of the PSM filter in real applications, where statistical information about the given corrupted images may be unavailable. While our parameter selection is based on the experiments on a small set of images such as "bridge" and "Lena", the results on other images are also good.

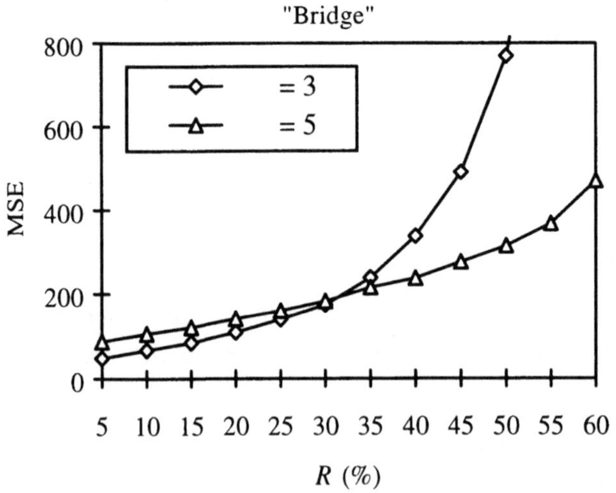

Figure 14.4. The effects of W_D with respect to MSE, where $W_F = 3$, $N_D = 3$ and $T_D = 50$

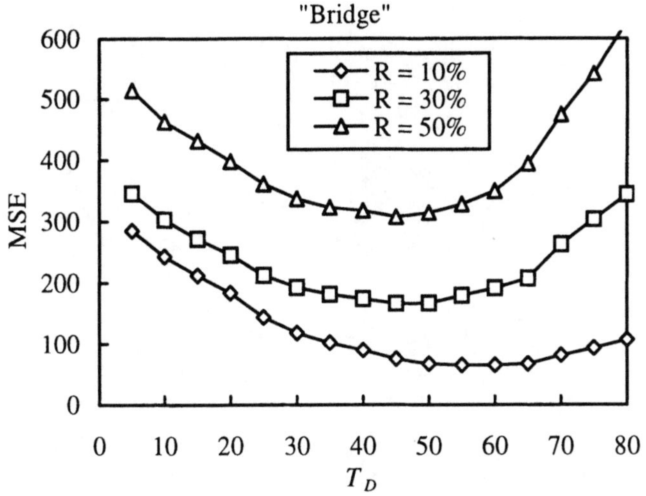

Figure 14.5. The effects of T_D with respect to MSE. For R = 10%, $W_F = 3$, $W_D = 3$ and N_D =3; For R = 30%, $W_F = 3$, $W_D = 5$ and $N_D = 3$; For R = 50%, $W_F = 3$, $W_D = 5$ and $N_D = 3$

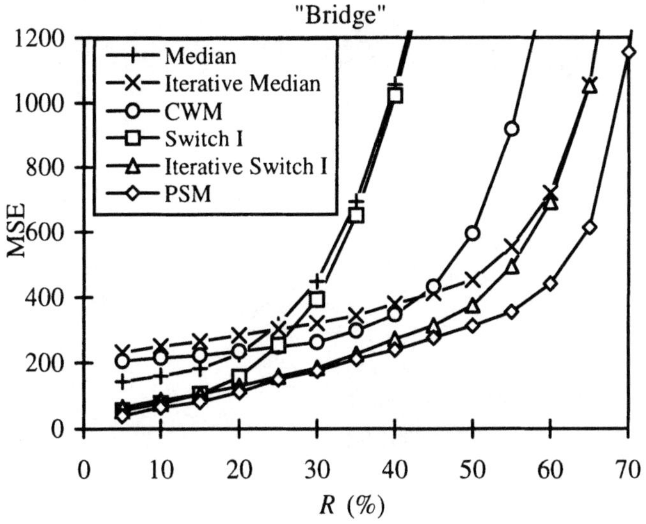

Figure 14.6. A comparison of different median-based filters for the restoration of corrupted image "Bridge" under a large range of impulse noise ratio

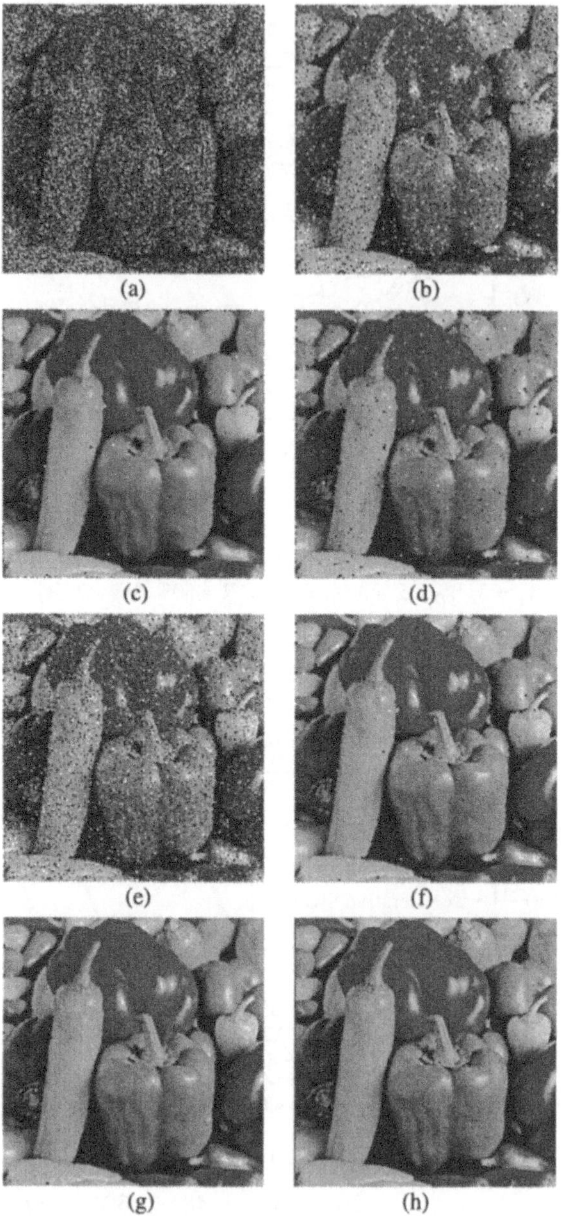

Figure 14.7. Restoration results of different median-based filters. (a) corrupted image "Peppers" with 50% salt-pepper noise, (b) median filter with 3×3 window size, (c) iterative median filter with 3×3 window size and 8 iterations, (d) center weighted median (CWM) filter with 5×5 window size and a center weight of 3, (e) switch I median filter with 3×3 window size, (f) iterative switch I median filter with 3×3 window size and 8 iterations, where the noise detection threshold is 40, (g) the PSM filter, and (h) original image of "Peppers"

We test our PSM algorithm and compare it with other well known median-based filters, which are the simple median filters, the iterative median filter (iteratively apply the simple median filter), the Center Weighted Median (CWM) filter, the switch I median filter and the iterative switch I median filter (iteratively apply the switch I median filter). The experiments are carried out on several 512×512, 8bits/pixel gray scale images. We provide the MSE performance in Figure 14.6 where the original test image "Bridge" is corrupted with different impulse noise ratios ranging from 5% to 70%. The MSE curves demonstrate that our PSM algorithm is better than other median-based methods, especially when noise ratios are high. In Figure 14.7, we show the restoration results of different filtering methods for test image "Peppers" highly corrupted with 50% impulse noise. Both the simple 3×3 median filter and the switch I median filter can preserve image details but many noise pixels are remained in the image. The Center Weighed Median (CWM) filter performs better than simple median filter, but it still influences good pixels and misses many impulse pixels. The iterative median filter removes most of the impulses, but many good pixels are also modified, resulting in blurring of the image. Since the iterative switch I filter does not modify good pixels in the image, it maintains image details better than the iterative median filter, but many noise blotches still remained in the image. Dramatic restoration results are obtained by our PSM filter. It can remove almost all of the noise pixels while preserve image details very well.

14.5 Impulse Noise Detection and Removal Using Fuzzy Techniques

In this section, we present another new impulse noise removal algorithm which is shown in Figure 14.8. This algorithm starts by inputting the noisy image to a median filter. The output image of the median filter, together with the noisy image itself, is the input of our fuzzy impulse detection module. The goal of the fuzzy impulse detection module is to generate a fuzzy flag map which gives each pixel a fuzzy flag indicating how much it looks like an impulse pixel. This fuzzy flag map has two usage: 1) The fuzzy noise cancellation module utilizes it to recommend a new value for every pixel; 2) It is also as the basis of the switch unit which controls each pixel of the output restored image in two different cases, the recommended value of the fuzzy noise cancellation module or the input pixel value remaining unchanged. Finally, the output of the switch unit is our restored image.

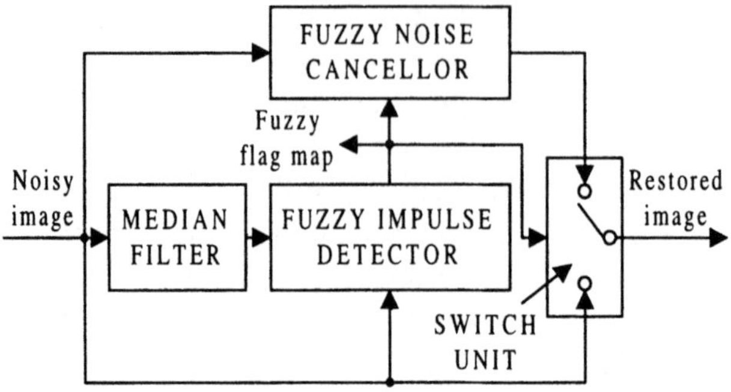

Figure 14.8. The fuzzy impulse noise removal system

Fuzzy Impulse Detection

Let $x_{i,j}$ and $y_{i,j}$ represents the pixel values at position (i, j) in the corrupted image and the restored image respectively. To judge whether $x_{i,j}$ is an impulse pixel, we get the median value of the samples in the $(2N_d+1)\times(2N_d+1)$ window centered about it, i.e.,

$$v_{i,j} = \text{med}\{\, x_{i-N_d,j-N_d}, \ldots, x_{i,j}, \ldots, x_{i+N_d,j+N_d} \,\}. \tag{14-24}$$

The difference between $v_{i,j}$ and $x_{i,j}$ provides us a simple and effective measurement to detect impulses: *If the difference between* $v_{i,j}$ *and* $x_{i,j}$ *is large, then it is an impulse pixel.* To give the pixel (i,j) a fuzzy flag indicating how much it looks like an impulse pixel, we define the following two-parameter membership function:

$$f_{i,j} = \begin{cases} 0 & \left|x_{i,j} - v_{i,j}\right| \le a \\ \dfrac{\left|x_{i,j} - v_{i,j}\right| - a}{b-a} & a < \left|x_{i,j} - v_{i,j}\right| < b \\ 1 & \left|x_{i,j} - v_{i,j}\right| \ge b \end{cases}, \tag{14-25}$$

where a and b are the two pre-determined parameters. On the contrary, we can use $(1 - f_{i,j})$ as a measurement to demonstrate how good is a pixel.

Fuzzy Noise Cancellation

According to our impulse noise removal system described in Figure 14.8, the noise cancellation scheme is applied to only the pixels look like impulses, i.e., if $f_{i,j} \le T_d$, then $y_{i,j} = x_{i,j}$; Otherwise, the fuzzy noise cancellation algorithm is employed to yield a new value for $y_{i,j}$ which is different from $x_{i,j}$. Here T_d is a given threshold value.

Our noise cancellation algorithm is based on a special kind of information redundancy — long range correlation within different parts of the image. For a pixel at position (i, j) to be modified, two $(2N_c+1)\times(2N_c+1)$ sized windows are employed: The first window is defined as a local window centered about the impulse pixel; The second window as a remote window located at a different place with its center at position (k, l). Since the whole image may contain a large number of complete $(2N_c+1)\times(2N_c+1)$ windows, the remote window should be chosen from one of them. In our algorithm, a candidate remote window must satisfy the following conditions: (1) It must be completely covered by a larger $(2M+1)\times(2M+1)$ ($M>N_c$) window called searching range window which is centered about the impulse pixel; (2) It is not the same as the local window, i.e., $i\neq k$ or $j\neq l$. All the $(2N_c+1)\times(2N_c+1)$ windows satisfying these requirements are subjected to a fuzzy window matching test. Before describing how the test is performed, however, we define a fuzzy pixel matching function based on the following fuzzy reasoning: If the difference between a pair of corresponding pixels in the local and remote windows is small, then the two pixels are well matched. The function is defined as:

$$p_{m,n}=\begin{cases}(T_m-\left|x_{i+m,j+n}-x_{k+m,l+n}\right|)/T_m & \left|x_{i+m,j+n}-x_{k+m,l+n}\right|<T_m \\ 0 & \left|x_{i+m,j+n}-x_{k+m,l+n}\right|\geq T_m\end{cases}, \qquad (14\text{-}26)$$

where T_m is a pre-defined parameter. *If a pair of corresponding pixels are well matched and both of the pixels are good, then the pair is a good matching pair. If most of the matching pixel pairs in the local and remote windows are good matching pairs, then the two windows are well matched.* Based on the above fuzzy rules, we use the following standard to determine how well a pair of local and remote windows are matched:

$$q_{(i,j),(k,l)}=\sum_{m=-N_c}^{N_c}\sum_{n=-N_c}^{N_c}p_{m,n}\cdot\min[(1-f_{i+m,j+n}),(1-f_{k+m,l+n})]\cdot(1-\delta_{m,n}), \qquad (14\text{-}27)$$

where

$$\delta_{m,n}=\begin{cases}1 & m=0\,\text{and}\,n=0\\ 0 & \text{otherwise}\end{cases}. \qquad (14\text{-}28)$$

Each of the candidate remote window will result in a $q_{(i,j),(k,l)}$, but only the one with the maximum $q_{(i,j),(k,l)}$ becomes our ultimate choice. Finally, the pixel value of (i,j) is replaced by a linear combination of its original value $x_{i,j}$ and the center pixel $x_{k,l}$ of the selected remote window:

$$y_{i,j}=[(1-f_{i,j})\cdot x_{i,j}+(1-f_{k,l})\cdot x_{k,l}]/(2-f_{i,j}-f_{k,l}), \qquad (14\text{-}29)$$

where the linear coefficients are determined on how good $x_{i,j}$ and $x_{k,l}$ are.

Experiment Results

Some computer simulations are carried out to assess the performance of our method. The original test image is "Lena" of size 512×512 (8bits/pixel). The corrupted images are generated using both fixed-valued impulse noise (equal values of 0 or 255 with equal probabilities) and random-valued impulse noise (random values uniformly distributed between 0 and 255). We use the proposed approach to remove noises from the corrupted images. Usually, the best restoration results are obtained after 2 or 3 iterations. Figure 14.9 gives the restoration result for the face region of "Lena" where the image is corrupted by 20% random valued impulse noise. The restored image appears very good subjective quality.

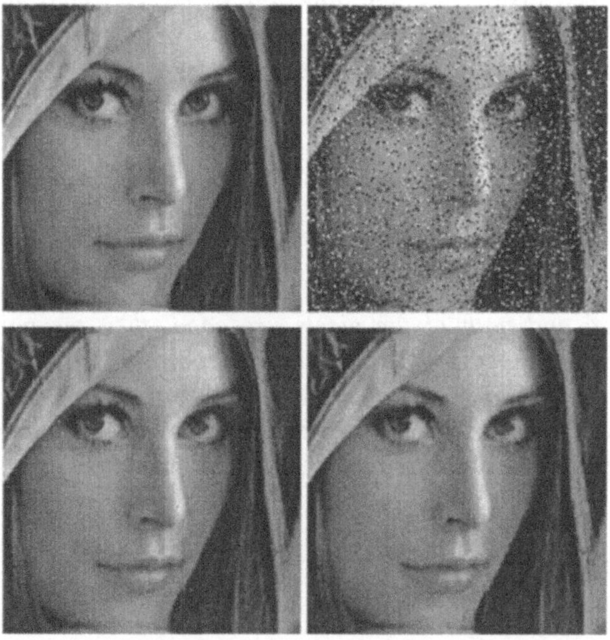

Figure 14.9. Restoration performance. Top-left: original face region of "Lena"; Top-right: corrupted image by 20% random-valued impulse noise; Bottom-left: after the first iteration; Bottom-right: restored image after the second iteration

To make a comparison with other published algorithms, peak signal-to-noise ratio (PSNR) is used to give a quantitative evaluation. In [11], Abreu et al. reported many restoration results in PSNR for images corrupted by both 20% fixed-valued and 20% random-valued impulse noises. We list some of those data in Table 14.2 and add the result of our algorithm at the end of the table. Clearly, the proposed algorithm outperforms all the other methods including those published in [11] which have, as far as we know, the best restoration results in the literature.

Table 14.2. Comparative restoration results in PSNR for 20% impulse noise for image "Lena"

Algorithm	Fixed-valued impulses[1]	Random-valued impulses[2]
Median filter (3×3)	28.57 dB	29.76 dB
Median filter (5×5)	28.78 dB	28.59 dB
Median filter with adaptive length[3] [9]	30.57 dB	31.18 dB
Rank conditioned rank selection filter[4] [10]	31.36 dB	30.78 dB
Abreu et al. (M=1296) (inside training set)[3,5] [11]	35.70 dB	33.37 dB
Our new fuzzy approach	36.47 dB [6]	33.78 dB [7]

1. Impulses take on only the values 0 or 255.
2. Impulses are uniformly distributed between 0 and 255.
3. Implemented recursively, i.e., the modified pixel values are immediately used in the process of the following pixels.
4. Implemented non-recursively using 9×9 window for fixed-valued impulses, and recursively using 3×3 window for random-valued impulses. M = 2 (M as defined in [12]).
5. M as defined in [11].
6. $N_d = 1$, $a = 24$, $b = 44$, $T_d = 0.3$, $N_c = 2$, $T_m = 28$, $M = 15$, after 3 iterations.
7. $N_d = 1$, $a = 8$, $b = 28$, $T_d = 0.2$, $N_c = 2$, $T_m = 31$, $M = 12$, after 2 iterations.

14.6 Conclusion

In this chapter, we introduce a new approach to reduce blocking artifacts from block-coded images. Different from traditional approaches, our algorithm is implemented by employing a special kind of information redundancy — piecewise similarity within natural images. Experiments on JPEG decoded images indicate that both PSNR and visual quality are improved. In our approach, finding an ideal matching vector $\boldsymbol{y}$ is a high time consuming procedure because most of the calculations are discarded after the best matching result is obtained. For real time applications, more detailed studies on fast searching technique are needed.

This chapter also shows that main advantage of PSM filter is that some impulse pixels located in the middle of large noise blotches can be properly detected and filtered. Therefore, the better restoration results are expected, especially for the cases where the images are highly corrupted. As another new impulse noise removal method, the usage of fuzzy techniques provides us a tradeoff between considering as much as possible good information and avoiding the influence of bad information. Experimental results indicate that the proposed method provides significant improvement over other algorithms in terms of both subjective and objective evaluations.

References

[1] H.C. Reeve III and J.S. Lim, "Reduction of blocking artifacts in image coding," *Optical Engineering*, 23(1):34-37, Jan./Feb. 1984.

[2] H.S. Malvar and D.H. Staelin, "The LOT: transform coding without blocking effects," *IEEE Trans. Acoust., Speech, Signal Processing*, 37: 553-559, Apr. 1989.

[3] A. Zakhor, "Iterative procedures for reduction of blocking effects in transform image coding," *IEEE Trans. Circuits and Systems for Video Technology*, 2(1):91-95, Mar. 1992.

[4] Y. Yang, N.P. Galatsanos and A.K. Katsaggelos, "egularized reconstruction to reduce blocking artifacts of block discrete cosine transform compressed images," *IEEE Trans. Circuits and Systems for Video Technology*, 3(6):421-432, Dec. 1993.

[5] M. Crouse and K. Ramchandran, "Nonlinear constrained least squares estimation to reduce artifacts in block transform-coded images," in *Proc. ICIP-95*, 1: 462-465, Oct. 1995.

[6] J. Luo, C.W. Chen, K.J. Parker and T.S. Huang, "Artifact reduction in low bit rate DCT-based image compression," *IEEE Trans. Image Processing*, 5(9):1363-1368, Sep. 1996.

[7] A.E. Jacquin, Image coding based on a fractal theory of iterated contractive image transformation, *IEEE Trans. on Image Processing*, 1(1):18-30, Jan. 1992.

[8] T. Sun and Y. Neuvo, "Detail-preserving median based filters in image processing," *Pattern Recognition Letters*, 15:341-347, Apr. 1994.

[9] H.M. Lin and A.N. Willson: "Median filters with adaptive length", *IEEE Trans. Circuits and System*, 35(6):675-690, June 1988.

[10] R.C. Hardie and K.E. Barner: "Rank conditioned rank selection filters for signal restoration," *IEEE Trans. Image Process.*, 3 (2):192-206, Mar. 1994.

[11] Abreu E., Lightstone M., Mitra S.K. and Arakawa K.: "A new efficient approach for the removal of impulse noise from highly corrupted images," *IEEE Trans. Image Process.*, 5(6):1012-1025, June 1996.

[12] D.R.K. Brownrigg, "The weighted median filter," *Communications of the ACM*, 27(8):807-818, Aug. 1984.

[13] I. Pitas and A.N. Venetsanopoulos, *Nonlinear digital filters: Principles and Applications*, Boston: Kluwer Academic Publishers, 1990.

[14] D.R.K. Brownrigg, "The weighted median filter," *Communications of the ACM*, 27(8):807-818, Aug. 1984.

[15] Z. Wang and D. Zhang, "Restoration of impulse noise corrupted image using long-range correlation," *IEEE Signal Proc. Lett.*, 5(1), 1998.

[16] D. Zhang and Z. Wang, "Impulse noise detection and removal using fuzzy techniques," *Electronics Lett.*, 33:378-379, Feb. 1997.

Chapter 15

IMAGE RESTORATION FROM INTERNET TRANSMISSION CORRUPTION

In this chapter, we present a new algorithm which can remove impulse noise from corrupted images while preserving details. In Section 15.2, the algorithm is fundamentally different from the traditional methods in that it can utilize the information of not only a local window centered about the corrupted pixel but also some remote regions in the image. Experimental results indicate that our algorithm outperforms many existing techniques in Section 15.3. Its performance was analyzed in Section 15.4.

15.1 Introduction

We would like to start this paper by doing a simple test. Let us look at two pictures that are shown as Figure 15.1(a) and Figure 15.1(b). It can be observed that the middle block regions of these two pictures are missing. Now the questions are: "What should be in the lost blocks? Can you give a good guess?" When we asked these questions to dozens of people, all of them gave us almost the same answers. That is, it seems difficult to guess what in the first picture should be, but what in the second picture can be easily imagined. People are not surprised before we told them that actually the lost blocks in these two pictures are exactly the same block removed from the same standard image. The only difference is that in Figure 15.1(a), the block is very closely observed, while in Figure 15.1(b), we observe the block from a remote position so that a much larger background region can also be seen. So, why people can give much better estimation of the lost block from the second picture than from the first picture? In our opinion, at least two conclusions can be drawn from this test. First, there exists abundant long-range correlation within natural images which can be viewed as a special kind of information redundancy. Second, the human vision systems composed of our eyes and brains can and do use such kind of correlation to interpret and restore image information.

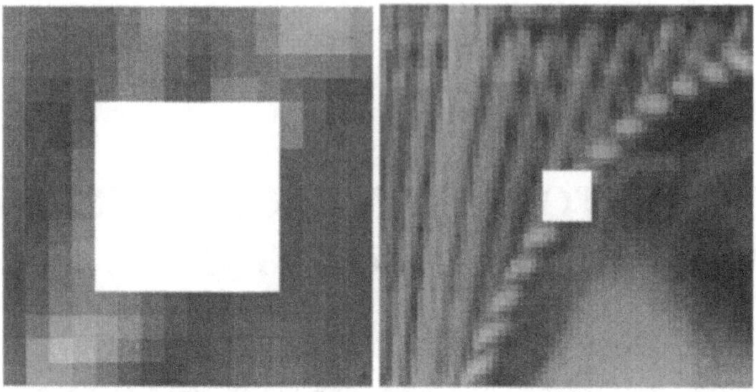

(a) (b)

Figure 15.1. The same lost block under different scales of backgrounds. (a) in a local region background, (b) in a large region background observed from a remote position

Now let us come to the traditional image restoration and enhancement techniques. Basically, they can be classified into three categories — pixel point processing method, pixel group processing method and frequency domain method. In the first method, the gray level of each pixel in the input image is modified to a new value, often by a mathematical or logical relationship, and placed in the output image at the same spatial location. All pixels are handled individually [5]. Typical examples are histogram sliding and stretching algorithms and binary contrast enhancement approaches. In the second method, pixel group processing operates on a group of input pixels surrounding a center pixel, resulting in the output center pixel value. Examples are low-pass and high-pass linear spatial filters, gradient operator-based edge detection/enhancement algorithms and the median-based filters, etc. In the third method, a frequency transform decomposes an image from its spatial-domain form of brightness, into a frequency-domain form of fundamental frequency components [5]. The real image restoration and enhancement processing is conducted by modifying the frequency components. To reconstruct the image, an inverse frequency transform converts an image from its frequency domain form back to a spatial form. The most common transform is the Fourier transform. There are also other transforms, such as the Hadamard, Harr, slant, Karhunen-Loeve, sine, and cosine transforms [5].

The limitation of traditional image restoration approaches is obvious because whatever they belong to which of the three above mentioned methods, only the pixels in a very limited local region are directly used as the information source to create the new value of a pixel. Although the frequency transform method can, in some extent, make use of the information, such as the magnitude of the energy on a certain frequency, of a large area, the information of remote regions are used only statistically but not directly. Consequently, traditional methods are impossible to simulate the human vision systems in utilizing long-range correlation in the images. In contrast, our new algorithms to be presented in this paper is just based on the employment of such kind of long-range information redundancy.

It should be mentioned that in Jacquin's fractal block coding (FBC) algorithm [6-7], some kinds of block-wise self-similarities had been used for the compression of images. The concept of self-similar in the FBC algorithm is very flexible. In some cases, it means an image block is very similar to some part of itself. In some other cases, it can also mean a small image block is similar to a remote larger block in the same image. We consider this second kind of block-wise similarity as a special form of what we have mentioned the long-range correlation. Another major contribution of Jacquin is that he introduced a practical way to find long-range block-wise similarities. Our approaches use the similar ways to find long-range correlation in images. However, our algorithm has many differences in comparison with FBC. First, the goal of our method is for information restoration rather than image compression. The long-range correlation between image pieces is used for recovering damaged image pixels, instead of removing redundancy to compress the image. Second, our method can not be called *fractal* because the word "fractal" in "fractal image coding" means self-similarity at different scales, while we are trying to use long-range similarities at the same scale.

Images are often corrupted by impulse noise due to errors generated in noisy sensors or communication channels. So far many techniques have been proposed to remove impulse noise from the corrupted images [1-4]. A general framework for them can be described as follows: For each pixel, we extract a window (usually with a size of 3×3, 5×5 or 7×7) centered about it from the image. Based on the information within the window, a noise cancellation scheme is then applied to replace the pixel with a new value, which makes it comply with some pre-defined constraints on the local window. Nevertheless, a drawback of this framework is that it can "see" only local information. Because the window size is often too small to reflect the real structure of the local region, the noise cancellation filters developed on them are not very effective in preserving many detail areas. In this chapter, we propose a fundamentally different technique where the new value of a corrupted pixel is determined by long-range correlation between its neighborhood window and some remote regions in the image.

15.2 Restoration Algorithm

Our algorithm is composed of two parts — impulse detection and noise cancellation. Many previously published algorithms such as those in [3,4] used an impulse detector to determine whether a pixel should be modified. A difference in our algorithm is that the detection results are also used to help the process of the second part — noise cancellation.

Impulse Detection

The impulse detection scheme used by our algorithm is Sun and Neuvo's switching I method [3] which can be briefly described as follows:

Let x_{ij} and $x_{ij}^{(new)}$ represent the pixel values at position (i, j) in the corrupted image and the restored image, respectively. The goal of the impulse detector is to generate a binary flag map where each pixel (i, j) is given a binary flag f_{ij} indicating whether it is considered as an impulse, i.e., $f_{ij} = 1$ means (i, j) is a corrupted pixel and $f_{ij} = 0$ means (i, j) is noise-free. In Sun and Neuvo's switching I scheme [3], they used the difference between the pixel value itself and the median value of a local window centered about it as the measurement to detect impulses. This measurement is easy to operate and is effective when the image is slightly contaminated with impulse noise. However, it can not perform well when noise ratio is high. To further improve the detection accuracy, we developed a modified version of Sun and Neuvo's method [5]. In this chapter, we use such an improved technique to generate the binary flag map.
During the noise filtering procedure, the good pixels with $f_{ij}=0$ are unaltered. That is,

$$x_{ij}^{(new)} = x_{ij}. \qquad (15\text{-}1)$$

Noise Cancellation

The noise cancellation scheme is only applied to those pixels considered as impulses ($f_{ij}=1$). For an impulse pixel at position (i, j), two $(2N_c+1)\times(2N_c+1)$ sized windows are employed: The first window is the local window centered about the impulse pixel; The second window is a remote window located at a different place in the image with its center at position (k, l). Since the whole image may contain a large number of complete $(2N_c+1)\times(2N_c+1)$ windows, the remote window should be selected from one of them. In our algorithm, a candidate remote window must satisfy the following conditions:

It is not the same as the local window, i.e., $i \neq k$ or $j \neq l$.

It must be completely covered by a larger (2M+1)×(2M+1) ($M > N_c$) window called search range window which is centered about the impulse pixel (i, j).

Its center (k, l) is a good pixel, i.e., $f_{kl} = 0$.

All the $(2N_c+1)\times(2N_c+1)$ candidate remote windows will compete for the best match to the local window. The measurement is based on the Mean Square Error (MSE) in the good part of the local window and the candidate remote window. That is,

$$MSE_g=\frac{\sum_{m=-N_c}^{N_c}\sum_{n=-N_c}^{N_c}(1-f_{i+m,j+n})\cdot(1-f_{k+m,l+n})\cdot(x_{i+m,j+n}-x_{k+m,l+n})^2}{\sum_{m=-N_c}^{N_c}\sum_{n=-N_c}^{N_c}(1-f_{i+m,j+n})\cdot(1-f_{k+m,l+n})}. \quad (15\text{-}2)$$

Note that the square error of a pixel pair will be computed only if both of its two corresponding pixels in the local and remote windows are good. Each of the candidate remote windows will result in MSE_g and the one with the minimal MSE_g becomes the winner. Finally, the corrupted pixel is replaced by the center pixel of the winning remote window:

$$x_{ij}^{(new)} = x_{kl}. \quad (15\text{-}3)$$

15.3 Experimental Results

Some computer simulations are carried out to assess the performance of our method. The original test images are some standard 8bits/pixel gray scale images. Two types of impulse noises are tested. The first is fixed-valued impulse noise where the impulses take on the values of 0 or 255 with equal probabilities. The second is random-valued impulse noise where the impulse values are uniformly distributed between 0 and 255. Peak Signal-to-Noise Ratio (PSNR) is used to give a quantitative evaluation on the filtering results. In this chapter, we always use the same set of parameters, $N_c = 3$ and $M = 10$, in all the experiments.

In Figures 15.2–15.4, we give some enlarged areas of our test images to show how the proposed algorithm performs on different kinds of image details. The visual qualities of the restored images are relatively good considering the abundance of image details and the high noise probabilities. Restoration performance for an enlarged area from image "Barb" (Figure

15.2). (a) Image corrupted by 10% fixed-valued impulse noise; (b) Restored image; (c) The original image area. Restoration performance for an enlarged area from image "Boats" (Figure 15.3). (a) Image corrupted by 20% random-valued impulse noise; (b) Restored image; (c) The original image area. Restoration performance for an enlarged area from image "Baboon" (Figure 15.4). (a) Image corrupted by 30% fixed-valued impulse noise; (b) Restored image; (c) The original image area.

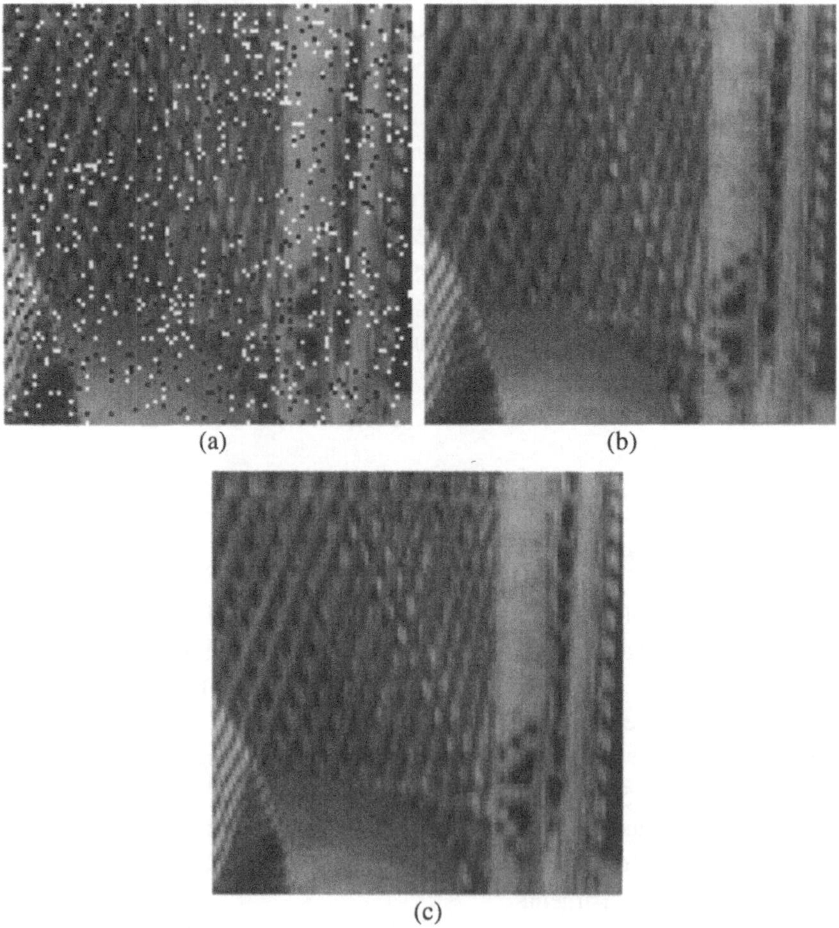

Figure 15.2. Restoration performance for an enlarged area from image "Barb". (a) Image corrupted by 10% fixed-valued impulse noise, (b) Restored image, and (c) The original image area

(a) (b) (c)

Figure 15.3. Restoration performance for an enlarged area from image "Boats". (a) Image corrupted by 20% random-valued impulse noise, (b) Restored image, and (c) The original image area

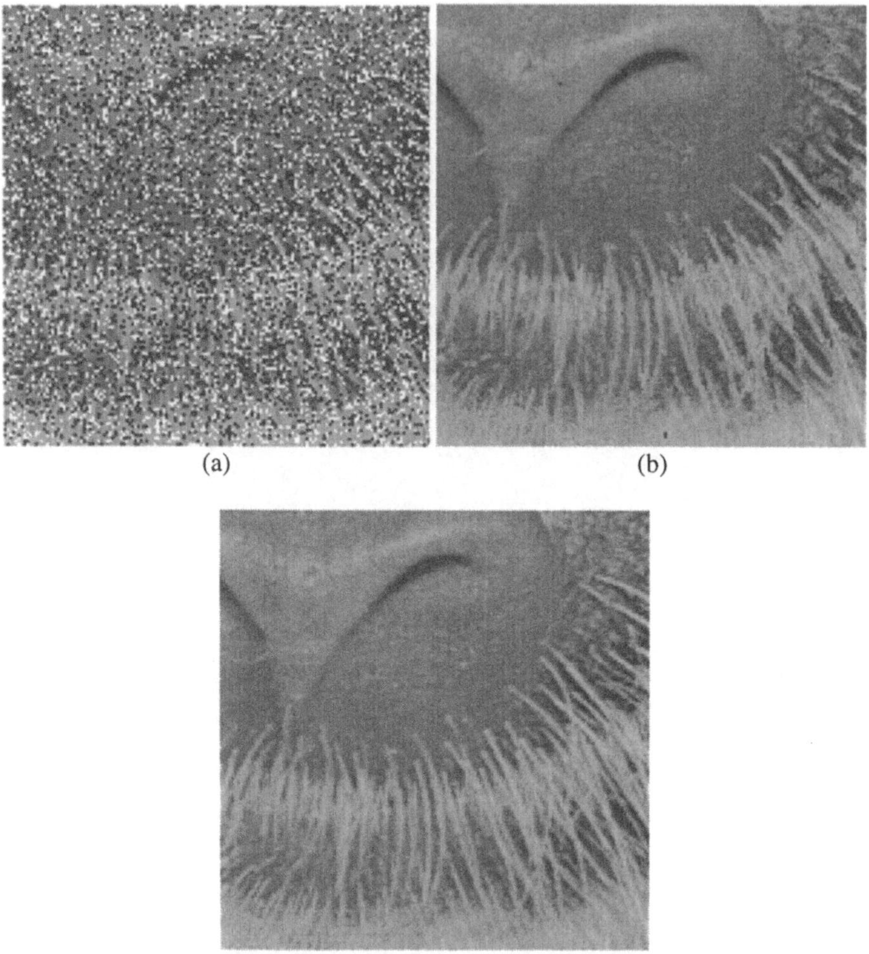

(a) (b)

(c)

Figure 15.4. Restoration performance for an enlarged area from image "Baboon". (a) Image corrupted by 30% fixed-valued impulse noise, (b) Restored image, and (c) The original image area

15.4 Performance Analysis

In [4], Abreu et al. reported many restoration results in PSNR for images corrupted by both 20% fixed-valued and 20% random-valued impulse noises. We list some of those data in Table 15.1 and add the results of our algorithm at the end of the table. For fixed-valued noise, our algorithm provides significant improvement over all the other approaches, while for random-valued noise, the result of our algorithm is also the best. Only Abreu et al.'s approach with inside training set [4] is close to our algorithm. In Table 15.2, we show the filtering results for image "Lena" corrupted by random-valued impulse noise with various probabilities ranging from 10% to 30%. The results of Abreu et al.'s approach are also given [4]. In most cases, the performance of the proposed algorithm is close to the best result of Abreu et al.'s approaches. Notice that our algorithm does not include any training procedure.

Table 15.1. Comparative restoration results in PSNR for 20% impulse noise for image "Lena"

Filtering Algorithm	Fixed-valued Impulses	Random-valued Impulses
Median filter (3×3)	28.57 dB	29.76 dB
Median filter (5×5)	28.78 dB	28.59 dB
Median filter with adaptive length[1] [1]	30.57 dB	31.18 dB
Rank conditioned rank selection filter[1] [2]	31.36 dB	30.78 dB
Sun and Neuvo, Switch I median filte[1] [3]	31.97 dB	31.34 dB
Sun and Neuvo, Switch II median filter[1] [3]	29.96 dB	32.04 dB
Abreu et al. (M=2, no training)[1] [4]	33.47 dB	32.47 dB
Abreu et al. (M=1296, outside training set)[1] [4]	34.65 dB	32.95 dB
Abreu et al. (M=1296, inside training set)[1] [4]	35.70 dB	33.37 dB
Our new approach	36.95 dB	33.43 dB

[1] See Reference [4] for more details with regard to methods and parameter selections.

Table 15.2. Comparative filtering results in PSNR for image "Lena"

Filtering Algorithm	Percentage of Random-valued Impulse Noise				
	10%	15%	20%	25%	30%
Abreu et al. (M=2, no training)[1] [4]	35.18 dB	33.94 dB	32.47 dB	31.18 dB	29.87 dB
Abreu et al. (M=1296, inside training set)[1] [4]	36.02 dB	34.44 dB	33.37 dB	31.77 dB	30.49 dB
Abreu et al. (M=1296, outside training set)[1] [4]	36.64 dB	34.72 dB	32.95 dB	31.52 dB	29.99 dB
Our new approach, 1 iteration	36.69 dB	34.83 dB	33.43 dB	31.76 dB	30.01 dB
Our new approach, 2 iterations	36.11 dB	34.71 dB	33.75 dB	32.54 dB	31.50 dB

[1] See reference [4] for more details with regard to methods and parameter selections.

It should be mentioned that the restoration results may be further improved simply by iteratedly applying the proposed algorithm, especially when the noise probability is high. For example, when image "Lena" is corrupted with 20% random-valued impulse noise, an additional iteration can raise PSNR from 33.43 dB to 33.75 dB. The image of Lena and its experimental results illustrate in Figure 15.5. In the last row of Table 15.2, we list the PSNR performance after 2 iterations.

Comparative restoration results in PSNR for 20% impulse noise for image "Lena". For fixed-valued impulse noise, impulses take on only the values 0 or 255 with equal probability. For random-valued impulse noise, impulse values are uniformly distributed between 0 and 255. Comparative filtering results in PSNR for image "Lena" corrupted with various percentages of random-valued impulse noise.

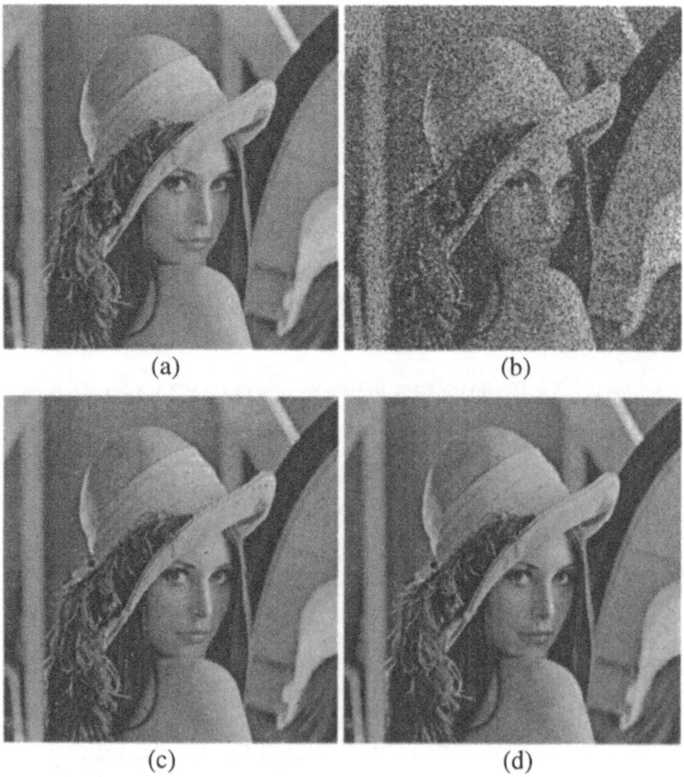

Figure 15.5. Restoration performance for image Lena". (a) original image, (b) corrupted image by 20% fixed-valued impulse noise, PSNR=12.41dB, (c) restored image after the first iteration, PSNR=31.73dB, and (d) restored image after the third iteration, PSNR=36.96dB

15.5 Conclusion

In this chapter, we present a new impulse noise removal scheme by employing long-range correlation in the image. The proposed filtering algorithm breaks through the traditional framework in that it can make use of both local and remote information in the image. Experimental results indicate that the proposed algorithm provides major improvement over many other well-known methods.

References

[1] R.C. Hardie and K.E. Barner, "Rank conditioned rank selection filters for signal restoration," *IEEE Trans. on Image Process.*, 3(2):192-206, Mar. 1994.

[2] T. Sun and Y. Neuvo, "Detail-preserving median based filters in image processing," *Pattern Recognition Letters*, 15:341-347, Apr. 1994.

[3] E. Abreu, M. Lightstone, S. K. Mitra and K. Arakawa, "A new efficient approach for the removal of impulse noise from highly corrupted images," *IEEE Trans. on Image Process.*, 5(6):1012-1025, June 1996.

[4] D. Zhang and Z. Wang, "Impulse noise removal using polynomial approximation," *Optical Engineering*, 37(4):1275-1282, 1998.

[5] G.A. Baxes, *Digital Image Processing:Principles and Applications*, John Wiley & Sons, Inc., 1994.

[6] A. Jacquin, "Image coding based on a fractal theory of iterated contractive image transformation," *IEEE Transactions on Image Processing*, 1(1):18-30, Jan. 1992.

[7] Y. Fisher, ed., *Fractal Image Compression - Theory and Applications*, New York: Spring-Verlag, 1994.

[8] G. Walleye, "The JPEG still image picture compression standard", *Commun. ACM*, 34(4):30-44, Apr. 1991.

[9] D. Le Gall, "MPEG: A video compression standard for multimedia applications", *Commun. ACM*, 34(4):46-58, Apr. 1991.

[10] M. Liou, "Overview of the p×64 kbit/s video coding standard", *Commun. ACM*, 34(4):59-63, Apr. 1991.

[11] Y. Wang and Q. Zhu, "Signal loss recovery in DCT-based image and video codecs", in *SPIE Proc. Visual Commun. Image Processing*, 1605:667-678, Nov. 1991.

[12] H. Sun, K. Challapali, and J. Zdepski, "Error concealment in digital simulcast AD-HDTV decoder", *IEEE Trans. on Consumer Electronics*, 38(3):108-118, Aug. 1992.

[13] W. M. Lam and A. R. Reibman, "An error concealment algorithm for image subject to channel errors", *IEEE Trans. on Image Processing*, 4(5):533-542, May 1995.

[14] X. Lee, Y.Q. Zhang, and A. Leon-Garcia, "Information loss recovery for block-based image coding techniques — a fuzzy logic approach", *IEEE Trans. on Image Processing*, 4(3):259-273, Mar. 1995.

[15] H. Sun and W. Kwok, "Concealment of damaged block transform coded images using projections onto convex sets", *IEEE Trans. on Image Processing*, 4(4):470-477, Apr. 1995.

[16] S.S. Hemami and T.H.Y. Meng, "Transform coded image reconstruction exploiting interblock correlation", *IEEE Trans. on Image Processing*, 4(7):1023-1027, July 1995.

[17] H.M. Lin and A.N. Willson, "Median filters with adaptive length", *IEEE Trans. on Circuits and Systems*, 35(6):675-690, June 1988.

[18] Z. Wang and D. Zhang, "Restoration of impulse noise corrupted images using long-range correlation," *IEEE Signal Processing Letters*, 5(1):5-8, 1998.

[19] H.C. Reeve III and J.S. Lim, "Reduction of blocking artifacts in image coding," *Optical Engineering*, 23(1):34-37, Jan./Feb. 1984.

[20] H.S. Malvar and D.H. Staelin, "The LOT: transform coding without blocking effects," *IEEE Trans. Acoust., Speech, Signal Processing*, 37: 553-559, 1989.

[21] A. Zakhor, "Iterative procedures for reduction of blocking effects in transform image coding," *IEEE Trans. Circuits and Systems for Video Technology*, 2(1):91-95, Mar. 1992.

[22] Y. Yang, N.P. Galatsanos and A.K. Katsaggelos, "Regularized reconstruction to reduce blocking artifacts of block discrete cosine transform compressed images," *IEEE Trans. Circuits and Systems for Video Technology*, 3(6):421-432, Dec. 1993.

[23] M. Crouse and K. Ramchandran, "Nonlinear constrained least squares estimation to reduce artifacts in block transform-coded images," in *Proc. ICIP-95*, 1:462-465, Oct. 1995.

[24] Y.Q. Zhang, R.L. Pickholtz and M.H. Loew, "A new approach to reduce the 'blocking effect" of transform coding," *IEEE Transactions on Communications*, 41(2):299-302, Feb. 1993.

[25] J. Luo, C.W. Chen, K.J. Parker and T.S. Huang, "Artifact reduction in low bit rate DCT-based image compression," *IEEE Trans. Image Processing*, 5(9):1363-1368, Sep. 1996.

Chapter 16

ENCRYPTION CODING FOR IAP DATA

Storing and transmitting IAP data in the Internet environment is different from the traditional communication due to the open nature of the Internet. Data encryption coding is desirable, and sometimes necessary, to ensure security for certain applications. Various encryption coding methods have been proposed to protect multimedia data on the Internet. A strong encryption should be almost impossible to break with the current computer technology within the time period that the encrypted data are valid or useful. Secret-key and public-key encryption algorithms handle applications with different coding needs. Section 16.1 briefly describes basic concepts of encryption. A number of well-known secret-key and public-key encryption algorithms are discussed in Sections 16.2 and 16.3, respectively. Then we concentrate on a *partial encryption* scheme for images and videos. Section 16.4 is on previous attempts in combining compression and encryption, and the general effects of partial encryption. Sections 16.5 and 16.6 present partial encryption methods of quadtree compressed and wavelet compressed images. Partial encryption of videos is given in Section 16.7.

16.1 Introduction

Accidental hardware damage or intentional tampering have always been a risk for stored and transmitted data. Because of the open access of the Internet, shared IAP data and software face the risk of being deleted or modified. IAP data transmission faces interception (accidental or intentional unauthorized access) and interruption (making access unavailable to authorized users). The goal of data encryption is to keep *Confidentiality* (no unauthorized access), *Integrity* (unmodified), and *Availability* (assets availability to authorized users), for data storage and communication. Figure 16.1 depicts some basic terminologies in data encryption.

The technology of keeping message or data secure is called *cryptography*. In other words, cryptography is the science and art of secure

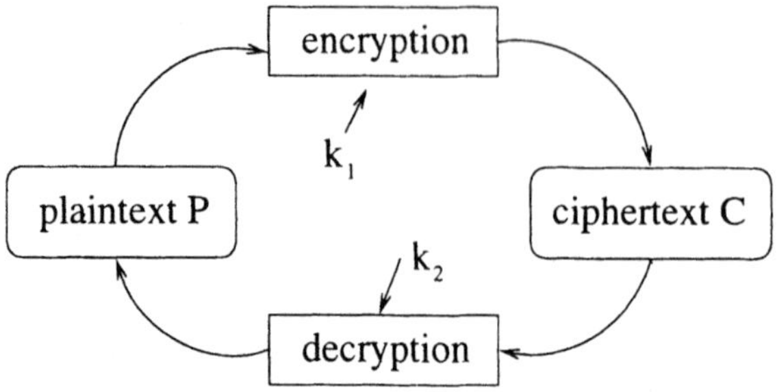

Figure 16.1. Basic terminologies in data encryption

writing. The original data to be secured is called *plaintext*, or *cleartext.* A mathematical function used for encryption and decryption is called *cryptographic algorithm* or *cipher*, which transforms plaintext into *ciphertext.* The art and science of breaking ciphertext is usually called *cryptanalysis.* The branch of mathematics embodying both cryptography and cryptanalysis is *cryptology.* There are many kinds of ciphers. In a *symmetric algorithm* (also called *secret-key algorithm*), k_1 can be calculated from k_2 and vice versa. Often, $k_1 = k_2$. In a *public-key algorithm*, k_2 cannot be calculated from k_1. Often, k_1 is public (called the public key), while k_2 is kept private. A secrete-key system is like a physical safe. A public-key system resembles a mailbox, which receives messages from public but can only be opened by one person. One important use of encryption is *digital signature*: a user can sign his message or data, nobody else can forge his signature. Not even the receiver. A judge can prove that the sender indeed signed that message. For example, one can use a public key algorithm for signature: the message is encrypted with the private key and decrypted with the public key.

One example of encryption is a *simple substitution cipher* ([9] p62-67): replacing each value (or character) in the plaintext with a corresponding value (or character) to form the ciphertext. If both the plaintext alphabet and the ciphertext alphabet are English letters, and the replacement rule is a shift of 3 (e.g., replacing "a" with "d", replacing "n" with "q"), this cipher is the famous *Caesar Cipher*, actually used by Julius Caeser. Another substitution cipher is the *simple XOR cipher* that performs an exclusive-OR operation between a key K and the plaintext P to produce ciphertext C : $C = P \oplus K$. A *one-time pad* encryption scheme is to use a key (a set of non-repeating random letters) to perform modular operations with the plaintext to produce ciphertext. Using English alphabet and "mod 26", we have, for example, $B + N$ mod $26 = P$. Each key is used only once. After decrypting the message, the key is destroyed.

Let's look at the cryptanalysis side. The enemy (opponent) of data security is also called *attacker*, eavesdropper, or intruder. The attacker has the complete knowledge of the entire encryption algorithm except the key. He wants to deduce the key or, equivalently, an inference from the ciphertexts to plaintexts. There are different kinds of attacks, such as:

- Ciphertext-only attack: the attacker knows the ciphertext of a number of messages produced from the same encryption algorithm.
- Known-plaintext attack: the attacker knows several pairs of plaintext and corresponding ciphertext.
- Chosen-plaintext attack: the attacker can choose the plaintext to input to the encryption algorithm and obtain the corresponding ciphertext.
- Chosen-ciphertext attack: the attacker can choose ciphertext to be decrypted and obtain the corresponding plaintext.

The attackers are often armed with powerful computers, sometimes multi-processor systems or even special-purpose hardware equipments. The *strength* of an encryption system is its ability to stand against various types of attacks.

One-time pad is the only encryption scheme that is *unconditionally secure*. Any other encryption algorithm can be broken given enough time and computing resources. Cryptography is mostly concerned with the cryptosystems that are *computationally secure*, that is, they are computationally infeasible to break with the available computation power. People measure the complexity of an attack in terms of data needed, time needed and memory needed [24], or the minimum of those three. Real attacks could take advantage of trade-offs between the three. For simplicity, we only consider the computation time requirement here. We use the term *work factor*, denoted by W, for the amount of computation, measured in the number of operations (e.g., addition, multiplications, etc.), required to break an encrypted message or data, that is, to recover the encryption key. The available computation power, P, can be expressed as a product of the number of processors N_p and the speed of each processor, S_p. Thus, $P = N_p S_p$ is the number of operations a cryptanalyst could carry out in a unit time, say, a second, assuming that there is no need for synchronization between processors and no other sequential overhead at all. Because processor speeds and storage capacities keep increasing rapidly, P should be a function of time. Let P_i represent the computation power available during year i (through out the entire year).

If y is the number of seconds in a year, the total number of operations can be carried out within n years should be

$$P(n) = \sum_{i=1}^{n} yP_i. \qquad (16\text{-}1)$$

And we assume that verifying the result of a test (checking a potential key) takes no time. From this point of view, $W > P(n)$ means "computationally secure" up to n years, and $W = \infty$ means "unconditional secure".

Consider the case where the processor speed doubles every other year, and the cryptanalysts upgrade their equipment accordingly, i.e.,

$$\begin{aligned} P_1 &= P_2,\ P_3 = P_4 = 2P_1,\ P_5 = P_6 = 4P_1, \quad \cdots \\ P_{2k-1} &= P_{2k} = 2^{k-1}P_1, \quad \cdots \\ P(n) &= 2yP_1(1 + 2 + 4 + \cdots + 2^{k-1}) \\ &= 2yP_1(2^k - 1) \approx 2^{25+k+1}P_1. \end{aligned} \qquad (16\text{-}2)$$

for $n = 2k$ and $y \approx 2^{25}$.

With one thousand ($10^3 \approx 2^{10}$) processors and one billion ($10^9 \approx 2^{30}$) operations per second per processor, $P_1 = 2^{40}$. According to Equation (16-2), an exhaustive key search of all possible keys of length 128 bits would take $2 \times (128 - 40 - 25 - 1) = 124$ years. However, predicting future computation powers is impossible. The future special-purpose equipments can be vastly different from anything we already have. It is a common believe that an encryption key must be at least 128 bits long to keep data secure for about 100 years [24], which happens to agree with our previous example. Due to the fast development of PRIP and Internet technology, new software products are becoming available everyday, data are easier to generate and obtain, thus the true value of the encrypted data decreases rapidly. In other words, n can be relatively small. Later sections of this chapter present a "partial encryption" scheme which encrypts only a part of the image/video *data structure* in such a way that an attacker would have great difficulty recovering the original data although a major part of the data is not encrypted at all. Using the clear (unencrypted) part of the data to decode the encrypted part takes a relatively long time, say, ten years, which could be longer than the time period that the original image itself is useful.

16.2 Secret-key Encryption Algorithms

DES (Data Encryption Standard), designed by IBM cryptographers, is a popular secrete-key encryption algorithm, which has been a U.S. and international standard for many years. DES employs a conceptually simple *block cipher* where the plaintext is divided into blocks of 64 bits each. Each block is "mixed" with a key of 56 bits. Because of the short key length, DES can be broken within hours or even minutes with a powerful computer, such as the DES-cracking machine built by Harris Corp using a Cray Y-MP. However, DES is still used in textbooks as an example to demonstrate the idea of mixing the key with each block of the plaintext data.

Table 16.1. Initial Permutation in DES

58	50	42	34	26	18	......	15	7
↓	↓	↓	↓	↓	↓		↓	↓
1	2	3	4	5	6	......	63	64

The mixing process involves 16 rounds of splitting, shifting, permutation, repeating, and exclusive OR (XOR) operations. The result of the above mixing operation is a "big mess" that cannot be easily recovered without knowing the key. Figure 16.2 shows the mixing operation of each 64 bit block. The initial permutation (IP) can be seen in Table 16.1. Between IP and IP^{-1}, each of the 16 rounds operates on the output of the previous round and a different 48-bit key (derived from the initial key K) is used. The input of round i is divided into two halves: L_{i-1} and R_{i-1}, each has 32 bits. R_{i-1} goes through the following operations which are depicted in Figure 16.3.

- "E" expands a 32-bit block into 48-bit block.
- "$\oplus$ is a bit-wise exclusive-OR operation involving a 48-bit key K_i.
- "S" consists of eight small S_k boxes, $k = 1,., 8$. Each S_k box takes a 6-bit input and produces four bits out.
- "P" permutes the 32-bit result of "S".

During the expansion "E" from 32 bits to 48 bits, some bits of R_{i-1} are repeated, some permuted. In the last round, the left and right halves are not switched. To generate the keys of every round, the initial key K is broken into two 28-bit halves. Those two halves are shifted. A subset of the 48 bits are selected from the shifted 56 bits. The reason behind all those mixing operations (shifts, repeats) is to spread the dependency of the output bits on the input bits, which is called an avalanche effect. Every bit of the ciphertext depends on every bit of the plaintext, and also depends on every bit of the key. DES intends to reach this dependency as early as possible.

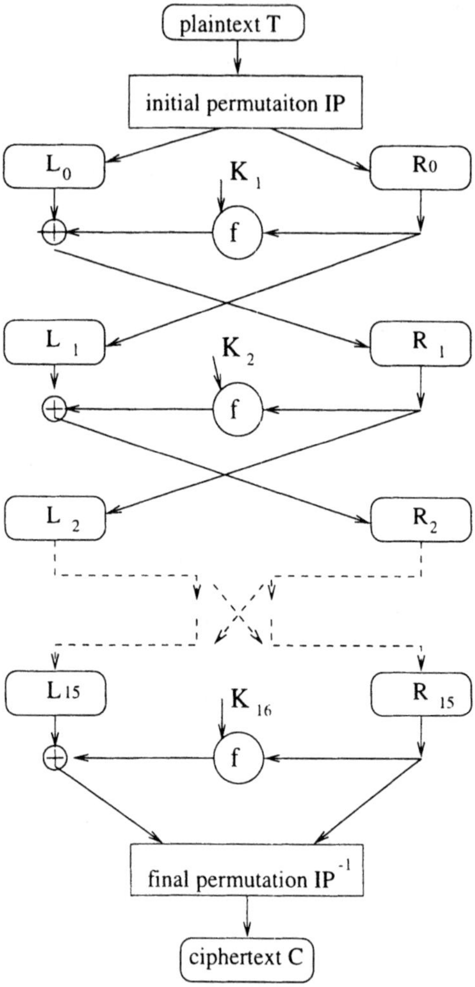

Figure 16.2. Mixing operations of each 64 bit block in DES

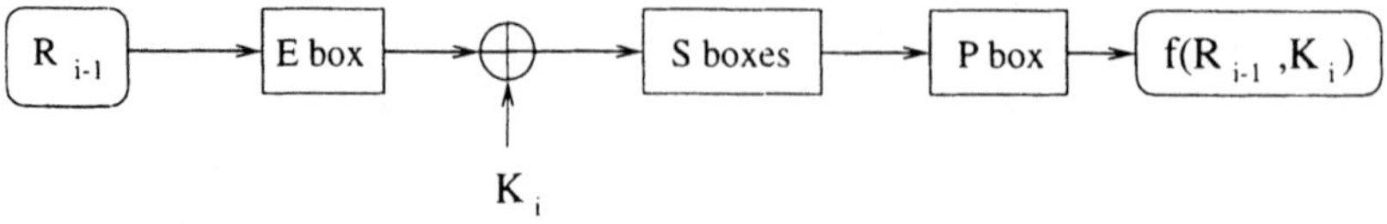

Figure 16.3. The operations on the right half of a block in DES

Numerous software and hardware implementations of DES and its variants have been reported in the literature [24]. On an IBM 3090, a DES program performs 32,000 encryptions per second. DES can also encrypt 84,000 blocks per second. Since early 1980s, there have been DES special hardware chips manufactured by AMD, Wstern Degital and Newbridge [24].

In 1991 [16], another secrete-key cipher, using a 128-bit key, was proposed and called PES (Proposed Encryption Standard), which was modified in 1991 and was called IPES (Improved PES). In 1992, the name was changed again to *IDEA (International Data Encryption Algorithm)*. This algorithm has a solid theoretical foundation and is considered to be an extremely secure block cipher. The "mixing" operations include XOR, addition modulo 2^{16}, and multiplication modulo $2^{16}+1$. No permutations involved.

Each data block of 64-bits is divided into four 16-bit sub-blocks. Each of the eight rounds of operations applies XOR, addition and multiplication to those four sub-blocks. Between the rounds, the middle two sub-blocks are switched. At the last round, a final output transformation is performed that involves multiplication and addition, but not XOR. The decryption process is exactly the same with the subkeys reversed.

Although multiplying 32-bit numbers takes up to 10 machine cycles on a Pentium, software implementations of IDEA are still much faster than DES. It can encrypt 2400 Kb per second on a 66 MHz 486 machine. VLSI chips developed in Zurich can encrypt 177 Mbps with a clock rate of 25 MHz. The work factor W of breaking IDEA is 2^{128}. The choice of the key may be the weak point of the system. Attention has been given to avoid "weak keys" [24].

16.3 Public-key Encryption Algorithms

A public-key encryption system uses one key for encryption and another key for description. The two keys appear to be "totally unrelated" and cannot be easily generated or inferred from each other. The encryption key is public, can be published in a phone book or posted on Web pages. The decryption key is kept private. Many public-key encryption algorithms have been proposed. Almost all of them require much more computation than secret-key algorithms. Many of them require a long key or produce a large ciphertext, therefore not useful in real applications. And most of them are not even secure. The few practical and secure public-key algorithms can be used for encryption and digital signature.

Public-key encryption is built on the concept of *one-way functions.* A one-way function is relatively easy to compute but significantly harder to undo or reverse. For some one-way functions, there is a secret "trap door" that allows the computation in the other direction.

One of the most well-known public-key algorithm is RSA [22]. Two large prime numbers of over 100 digits long, p and q, are chosen. The product is $n = pq$ and $\phi(n) = (p-1)(q-1)$. A number, e, which is relative prime to $\phi(n)$ is chosen as the encryption key. The decryption key, d, is chosen so that $e \times d = 1 (\mod \phi(n))$. While d is kept secret, e and n are public. The plaintext is divided into blocks smaller than n. If the plaintext block is m, the ciphertext is $c = m^e (\mod n)$. To decrypt, $m = c^d (\mod n)$. Take small integers as an example: $p = 3$, $q = 5$, $n = 15$, $\phi(n) = 8$, $d = 11$, and $e = 3$. If $m = 2$, then $c = 2^3 (\mod 15) = 8$, and $8^{11} (\mod 15) = 8589934592 (\mod 15) = 2$.

Calculating d from e is easy only if p and q are available. The security of RSA depends on the difficulty of factoring n into p and q. The best existing algorithm of factorization cannot handle n of 200 digits in any reasonable amount of time. Many software and hardware implementations of RAS [21, 28] have been proposed. Using hardware, RSA is 1000 times slower than DES. Because of the heavy computation load of a public key algorithm, it is only suitable for encrypting a small amount of data. It can be used for transmitting through the Internet the keys of a secret-key encryption algorithm, such as IDEA.

RSA is also suitable for digital signature. The sender of a message or data item can use his/her own secret key to encrypt the message, and the receiver can decrypt the message using the sender's public key. Even the receiver cannot forge the ciphertext without knowing the sender's secret key.

16.4 Image and Video Encryption Coding

Although one can use general encryption methods and treat IAP data as they are text messages, researchers have been trying to take advantage of the special characteristics of image and video data. On the other hand, the processing time for encryption and decryption is one of the difficulties in real-time image and video communication over open channels and the Internet. For example, MPEG-2 compression produces output at a bit rate of 10 Mb/s or higher [19]. Compression algorithms for high-quality video sequences may generate even higher bit rates. Very often, compression and decompression algorithms can barely keep up with the required bit rate even with special-purpose hardware devices. The additional processing required by encryption and decryption makes real-time secure video transmission difficult or impossible. Although hardware acceleration for encryption exists, an efficient software implementation is still much cheaper and more flexible. For almost a decade, methods have been proposed to speed up or simplify the encryption and decryption operations for IAP data. They have combined compression and encryption together to reduce the overall processing time, but most of the methods are either insecure or too computationally intensive. This section gives a brief review of previous methods, and presents a *partial encryption* scheme for image and video data [5, 4]. This scheme is based on a hierarchical data structure (a "tree"). Both the quadtree compression algorithm and wavelet compression algorithm use tree data structures, although they are for different purposes and implemented in different fashions. The actual algorithms and the security issues are discussed in detail in Sections 16.5 and 16.6.

Previous Attempts to Combine Compression and Encryption

Researchers have found inadequacies in the current encryption technology and proposed methods to combine compression and encryption into a single process to reduce the total processing time.

Jones [12] proposed an adaptive symbol encoding algorithm which encrypts by keeping the initial model secret. He observed that in adaptive Huffman coding [10] and arithmetic coding [31], errors in the first few bits of the encoded data can ruin the synchronization between the encoder and the decoder, and make the remaining data undecodable. His adaptive compression algorithm uses a string of symbols as a key which determines the initial model. Because there are sequences of input symbols that can expose the current state of the model, this algorithm is vulnerable to chosen-plaintext attacks [11].

Liu *et al.* [17] combines adaptive arithmetic coding with encryption. Besides hiding the initial parameters of the algorithm, the current interval (after coding each symbol) is secretly adjusted. The compression performance is 2% worse than that of the original arithmetic coding algorithm [31], and it is approximately twice as slow.

An image scrambling algorithm was proposed by Bourbakis and Alexopoulos [2]. Hierarchical scan patterns defined by the SCAN language are used along with run-length encoding. A substitution is performed on each pixel based on an additive noise vector that is part of the key. The number of SCAN patterns for an image of dimensions 512×512 is approximately $6.6 \times 10^{10} < 2^{36}$ [2]. It is obviously too weak to withstand attacks by an exhaustive key search [4].

A video encryption algorithm is developed by Matias and Shamir [18], which scrambles each frame by a secret space-filling curve. This algorithm is a transposition cipher, thus is vulnerable to known-plaintext and chosen-plaintext attacks [4]. Bertilsson *et al.*'s ciphertext-only attack [1] can take advantage of the temporal correlation among consecutive frames.

Chang and Liu [3] proposed an encryption scheme working with lossless quadtree image compression. The four children of each internal node are permuted according to an encryption key. The key length is a linear function of the image size: $\lceil \log_2(24)(4^n - 1)/3 \rceil$ bits for a $2^n \times 2^n$ image. Numerous attacks on this algorithm are available [4], such as key space reduction (many keys produce the same output on the same input), histogram attacks, known-plaintext attacks and chosen-plaintext attacks.

Although the above methods are either insecure or too computationally expensive, they do represent a strong effort in combining compression with encryption and reducing the overall processing time, which can be desirable for managing IAP data on the Internet.

Partial Encryption: Its Effects and Applications

The first step of image compression is a mapping from the original pixel values to another set of numbers, such as transform coefficients or run-lengths. This new set of numbers can be considered as several logical parts. If some parts can be used to reconstruct the image approximately without the other parts, they are called "important". The parts that do not provide enough information to approximate the original image without the "important" parts are called "unimportant". The term "information" are used loosely here, not referring to the concept defined mathematically by information theory. And we consider all important parts as *one* important part, and the remaining parts are grouped into one unimportant part, for simplicity. If the important part is relatively small, compared to the entire compressed image, the following encryption scheme, as shown in Figure 16.4, may be feasible:

Partial Encryption of Images:

(1) The compression algorithm decomposes the image into an important part and an unimportant part.

(2) Encrypt the important part.

(3) Transmit (or store) the unimportant part without encryption.

Some compression algorithms do not produce "important" and "unimportant" parts, therefore the above partial encryption scheme is not feasible. The DCT-based JPEG [20] is one such example. Encrypting only low-frequency DCT coefficients, as much as 50% of them, will still reveal the outlines of the image objects, as shown in Figure 16.5.

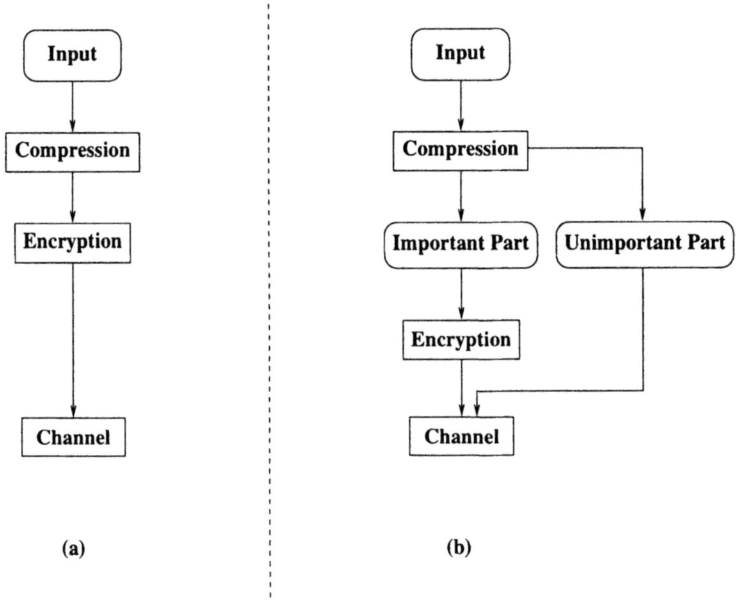

Figure 16.4. A comparison between (a) the traditional approach to secure image and video communication and (b) the proposed approach

The hierarchical data structure ("tree") commonly used in data decomposition is a natural choice for dividing data into important and unimportant parts. The "abstract" tree structure, i.e., the basic "shape" of the tree is considered important since it provides a general layout of the objects in an image. The leaves of the tree give the detailed properties of image regions and cannot be used to approximate the image without the tree structure. Encrypting only the tree structure indeed hides crucial information for image reconstruction. For the quadtree compression method discussed previously, with a typical image, 13%–27% of the output is for the tree structure itself, and thus will go through encryption. Less than 2% is encrypted for a 512×512 image compressed by an EZW-based wavelet algorithm (such as SPIHT or some modified version of it). Both quadtree and wavelet tree are suitable for low bit rate applications (better than DCT). The relative size of the important part of the compressed image is directly proportional to the amount of encryption and decryption time required. The applications using low bit rate compression algorithms would result in a smaller portion of the data to be encrypted. In fact, the encrypted part may be so small that a public-key encryption can be applied directly so that the implementation and operating costs of a secret-key encryption can be completely eliminated, as illustrated in Figure 16.6.

(a) Original image

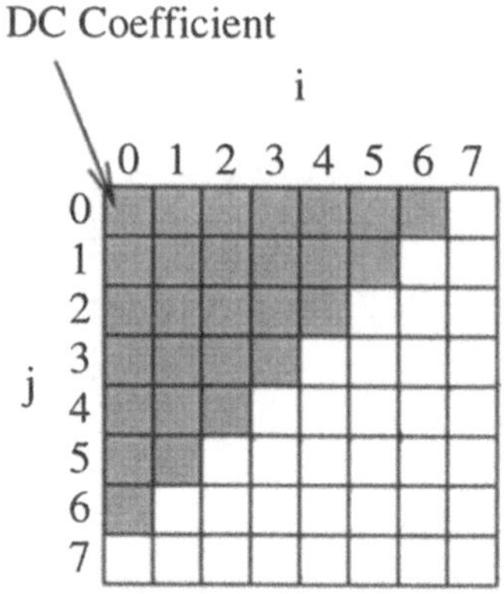

(b) Only the shaded DCT coefficients are encrypted

(c) Reconstructed image when $i+j=4$

(d) Reconstructed image when $i+j=7$

Figure 16.5. Image "Lena" and reconstructed images (after contrast enhancement) using the unencrypted DCT coefficients

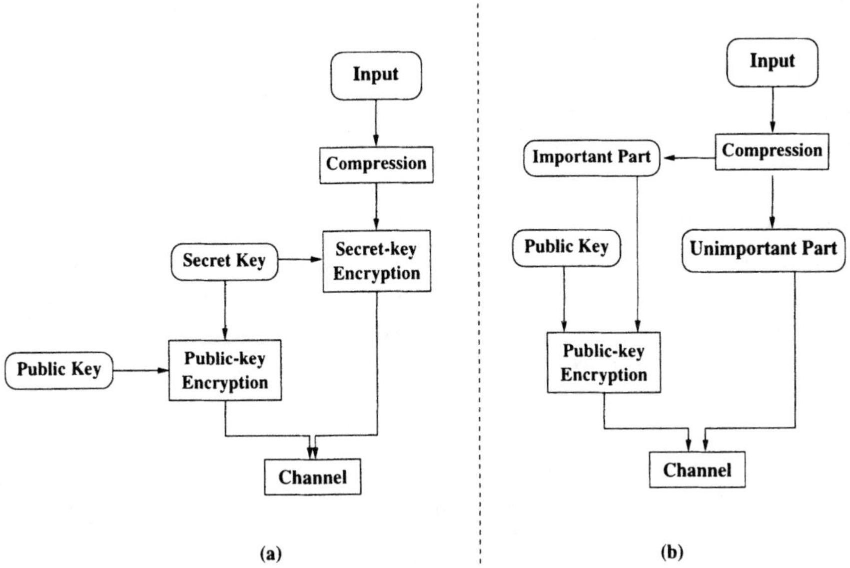

Figure 16.6. A comparison between (a) the traditional approach to secure image and video communication and (b) the proposed approach when public-key encryption can be applied directly to the important part

Because of the reduction in the encryption and decryption time, some real-time secure video communication and processing might become possible. In some cases, partial encryption allows the important part to be encrypted while the unimportant part is transmitted concurrently, which makes the encryption time negligible.

The partial encryption study provided us with insight on IAP data storage and transmission. The important part often gives important visual information about an image. For example, the important part in quadtree coding reveals the basic shape of objects in an image. A progressive transmission or an information prioritization may be implemented accordingly: more bandwidth can be allocated for the important part, and more careful error-correction should be applied to it as well, which may be useful or crucial in an open channel such as the Internet. In a distributed image and video retrieval, the small important parts can be stored locally in a catalogue, and the large unimportant parts can be transmitted without encryption when they are needed.

Table 16.2. Approximate upper bounds on the relative quadtree size in lossless quadtree compression on b-bit images

b	2	3	4	5	6	7	8
Quadtree Size (%)	40.0%	30.8%	25.0%	21.1%	18.2%	16.0%	14.3%

16.5 Partial Encryption of Quadtree Compressed Images

This section discusses the issues involved in partial encryption of quadtree compressed images: why it is feasible, how the leaf values should be transmitted (or stored) and how secure this scheme actually is.

Quadtree Structure and Leaf Values

In quadtree image compression, two logical parts are produced—the tree structure and the parameters describing each node. Any nonempty quadtree will have $4k+1$ nodes for some non-negative integer k. Among the nodes, k of them are internal and the others are leaf nodes. With the binary image in Figure 16.7 and its quadtree in Figure 16.8, $k = 5$. To represent a quadtree structure with $4k+1$ nodes, at most $4k+1$ bits are needed to indicate whether each node is an internal node or a leaf. To describe a leaf node, which corresponds to a square block of the image, many types of parameters have been used, such as the first-order polynomial models ($f(x, y) = a + bx + cy$) [30]. Our discussion is focused on the simplest model where each block is described by a single parameter, the average intensity. Similar arguments apply to other types of parameters. In a lossless quadtree compression, each leaf value is represented by the same number of bits. Using a single number (block intensity) of b bits for each leaf, $b(3k+1)$ bits would be used. The ratio of the quadtree size over the total size of the compressed image data (tree structure plus leaf values) is

$$S_r = \frac{4k+1}{b(3k+1)+4k+1}. \tag{16-3}$$

Those relative quadtree structure sizes for various b values are given in Table 16.2. For a typical image of 256×256 or larger, k is above 1000, thus

$$S_r \approx \frac{4}{3b+4}. \tag{16-4}$$

The observation that a relatively small number of bits are used for the tree structure is the base for the consideration of a partial encryption. Knowing only the intensity of each block does not allow one to learn much about the original image, as the location and size of each block are unknown. In a lossy compression, more bits are used for the leaves representing larger image blocks. Consider the bit allocation used by Shusterman and Feder [27], and let the root node being level 0, and the children of the root as level 1, etc.:

$$b_i = \frac{1}{2}\log\left(\frac{\sigma_i^2 L}{4^i D}\right), \tag{16-5}$$

where b_i is the number of bits used to represent each leaf value at level i, σ_i^2 is the variance of the leaf values at level i, L is the total number of leaf nodes in the quadtree (L_{qt} in [27]), and D is a user-defined constant to control the bit rate. The decoder must have the b_i values in order to separate the individual leaf values. The bit allocation can be represented efficiently, and it is also included in the encrypted part.

Table 16.3. Relative quadtree size in lossy quadtree compression

Image	Dimensions	bpp	Tree Size (bytes)	Tree Size (%)
sunset	256 × 256	0.542	859	19.4%
bridge	256 × 256	1.826	2178	14.6%
camera	256 × 256	0.877	1035	14.4%
bay	256 × 256	0.933	1371	17.9%
bird	256 × 256	0.370	643	21.2%
airfield	512 × 512	1.323	6244	14.4%
airplane	512 × 512	0.530	3601	20.7%
barbara	512 × 512	1.210	5524	13.9%
boat	512 × 512	0.673	4352	19.7%
couple	512 × 512	0.956	5064	16.2%
crowd	512 × 512	0.813	5232	19.6%
festung	512 × 512	0.655	3922	18.3%
goldhill	512 × 512	0.631	4825	23.3%
io	512 × 512	0.784	4188	16.3%
lax	512 × 512	1.155	6331	16.7%
lena	512 × 512	0.547	3537	19.7%
man	512 × 512	0.852	4974	17.8%
mandrill	512 × 512	1.913	8168	13.0%
peppers	512 × 512	0.516	3388	20.0%
sailboat	512 × 512	0.671	4621	21.0%
shepherd	512 × 512	1.502	7083	14.4%
washsat	512 × 512	**0.132**	**2420**	**56.1%**
woman1	512 × 512	0.757	4186	16.9%
woman2	512 × 512	0.296	2290	23.6%
zelda	512 × 512	0.344	3027	26.8%

The relative quadtree structure size is small if there are many leaf nodes at low levels. It is difficult to analyze the size of the quadtree without the knowledge of the bit allocation as well as the distribution of leaf nodes among the different levels. Table 16.3 shows the results obtained from test images. The relative quadtree size of all but one image is between 13%–27%, with the exception of "washsat" image, which has a relative quadtree size of 56.1%. Image "washsat" is a low-contrast

0	0	1	1	1	1	0	0
0	0	1	1	1	1	0	0
0	0	1	1	1	0	1	1
0	0	0	0	1	0	1	1
0	0	0	0	1	1	1	1
0	0	0	0	1	1	1	1
0	0	0	0	1	1	1	1
0	0	0	0	1	1	1	1

Figure 16.7. A binary image segmented iteratively into quarters

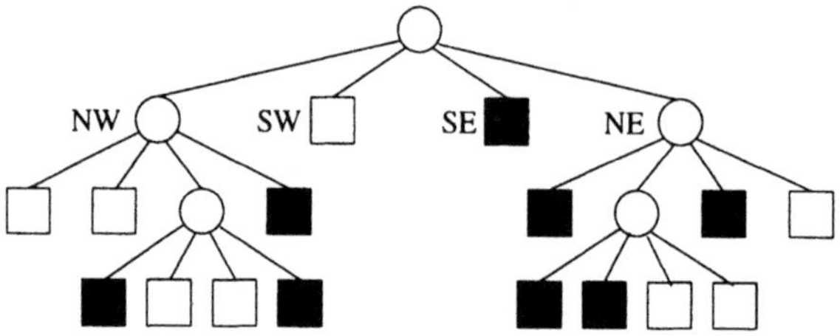

Figure 16.8. The quadtree representation for the binary image of Figure 16.7. The leaf nodes can be listed by *Leaf Ordering I* as 00-1001-1-01-1-1100-10, and can also be listed by *Leaf Ordering II* as 11100010-011001-01

image, so that the values σ_i^2 in (16-5) are small. Hence, many leaf values are represented by one bit.

Similar analysis holds when other parameters are used to describe the blocks associated with the leaf nodes. For example, for the first-order model $f(x, y) = a + bx + cy$ in [30], at approximately 0.5 bpp, the quadtree is 8.4% for the "lena" image and 11.7% for the "boat" image.

The Transmission Order of the Leaf Values

The leaf values must be transmitted in some order. Since the leaves are not encrypted, the transmission ordering of the leaves could give away crucial information. For example, the 8×8 binary image in Figure 16.7 can be encoded as the quadtree shown in Figure 16.8. Let's name the branches of each quadtree node NW, SW, SE, and NE, sequentially, and use "1" for a black leaf, "0" for white. The inorder traversal of the quadtree [15] will encode the leaf values of the quadtree in Figure 16.8 as 00-1001-1-01-1-1100-10. This is called *Leaf Ordering I.* We can also concatenate the leaf values from the highest level to the lowest, one level at a time, just the opposite to breadth-first traversal. Within each level, the blocks corresponding to the leaf values are ordered by the raster scan: each row of blocks is ordered left to right, and the rows are ordered from top to bottom. The leaf values are ordered according to the order of the corresponding blocks. Consider the quadtree in Figure 16.8 again. At Level 1, there are two leaf nodes, each corresponds to a square subimage of 4 by 4. Those nodes are recorded as "01". At Level 2, a sequence "011001" is used to represent the 2 by 2 blocks in scanning order. At Level 3, the eight pixels are encoded as "11100010". Concatenating the levels together, from the leaves farest away from the root to the root, i.e., from Level 3 to Level 1, we obtain "11100010-011001-01". That ordering is called *Leaf Ordering II.* These two orderings are equivalent in concisely represent the leaf values, but behave quite differently from the encryption point of view. It will be shown in the next section that Leaf Ordering I is not as secure as Leaf Ordering II.

How Secure Is It

The security of the quadtree partial encryption is examined in this section. We first present several properties of quadtrees about the number of possible trees, and then discuss the infeasibility of attacks based on exhaustive tree enumeration. Next, we deal with the attacks on lossless and lossy quadtree coding using different leaf orderings. Many of the results are generalized from those given in Section 2.3 of [15].

The cryptanalyst has a complete knowledge of all the leaf nodes and tries to figure out the quadtree structure. Using tree enumeration, a cryptanalyst may generate all possible quadtrees with specified parameters (e.g., the maximum height of the tree and the number of leaf nodes), and match the result tree with the leaf values until the correct image is obtained. We are interested in the relation between the maximum number of quadtrees and the tree parameters.

Theorem 1 *There is a one-to-one correspondence between quadtrees of height $h+1$ with $4k+1$ nodes and 4-ary trees having k nodes and a height of h.*

Here, a 4-ary tree is a rooted tree with every node having at most four children.

Corollary 1 *Let $a_{k,h}$ denote the number of quadtrees having $3k+1$ leaf nodes and a maximum height of $h+1$. This number $a_{k,h}$ is the same as the number of 4-ary trees with k nodes and a maximum height of h.*

Similar to the analysis of general trees found in [8], the following theorem provides a way to calculate $a_{k,h}$.

Theorem 2 *If $g_h(z) = \sum_k a_{k,h} z^k$ is the generating function of $a_{k,h}$ for height h, we have*

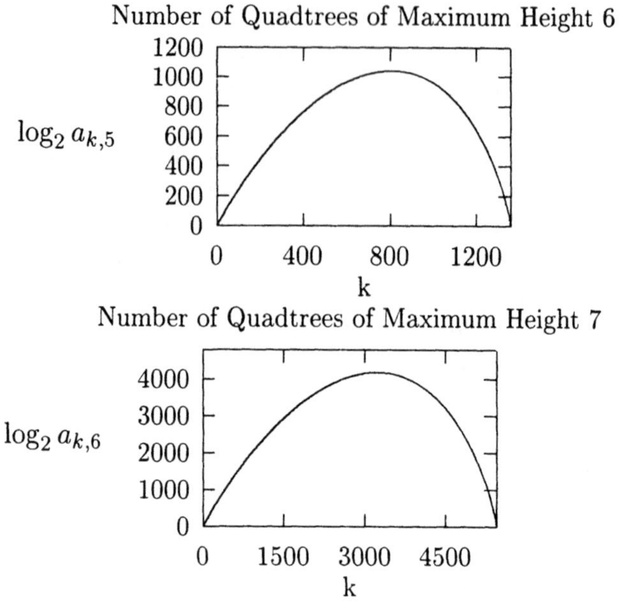

Figure 16.9. Plots of $\log_2 a_{k,h}$ for $h = 6, 7$

$$g_h(z) = \begin{cases} 1 + z & \text{if } h = 0, \\ 1 + z(g_{h-1}(z))^4 & \text{if } h > 0. \end{cases} \tag{16-6}$$

For an image of dimensions $2^n \times 2^n$, the maximum height of the quadtree is n. In the case of a lossless compression, the number of leaf nodes in the quadtree can be obtained from the total number of bits for leaves. In the case of a lossy compression, a range for the number of leaf nodes can be determined. Suppose that the cryptanalyst figured out that the number of leaf nodes is L, the number of such quadtrees is $a_{k,h}$ for $k = (L-1)/3$ and $h = n-1$. For $h = 6$ and $h = 7$, the values $\log_2 a_{k,h}$ for different k's, calculated by Theorem 2, are plotted in Figure 16.9. Unless k is very small (almost an empty tree) or k very large (almost a complete tree), $a_{k,h}$ is at least two to the hundreds. For the typical images in the testing set reported in [4], k takes a value close to the middle point of the curve [4]. Such a large number of possible quadtrees makes tree enumeration infeasible.

Suppose that the cryptanalyst also knows the number of leaves at every level, thus the number of possible quadtrees can be reduced by examining the locations of the leaf nodes at each level. That is, the number of possible quadtrees is

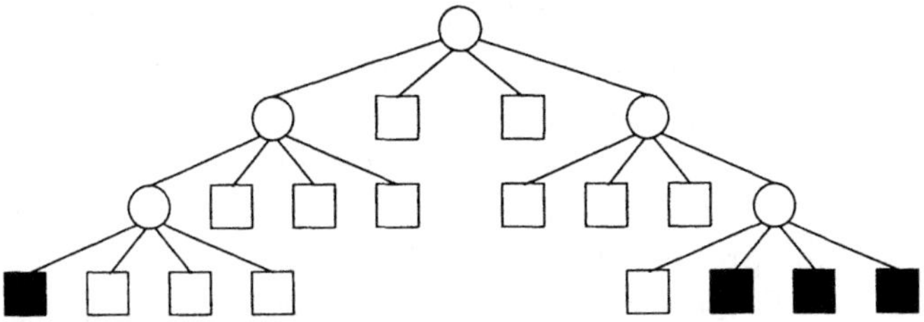

Figure 16.10. A quadtree with a run of length 11

$$\prod_{i=1}^{n} \binom{m_i}{L_i} \qquad (16\text{-}7)$$

where m_i is the number of possible locations at level i, and L_i is the number of leaves at level i. For the "lena" image, the number of possible quadtrees is 2^{23579}, even with that extra information on L_i. Other images give similar results.

Knowing that the tree enumeration is infeasible, the cryptanalyst may turn to the ordering of the leaf nodes. If Leaf Ordering I (the traditional inorder traversal) is used, the values of sibling leaf nodes are closed together in the encoded data. This fact gives away crucial information about image regions.

Let us still assume the NW, SW, SE, NE sequence among the quadrants. The first leaf value of the entire sequence must correspond to a block containing the NW corner of the image, and the last leaf must be related to the NE corner of the image. If the image has a somewhat uniform background that includes the image corners, giving away information about the background may help reveal the foreground objects.

In the case of a lossless quadtree compression, equal number of bits are used for each leaf, so that it is straightforward to separate the encoded data into individual leaf values. A sequence of identical leaf values, called a *run*, can be used in cryptanalysis. Figure 16.10 shows a quadtree with a run of length 12. In this particular run, the levels of the leaves decreases first, then increases, and the direction change (from decrease to increase) happens only once. Once the levels start increasing, they cannot decrease until all four sibling leaves are encountered in the run, which is impossible, because those four would have been merged into one single node. As a result, long runs help recovering homogeneous regions and thus reduce the number of quadtrees that need to be examined in an exhaustive search. Algorithms are given for revealing such regions from runs [4]. Those algorithms can also be used in a known-plaintext attack. If a known non-homogeneous image portion sent through the quadtree coder to produce leaf nodes, which is a substring of the leaf values of the entire image. The runs before and after the substring can be used to extend the known image portion. The minimum dimensions of the blocks represented by the leaves in a run can be determined. Especially, long runs may be used to obtain homogeneous regions at the corners therefore the shapes of foreground objects can be seen.

When Leaf Ordering I is used in lossy quadtree compression, and a variable number of bits are used to represent leaf values, the cryptanalyst cannot easily obtain the individual leaf values, and cannot easily recognize runs. If the bit allocation for each level is distinct, there are at more $12! < 2^{29}$ orderings of the b_i values to reach the correct bit allocation. Once that ordering is obtained, the level at which each leaf value is located is also known. As a result, the complete quadtree can be determined [4].

The above attacks may or may not completely recover the entire image, but enough information about the image may be revealed. Therefore, Leaf Ordering I is NOT recommended for quadtree compression.

Leaf Ordering II is more secure for both lossless and lossy compression. In the lossless case, leaf values of sibling nodes may be far apart. Actually, the number of leaf values between two sibling nodes could be as many as the number of possible blocks in a row. The first and last leaf values do not correspond to fixed pixel locations. A known image portion does not correspond to a substring of the leaf values of the whole image, so that the known portion cannot be easily extended. In the case of lossy compression, Leaf Ordering II allows the individual leaves to be separated without compromising security. The same attack based on bit allocation can only give the number of leaf nodes at each level, and the number of possible quadtrees is still large enough [4].

Leaf Ordering II can easily be used in a bottom-up quadtree. At each level, the leaves are examined for merging in the spatial order described by Leaf Ordering II. If a leaf node is not merged with siblings, the leaf value is transmitted or stored. The computational overhead of using quadtree partial encryption is negligible.

In fact, the raster scan order used in Leaf Ordering II could be substituted by any other permutation of the blocks within each level, as long as it does not reveal the correspondence between any two given leaves and the sibling nodes. One may even use a secret permutation of the leaves to add more security, although the leaf values themselves are not encrypted. However, the crucial reason of the security of the partial encryption is still the hiding of the tree structure. Without the tree, the cryptanalyst only has a pile of leaves at most. There are just too many possible trees that match the same distribution of the leaves but have totally different block locations.

16.6 Partial Encryption of Wavelet Compressed Images

In a wavelet compression algorithm based on zerotrees, the wavelet coefficients are organized in a tree structure. The "significance" of a coefficient set indicates whether the set needs to be "decomposed" further, which is similar to the homogeneity criterion in quadtree decomposition. Although many other zerotree-based wavelet algorithms [7, 13, 14, 26] behave similarly from the partial encryption point of view, we focus on the Set Partitioning in Hierarchical Trees (SPIHT) algorithm [23] here. In the SPIHT algorithm, after several levels of wavelet transform, each 2×2 square of coefficients at the root level ("LL") corresponds to three trees of coefficients of other levels. At location (i, j), $c_{i,j}$ represents the coefficient, $O(i, j)$ denotes the set of coordinates of the children of $c_{i,j}$, $D(i, j)$ denotes the set of coordinates of all descendants of $c_{i,j}$, and $L(i, j) = D(i, j) - O(i, j)$. The magnitude of a coefficient is compared against a threshold T. If it is greater than T, it is considered significant. Three lists are used: list of insignificant sets (LIS), list of insignificant pixels (LIP), and list of significant pixels (LSP). The LIS has two types of entries, for $D(i, j)$ and $L(i, j)$. The LIP has insignificant coefficients that do not belong to the sets in LIS. And the LSP has the actual significant coefficients. The significance information of the sets is used heavily by the SPIHT algorithm to determine the tree structures, and the execution of the algorithm depends strongly on the structure of the zerotree. If a small amount of significance information at the beginning of the encoded data is incorrect, the entire decoding process can be ruined [6, 23]. To interpret the bits in the encoded string, the decompression algorithm must know which type the bits are: sign bits, refinement bits, significance of pixels, or significance of sets. Incorrect significance bits can cause future bits to be misinterpreted.

Our partial encryption scheme only encrypts the significance information related to pixels or sets in the two highest pyramid levels, and encrypt the parameter n that determines the initial threshold. That is, we encrypt the significance information $S_n(i, j)$, $S_n(\mathcal{D}(i, j))$, and $S_n(\mathcal{L}(i, j))$ if and only if (i, j) is in the two highest pyramid levels. For the root level of dimension 8×8, the significance information is encrypted when $0 \leq i, j < 16$. The pixels and sets of other levels are produced by decomposing sets in the two highest pyramid levels. The states of the lists LIP, LIS, and LSP are constantly updated by the algorithm according to the significance information. If the states of the lists are incorrect at the beginning of the algorithm, it is hard to recover. The size of the encrypted part, the top two levels of the pyramid, should be at least $64 + 96 = 160$ bits (the proof is in [4]). In most cases, 6 to 10 passes are performed for an image compressed to 0.8 bpp, which gives an upper bound of about 5200 bits on the size of the encrypted part. Table 16.4 shows the actual sizes obtained at various bit rates for some typical images. The size of the encrypted part is less than 7% of the compression output for a 256×256 image, and less than 2% for a 512×512 image.

Table 16.4. The size of the encrypted part in an image compressed by SPIHT

		0.80 bpp		0.60 bpp		0.40 bpp	
Image	Dimensions	Bits	%	Bits	%	Bits	%
bay	256 × 256	1594	3.0%	1556	4.0%	1471	5.6%
bird	256 × 256	1895	3.6%	1830	4.7%	1717	6.6%
sunset	256 × 256	1769	3.4%	1761	4.5%	1723	6.6%
bridge	256 × 256	1509	2.9%	1487	3.8%	1478	5.7%
camera	256 × 256	1752	3.3%	1724	4.4%	1656	6.3%
airfield	512 × 512	1653	0.8%	1653	1.1%	1642	1.6%
airplane	512 × 512	1710	0.8%	1704	1.1%	1680	1.6%
barbara	512 × 512	1722	0.8%	1716	1.1%	1709	1.6%
couple	512 × 512	1634	0.8%	1624	1.1%	1617	1.5%
boat	512 × 512	1841	0.9%	1835	1.2%	1805	1.7%
crowd	512 × 512	1674	0.8%	1670	1.1%	1670	1.6%
festung	512 × 512	1770	0.8%	1744	1.1%	1720	1.6%
goldhill	512 × 512	1741	0.8%	1729	1.1%	1726	1.6%
io	512 × 512	1730	0.8%	1724	1.1%	1720	1.6%
lax	512 × 512	1561	0.7%	1561	1.0%	1535	1.4%
lena	512 × 512	1684	0.8%	1676	1.1%	1670	1.6%
man	512 × 512	1570	0.7%	1566	1.0%	1566	1.5%
mandrill	512 × 512	1533	0.7%	1516	1.0%	1510	1.4%
peppers	512 × 512	1647	0.8%	1647	1.0%	1647	1.6%
sailboat	512 × 512	1748	0.8%	1741	1.1%	1734	1.7%
shepherd	512 × 512	1596	0.8%	1596	1.0%	1590	1.5%
washsat	512 × 512	1435	0.7%	1435	0.9%	1435	1.4%
woman1	512 × 512	1658	0.8%	1657	1.1%	1651	1.6%
woman2	512 × 512	1884	0.9%	1884	1.2%	1883	1.8%
zelda	512 × 512	1808	0.9%	1808	1.2%	1805	1.7%

Without the significance information of the two highest pyramid levels, an exhaustive search requires testing at least 2^{160} possibilities. Recall that the key length for the secret-key encryption algorithm IDEA is 128 bits. Figure 16.11 shows the reconstructed "lena" images when only k encrypted bits are received and interpreted correctly by the decoder. When $k \geq 160$, a rough shape of the image begin to appear.

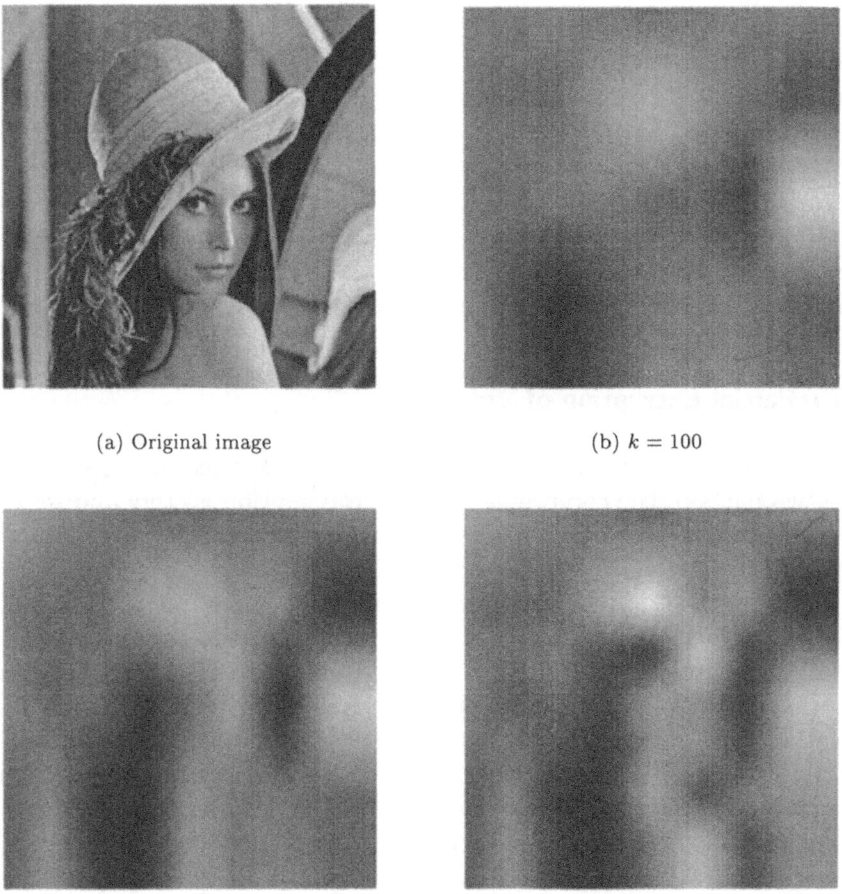

(a) Original image

(b) $k = 100$

(c) $k = 140$

(d) $k = 180$

Figure 16.11. Reconstructed images using only the first k encrypted bits

In summary, without the significance information, the decoder cannot determine the type of transmitted bits, and cannot locate the bits where a sorting pass or a refinement pass starts. If the initial updates to the LSP are not known, it is difficult to determine the order in which the coefficients are refined. Given one encrypted part, there are many possible unencrypted parts that can match with it. On the other hand, one can generate a large number of encrypted parts that match a given unencrypted part by translating the significant branches. The encrypted parts of two similar images may be dramatically different. Substituting the important part of one image into another will not give any meaningful approximation.

One can add a comparison on the coordinates (i, j) before each significance bit is transmitted in the SPIHT algorithm in order to perform the partial encryption. This straightforward modification take very little time. Actually, we are unable to detect any increase in running time due to the additional comparisons in our experiments.

16.7 Partial Encryption of Videos

The partial image encryption scheme can be extended to videos. There are two parts in the compressed video data: motion vectors and residual errors. For low-resolution videos, all motion vectors must be encrypted, especially if the encryption is activated after the video transmission has started and the cryptanalyst already obtained some initial frames. For higher resolution videos, not all motion vectors have to be completely hidden. Motion compensation algorithms usually divide the current frame into blocks of fixed size, and merge multiple blocks with similar or identical motion vectors. Schuster and Katsaggelos [25] compute the motion vectors for fixed-sized blocks, say 8×8, and merges the blocks using a quadtree. The quadtree partial encryption for still images, described in previous sections, can be adapted to encode motion vectors. Here, the leaves are the motion vectors and they can be transmitted without encryption. Only the quadtree structure is hidden. The motion vectors are encoded one level at a time using Leaf Ordering II. For high and medium resolution videos, the maximum height of the quadtree is still large enough that an exhaustive tree enumeration is infeasible.

The residual errors must be encrypted, otherwise they can easily reveal outlines of moving objects that are not perfectly described by the motion vectors, as can be seen in Figure 16.12. A quadtree algorithm or a wavelet algorithm can be used to compress the residual error image. The partial encryption schemes for quadtree and wavelet image coding can be applied directly here.

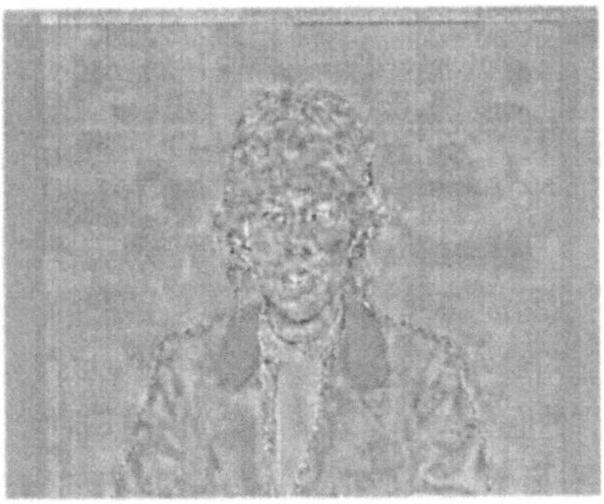

Figure 16.12. Residual error for frame 2 (after contrast enhancement) of the "claire" sequence

The number of bits used for each motion vector can be used to estimate the relative size of the quadtree of motion vectors. If each motion vector is represented by six bits, the quadtree structure is at most 18.2% (Table 16.2) of the motion compensation output. As indicated in Table 16.5, in the case of residual error image, the relative size of the encrypted part is similar to the case of a still image. The results for the first 10 frames of each video are shown and the rests are similar. With an accurate motion estimation, residual errors are small, thus the relative sizes of the encrypted parts in the quadtree are slightly larger than those in still image compression. Because of the small variance of the leaf values, a small number of bits can be used to represent each leaf value. When the SPIHT is used with partial encryption, the size of the encrypted part is similar to the case of still image compression.

Table 16.5. Sizes of the encrypted part of the residual error for two test video sequences: "football" sequence (720×496 frames) and "claire" sequence (360×288 frames). Motion block size 8×8

	football				claire			
	Motion		residual		Motion		residual	
Frame	Bytes	%	Bytes	%	Bytes	%	Bytes	%
2	1808	28.8%	146	0.6%	90	27.0%	141	2.2%
4	2124	29.0%	143	0.5%	201	26.7%	140	2.1%
6	2425	27.8%	149	0.6%	212	26.9%	141	2.2%
8	2473	24.0%	135	0.5%	226	28.8%	140	2.1%
10	2646	27.9%	137	0.5%	256	28.0%	136	2.1%

As discussed in Sections 16.5 and 16.6, large homogeneous regions in the input image produce long runs of leaf values in quadtree coding using Leaf Ordering I. It is also true in the case of video partial encryption. A large number of motion vectors belonging to the same object

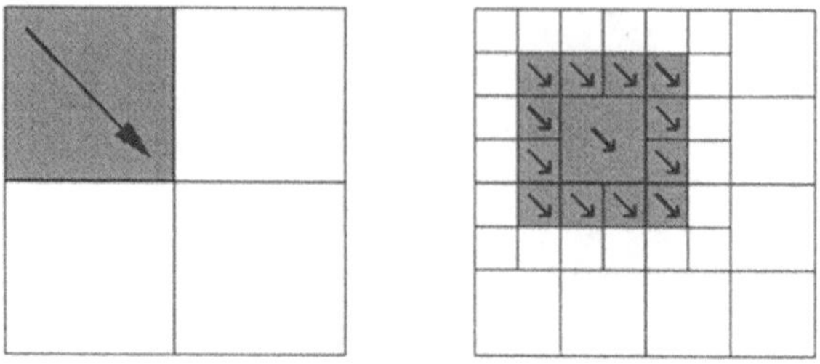

Figure 16.13. Motion vector quadtrees change a great deal when objects move

are almost identical, thus large homogeneous regions exist in the motion vector "image". Therefore, it is critical to use Leaf Ordering II.

The security of the partial encryption also depends on the inability of a cryptanalyst to take advantage of the temporal correlation between consecutive frames. Experiments have indicated that much of the frame correlation is lost in both the encrypted part and the unencrypted part. Since the motion vector frames are extremely sensitive to the placement of the moving objects [29] as shown in Figure 16.13, the quadtrees of consecutive motion vector frames are drastically different. Zerotrees are also highly sensitive to the location of moving objects, therefore consecutive error frames produced by SPIHT are also totally different.

The encryption of the important part can often be performed in parallel to the transmission of the unencrypted part. Even if they are carried out sequentially, the overhead of separating the important part from the unimportant part is negligible, similar to the case of still image compression and encryption.

16.8 Conclusion

In this chapter, we have discussed the need of encryption coding of IAP data for Internet computing. After briefly introducing basic concepts of cryptography and some secret-key and public-key encryption algorithm, we focus on methods aimed at combining compression and encryption in order to speedup or simplify the encryption process. One such method is partial encryption based on hierarchical data structures employed in quadtree and wavelet coding. The output of a compression algorithm is decomposed into the tree structure itself and the detailed information (e.g., leaves). Only the tree structure is encrypted. In both still image and video coding, the partial encryption scheme significantly reduces the encryption/decryption time with little reduction of the compression performance and data security. The main limitation of partial encryption is that every compression algorithm requires a different encryption scheme. One possible future research topic could be the identification of the "driving" part of decompression in a general coding algorithm. That is, the branch of execution of the decompression algorithm heavily depends on a portion of the compressed data, and that portion should be considered "important" and should be encrypted.

References

[1] M. Bertilsson, E.F. Brickell, and I. Ingemarsson. Cryptanalysis of video encryption based on space-filling curves. In *EUROCRYPT '89*, pages 403–411, 1990.

[2] N. Bourbakis and C. Alexopoulos. Picture data encryption using scan patterns. *Pattern Recognition*, 25(6):567–581, 1992.

[3] H.K.-C. Chang and J.-L. Liu. A linear quadtree compression scheme for image encryption. *Signal Processing: Image Communication*, 10(4):279–290, Sep. 1997.

[4] H. Cheng. Partial encryption for image and video communication. Master's thesis, Univ. of Alberta, 1998.

[5] H. Cheng and X. Li. On the application of image decomposition to image compression and encryption. In *Communications and Multimedia Security II*, pages 116–127, 1996.

[6] C.D. Creusere. A new method of robust image compression based on the embedded zerotree wavelet algorithm. *IEEE Trans. Image Processing*, 6(10):1436–1442, Oct. 1997.

[7] E.A.B. da Silva, D.G. Sampson, and M. Ghanbari. A successive approximation vector quantizer for wavelet transform image coding. *IEEE Trans. Image Processing*, 5(2):299–310, Feb. 1996.

[8] N.G. de Bruijn, D.E. Knuth, and S.O. Rice. The average height of planted plane trees. In R. C. Read, editor, *Graph Theory and Computing*, pages 15–22. Academic Press, 1972.

[9] D. Denning. *Cryptography and Data Security*. Addison-Wesley Publishing, 1982.

[10] D.A. Huffman. A method for the construction of minimum-redundancy codes. *Proc. IRE*, 40(2):1098–1101, Sep. 1952.

[11] D. Jones. Data compression and encryption algorithms. World Wide Web. http://www.cs.uiowa.edu/~jones/compress/.

[12] D. Jones. Applications of splay trees to data compression. *Commun. ACM*, pages 996–1007, Aug. 1988.

[13] J. Knipe. A comparison of improved spatial and transform domain compression schemes. Master's thesis, Univ. of Alberta, 1996.

[14] J. Knipe, X. Li, and B. Han. An improved lattice vector quantization based scheme for wavelet compression. *IEEE Trans. Signal Processing*, 46(1):239–243, Jan. 1998.

[15] D.E. Knuth. *The Art of Computer Programming: Fundamental Algorithms*, volume 1. Addison-Wesley, 3rd edition, 1997.

[16] X. Lai and J. Massey. A proposal for a new block encryption standard. In *Advances in Cryptology - EUROCRYPT '90 Proceedings*, pages 389–404. Springer-Verlag, 1991.

[17] X. Liu, P.G. Farrell, and C.A. Boyd. Resisting the Bergen-Hogan attack on adaptive arithmetic coding. In *Cryptography and Coding: 6th IMA Intl. Conf.*, pages 199–208, 1997.

[18] Y. Matias and A. Shamir. A video scrambling technique based on space filling curves. In *CRYPTO '87*, pages 398–417, 1988.

[19] J.L. Mitchell, W.B. Pennebaker, C.E. Fogg, and D.J. LeGall. *MPEG Video: Compression Standard.* Chapman & Hall, 1996.

[20] W.B. Pennebaker and J.L. Mitchell. *JPEG Still Image Data Compression Standard.* Van Nostrand Reinhold, 1993.

[21] R.L. Rivest. A description of a single-chip implementation of the rsa cipher. *LAMBDA Magazine*, 1(3):14–18, 1980.

[22] R.L. Rivest, A. Shamir, and L.M. Adleman. A method for obtaining digital signatures and public-key cryptosystems. *Communications of the ACM*, 21(2):120–126, 1978.

[23] A. Said and W.A. Pearlman. A new, fast, and efficient image codec based on set partitioning in hierarchical trees. *IEEE Trans. Circ. and Syst. for Video Technol.*, 6(3):243–250, June 1996.

[24] B. Schneier. *Applied Cryptography.* John Wiley & Sons, 1996.

[25] G.M. Schuster and A.K. Katsaggelos. *Rate-Distortion Based Video Compression: Optimal Video Frame Compression and Object Boundary Encoding.* Kluwer Academic Publishers, 1997.

[26] J.M. Shapiro. Embedded image coding using zerotrees of wavelet coefficients. *IEEE Trans. Signal Processing*, 41(12):3445–3462, Dec. 1993.

[27] E. Shusterman and M. Feder. Image compression via improved quadtree decomposition algorithms. *IEEE Trans. Image Processing*, 3(2):207–215, Mar. 1994.

[28] K. Smith. Watch out hackers, public encryption chips are coming. *Electronics Week*, 20:30–31, 1985.

[29] P. Strobach. Tree-structured scene adaptive coder. *IEEE Trans. Commun.*, 38(4):477–486, Apr. 1990.

[30] P. Strobach. Quadtree-structured recursive plane decomposition coding of images. *IEEE Trans. Signal Processing*, 39(6):1380–1397, June 1991.

[31] I.H. Witten, R. Neal, and J.G. Cleary. Arithmetic coding for data compression. *Commun. ACM*, 30:520–540, June 1987.

INDEX

A

Active contour, 4, 135
Adaptive order PA (AOPA), 6, 121-130
Addressing Function, 168

B

Bayesian estimation, 63
Best Neighborhood Matching (BNM), 6-8, 97, 99, 100, 101, 103, 105, 107-110, 151-157, 164
Bit Reversal, 223, 225, 226, 234, 259
Bit allocation, 281, 346, 347, 352
Binary
  image, 16, 38, 268, 348
  morphology, 6, 33, 38, 39
Bit plane, 137
Block-based, 78, 79, 85, 87, 97, 98, 111, 112, 151, 164, 297
Block-encoded, 9, 297
Block-wise, 98, 319
  luminance transformation, 99, 100
  similarity, 97, 98, 152, 298, 319
Blocking artifact, 297, 313, 314
Blocking effect, 297, 298, 300, 301, 314, 328, 329
Blur, 35, 64, 116, 127, 309
Boundary, 2, 9, 37, 71, 90, 100, 105, 154, 161, 297, 298, 300, 360
BPC Permutations, 225, 226, 234, 235, 259, 261, 262
Brightness, 318

C

Cache, 180, 195-220
  Column Associative Cache, 217
  One's Complement Cache, 217
  Skewed Associative Cache, 217
  Victim Cache, 217
Camera, 1, 16, 39, 135, 266, 347, 354
Cartesian, 79
Center Weighted Median (CWM), 308, 309
The Chinese Remainder Theorem, 168, 169, 172, 173, 174, 190, 192
Circuit Switch, 221, 222, 248, 251, 157, 258, 260
Circulation Operation, 245, 248, 252
Closing, 201
Clustering, 3, 4, 113, 191, 200, 201-203, 219
Co-occurrence matrix, 18
Gray code, 41, 182
Codebook, 268, 281, 285-289, 292
Color, 9, 15, 16, 18, 111, 123, 134, 137, 145, 146, 265, 267
Communication, 95, 97, 115, 154, 160, 163, 221, 222, 223, 236, 237, 248-250, 258-260, 303, 315, 319, 329
Complete Residue System (CRS), 224, 225, 233, 257
Compression
  data, 95,
  ratio, 7, 77, 78, 91, 92, 93, 98, 267, 291
  standards, 71, 97, 151
Computer vision, 1, 2, 134, 135, 191, 261
Congestion, 222
Consistent labeling problem (CLP), 55-57
Contour, 4, 135
Contraction Mapping Theorem, 81
Convolution, 20, 64, 201
Coordinate descending mutation, 6, 63, 64, 65, 74
Correlation, 20, 111, 112, 132, 151, 152, 164, 266, 310, 315, 342, 358
Cosine transform, 3, 268, 314, 318, 328
Covariance matrix, 203, 204
Crossbar, 141, 143, 144
Curvature, 116, 121

D

D-ordered p-vector, 169, 170, 171
Decoder, 90, 93, 95, 112, 285, 328, 341, 347, 354, 356
Decoding, 2, 7, 9, 77, 81, 85, 86, 89, 90, 92, 297, 301, 353

Detour Dimension, 237
Digital image, 75, 95, 97, 137, 193, 219, 327
Dilation, 38-41, 201
Discrete Cosine transform (DCT), 3, 78, 267-269, 277, 280, 282, 292, 342, 343, 344
Discrete Fourier transform (DFT), 24
Distance measure, 169
Distortion, 46, 271, 275

E

Edge
  detection, 22, 23, 36, 37, 41, 115, 135, 303, 318
Eigenvalue, 205
Eigenvector, 205
Encoder, 78, 90, 267, 280, 341
Encoding, 2, 7, 77, 78, 81-93, 267-269, 297, 341
Encryption, 9, 331,-336, 339-346, 349, 350, 353, 356-359
Enhancement, 318
Erosion, 23, 38, 39, 40, 201
Error concealment, 7, 97, 98, 107, 110, 112, 151, 152, 165, 328
Euclidean geometry, 77
Evolution strategy(ES), 6, 63, 64, 103
  best-neighborhood-matching (ES-BNM), 98, 104, 105, 109-111
Exchange Operation, 237, 242, 245
Exclusive-OR, 175, 187, 236, 334, 337
  Bitwise Exclusive-OR, 175, 176, 177, 209
  Exclusive-OR gate, 247

F

Fast Fourier transform(FFT), 16, 24-26, 30, 191, 193, 198, 201, 210, 214, 216, 247
Feature, 3-5, 16, 21, 36, 121, 135, 177, 178, 180, 183, 188, 198, 199, 203, 207, 210, 211, 217, 218, 221, 248, 266
Filter
  low-pass, 34, 35, 98, 135
  high-pass, 34, 35, 135
  median, 9, 21, 116, 127, 129, 130, 131, 297, 303, 308, 309, 313, 315, 325
  linear, 6, 33, 34, 35, 38, 39
  non-linear, 38, 39
  morphological, 6, 23, 33, 38, 39, 40
Fixed-order PA (FOPA), 121, 125-127
Fourier transform, 16, 18, 22, 24, 268, 319
Fractal
  Block Coding (FBC), 78, 79, 92, 93, 95, 98, 298, 319
  Block Coding in Residue Domain (FBCRD), 89, 95
  code, 7, 77, 78, 82, 85, 88, 90, 92
  decoder iteration, 90
  image compression, 77, 93, 94, 95, 112, 327
  transformations, 78,
Non-fractal-coded, 7, 78, 85, 90, 93
Fuzzy
  approach, 127, 313
  flag map, 309
  impulse detection, 298, 309, 310
  logic, 108, 112, 164, 328
  noise cancellation, 298, 310

G

Gaussian
  distribution, 287
  mutation, 64, 65, 68, 75, 103, 104
Generation Matrix, 182
GF(2), 247
Gray
  level, 2, 15, 16, 17, 23, 24, 63-65, 69, 71, 72, 74, 88, 89, 100, 108, 116, 117, 121, 125, 137, 150, 161, 199, 265, 266, 267, 271, 292, 318
  scale, 77, 91, 98, 301, 303, 309, 321
Greatest Common Divisor (GCD), 170

H

High-level processing, 15
High-pass filter, 34, 35, 135
Histogram, 2, 3, 18, 23, 26, 268, 342
  array, 3
  transformation, 2
  equalization, 2, 199
HNN, 68, 69, 71-74
Hopfield network, 70, 71

Hough transform, 4, 33, 41, 42, 44, 46-48, 50, 52, 53, 55, 198, 206, 207
adaptive Hough trandform, 55
probabilistic Hough transform, 55
pyramid Hough transform, 55
randomized Hough transform, 61
Hybrid
evolution strategy, 7, 63, 64, 66
fractal image coding, 78, 85
system, 78, 79, 91-94
Hypercube, 192-194, 221, 222, 224-226, 232, 233, 235, 240, 242, 247, 248, 252, 258-261

I

I/O, 159, 160
Image and pattern (IAP), 1, 2, 6-9, 15, 18, 27, 29, 30, 33, 56, 134, 142, 146, 265-267, 292, 331, 340-342, 345, 358
Internet, 1, 4-9,16, 59, 133-136, 142, 144-146, 256, 317, 331, 336, 340, 342, 345, 358
Image
analysis, 1, 5, 146
coding, 6, 7, 15, 77-79, 81, 85, 86, 89, 92-95, 97, 98, 111, 137, 268, 269, 297, 319, 356
compression3, 7, 16, 77, 78, 93-95, 98, 201, 267, 268, 281, 282, 292, 298, 319, 342, 346, 357, 358
encryption, 356
partitioning, 85-88, 90
processing, 1, 2, 5, 6, 15, 33, 77, 134-137, 139, 141, 167, 189, 190, 197, 198, 213, 216, 259, 266
restoration, 2, 3, 6, 9, 63-65, 67-71, 74, 151, 152, 155, 156, 158, 160, 164, 317, 318
segmentation, 2, 3, 5, 6, 33, 55, 115, 135, 145, 267, 303
Impulse
noise, 6, 7, 9, 115, 116, 118, 119, 121, 122, 124-132, 297, 298, 303, 307, 309, 310, 312, 313, 317, 319, 320
detection, 7, 115, 117, 131, 298, 303-305, 309, 310, 320
detector, 7, 115-118, 298, 320
Intensity, 266, 346
Iterated Function System (IFS), 77, 80, 82

J

JPEG, 77, 92, 93, 97, 297, 300-302, 313
Jump and look all round Best Neighborhood Matching (JBNM), 8, 151-158, 164
parallel (PJBNM), 152, 158-164

K

Knowledge base, 267

L

Labeling, 2, 5, 6, 18, 33, 34, 55-58, 200, 204, 266
Laplacian
mask, 124
filter, 124
LBG, 78, 285
LC Permutations, 175, 235, 248, 249, 260
Line detection, 50, 51, 53
Local data movement, 19

M

Mapper, 267, 268
Mapping, 2, 6, 7, 267, 268, 342
Matrix, 175-178, 182, 184, 188
Master Reading a file then Distributing it (MRD), 160
Mean Square Error (MSE), 6, 63, 88, 89, 99, 100, 103, 152, 153, 274, 275, 281, 305, 306, 307, 309, 321, 352
Weighted (WMSE), 298, 299
Median filter, 9, 21, 116, 127, 129, 130, 131, 297, 303, 308, 309, 313, 315, 325
Miss, 197, 201, 208, 216, 217
Compulsory Miss, 197
Capacity Miss, 197
Conflict Miss197-199, 201, 214, 216, 217
Modified evolution strategy (MES), 6, 63
Morphology, 135
Motion, 265, 266, 356-358

N

Neighborhood mean filter, 116, 121
Neighborhood operation, 20, 21
Network Conflicts, 221, 222, 258
Neural evolution algorithm(NEA), 63, 67, 68, 71-75
Noise cancellation, 7, 115, 298, 309, 310, 319, 320

O

Opening, 201
Optimization criteria, 63, 64, 67

P

Packet Switch, 221, 226, 248, 257, 260
Parallel
  algorithm, 8, 19, 21, 22, 26-30, 34, 39, 55, 57-59, 134, 136-139, 143, 151, 158, 159, 160, 162, 163, 178, 191, 358
  JBNM (PJBNM), 152, 158-164
  processing, 7, 151, 157, 159, 160, 162, 163, 178, 191,
  Reading from Control node(PRC), 159, 160
Parallel Memory System, 167-170, 172, 173, 175, 189, 190, 210, 221
Partial encryption, 9, 331, 336, 342, 345, 346, 349, 352, 353, 356, 358
Partial fractal mapping, 6, 7, 77-79, 81-83, 93
Pattern
  analysis, 5, 203
  matrix, 18, 29, 204
  recognition, 1, 2, 4, 5, 189, 198, 213, 216, 259, 267
Pattern Recognition and Image Processing (PRIP), 1, 2, 4-6, 8, 9, 15, 18, 19, 21, 26, 27, 29, 30, 33, 34, 39, 59, 134, 135, 136, 198, 199, 201, 204, 206, 216, 217
PEACE Machine, 211-241, 218
Peak signal-to-noise ratio(PSNR), 69, 71-74, 91, 93, 105, 107, 108-110, 121, 122, 125, 127, 155-157, 164, 272, 274, 275, 277-280, 289, 290, 301, 312, 313, 321, 324-326
Perfect Shuffle, 223, 225, 226, 234, 260
Piecewise similarity, 9, 297, 298, 313
Polynomial approximation (PA), 6, 115, 116, 119, 121, 131,
  fixed-order (FOPA)121, 125-127
  adaptive order (AOPA) , 6, 121-130
Post-processing, 297, 301, 302
Predictive coding, 267, 268
Progressive Switching Median (PSM), 9, 298, 305, 306, 308, 309, 310, 314
Proximity matrix, 4, 19, 200

Q

Quadtree, 7, 9, 77, 92-95, 265, 267-281, 289, 292, 331, 341-353, 357
Quantization, 9, 71, 201, 265, 267, 269, 280, 281, 285, 287, 289
Quantizer, 267

R

Rate distortion, 275
Recognition, 115, 189, 198, 201, 204, 213, 217
Redundancy, 3, 7, 77, 97, 98, 266, 267, 298, 310, 313, 317, 319
Region, 2, 3, 7, 9, 21, 23, 26, 27, 30
  growing, 3, 23, 26, 27, 30, 87
Resolution, 16, 42, 44, 45, 134, 145, 265, 281, 282, 284, 356
Restoration, 2, 3, 6, 7, 9, 63-65, 67-72, 102, 103, 105, 108, 111, 127, 132, 151, 152, 156, 158, 164
Reuse Ratio, 198, 199, 201-204, 213, 217
Rotation, 3, 29, 48, 80, 142, 191, 205, 272

S

Sampling, 3
Scaling, 89-91
Scene, 1, 2, 5, 15-17, 39, 55, 274
Segmentation, 2-6, 33, 55, 85, 115, 135, 145, 267, 303
Self-similarity, 97, 98, 319
Shape, 4, 5, 20, 28, 41, 44, 46, 48-52, 77, 111, 146, 179-181, 266, 277, 287, 298,

300, 342, 345, 352, 354
Skeleton, 2
Skew, 169, 171, 174, 190, 217
Skewing Scheme, 168-170, 175, 180, 182, 188, 189-191
Linear Skewing Scheme, 169
XOR Scheme, 175, 176, 190, 210
EE Scheme, 176, 184, 210
MG Scheme, 181-186
LR Scheme, 210
Skewing Function, 168, 169
Smoothing, 9, 274, 297
Sobel operator, 86,
Spatial, 2, 3, 9, 18-20, 23, 27, 33-35, 39, 41, 80, 98, 151, 152, 265, 297, 318
Standard deviation, 103
Stereo, 135
Structuring element, 23, 38
Survival of the Fittest, 63, 64, 66, 67, 69, 74, 104

T

Template matching, 20, 36, 41, 42, 201
Texture, 23, 78, 107, 108, 135, 146, 154, 291
Thinning, 5, 201
Threshold, 3, 39, 40-42, 44, 46, 51, 53, 87-92, 117, 125, 199, 269, 271, 274-277, 280-282, 284, 286, 287, 289, 305, 308, 310, 353
Threshlding, 3, 41, 199
Transform
Cosine, 3, 268, 318
Fourier, 16, 18, 22, 24, 268, 319
Hough, 4, 33, 41, 42, 44, 46-48, 50, 52, 53, 55, 198, 206, 207
Wavelet,201, 268, 269, 281, 353
Transformation Matrix, 236-240, 246, 247, 252-256
Transposition, 175
Tree, 1, 3, 7, 9, 18, 24, 30, 36, 44, 56-59, 142, 204, 265, 268, 269, 271, 272, 277, 281, 341, 343, 346

V

Virtual Modular Operation (VMOD), 224
Vector Quantization (VQ), 9, 201, 265, 267, 268, 281, 285-287, 289
Lattice, 281, 285, 286, 287

W

Weighted Mean Square Error (WMSE), 298
Window, 9, 34, 116-118, 124, 127, 131, 135, 152
Wormhole Routing, 222, 248, 258, 260

X

X-ray, 5
XOR, 8, 167, 175-177, 183, 184, 189-191, 209-212, 217, 218, 238, 334, 337, 339
XOR Mapping, 209, 212, 217

Z

Zerotree, 282, 284, 353, 358

David Zhang graduated in computer science from Peking University in 1974 and received the MSc and PhD degrees in computer science and engineering from Harbin Institute of Technology in 1983 and 1985, respectively. From 1986 to 1988, he was a postdoctoral fellow at Tsinghua University and became an associate professor at Academia Sinica, Beijing, China. He received his second PhD in electrical and computer engineering at University of Waterloo, Ontario, Canada, in 1994. Currently, he is a professor in Hong Kong Polytechnic University, Hong Kong. He is Founder and Director of Biometrics Technology Centre supported by UGC/CRC, Hong Kong Government. He also is Founder and Editor-in-Chief, *International Journal of Image and Graphics*, and an associate editor, *Pattern Recognition,* and other five international journals. His research interests include automated biometrics-based identification, neural systems and applications, and parallel computing for image processing & pattern recognition. So far, he has published over 170 papers including six books around his research areas. Prof. Zhang is a senior member of IEEE.

Xiaobo Li graduated from Peking Polytechnic University, China, in 1975, and worked as a technician/engineer in hardware and software design for industry from 1976 to 1979. He received the MSc and PhD degrees in computer science from Michigan State University, USA, in 1981 and 1984, respectively. After working as a visiting assistant professor at Wichita State University for two years, he jointed the University of Alberta, Canada, in 1986, where he is currently a professor. His research interests include pattern recognition, image analysis, and parallel processing. He is a senior member of IEEE and an associate editor for *Pattern Recognition* and *International Journal of Image and Graphics*.

Zhiyong Liu graduated from Department of Telecommunication Technology in 1970, received the MSc Degree there in 1983, and worked as an assistant professor in Department of Computer Science and Technology in 1984, Northwest Telecommunication Institute, Xi'an, China, respectively. He obtained his PhD Degree in Computer Science from the Institute of Computing Technology, Chinese Academy of Sciences, Beijing China, in 1987. Then, he worked in the Institute of Computing Technology and currently is a professor, as well as a Deputy Chairman (Standing) of the Directorate of Information Sciences, National Natural Science Foundation of China. His research interests include computer algorithms and architectures, parallel processing, image processing, and interconnection networks.

GPSR Compliance

The European Union's (EU) General Product Safety Regulation (GPSR) is a set of rules that requires consumer products to be safe and our obligations to ensure this.

If you have any concerns about our products, you can contact us on ProductSafety@springernature.com

In case Publisher is established outside the EU, the EU authorized representative is:

Springer Nature Customer Service Center GmbH
Europaplatz 3
69115 Heidelberg, Germany

Batch number: 10704033

Printed by Printforce, the Netherlands